CONGRESS

BENJAMIN GINSBERG

KATHRYN WAGNER HILL

Congress

THE FIRST BRANCH

Yale

UNIVERSITY PRESS

NEW HAVEN & LONDON

Published with assistance from the foundation established in memory of
Philip Hamilton McMillan of the Class of 1894, Yale College.

Yale University Press books may be purchased in quantity for educational,
business, or promotional use. For information, please e-mail
sales.press@yale.edu (U.S. office) or sales@yaleup.co.uk (U.K. office).

Set in Times Roman type by Integrated Publishing Solutions,
Grand Rapids, Michigan.
Printed in the United States of America.

Library of Congress Control Number: 2019930485

ISBN 978-0-300-22053-7 (paperback : alk. paper)

A catalogue record for this book is available from the British Library.

This paper meets the requirements of ANSI/NISO Z39.48-1992
(Permanence of Paper).

10 9 8 7 6 5 4 3 2 1

In memory of our teacher and friend,
Theodore J. Lowi

CONTENTS

Congress: The First Branch

AMERICA'S CONGRESS IS OFTEN CASTIGATED for being slow and unproductive, a victim of cumbersome procedures and partisan intransigence. One frequently cited book called Congress the "broken branch" of government.[1] Another well-known volume, sharply critical of the Congress, called for "a new political order in which government is centered on the executive."[2]

The idea that Congress is "broken" is misleading and actually does little service to the cause of popular government in the United States. Congress is far from perfect. Yet, warts and all, Congress is the national government's most democratic political institution. Some may wish to award this distinction to the president, who, of course, can claim to be the only official elected by the citizenry as a whole. Nevertheless, it is Congress that collectively reflects the diversity of the nation's citizenry. No president, whether Democrat or Republican, can actually represent more than a small fraction of the nation's disparate groups, interests, and political and social forces. As a body, the Congress represents many, even if not all, Americans.

Only the Congress, moreover, governs in anything approaching a democratic and pluralistic manner. The congressional process, to be sure, seldom conforms to some idealized conception of democratic government. Some members of Congress are venal, inept, or indolent. Rates of incumbency are very high. The appearance of public deliberation can mask behind-the-scenes deals and bargains among small numbers of powerful insiders. House and Senate rules can allow the wishes of entrenched political forces and well-situated economic interests to prevail against the welfare of the more general public. All this is true.

Yet, at its core, the congressional policy-making process frequently includes open hearings, public debate, and vigorous contention among a host of fractious groups. Though a small number of congressional hearings are closed, usually because executive branch witnesses claim national security concerns, the great majority of committee and subcommittee hearings are open to the public and to the press. Many hearings involve a parade of dozens, even hundreds, of witnesses from corporations, interest groups, and the administration. Even concerned cit-izens arrive on Capitol Hill to make their views known. It is unusual for any representative of any group, however small, to be denied an opportunity to testify.[3] In the contemporary Congress, floor debate is not an empty exercise. Especially in the Senate, it can be lengthy and rancorous. Floor amendments are offered in both houses and often win acceptance. In short, despite its many imperfections, the U.S. Congress is a democratic decision-making body.

And whatever Congress's shortcomings as a democratic policy-making body, its credentials shine by comparison to those of the White House. Presidential decision-making generally takes place in private and is often shrouded in se-crecy. Recent presidents have vehemently asserted that the secrecy of the pro-cesses leading up to their decisions is shielded by executive privilege. Not only are the deliberations for presidential decision-making often removed from the public domain, but even the decisions themselves are sometimes not revealed to the public or even to the Congress. Many so-called national security direc-tives issued by presidents in recent years have been used to initiate secret missions by intelligence and defense agencies.[4] For many years, too, presidents have signed secret executive agreements with other governments, obligating the United States to various forms of action without congressional knowledge, much less approval. In 2015, for example, President Barack Obama (D) re-sisted efforts by members of Congress to obtain the text of his proposed Trans-Pacific Partnership (TPP), a pending trade deal with twelve other nations. The president said the negotiations were confidential for national security reasons, though Congress would eventually be asked to approve the deal in the form of a congressional-executive agreement. President Donald Trump (R) reversed President Obama's stance on the TPP, which is another aspect of presidential actions, namely that the new chief executive can easily reverse decisions of his predecessor. Like presidents before him, President Trump also pursues foreign policy objectives without consulting Congress, such as his negotiations with

North Korea over denuclearization of that country (see chapter 7 for more on executive agreements and Congress and foreign policy).

Many of the characteristics of Congress with which Americans are so impatient stem directly from the institution's democratic nature. Members of Congress are elected individually and are likely to bicker, delay, and compromise because they represent a variety of different groups and interests that demand that their perspectives be voiced and insist that their narrow and even selfish interests be considered when decisions are made. Sometimes this individualism can produce collective-action problems as members are impelled to focus on their own particular interests rather than the general good. Congress can become "gridlocked" and slow to act, particularly when Americans are themselves deeply divided. The legislative process is complicated because a representative assembly must find ways of balancing minority rights and majority rule and develop mechanisms for reaching decisions while still allowing competing claims to be heard and taken into account. In short, Congress is slow to act, cumbersome in its procedures, and contentious in its discussions because it is a democratic decision-making body. Many who disparage Congress are, in effect if not intent, disparaging popular government.

The framers of the Constitution were certainly familiar with the inefficiencies of representative assemblies. They were conscious of the inclinations of some delegates to put parochial interests ahead of the collective good and of the tendency of others to engage in interminable partisan squabbling.[5] The framers, however, were not particularly troubled by these proclivities. "In the legislature," wrote Alexander Hamilton, "promptitude of decision is oftener an evil than a benefit. The differences of opinion, and the jarring of parties in that department of the government, though they may sometimes obstruct salutary plans, yet often promote deliberation and circumspection, and serve to check excesses in the majority."[6] And despite their awareness of the defects of popular assemblies, the framers placed what they viewed as the central power of government— the legislative power, or power to make the law—in the hands of just such a body.

Representation

The U.S. Congress is a representative institution. Each of its members is expected to speak on behalf of the views and interests of numerous constituents when decisions are made in the Capitol. In ancient Athens, democracy entailed the assembly of all citizens, the "ecclesia," in which all citizens might express their views and vote. This sort of assembly was possible within the context of a small city-state. However, one could hardly expect all the citizens of the United States to gather in an amphitheater to engage in political debate. Even today, when technology might permit the construction of an electronic version of the ecclesia, could hundreds of millions of citizens engage in the discussion, deliberation, and compromise needed to produce effective government?

Representation is a rather complex idea. How can one individual represent another, much less many thousands of others? Let us count the ways. One form of representation might be based on some common identity. That is, a representative might be so close to the district's voters in terms of ethnicity, gender, religion, education, place of origin, philosophical perspective, and so forth that the representative and constituents are likely to have common views and interests. Congressional and senatorial candidates often appeal to voters on the basis of such social and political identities, claiming that they share some salient trait with those they hope to represent and that they are, as a result, likely to be sympathetic to their needs. Since constituencies are diverse, candidates for office often find it expedient to point to elements in their backgrounds that might simultaneously tie them to several constituency groups.

A common identity between representatives and constituents seems to increase the chance that the former will show sympathy for the interests of the latter. For example, of the fifty women serving in a recent Congress, forty received perfect 100 percent ratings from the National Organization for Women (NOW) based on their roll-call votes on issues said to be of interest to women.[7] Common identity, however, is not a guarantee that such a relationship will exist. Seven of the women serving in the same Congress received scores of 50 percent or below on women's issues, with one congresswoman, Marsha Blackburn (R) of Tennessee, earning a rock-bottom 13 percent score.

A second way in which representatives can be tied to constituents is called *agency representation*, indicating that the representative, regardless of similarity of identity, serves as an agent for his or her constituents in much the same way that attorneys or accountants might serve as agents for their clients. Presumably, patients seek the services of physicians who have the skill to help them and are not particularly concerned with finding a physician who shares their own ethnic identity. Similarly, voters may wish to be represented by individuals able to press their claims with care and skill rather than those who merely share their own ethnicity, gender, or religion.

Agency representation can take two forms. The agent may seek to learn and follow the wishes of the client and act accordingly. In the case of Congress, representatives may make an effort to learn their constituents' views and serve as spokespersons for these views on Capitol Hill. Such representatives are sometimes said to see themselves as their constituents' *delegates* to Washington. Alternatively, an agent may act in what he or she perceives to be the client's best interests, even if the client is misinformed or unaware of those interests. In the case of Congress, representatives may view it as their responsibility to make use of their own experience and expertise to promote their constituents' interests whether or not constituents agree with or even understand these efforts. Such members of Congress are sometimes called *trustees* for their districts.

At the heart of agency representation is the idea that representatives are effectively employed by the constituency. Whether they comport themselves as trustees or delegates, representatives must stand for election and can be sent packing if voters are unsatisfied with their performance. As Alexander Hamilton observed, elected representatives are "compelled to anticipate the moment when their power is to cease, when their exercise of it is to be reviewed, and when they must descend to the level from which they were raised; there forever to remain unless a faithful discharge of their trust shall have established their title to a renewal of it."[8] A number of empirical studies have suggested that representatives do, indeed, pay attention to their constituents' views as well as to their interests.[9]

Collective Representation

Both identity and agency representation are usually thought of in terms of the relationship between the representative or senator and the voters of his or her own district or state. Yet congressional representation can also be seen as a collective matter. Citizens may look to representatives from other districts or senators from other states or even Congress as a whole to speak for them. Indeed, if citizens are so inclined, they may contribute money or volunteer to work in campaigns outside their own state or district. Much of the funding for congressional campaigns today comes from ideologically motivated "super PACs" (see chapter 3) that contribute funds to many candidates in an attempt to influence the partisan makeup of the Congress. For their part, many Americans focus more on the character and composition of the Congress as a collective body than on the behavior of their own representative. Many, in fact, cannot name their own representative.[10]

To be sure, the distribution of some social characteristic or political perspective within the Congress may not accurately reflect that trait's distribution in the American populace. Women, for example, constitute slightly more than 50 percent of America's population but only about 24 percent of the membership of Congress. This difference may reflect the persistence of gender-based social discrimination or the fact that for many female voters, gender is only one of several salient determinants of the voting decision. In either event, it seems unlikely that a representative body can fully reflect all the social traits and political preferences of 328 million Americans. If voters focus on one social trait, they will inevitably reduce the incidence of another. Even if we chose members of Congress through a lottery, some social or political features of the public would be underweighted or ignored.

Yet very few social, religious, ethnic or other sociological features of the American public are entirely missing from the Congress. Take the matter of religion. Many Americans are formally represented by a senator or House member who does not share their own religious identity. And some denominations are overrepresented and others a bit underrepresented in Congress relative to their percentage of the general population. Nevertheless, few Americans can fail to find some member of Congress who does not share their own faith and might be available to serve as a champion for that faith's adherents. For example, as we can see from table 1.1, as of 2019 there were only three Muslim members of Congress, André Carson (D-IN), Rashida Tlaib (D-MI), and Ilhan Omar (D-MN); but they make a point of serving as national spokespersons for Muslim concerns.

Of course, the way in which congressional district boundaries are drawn can also affect the social and political makeup of the Congress. Efforts to shape the composition of the Congress and to alter the relative influence of competing political forces by manipulating district boundaries is called *gerrymandering*. We will return to this topic in chapter 3.

Creating the Congress

The issue of representation was very much on the minds of the members of America's Constitutional Convention of 1787. The framers viewed a represen-

Table 1.1. Religious Affiliations of Members of the 116th Congress

Religion	House		Senate		U.S. Adults
	Number	%	Number	%	%
Christian	385	88.7	86	86.0	71
Protestant	233	53.7	60	60.0	48
Catholic	141	32.5	22	22.0	21
Mormon	6	1.4	4	4.0	2
Orthodox Christian	5	1.2	0	0	<1
Jewish	26	6.0	8	8.0	2
Buddhist	1	0.2	1	1.0	1
Muslim	3	0.7	0	0	1
Hindu	3	0.7	0	0	1
Unitarian Universalist	2	0.5	0	0	<1
Unaffiliated	0	0	1	1.0	23
Other faiths	0	0	0	0	2
Don't know/refused	14	3.2	4	4.0	1
Total	435	100	100	100	100

Source: Based on *Faith on the Hill: The Religious Composition of the 116th Congress* (Washington, DC: Pew Research Center, 2019).

tative assembly as the cornerstone of the republic they hoped to establish. They thought a representative assembly would give voice to the variety of sectional, economic, and social interests clamoring for attention in the new nation. The framers also understood that representation served the interests of the government as much as those of the governed. Citizens who thought they had a voice in the government would, the framers believed, also view that government as an institution worthy of their support. Most delegates recognized that the power and stability of the new government and its ability to compete with the states for popular affection would be enhanced if citizens saw the national government as effectively representing their own views and interests. James Wilson of Pennsylvania, for example, said that he favored "raising the federal pyramid to a considerable altitude," and for that reason he wished to give it "as broad a base as possible."[11] In other words, a broadly representative body would strengthen the new government by building popular "confidence" in it. Moreover, by explicitly placing (as we shall soon see) most of the powers of the new government in the hands of the representative assembly, the framers were, in effect, announcing to the citizenry that the new government was to be a government of the people.

There were, as readers will recall, many views about how a representative assembly should be constituted. Most delegates to the Constitutional Convention, familiar with British practice, favored the principle of bicameralism. One exception was Benjamin Franklin, who supported the idea of a unicameral legislature, which he called the "House of Legislation."[12] Franklin had apparently been satisfied with the unicameral Congress of the Confederacy, which had been the sole national body established under the Articles of Confederation. Most delegates, however, looked to the British example. The British Parliament was divided into two houses, the House of Commons, elected on the basis of a very narrow suffrage and representing mainly important commercial and mercantile interests, and a House of Lords, in which sat members of the hereditary aristocracy. Many thought that the conservative Lords and the more active and energetic Commons checked one another's worst tendencies and brought a balance of progress and stability to Britain.

After much debate and compromise, delegates agreed that the American version of a bicameral assembly was to be a Congress of the United States, consisting of a House of Representatives and a Senate. The House, by tradition (though not constitutional fiat) called the lower chamber of Congress, would represent the people of the United States. The Senate, or upper chamber, would be chosen by and presumably reflect the views of the state legislatures. Members of the House would be chosen every two years, but senators would serve six-year terms. Only one-third of the members of the Senate would be chosen at any one time. The purpose of "staggered terms" was to better insulate the Senate and, hence, the government from sudden swings in the political climate. For the first Senate selections, one-third of the senators were chosen for two years, one-third for four years, and one-third for six years, thus putting into place the system of staggered six-year terms.

Members of the House are to be at least twenty-five years of age, to have been citizens of the United States for at least seven years, and to reside in the state from which they are elected. Note that representatives are not required to live in their districts, though most do. When the Constitution was adopted, some states elected their representatives on a statewide at-large basis, so requiring representatives to live in their districts would have made no sense. Since 1967, at-large elections for members of Congress have been prohibited except, of course, in the states that are entitled to only one representative. The framers thought that the Senate, with its longer terms, would be a more deliberative body than the House. Consistent with that idea, the Constitution requires senators to be older—at least thirty—than members of the House, and to have been citizens for at least nine years. Senators must be residents of the state they represent.

This idea of a Senate representing the states may seem somewhat odd today when the states have receded in importance politically and few members of our geographically mobile citizenry regard loyalty to the state in which they currently happen to live as a significant political identification. In the world of 1787, however, citizens were both physically and emotionally attached to their states. The state governments, for their part, were well-established political institutions and, like the national governments of Europe today, were not eager to completely surrender their sovereignty to an upstart central government. Some nationalists among the convention's delegates hoped the federal government would supplant the states. Many delegates, though, viewed the new Constitution more as a compact among the states than the basis for a unitary national regime. Hence, allowing the state legislatures a voice in the governance of the new nation reflected the political realities of the time. It was not until the ratification of the Seventeenth Amendment in 1913 that senators came to be elected directly by the people. This amendment both reflected and accelerated the decline of the states as autonomous governmental entities.[13]

A number of delegates, mainly from the smaller states, argued that whether representatives were to be chosen by the people or the legislatures, each state should be entitled to equal representation in each house of Congress. Delegates from the larger states retorted that in both houses of Congress representation should be based upon population. Under the terms of the so-called Great Compromise, the delegates settled upon the principle of equality of representation in the Senate and representation based upon population in the House. Accordingly, the Constitution assigned each state two senators regardless of its size. The initial Senate seated twenty-six members, and today, of course, the fifty states are together represented by one hundred senators.

Representation in the lower house was to be based upon population. Initially, states were assigned one House member for every thirty thousand inhabitants, with a minimum of one for each state. Delegates from the southern states argued that slaves should be counted toward the total. Delegates from the northern states rejected this idea. The delegates reached a compromise on this point as well and agreed that for the purpose of determining the size of their House delegations, states would be credited for three-fifths of their black slaves. Some delegates viewed this "three-fifths compromise" as immoral but allowed expedience to triumph over principle.

The initial House seated 59 members. This number increased as the nation's population grew. In 1911, the size of the House was set by law at 435 members, where it remains today. The most populous state, California, boasts 53 representatives, while seven other states possess only 1 representative each. These numbers are adjusted after each decennial census, with states gaining or losing seats as their populations rise or fall relative to the other states. Each congressional district now represents about 711,000 people. In addition to the 435 voting members of Congress, there are 6 delegates from the District of Columbia and the U.S. territories, who can speak and serve on committees but are not entitled to cast votes on the floor of the House.

Though members of the lower house of Congress were to be selected by the people, some Constitutional Convention delegates were distrustful of the idea of allowing ordinary citizens too great a voice in public affairs. Elbridge Gerry of Massachusetts, for example, declared that ordinary citizens were too easily "misled into the most baneful measures and opinions."[14] He favored restrictions on the suffrage, or some form of indirect election. Most, however, agreed with James Madison, who considered "popular election of one branch of the national legislature as essential to every plan of free government."[15] In 1787 most state legislators were popularly elected, though the states imposed a variety of limitations upon the suffrage, including property qualifications. Constitutional Convention delegates understood that if citizens had the right to vote for state legislators but not for members of the federal Congress, they would continue to give their political support to the states rather than the new national government. Accordingly, the Constitution provides that all those citizens eligible to vote for state legislators are also eligible to vote for members of the House of Representatives. As property qualifications disappeared, this provision gradually brought about white manhood suffrage and, eventually, universal suffrage as African Americans and women won the right to vote.

Representation and Governance

When Americans lambaste the Congress they perhaps fail to realize what a rare and even precious institution it is. America's Congress is one of the few representative bodies in the world that actually govern. Most of the world's representative bodies only represent. That is, their sole governmental function consists of affirming and legitimating the national government's decisions by conveying the impression that the government has secured the consent of the peoples' representatives. In the former Soviet Union, for example, the nation's representative assembly, the Supreme Soviet, was carefully designed to precisely reflect the USSR's many ethnic groups. Unfortunately, however, the Supreme Soviet possessed no power beyond the power to assent to the government's "proposals." Today, even European parliaments, which choose—and can depose—their nations' prime ministers, have few substantive powers of governance. The U.S. Congress, on the other hand, actually plays a significant role in the operations of the national government.

The Legislative Power

Congress's chief, but not only, power is the power to make the law. Article I, Section 1, of the Constitution declares that "All legislative Powers herein granted shall be vested in a Congress of the United States, which shall consist of a Senate and House of Representatives." Article I, Section 8, of the Constitution proceeds to identify these legislative powers, known collectively as the *enumerated powers* of Congress. In response to critics who asserted that the new government would be too powerful, the Constitution's framers averred that it would exercise only the powers enumerated in the Constitution. This claim turned out not to be entirely true.

Article 1, Section 8. Powers of Congress

To lay and collect Taxes, Duties, Imposts and Excises, to pay the Debts and provide for the common Defence and general Welfare of the United States; but all Duties, Imposts and Excises shall be uniform throughout the United States;

To borrow Money on the credit of the United States;

To regulate Commerce with foreign Nations, and among the several States, and with the Indian Tribes;

To establish an uniform Rule of Naturalization, and uniform Laws on the subject of Bankruptcies throughout the United States;

To coin Money, regulate the Value thereof, and of foreign Coin, and fix the Standard of Weights and Measures;

To provide for the Punishment of counterfeiting the Securities and current Coin of the United States;

To establish Post Offices and Post Roads;

To promote the Progress of Science and useful Arts, by securing for limited Times to Authors and Inventors the exclusive Right to their respective Writings and Discoveries;

To constitute Tribunals inferior to the supreme Court;

To define and punish Piracies and Felonies committed on the high Seas, and Offences against the Law of Nations;

To declare War, grant Letters of Marque and Reprisal, and make Rules concerning Captures on Land and Water;

To raise and support Armies, but no Appropriation of Money to that Use shall be for a longer Term than two Years;

To provide and maintain a Navy;

To make Rules for the Government and Regulation of the land and naval Forces;

To provide for calling forth the Militia to execute the Laws of the Union, suppress Insurrections and repel Invasions;

To provide for organizing, arming, and disciplining, the Militia, and for governing such Part of them as may be employed in the Service of the United States, reserving to the States respectively, the Appointment of the Officers, and the Authority of training the Militia according to the discipline prescribed by Congress;

To exercise exclusive Legislation in all Cases whatsoever, over such

District (not exceeding ten Miles square) as may, by Cession of particular States, and the Acceptance of Congress, become the Seat of the Government of the United States, and to exercise like Authority over all Places purchased by the Consent of the Legislature of the State in which the Same shall be, for the Erection of Forts, Magazines, Arsenals, dock-Yards, and other needful Buildings; And

To make all Laws which shall be necessary and proper for carrying into Execution the foregoing Powers, and all other Powers vested by this Constitution in the Government of the United States, or in any Department or Officer thereof.

Notice that these enumerated powers constitute a list of many of the most important powers of government. First, the Constitution assigns Congress the power to raise and spend money "for the common Defence and general Welfare of the United States." In other words, it is Congress, and not the president or the judiciary or the states, that is to determine what revenues are needed by the federal government and how these are to be spent. This "power of the purse," reinforced by Article I, Section 9, which prohibits drawing money from the Treasury without a congressional appropriation, is in some respects the central power of government. Without revenues there can be no government, and the institution that determines how these revenues should be spent seems, of necessity, to be the most important institution of government. The framers were aware of the fact that it was the British Parliament's growing control of the power of the purse that had allowed that body to increase its influence vis-à-vis the Crown. By placing this power in the hands of the Congress, the framers underlined their intention to make the legislative branch the most influential element of the government. As we shall see, Congress jealously guarded its power of the purse until 1921, when it created the Bureau of the Budget (BOB) in the executive branch. The creation of this bureau, now called the Office of Management and Budget (OMB), began a shift of power that has given presidents a good deal of influence over the federal budget and left Congress to bargain with the White House over matters that once were its sole prerogative.

It is very important also to take careful note of the very last power enumerated by Article I, Section 8, the so-called "necessary and proper" clause. This simple phrase creates a second, and very important, set of congressional powers. These are the *implied powers* of Congress. An implied power is one that is not specifically enumerated in the Constitution but can be said to be necessary and proper for the execution of one of the enumerated powers and hence implied. This idea was forcefully articulated by Chief Justice John Marshall in his decision in the case of *McCulloch v. Maryland*,[16] interpreting the Constitution's so-called Commerce Clause.

Article I, Section 8, assigns Congress a good deal of power over the nation's economy. In particular, in the Commerce Clause, Congress is given the power to regulate international commerce and commerce between the states. This power is important because it is so encompassing. Virtually every activity in which we engage could be said to have some relationship to commerce. Raw materials and manufactured goods travel across state and national boundaries before reaching consumers. Messages travel across the nation and across the globe. Interpreted broadly, everything is commerce and, thus, subject to regulation by the Congress. How broadly should the commerce power be construed?

Very broadly indeed, said Chief Justice John Marshall in the 1819 case of *McCulloch v. Maryland.* The *McCulloch* case involved an effort by the state of Maryland to impose a tax on the Baltimore branch of the Bank of the United States. Marshall determined that the Constitution's Supremacy Clause meant that no state had the power to tax or otherwise impede or control any arm of the federal government. At the same time, Marshall considered whether Congress actually had the power to charter a bank. Though Article I, Section 8, lists many powers, nowhere does it refer to the power to establish a bank. How could a government of enumerated powers exercise a power that was not enumerated?

Marshall was a nationalist, and his answer to this question represented a strong assertion of the power of Congress and the national government. According to Marshall, the "necessary and proper" clause of Section 8 meant that if Congress was pursuing a purpose within the scope of its Constitutional powers it might enact laws "necessary and proper" to achieve this purpose so long as these laws were not, themselves, prohibited by the Constitution. Marshall wrote, "Let the end be legitimate, let it be within the scope of the constitution, and all means which are appropriate . . . which are not prohibited . . . are constitutional."[17] In other words, the list of enumerated congressional powers was a foundation of, rather than a limitation upon, congressional power. In the case at hand, Marshall averred that Congress had chartered a bank as a reasonable way of achieving its constitutionally sanctioned purpose of regulating commerce. And, since nowhere in the Constitution was this action prohibited, it was valid. In his decision, Chief Justice Marshall made the power to regulate commerce a bedrock of congressional power. More than two centuries later, in statute after statute, Congress cites the commerce power as the basis for its actions in realms from Antarctic exploration through zoonotic infections.

Even more important, Marshall's decision underlined the idea that the Constitution implied congressional powers that were not specifically enumerated in the document. This idea of implied powers has encouraged Congress to legislate in many realms not mentioned in or anticipated by the Constitution. It seems unlikely that the framers, who lived in the age of the horse and buggy, would have anticipated the need for anything like the National Aeronautics and Space Act, creating NASA, but the members of Congress had no difficulty assuming that somewhere in Article I, Section 8, this power was implied.

Foreign and Military Policy

Article I, Section 8, also gives Congress important military and foreign policy powers, including the power to declare war, to raise armies, to regulate commerce with foreign nations, and, in the case of the Senate, the power to ratify treaties and concur in the appointment of ambassadors. It is Congress, moreover, that must appropriate the funds to pay for all these activities.

Of course, from the earliest years of the Republic, presidents and their advisers have asserted that they, and not the Congress, were mainly responsible for America's foreign and military policies. President George Washington's efforts to assert the primacy of the presidency in the foreign policy arena were strenuously defended by Alexander Hamilton. Writing under the pseudonym *Pacificus* in a series of 1793 articles in the *Gazette of the United States,* Hamilton argued that the direction of foreign policy was inherently an executive function.[18] Hamilton asserted, moreover, that the federal Constitution gave presidents the power of initiative in foreign policy. The specific grants of power in the Constitution and their logical implications, he wrote, gave the executive the right to "determine the condition of the nation . . . [and, if necessary] . . . to establish an antecedent state of things."[19] In other words, the president was free to undertake actions based upon his judgment of the national interest and, if he deemed it appropriate, to confront the Congress and other governmental agencies with faits accomplis.[20]

Writing in response to Hamilton's *Pacificus* letters, James Madison, using the pen name *Helvidius,* took issue with Hamilton and argued that the president's powers in foreign affairs were instrumental only. That is, it was Congress's constitutional role to determine the substance and direction of American foreign policy, while the task of the president was limited to implementing the will of the legislature.[21] The Constitution, as noted earlier, assigns the Congress specific powers in the realm of foreign affairs, including the power to declare war, the power to raise armies, and the power to regulate foreign commerce. On the basis of this constitutional authority, Congress has enacted numerous pieces of trade legislation; authorized the recruitment, training, and equipment of military forces; and, on at least one occasion—the War of 1812—declared war despite the concerns of the president.

Presidents have, of course, worked to increase their power over foreign commerce and have engaged in pitched battles with Congress over this matter. In 2015, for example, Congress and President Obama battled over the president's plan to increase executive power in the trade realm. For its part, Congress has occasionally sought to use its constitutionally mandated powers to claim additional powers as well. For example, when Congress declared war against Spain in 1898, it included recognition of the independence of Cuba in its resolution, even though President McKinley was opposed to recognition of the Cuban insurgent government.[22] Article II, Section 3, of the Constitution seems to give this power of recognition to the executive by authorizing the president to receive ambassadors.

Through its general legislative powers, moreover, Congress can exercise broad influence over foreign policy. Congress may, for example, refuse to appropriate funds for presidential actions it deems to be unwise or inappropriate. Thus, in 1796, the House of Representatives was asked to appropriate funds to implement the Jay Treaty with England. Opponents of the treaty demanded that the House be given all papers and records pertaining to the negotiating process—a demand rejected by President Washington. The House narrowly approved funding but accompanied its acquiescence with a resolution affirming its right to refuse appropriations for the implementation of any treaty to which a majority of its members objected.[23] And on several occasions over the years, the House has indeed refused to appropriate funds needed to implement treaties negotiated by the president and ratified by the Senate.[24] In 2015, the Congress threatened but ultimately refrained from seeking to withhold funds for implementing President Obama's proposed nuclear agreement with Iran unless legislators' terms for such an agreement were met.

This power of the purse also extends to military action. Not only does Congress have the constitutional power to declare war, but under its general legislative powers it must appropriate the funds needed to support military activities. In *Federalist* 69, Hamilton argues that Congress's power of the purse provides it with an ultimate check on the president's power as commander in chief.[25] This principle was illustrated during the Reagan administration when Congress enacted the so-called Boland Amendments. This legislation prohibited the president from using any funds to provide military support for right-wing "Contra" guerrilla forces in the civil war then raging in the nation of Nicaragua. The administration's response was to seek funds from Saudi Arabia, the Sultan of Brunei, and even from private individuals. This attempt to circumvent Congress's authority sparked the 1986 congressional Iran-Contra investigations, which led to criminal convictions for several high-ranking administration officials.

If foreign policy entailed only matters of trade, recognition, international accords, and other peacetime pursuits, the constitutional struggle between the president and Congress might have gone on indefinitely without any conclusive resolution. Unfortunately, however, throughout the nation's history, war and military affairs have been central foci of American foreign policy. Though the United States has fought only five formally declared wars, American armed forces have been involved in hundreds of military actions and "small wars" in every corner of the world.[26] America's first small war, the 1801–1805 naval campaign against the Barbary States, involved a handful of ships and generated few casualties. Other "small" wars have been quite large. American military action in Korea and Vietnam required the mobilization of hundreds of thousands of troops and resulted in tens of thousands of casualties.

Whether declared or undeclared, large or small, war has been the crucible of presidential power. During the nineteenth and early twentieth centuries, wartime expansion of presidential power tended to be temporary, generally limited to the duration of the war. In some respects, as we shall see in chapter 7, war mobilized the populace and empowered the Congress as much as it strengthened the presidency. Beginning with the Cold War, however, and perhaps even more markedly in recent years, preparation for war has helped presidents to substantially reshape the constitutional balance of power among the major institutions of government.

Additional Legislative and Nonlegislative Powers of Congress

In addition to the powers enumerated or implied by Article I, Section 8, other articles of the Constitution also assign powers to the national legislature. Some of these powers, like the impeachment power, the power to admit new states to the Union, the power to break ties in the Electoral College, and the power to propose constitutional amendments, do not pertain to making law, hence are sometimes called *"non-legislative powers."* The difference, however, between a legislative and nonlegislative power is sometimes subtle, since the exercise of nonlegislative powers may involve or result in legislation. For example, Congress's power to regulate the selection of presidential electors, a nonlegislative power, would generally entail the enactment of legislation to be exercised effectively.

Congressional Powers Found Outside Article I, Section 8, Summarized

No State shall, without the Consent of the Congress, lay any Imposts or Duties on Imports or Exports, except what may be absolutely necessary for executing it's inspection Laws: and the net Produce of all Duties and Imposts, laid by any State on Imports or Exports, shall be for the Use of the Treasury of the United States; and all such Laws shall be subject to the Revision and Controul of the Congress.

The Congress may determine the Time of chusing the Electors, and the Day on which they shall give their Votes; which Day shall be the same throughout the United States.

The power to choose the president if no candidate wins a majority in the Electoral College.

[If the president vetoes a bill] if approved by two-thirds [of both houses of Congress] it shall become a law.

No money shall be drawn from the Treasury without an appropriation from Congress.

The Senate is empowered to confirm presidential appointments and treaties, the latter by a two-thirds vote.

In Case of the Removal of the President from Office, or of his Death, Resignation, or Inability to discharge the Powers and Duties of the said Office, the Same shall devolve on the Vice President, and the Congress may by Law provide for the Case of Removal, Death, Resignation or Inability, both of the President and Vice President, declaring what Officer shall then act as President, and such Officer shall act accordingly, until the Disability be removed, or a President shall be elected.

The judicial Power of the United States, shall be vested in one supreme Court, and in such inferior Courts as the Congress may from time to time ordain and establish.

The Trial of all Crimes, except in Cases of Impeachment, shall be by Jury; and such Trial shall be held in the State where the said Crimes shall have been committed; but when not committed within any State, the Trial shall be at such Place or Places as the Congress may by Law have directed.

The Congress shall have Power to declare the Punishment of Treason, but no Attainder of Treason shall work Corruption of Blood, or Forfeiture except during the Life of the Person attainted.

Full Faith and Credit shall be given in each State to the public Acts, Records, and judicial Proceedings of every other State. And the Congress may by general Laws prescribe the Manner in which such Acts, Records, and Proceedings shall be proved, and the Effect thereof.

New States may be admitted by the Congress into this Union;

The Congress shall have Power to dispose of and make all needful Rules and Regulations respecting the Territory or other Property belonging to the United States; and nothing in this Constitution shall be so construed as to Prejudice any Claims of the United States, or of any particular State.

The Congress, whenever two thirds of both Houses shall deem it necessary, shall propose Amendments to this Constitution, or, on the Application of the Legislatures of two thirds of the several States, shall call a Convention for proposing Amendments, which, in either Case, shall be valid to all Intents and Purposes, as Part of this Constitution, when ratified by the Legislatures of three fourths of the several States, or by Conventions in three fourths thereof, as the one or the other Mode of Ratification may be proposed by the Congress

The House of Representatives shall chuse their Speaker and other Officers; and shall have the sole Power of Impeachment . . .

The Senate shall have the sole Power to try all Impeachments. When sitting for that Purpose, they shall be on Oath or Affirmation. When the President of the United States is tried, the Chief Justice shall preside: And no Person shall be convicted without the Concurrence of two thirds of the Members present.

The Times, Places and Manner of holding Elections for Senators and Representatives, shall be prescribed in each State by the Legislature thereof; but the Congress may at any time by Law make or alter such Regulations, except as to the Places of chusing Senators.[27]

Among these non–Section 8 powers, some are especially noteworthy. One is the amendment power. Congress may, by a two-thirds vote of both houses, propose amendments to the Constitution and present them for ratification by the state legislatures. Ratification requires approval by three-fourths of the legislatures. Since the nation's founding, some eleven thousand amendments have been proposed in the Congress and thirty-three sent to the states for ratification. Of these, twenty-seven have actually been ratified and added to the Constitution. Of course, under the terms of Article V, the Constitution may also be amended by a convention of the states, but this route has never been taken.

Also noteworthy is the fact that the Constitution assigns Congress a good deal of authority over the composition of the other two branches of government. The executive and the judiciary, for their parts, can block acts of Congress but are assigned no power over the organization or composition of the legislative branch. This institutional asymmetry is one indication of the framers' assumption that the legislature was to be the chief branch of American government. Let us consider the ways in which Congress can shape and reshape the judiciary and the executive.

Congressional Power and the Judiciary

The Senate must consent to all federal judicial appointments, as will be discussed further. Moreover, while the Constitution created the Supreme Court, the framers empowered Congress to establish "inferior" courts. As a result, today's elaborate federal judicial system, consisting of federal appeals courts, district courts, and specialized tribunals, is a product of congressional mandate and can be altered by the Congress as it has been many times in American history. Congress is also constitutionally empowered to impeach federal judges. Impeachment is a two-step process consisting of an indictment issued by the House and a trial by the Senate. Over the years, fifteen federal judges have been impeached by the House of Representatives, and eight have been convicted after trials by the Senate. Four were acquitted and three resigned rather than face the process. These numbers include Supreme Court Justice Samuel Chase, who was impeached but not convicted in 1804. The most recent jurist to be impeached, Thomas Porteous, federal judge of Louisiana, was convicted by the Senate in 2010 of taking bribes and removed from the bench. One federal judge, Alcee Hastings of Florida, who was removed from office by the Congress in 1989, had the last laugh when he was elected to Congress, where he has served since 1993.

Congress can also enact legislation designed to alter the jurisdictions of federal tribunals, the rules of the judicial process, and the flow of cases through the appellate process. Often, congressional efforts to control the courts lead to judicial resistance and institutional struggles. For example, in the Sentencing Reform Act of 1984 Congress created the U.S. Sentencing Commission, which in turn issued a set of mandatory sentencing "guidelines," adopted by Congress in 1987, that effectively abolished federal judicial discretion in sentencing. When handing down sentences, federal judges were required to consult an elaborate table that took account of the severity of the crime and the perpetrator's prior record to determine the offender's precise sentence. A history of prior convictions could greatly enhance the sentence meted out for any given crime, so that individuals convicted of several minor crimes might find themselves behind bars for decades. Many states adopted their own versions of these guidelines to govern state criminal proceedings.

The nominal purpose of the mandatory guidelines was to ensure uniformity of sentencing across jurisdictions. The adoption of the Sentencing Reform Act, however, reflected a congressional view that some federal judges were too lenient in their handling of serious offenders.[28] Accordingly, Congress decided to take matters into its own hands and eliminate judicial discretion in this realm. Federal judges chafed at this intrusion into what they saw as their domain and sought an opportunity to reassert their own roles in the sentencing process. Such an opportunity presented itself in 2005 in the case of *U.S. v. Booker.*[29] Freddie Booker had been found guilty by a federal jury of selling cocaine. Adhering to the sentencing guidelines, which penalized Booker for prior convictions, a federal judge sentenced Booker to thirty years in prison. Booker's attorney appealed, asserting that the mandatory guidelines had violated Booker's Sixth Amendment right to a trial by jury because his sentence had been based upon facts never presented to the jury. A federal appellate court and the U.S. Supreme Court agreed, striking down the mandatory sentencing procedures.

Conflicts between Congress and the Supreme Court are not unusual, and the Court, which is usually reluctant to oppose the White House, often seems only too happy to strike down congressional enactments. In chapter 9 we shall consider the causes and consequences of what often seems a strained relationship between the legislative and judicial branches of America's government. While the framers saw the Supreme Court as providing a balance between Congress and the executive, the Court has often unbalanced this relationship by adding its weight to the authority of the president.

Congressional Power and the President

The Constitution authorizes Congress to regulate the selection, fitness for office, impeachment, and removal of the president. Thus, Congress is to develop rules concerning the schedule for the selection of presidential electors. Congress is empowered to develop rules governing presidential disability and succession. And Congress is empowered to remove the president from office through the process of impeachment. By statute, Congress has set the procedures governing the meetings of presidential electors and the manner in which their votes are tallied and reported. Congress has legislated a number of times on the matter of presidential succession and removal, though today these matters are mainly governed by the Twentieth and Twenty-Fifth Amendments, ratified in 1933 and 1967 respectively.

As to presidential impeachment, the framers viewed the threat of impeachment as an important check upon executive power. Article II, Section 4, of the Constitution provides that a president may be impeached for "high crimes and misdemeanors." Such offenses are to be charged by the House and tried in the Senate, with the chief justice presiding and a two-thirds vote needed for conviction. At the Constitutional Convention, James Madison said it was "indispensable that some provision should be made for defending the Community against the incapacity, negligence or perfidy," of the chief executive.[30] Elbridge Gerry concurred on the necessity of impeachments, saying, "A good magistrate will not fear them. A bad one ought to be kept in fear of them."[31] During the course of American history, only two presidents, Andrew Johnson (D) and Bill Clinton (D), have been impeached by the House, though neither was convicted by the Senate. Johnson's impeachment was triggered by his opposition to congressional Reconstruction policy, and Clinton's by charges of sexual improprieties. A third president, Richard Nixon (R), would almost certainly have been impeached for his misdeeds in the Watergate affair, but Nixon chose to resign to avoid the impeachment process.

Congress's Implied Powers over the Executive

Some powers over the executive branch claimed and exercised by Congress are not explicitly granted by the Constitution. One of the most important of these implied powers is the power to create the executive departments of the federal government. Each of the federal government's great cabinet departments and most of its other agencies were created by acts of Congress. Nowhere, however, does the Constitution specifically authorize Congress to establish such agencies. Article II, Section 2, of the Constitution merely states that the president shall have the power to appoint, with the advice and consent of the Senate, ". . . Officers of the United States, whose Appointments are not herein otherwise provided for, and which shall be established by Law: but the Congress may by Law vest the Appointment of such inferior Officers, as they think proper, in the President alone, in the Courts of Law, or in the Heads of Departments." This language seems to imply the existence of federal officials appointed by the president with senatorial consent to head departments. It follows logically, if not inexorably, that there must exist departments for them to head.

This language seemed to be sufficient for the first Congress, meeting in 1789, to create the Departments of State, Treasury, and War (now Defense). In 1792, Congress established the Post Office Department (now the quasi-independent U.S. Postal Service) and the Department of the Navy (now part of Defense). Today, the executive branch consists of fifteen government departments as well as sixty-seven independent agencies and a host of boards, commissions, and quasi-public entities. Each of these departments and agencies consists, in turn, of many other offices, bureaus, services, agencies, authorities, commissions, and other subdivisions—more than five hundred altogether. All of America's cabinet departments and about half the other agencies were created by acts of Congress. The act establishing an agency is called its "organic statute." The remaining agencies were created by executive order, by the orders of department secretaries, or through the reorganization of existing agencies.[32] Major agencies created by executive order include the Environmental Protection Agency (EPA), the Federal Emergency Management Agency (FEMA), and the Drug Enforcement

Administration (DEA). Presidents have claimed the power to create agencies, and Congress has acquiesced by providing funding.

Ironically, even though most agencies of the executive branch were created by Congress, most presidents subscribe to the theory of the *unitary executive*.[33] Unitary-executive theory holds that all executive power inheres in the president except as explicitly limited by the Constitution.[34] Proponents of this theory claim that the unitary executive is implied by Article II of the Constitution, the so-called Vesting Clause, which vests the executive power in a president of the United States of America. According to some proponents of the unitary-executive view, the president is effectively a sovereign subject only to a small number of legislative restraints, such as Congress's control of revenues, its impeachment power, and its power to override presidential vetoes. Some proponents of unitary-executive theory also subscribe to a theory of *departmentalism* (to be discussed more fully in chapter 9), averring that presidents have their own power to interpret the Constitution as it applies to the executive branch and need not necessarily defer to the judiciary.

Both unitary-executive theory and a departmentalist claim were articulated by President George W. Bush when he signed the Defense Appropriations Act that included language on the treatment of terrorist suspects—the so-called antitorture provision introduced by Senator John McCain, which the president had opposed. In his signing statement, Bush declared that he would construe the portion of the act relating to the treatment of detainees "in a manner consistent with the constitutional authority of the President to supervise the unitary executive branch and as Commander in Chief and consistent with the constitutional limitations on the judicial power."[35] The president was claiming, in other words, that particularly in the military realm, he possessed the authority to execute acts of Congress according to his own understanding of the law, the Constitution, and the nation's interests.

Oversight of the Executive: Congress versus the White House

When it comes to management of the executive branch, the implied powers of Congress clash with the implied powers of the president. Congress, as we shall see in chapter 8, claims the implied power to engage in oversight and investigation of the activities of the executive branch. Like the executive branch itself, oversight is not mentioned in the Constitution, but Congress reasonably asserts that oversight is implied by its enumerated powers, including the power to appropriate funds, to raise and support armies and navies, and even to impeach judges and presidents. It seems reasonable to assert that Congress could not fulfill any of these constitutional responsibilities without holding hearings and conducting investigations. Indeed, if the Constitution implies that Congress has the power to create an executive branch, surely it also implies that Congress has the power to monitor the activities of its own creation.

Nevertheless, when it suits their purposes, presidents will seek to resist efforts at congressional oversight, citing executive privilege or national security concerns to block congressional inquiries. In this clash between the implied powers of Congress and the implied powers of the president, the advocates of presidential power claim the support of no less an authority than Alexander Hamilton, who pointed out that Article I, Section 1, of the Constitution limited congressional powers to those "herein granted," while no such limitation is attached to the executive powers of the president, which are, writes Hamilton, subject only to specific qualifications and limitations. Thus, if we agree with Hamilton, the idea of implied presidential power might carry more weight than the concept of implied congressional power.[36] However, another famous authority on government, the British philosopher John Stuart Mill, saw oversight of the executive as among the chief duties of legislative assemblies.[37] In the 1927 case of *McGrain v. Daugherty,* the Supreme Court agreed with Mill's position, stating that oversight was implied by Congress's legislative power, though it should concern only matters "on which legislation could be had."[38] This principle does not impose much of a constraint on oversight, since legislation "could be had" on just about any topic.

Accordingly, by statute, Congress has authorized House and Senate standing committees to oversee executive programs under their jurisdictions. And among the various provisions of the 1974 Congressional Budget and Impoundment Control Act was one authorizing congressional committees to conduct performance evaluations of executive agencies. By statute too agencies are required to furnish a variety of reports to Congress, and each agency's inspector general is required to inform Congress of serious management and performance problems within his or her agency. We will return to the topic of oversight and the role of Congress's watchdog agency, the Government Accountability Office (GAO), in chapters 4 and 6.

Inherent Powers

In addition to its enumerated and implied powers, Congress also claims to possess *inherent powers.* These inherent powers stem from the fact that the United States is a sovereign nation. Under international law and custom, sovereign states possess a number of inherent rights and powers. The most important of these are the right to engage in relations with other nations, the right of self-defense against attacks from other states, and the right to curb internal violence and unrest. The Constitution seems to bolster Congress's claim to exercise these inherent powers by assigning Congress the power to declare war, the power to punish crimes on the high seas and "offenses against the law of nations," the power to call out the militia to defend the nation against insurrections and invasions, the power to regulate commerce with other nations, and a number of other powers that seem relevant to American sovereignty.

However, presidents have claimed that it is the executive and not the Congress that should give effect to the nation's sovereign rights and powers. Presidents and their advisers are quick to point out that the executive power is vested by the Constitution in the president, who is acknowledged to have the power to "make" if not "declare" war, to negotiate treaties with other nations, and to see to it that the laws are faithfully executed. Thus, it might be said to be constitutionally implied that it is the president who possesses the inherent power to act to defend the nation, to conduct its foreign relations, and to safeguard law and order.

Most presidents believe that they and only they are constitutionally authorized to manage the nation's sovereign relations with foreign states. If challenged, presidents and their aides will cite the words of John Marshall's 1800 speech to the House of Representatives, in which the future chief justice called the president "the sole organ of the nation in its external relations, and its sole representative with foreign nations."[39] According to constitutional scholar Louis Fisher, Marshall meant that the president was the sole organ in *implementing,* not *making,* foreign policy.[40] Yet the Supreme Court took the more expansive view in its famous *Curtiss-Wright* decision, which cites Marshall in support of the idea that the president possesses broad inherent power in the making of foreign policy.[41]

Which of these views is correct? Do the powers inherent in national sovereignty belong mainly to Congress or to the president? Was Congress acting properly in 2015 when it ignored President Obama's objections and invited Israeli prime minister Benjamin Netanyahu to address a joint session? As we shall see in chapter 7, the answer to this question is generally the result of political struggle rather than constitutional debate.

Limits on Congressional Power

The Constitution not only enumerates congressional powers, it also lists a number of limits on the power of the legislative branch. For example, according to Article I, Section 9, except in the event of a national emergency, Congress is prohibited from suspending the writ of habeas corpus. This fundamental safeguard of liberty against the government's abuse of power means that individuals taken into custody by the authorities must promptly be brought before a magistrate and charged with an offense or released. Arrestees cannot be held indefinitely at the whim of the police. Congress is prohibited from enacting bills of attainder or ex post facto laws. That is, Congress cannot enact legislation declaring a person guilty without a trial or write laws that allow individuals to be punished for acts that were not criminal at the time of their commission. After the adoption of the Constitution, the Bill of Rights placed additional limits upon congressional power. The First Amendment declares, "Congress shall make no law respecting an establishment of religion, or prohibiting the free exercise thereof; or abridging the freedom of speech, or of the press; or the right of the people peaceably to assemble, and to petition the government for a redress of grievances." Of course, the precise meaning of the phrase "Congress shall make no law" has been debated in the courts for more than two centuries.

Checks and Balances

The framers were political realists and had little faith in what they called "parchment guarantees," that is, mere words. In the view of the nation's founders, without appropriate safeguards, any of the new government's institutions might pose a threat to citizens' liberties. What form, however, should such safeguards take? James Madison famously answered this question in *Federalist* 51, where he wrote, "But the great security against a gradual concentration of the several powers in the same department, consists in giving to those who administer each department the necessary constitutional means and personal motives to resist encroachments of the others."[42]

Consistent with this idea, the Constitution created three branches of government and assigned each branch a role in the operations of the others that would allow it to thwart the actions of the other branch. Thus, the president is required to submit appointments and treaties to the Congress, which may reject appointments and refuse to ratify treaties. The Congress can impeach and remove presidents and judges from office. The president nominates judges and may pardon persons convicted of crimes in federal court. The courts may overturn congressional and executive actions. The president may veto acts of Congress, and so forth.

Congress and Appointments

Among Congress's most important powers vis-à-vis the executive is the requirement that the president obtain senatorial consent for judicial appointments as well as those of major federal officers. Some 1200–1400 top federal officials require senatorial confirmation, and this is not always forthcoming. Over the course of American history, of some 500 cabinet nominations, 9 were rejected by the Senate and 12 were withdrawn in the face of Senate opposition.[43] Twelve of 151 Supreme Court nominations were rejected and 11 withdrawn by the president.[44] The Senate's confirmation power is more important than these numbers might suggest. Knowing that they will face Senate confirmation, presidents will seldom nominate individuals they think unlikely to be confirmed. In 2017, Senate Democrats delayed a number of Trump cabinet picks but were unable to actually block any appointees, though several nominees withdrew their names because their private financial commitments would have raised ethics concerns. Democrats used the confirmation hearings mainly to demonstrate to their constituents that they were willing to oppose the new president and to probe for weaknesses in the new administration. A Democratic filibuster briefly blocked the confirmation of President Trump's Supreme Court nominee Neil Gorsuch, but Republicans were able to change Senate rules to bring about Gorsuch's confirmation. After the retirement of Justice Anthony Kennedy in 2018, Trump nominated Appeals Court Judge Brett Kavanaugh to replace Kennedy on the High Court. Kavanaugh's confirmation hearings became a national drama stemming from controversy over allegations against him of sexual misconduct in high school and college along with concerns raised regarding his overall fitness for the Court. Kavanaugh was confirmed, though, by the narrowest margin.

Presidential nominations are first considered by the appropriate subject-matter committee of the Senate. If the committee schedules hearings, nominees are expected to testify. Other witnesses purporting to have knowledge of the nominee's fitness may testify for and against the nominee. A vote is taken to bring the nomination before the full Senate; the committee may or may not include a recommendation. When an appointment is presented to the Senate, there may be a debate, following which a majority of those senators present must agree to the motion "to advise and consent."

Not infrequently, the Senate will delay action on nominations, keeping a proposed appointment bottled up in committee, until the president accedes to some specific demand. This usually takes the form of a senator placing a "hold" on a nominee, slowing or even blocking further action. A hold is a procedure allowed under Senate rules and is virtually impossible to break if the senator placing the hold is a member of the majority party.

Traditionally, breaking a hold required a cloture vote with three-fifths of senators agreeing to end the hold. In 2013, however, when Democrats held a majority of seats in the Senate, but not three-fifths, majority leader Harry Reid crafted what he called the "nuclear option," allowing the Senate's leadership, at its discretion, to decide that a cloture vote (to force a vote by the chamber) for any given nominee would require only a simple majority. Reid said the rule change was justified because Republicans had blocked almost as many Obama nominees as the total blocked during previous presidencies since World War II. After the rules change, the stalled Obama nominees were confirmed by the full Senate. Democrats, however, soon had reason to question the wisdom of the 2013 rules change and in the future may want to change it back.

To begin with, in 2015, after the GOP took control of the Senate, Republican senators placed holds on a slew of President Obama's nominations. Republican leaders, naturally, were not about to use Reid's 2013 rule against their own members' holds, hence cloture for any of the Obama nominations would have required a three-fifths vote, nearly impossible to obtain in a chamber controlled by the Republicans. Accordingly, Senator Chuck Grassley (R) of Iowa placed holds on three senior State Department appointments, declaring they would not go forward until the department complied with Senate demands for documents relating to then Secretary of State Hillary Clinton's e-mails. Senator Ben Sasse (R) of Nebraska placed holds on all nominees to posts in the Department of Health and Human Services (HHS) until the administration agreed to provide information on various aspects of the implementation of the Patient Protection and Affordable Care Act. Senator Tom Cotton of Arkansas put holds on three ambassadorial appointments, demanding that the Secret Service conduct an investigation of leaks from that agency designed to embarrass a Republican congressman. By the end of the Obama administration, some one hundred presidential nominations plus Supreme Court nominee Merrick Garland, whom Senate Republican leaders simply refused to consider, remained on hold and would never be confirmed.

To make matters worse, from the Democratic perspective, in 2017, as the Trump administration put forward its choices for federal offices, Senate Democrats vociferously, but ineffectually, objected to quite a number of nominees for major and minor positions. Before 2013, Democrats might have filibustered some nominees and placed holds on others. Harry Reid's nuclear option, however, now gave the Senate's Republican leadership the power to defeat such tactics by declaring that cloture would require only a simple majority. Reid had exempted Supreme Court appointments from his rules change. But in 2017 Republicans extended the Reid rule to the High Court in order to overcome Democratic opposition to Trump nominee Neil Gorsuch. Later, Republicans were able to confirm the nomination of Brett Kavanaugh with only a two-vote majority. Had he been able to look into the future, Senator Reid might not have been so anxious to change the Senate's rules. Interestingly, James Wallner, a congressional scholar and former Senate aide, notes that senators are actually breaking the Senate rules every time they invoke the nuclear option instead of the existing process, which is required by Rule XXII for invoking cloture.[45] This means that the nuclear option can be reversed, as was done in the past when the chamber changed its cloture rules, but it is unlikely to happen while the Republicans are still in the majority.

Recess Appointments

In recent years severe partisan disagreements have led presidents often to resort to "recess appointments." These are authorized by Article II, Section 2, which states, "The President shall have Power to fill up all Vacancies that may happen during the Recess of the Senate, by granting Commissions which shall expire at the End of their next Session." Until recent years, recess appointments were made only between Senate sessions or when the Senate was adjourned for lengthy periods. In recent years, however, recess appointments have become more frequent and the Senate has resorted to a clever expedient. One senator is assigned the task of calling the chamber to order for a few moments every day for a pro forma session during periods of recess so that the president cannot claim the Senate was closed for business. Presidents have viewed this procedure as nothing more than a subterfuge, because the Senate was incapable of actually conducting business during these periods.

In 2012, President Obama thought to seize an opportunity when, during a ten-day recess, the Senate was not even in pro forma session during a three-day period. Obama quickly made three recess appointments to the National Labor Relations Board (NLRB). All three appointees had been blocked by Republican senators using a variety of procedural maneuvers. In a unanimous June 2014 decision, however, the Supreme Court ruled that a ten-day recess was "presumptively too short" to permit a recess appointment. The Court did not indicate how long a recess would be necessary to permit recess appointments by the president.

Another expedient to which presidents have resorted to circumvent senatorial power over appointments is the use of temporary appointees to fill executive branch posts. Currently, more than a dozen senior officials in the Departments of Justice, Treasury, Defense, and Health and Human Services whose appointments require Senate confirmation hold their positions on an "acting" basis. In most cases these are individuals who have been nominated by the president for a permanent position but have been awaiting Senate confirmation for many months. The appointment of an official to an "acting" slot prior to Senate confirmation is prohibited by the Federal Vacancies Reform Act of 1998. But presidents have become increasingly impatient with senatorial opposition and delay and have increasingly ignored the law, claiming that it is an unconstitutional intrusion upon the president's appointment powers. In 2016, however, the statute was upheld by the U.S. Court of Appeals for the District of Columbia, throwing into question not only the legality of the temporary appointees but also the validity of any decisions they might have made while in office. More litigation will undoubtedly result over this matter.[46]

Judicial Appointments

The Senate must confirm all federal judges. In the case of federal district and appellate judges, nominees are often blocked by holds and filibusters and the president is eventually forced to withdraw the name. More than sixty Obama nominees were kept in Senate limbo and eventually withdrawn. Many others would have been blocked if not for the Harry Reid nuclear option discussed earlier. Until the recent Merrick Garland case, delaying tactics have seldom been used in the case of Supreme Court justices. Instead, Supreme Court confirmations have produced epic battles between the Senate and the White House as Democrats and Republican have struggled to maintain or secure control of the High Court. In 1987, one Reagan nominee, Judge Robert Bork, was defeated in a 42–58 Senate vote, and a second, Judge Douglas Ginsburg, withdrew. Bork had been solicitor general during the Nixon administration and had been the official to actually fire Watergate special prosecutor Archibald Cox at Nixon's order. During the confirmation hearings, Democratic senators read passages from Bork's scholarly writings and judicial opinions that seemed to picture him as an extremist. Using this tactic against nominees came to be known as "Borking." Ginsburg withdrew from consideration in the face of allegations that he had smoked marijuana while a student.

George H. W. Bush encountered an unanticipated battle when he nominated Clarence Thomas to the Supreme Court. Bush calculated that Senate Democrats would be reluctant to attack an African American nominee even though Thomas was politically quite conservative. Democrats, indeed, hesitated but launched a campaign against Thomas centering around allegations from one of his former subordinates at the Equal Employment Opportunity Commission that Thomas had engaged in inappropriate sexually explicit banter with her. Thomas was confirmed after a nationally televised speech in which he accused his opponents of conducting a "legal lynching." Southern Democratic senators dependent upon the votes of African American constituents quickly ascertained that these constituents agreed with Thomas and so the senators gave him their support.[47]

During the Clinton administration, two individuals whom the president had introduced as nominees were forced to withdraw even before their nominations were formally sent to the Senate. In what the media dubbed "Nannygate," corporate lawyer Zoë Baird and federal judge Kimba Wood both asked the president to drop them from consideration when Republicans pointed to evidence that both might have employed undocumented immigrants as nannies for their young children. This was a sufficiently widespread practice among wealthy Americans that Senate investigators had no doubt that they would find it if they looked.

During the presidency of George W. Bush, Supreme Court nominee Harriet Miers was forced to withdraw from consideration. Miers, then White House counsel, had no judicial experience or experience in the constitutional areas dealt with by the Supreme Court. The Senate Judiciary Committee called her responses to questions inadequate, insufficient, and insulting and made it clear to the president that she would not be confirmed.[48]

In 2016, Justice Antonin Scalia died unexpectedly, creating the possibility that President Obama might make an appointment that would tip the ideological balance on the Court. The appointment of a liberal justice would give the Court's liberal wing the 5–4 majority that had previously been enjoyed by the conservative wing. Obama moved quickly to make an appointment, nominating Judge Merrick Garland, the well-respected chief judge of the U.S. Court of Appeals for the District of Columbia, often seen as the nation's second-most important federal court. Garland had been appointed to the court of appeals by President Bill Clinton and was generally viewed as a moderate-to-liberal Democrat. Senate Republicans responded to the threat of a shift in the balance of power on the Supreme Court by refusing to schedule hearings on the Garland nomination, effectively leaving it dead in the water. The Senate's Republican leadership hoped that the 2016 election might produce a Republican president who would then name a conservative justice. These hopes were realized when Donald Trump was elected and promised to choose a new justice in the Scalia mold. Trump fulfilled this promise when he nominated federal appeals court judge Neil Gorsuch, a conservative who, like Scalia, was an "originalist," interpreting the law in terms of the actual text and original meaning of the Constitution rather than taking the more liberal view of the Constitution as an evolving or "living" document. As we saw earlier, Gorsuch was confirmed after Republicans changed Senate cloture rules.

Keeping Congress in Check

While each branch is given some power over the two others, the framers were especially concerned about the Congress, and particularly the House of Representatives. The prior century of British history as well as the experience of the American states under the Articles of Confederation led the framers to believe that popularly elected legislative assemblies tended to be aggressive institutions inclined to use their connection to popular constituencies to aggrandize their own power. "The legislative department is everywhere extending the sphere of its activity," said James Madison, "and drawing all power into its impetuous vortex." For this reason, Madison thought special safeguards were needed to keep legislative power within bounds. "[W]here the legislative power is exercised by an assembly, which is inspired, by a supposed influence over the people, with an intrepid confidence in its own strength; . . . it is against the enterprising ambition of this department that the people ought to indulge all their jealousy and exhaust all their precautions."[49] To reduce this supposed threat, the framers gave the president a veto over acts of Congress, assigned the vice president the responsibility of presiding over the Senate, and hoped that the division of Congress into two separate houses, with a requirement that each must assent to any proposed legislation, would reduce the likelihood that the legislature would seek to add to its powers. The framers also thought staggered Senate terms, with only one-third of the members elected every two years, would ensure stability in the upper house of Congress even if the lower house fell victim to evanescent political whims and passions.

Subsequently, Chief Justice John Marshall claimed to find in the Constitution an implied judicial power to review acts of Congress and to invalidate those the High Court found unconstitutional. Interestingly, the framers did not fear the judiciary or the executive. "Executive usurpations," said Madison, were mainly to be feared from hereditary monarchs, not from the chief magistrates of republics.[50] Indeed, some of the framers feared that the executive was far too weak and would hardly play a role in the governance of the new nation. Rufus King of Massachusetts, for example, said he was concerned that, "an extreme caution in favor of liberty [in the construction of the executive] might enervate the government we were forming."[51]

Checks Unbalanced?

Was Madison correct? Is the Congress an "impetuous vortex" while the executive is politically supine? Surely not. The framers saw the world through the lens of their experience. Through a contemporary lens, though, it might seem to be the president whose power is ever expanding while that of the Congress wanes. There are a number of reasons for this phenomenon, which we will address in detail in chapter 6. For now, let us consider just one of the several constitutional factors that have gradually empowered the president and weakened the Congress. This is the principle of *execution.*

To state the matter simply, presidents derive power from their execution of the laws. Decisions made by the Congress are executed by the president, while presidents execute their own decisions. The result is an *asymmetric* relationship between presidential and congressional power. Whatever Congress does empowers the president; presidential actions, on the other hand, often weaken Congress. Congress has no executive power of its own. If it wishes to accomplish any goal, Congress must delegate power to the executive. Sometimes Congress accompanies its delegation of power with explicit standards and guidelines; sometimes it does not. In either eventuality, over the long term, almost any program launched by the Congress empowers the president and the executive branch more generally, whose funding and authority must be increased to execute the law.

Take, for example the 2010 Affordable Care Act. After much debate, Congress voted to enact a piece of legislation that would cost billions of dollars and have an enormous impact on the nation's health care system. Congress certainly had no capacity to execute and administer the new law. Whatever the impact of "Obamacare" on the health care system, the statute entailed an enormous grant of power and funding to the executive branch. Utilizing these grants of executive power, the Department of Health and Human Services went on to develop thousands of pages of rules and regulations, all having the force of law. Many rules were drafted in consultation with the White House, and while over the coming years HHS will use its own judgment in developing new regulations, presidents will intervene in the process as they see fit. Thus, in its attempt to promote health care, Congress inevitably added to executive and presidential power. The Affordable Care Act is hardly unique. Every congressional statute—and there are thousands—empowers the executive to do something. Some statutes give the executive more discretion in its use of power, some less, but the end result is always to increase the power of the executive by providing the executive with more authority, more money, more personnel, and more justification for subsequent action to enhance or improve the service being provided or regulation being imposed.

Congress's most important power vis-à-vis the executive is its "power of the purse." Article I, Section 9, of the Constitution declares, "No money shall be drawn from the Treasury, but in Consequence of Appropriations made by Law." When Congress writes legislation authorizing some program, it generally enacts an appropriation to pay the costs of the program for the next fiscal year. Except in the case of "entitlement programs," like Social Security, whose appropriations are automatically tied to a statutory formula, Congress must agree to appropriate new funds for existing programs on an annual basis. Congress has the constitutional power to reduce or cut funding for every executive branch program except the entitlements, and even these could, at least hypothetically, be altered or even abolished. Congressional Republicans, for example, periodically threaten to "privatize" Social Security. Article I, Section 8, further enhances Congress's power of the purse by assigning to Congress the power to levy taxes and borrow money. Without congressional approval, the executive could not pay its bills.

Article I, Sections 7 and 8, do give Congress powerful weapons to use in struggles against the executive. These weapons, though, can be difficult to wield. Once created, federal programs can quickly develop political constituencies from among beneficiaries and service providers, who will fight tooth and nail to protect their favorite programs from the budget ax. Take the amusing but typical case of "Super Twiggy," the cartoon squirrel. Super Twiggy was a character in web videos shown in Spain touting the health benefits of California-grown walnuts. Costing about $3 million to produce and air, the videos were part of a $200-million-per-year Agriculture Department marketing effort to promote U.S. farm products overseas. When the program was threatened with cuts, walnut growers, farm groups, and farm-state representatives came to its defense and saved the little squirrel, illustrating the difficulty of eliminating an established program.

Nevertheless, under the terms of the Budget Control Act of 2011, Congress did impose mandatory across-the-board spending cuts for almost all nonentitlement programs. The cuts, referred to as "budget sequestration," went into effect in 2013 and are scheduled to continue until 2021, slowing the rate of increase in federal spending. The 2011 Budget Control Act was itself reluctantly signed by President Obama in the face of a threat by House Republicans to use Congress's constitutional power over borrowing to refuse to raise the nation's debt limit and potentially produce a government default on some of its loans.

Thus, Article I, Sections 7 and 8, can give the Congress power to say no to the president. If, however, Congress decides it wants to accomplish something rather than be perceived as merely obstructionist—a source of gridlock, as critics like to say—it must resume empowering the executive. This is one of the great dilemmas of congressional power. As it seeks to govern, Congress may gradually surrender its power to govern.

A Brief History of Congress:
From First Branch to Second Fiddle

IN ARTICLE I, AS WE SAW, the Constitution's framers assigned most powers of governance to the Congress. During the early years of the Republic, Congress was indeed the dominant branch of American government and made certain to leave no doubt about its place in the constitutional order, generally keeping both the judiciary and the executive on short leashes. Thus, in 1804 the House impeached Supreme Court Justice Samuel Chase essentially for his vocal opposition to the policies backed by the Jeffersonian majority in Congress. Chase was acquitted by the Senate, but future justices were generally more careful about asserting their political views. Justice Ruth Bader Ginsburg's uncomplimentary remarks about Republican presidential candidate Donald Trump in 2016 were so exceptional as to generate a good deal of unfavorable media commentary.

As to the president, in the early years of the Republic, Congress demonstrated its disdain for the chief executive by refusing to appropriate funds for even one secretary or assistant to help presidents carry out their day-to-day tasks. As a result, presidents often greeted visitors personally and were responsible for their own correspondence and record keeping. George Washington resorted to the expedient of employing family members as informal private secretaries. According to administrative historian Leonard White, Congress believed that presidents did not play a sufficiently important role in the governmental process to merit a staff.[1] And, of course, by refusing to provide the chief executive with assistants, Congress hoped to make certain that presidents would have difficulty expanding their role.

Today, not only does the president command thousands of assistants, but many of the enumerated powers of Congress, such as the war power, for all intents and purposes have been captured by the executive. And while most judges are polite in their public utterances, the judiciary has few compunctions about striking down congressional actions and circumscribing congressional powers.

The Constitution may have given Congress very formidable formal powers, but, as the framers liked to say, facts asserted on "parchment" do not always hold true. Historically, Congress's ability to actually exercise its nominal powers has depended upon the legislature's ability to address three issues. The first of these is its *constituency*. Congress, or any legislative assembly for that matter, depends for its power on the support of significant groups in society. If important social forces and interests believe that the legislature actively represents their views and aspirations, they are likely to give it their support. If, on the other hand, the Congress lacks a strong constituency, it becomes more vulnerable to encroachments by other institutions.

The second issue influencing congressional power is *organization*. Congress, like any representative assembly, can be a chaotic body. Each member of an assembly is nominally equal to each and every other member. All are eager to assert their own views and to promote their individual interests. Left to itself, a legislative assembly can become a giant debating society, unable to reach any resolution or achieve any goals or purposes. Bringing order out of the chaos and maximizing the potential power of an assembly requires organization and leadership. If the assembly is to be more than a debating society, it must develop rules, institutional structures, and leadership arrangements to set a legislative agenda, end debate, and reach decisions. One form of organization that can help a representative assembly function more efficiently is the political party. Party leaders attempt to cajole and coerce their members into acting as a unified group in order to pursue some legislative agenda. These efforts are called party *discipline*. In June, 2015, for example, Republican Speaker of the House John Boehner punished several Republicans who had refused to follow his lead on an important piece of legislation by depriving them of subcommittee chairs and threatening further reprisals. Though members resent this sort of discipline, Congress is generally most effective when parties provide it with leadership and organizational coherence. At times, to be sure, party battles produce gridlock. And occasionally, if the president is an Andrew Jackson, who was both chief executive and party leader, strong parties can help the president bring Congress to heel as members of the president's party in Congress opt to support the president rather than to stand up for congressional power. Generally, however, strong parties organize and empower the Congress and allow it to compete more vigorously with the White House.

This brings us to the third problem Congress must solve in order to effectively exercise its formal powers. This is its *relationship to the executive.* Presidents often attempt to impose their own views on every aspect of governance. The Constitution, as presidential scholar Edward Corwin famously quipped, is an, "invitation to struggle."[2] In this struggle, the president has certain advantages. As we saw in chapter 1, the president gains power from executing the law. In addition, the president is a unitary actor not faced with the organizational problems that can plague a large representative assembly. Presidents, moreover, have the power of initiative and can sometimes force a reluctant Congress to follow in their wake. And, to make matters worse, the president's visibility can allow particularly talented chief executives to persuade their fellow citizens that they somehow embody the hopes and aspirations of the nation. When Congress encounters such a president—a Jackson or a Roosevelt—the legislature can be hard-pressed to compete with the executive for popular support. We will examine all these matters in more detail in chapter 6. Thus, while the Constitution nominally awarded to Congress more power than to the president, America's constitutional structure puts Congress at a disadvantage when it comes to the actual exercise of power. Congress must constantly struggle to avoid being marginalized by the executive branch.

As we examine the history of Congress, let us pay particular attention to issues of constituency, congressional organization, and the ways in which Congress and the executive have dealt with their constitutional invitation to struggle. Focusing on political changes outside Congress and institutional changes within Congress, the history of the legislative branch can be divided into six political eras. These are the Federalist and Jeffersonian eras, the Jacksonian era, the Civil War Congress, the Republican era, the "New Deal" and postwar period, and the contemporary period of congressional gridlock and presidential unilateralism.

During each of these periods we can find examples of congressional successes and achievements, but the overall picture is one of institutional retrocession. Beneath the surface of the day-to-day and even year-to-year flow of congressional history is a story of a long institutional retreat in the face of encroachments by the executive branch. Congress was the "first branch" but is in danger of becoming the "second fiddle" of American government.

The Federalist and Jeffersonian Eras

America's first elections under the new constitution were held in 1788. The Electoral College, as was expected, chose George Washington to be the nation's first president. Twenty-six senators were appointed by the state legislatures. Fifty-nine members were elected to the new House of Representatives. Some states had established congressional districts and asked voters within each district to choose a representative. Other states provided for statewide, at-large elections for members of the House. The 1842 Apportionment Act required the states to form districts within each state and to elect one member of Congress from each district. Some states ignored this law, and Congress never enforced it. But in 1967 Congress enacted legislation explicitly prohibiting at-large elections except in the seven least populous states entitled to only one representative each. Today, each state legislature divides the state into as many districts as the number of House members to which it is entitled on the basis of the most recent census, and candidates compete within each district for one congressional seat. Districting, as we shall see in chapter 3, causes enormous political controversies, and some reformers have even advocated a return to statewide, at-large elections.[3]

Members of the new House of Representatives began to assemble in New York, the nation's temporary capital, in March 1789. Subsequently, the government moved to Philadelphia for ten years, until it finally settled in Washington, D.C. in 1800. Even today, a small number of families—names like Bush and Clinton come to mind—seem to play outsize roles in American politics, and certainly in the world of the late eighteenth century, only a very small number of relatively wealthy, well-connected, and well-educated individuals could undertake political careers. Hence the same names—Madison, Jefferson, Hamilton, Adams, Monroe, Lee, Morris—seem to crop up in the Continental Congress, the Constitutional Convention, and the Congress of the United States. For the next half-century, until they were roughly shouldered aside by the new political forces of the Jacksonian era, small cliques of these competing notables would dominate American politics. The members of the first House were a rather distinguished group that included nine Constitutional Convention delegates. Indeed, one of Virginia's representatives was none other than James Madison, the Constitution's principal author. Most other representatives had served in the Continental Congress, the state ratifying conventions, and the various state legislatures. Senators arrived a bit later but were no less illustrious than their colleagues. Ten members of the new Senate had served in the Constitutional Convention; several had signed the Declaration of Independence, and most had served in their state legislatures.

It was not until April 1789, that each house achieved a *quorum*. The term "quorum" refers to the minimum number of senators or representatives needed for that house to officially function as a legislative body. A congressional quorum is defined by Article I, Section 5, of the Constitution as a majority of the house's members. For each house, the first order of business was the selection of leaders. The House of Representatives chose Frederick Muhlenberg of Pennsylvania as its Speaker, while the Senate named John Langdon of Pennsylvania, formerly a member of the Constitutional Convention, as its president pro tempore.

The matters of House and Senate leadership are treated differently by the Constitution. The leadership of the Senate is constitutionally defined. Article I, Section 3, names the vice president of the United States as the presiding officer of the Senate and avers that the Senate should elect a president pro tempore to preside in the absence of the vice president. Leadership of the House, on the other hand, is less precisely determined. Article I, Section 2, says only that the House of Representatives shall choose its own Speaker.

This difference in constitutional language has had important consequences for the powers that each chamber has allowed its leaders. Since Speakers are elected directly by the House, as we shall see in chapter 4, they have been entrusted with a great deal of power under House rules.

In its very first session, the House gave its Speaker the power to decide points of order, to appoint committees, to end debate by calling the question, and to announce the results of a vote. Senate rules, on the other hand, allow minimal power to its presiding officer, the vice president, whose political and partisan attachments may differ from those of a majority of the senators. Senate president pro tempore has become an honorific position generally held by the longest-serving member of the majority party, and sessions of the Senate are usually presided over by a junior member of the majority party who exercises little discretionary authority. Since 1920, each party in the Senate has formally elected a leader, and the leader of the majority party, known appropriately enough as the *majority leader,* wields considerable power in the upper chamber. We will learn more about House and Senate leaders in chapter 4.

The First Branch

In the early years, the Congress seemed rather amateurish, for want of a better term. Members frequently displayed a lack of decorum, resorting to taunts, insults, and occasionally physical violence against their political foes. With the exception of the first Congress, which met for seventeen months, Congress was seldom in session for more than half the year, as compared to modern Congresses, which are in session much of the year. Membership turnover in both the House and Senate was quite high, especially after the government moved to Washington. Life in the new capital was unpleasant, and few members cared to serve for more than one term. Senators often chose not to complete even one term and frequently resigned to pursue other opportunities.[4] As a result, over half the members of any given House in the early years were freshmen, lacking legislative experience. With its staggered terms, the Senate was a more stable body. But in both houses, leaders retained their positions for only short periods of time. The average length of service for a House Speaker before 1875, for example, was hardly more than three years.[5]

In the early years too most of the business of the Congress was undertaken by each house as a whole. Legislation was generally initiated by the House of Representatives, meeting as the Committee of the Whole. When a course of action was agreed upon, a bill might be sent to a temporary, ad hoc committee for refinement. Eventually, hundreds of ad hoc committees duplicated one another's efforts and competed for members' time and attention The completed measure would go to the Senate, where it would typically be considered by the entire body. This mode of legislating was cumbersome and time-consuming, as it required lengthy discussion among many members about the details of bills that today would be dealt with in the standing, subject-matter committees of the House and Senate. The House began to establish such committees in its first session, but by 1810 had only ten standing committees. The Senate established its first standing committee in 1816.

Despite these institutional shortcomings, members of the early Congresses took their legislative responsibilities seriously. The first Congress, in particular, compiled an extraordinary record. In its three sessions, the first Congress created the departments of State, War, and Treasury; began the creation of the federal court system; enacted tariff, copyright, and patent legislation; and established the Bank of the United States. Perhaps even more important, the first Congress proposed twelve amendments to the Constitution and sent these to the states for ratification. The first ten, known today as the Bill of Rights, are the cornerstones of civil liberties in America. Congress also proposed two other amendments. One of these proposals prohibited a sitting Congress from raising its own salary. This proposed amendment was unratified by the requisite three-fourths of the states and was forgotten for nearly two centuries until a University of Texas student, reading about the old proposal, launched a campaign that led to its ratification in 1992 as the Twenty-Seventh Amendment. The last proposal, establishing a precise formula for the apportionment of congressional districts, was never ratified.

Early Congresses also found themselves embroiled in battles with two particularly ambitious presidents, George Washington and Thomas Jefferson. Washington, America's first president, understood that his conduct in office would influence the way in which Americans viewed not only the presidency but the new nation as well. He made a point of touring the country, making public appearances, and always comporting himself with great dignity so as to build respect for his office.[6] Virtually everything Washington did set a precedent.[7] Washington's proclamation of American neutrality in the 1793 war between Britain and France, followed by the signing of the Jay Treaty in 1794, normalizing trade relations with England, began to establish the principle of presidential primacy in the realm of foreign relations. Washington sent regular messages to Congress and made an annual appearance and speech—the forerunner of today's State of the Union address.

Washington also sought to take firm control over major government appointments, including, in 1795, making the first "recess appointment," an appointment made while Congress was not in session, to avoid the need for Senate confirmation. Washington also made it a practice to call meetings of the secretaries of the new government's departments, laying the foundations for the president's cabinet. Washington invented the principle of "executive privilege" when he refused to give the House documents it requested regarding a diplomatic matter. Subsequent presidents expanded the idea that presidents were not obligated to give Congress records of their deliberations. The Supreme Court ultimately recognized the doctrine in the 1974 case of *U.S. v. Nixon,* when presidents were held to possess executive privilege, though, in the matter at hand, Nixon was ordered to give Congress the "Watergate tapes," which had recorded meetings in the Oval Office.[8]

Washington also assigned his Treasury secretary and loyal lieutenant, Alexander Hamilton, to lead the administration's supporters in the Congress. Washington saw his relationship with Hamilton as akin to that of a king to his prime minister and relied upon Hamilton, though not a member of Congress, to work with members to secure the success of the president's legislative programs. The administration's supporters began to call themselves *Federalists* to claim the mantle of the Constitution's proponents, though some had actually been Anti-Federalists during the ratification debates. These Federalists generally spoke for New England commercial interests and supported a program of protective tariffs to encourage manufacturing, assumption of the states' Revolutionary War debts, the creation of a national bank, and the resumption of trade relations with England.

While Hamilton was able to organize the administration's congressional supporters, his efforts also galvanized the administration's foes. These members of Congress looked to Secretary of State Thomas Jefferson for leadership and were known at first as the Jeffersonian Republicans, and later as the Democratic-Republicans. The Jeffersonian Republicans, who mainly represented southern agricultural interests, are the forebears of the contemporary Democrats, making today's Democratic Party the oldest political party in the world. The Jeffersonian Republicans favored free trade, the promotion of agriculture over commercial interests, and friendship with France.

In this battle, both sides sought to make use of congressional powers and, in so doing, often bolstered and better defined those powers. In the battle with President Washington over the Jay Treaty, the Senate ratified the treaty but the House made clear that it retained the power to refuse to appropriate funds in support of a presidential foreign policy initiative that did not have its backing. Congress, moreover, established the principle—one that persisted for many decades—that the president's veto power could be used only to protect the integrity of the executive branch. Presidents were not to veto bills simply because they disagreed with them. Washington assented to this principle, saying, "I never had such confidence in my own faculty of judging as to be over tenacious of the opinions I may have imbibed in doubtful cases."[9]

Congress, particularly its Jeffersonian members, was also sensitive to efforts by the executive to set its legislative agenda. Led by Secretary Hamilton, the Treasury Department in particular attempted to bring proposed legislation to the House as though it controlled Congress's legislative business. Representative Thomas Fitzsimons of Pennsylvania responded to one such effort by saying, "there was a degree of indelicacy, not to say impropriety, in permitting the heads of departments to bring bills before the House."[10]

Led by James Madison, the House fought vigorously to defend its power of the purse against what it saw as efforts by the executive to take the initiative in matters of taxation and spending. As early as 1790, Secretary Hamilton had begun to present reports and propose tax and spending legislation to the House. Jeffersonians in the House resisted as a matter of principle, with Madison declaring that the executive was attempting to usurp congressional authority. Abraham Baldwin of Georgia said firmly, "The laws should be framed by the legislature."[11] By 1794, the House was determined to refrain from even receiving recommendations from the Treasury secretary and, led by Albert Gallatin of Pennsylvania, one of the few Jeffersonians with a background in public finance, established its own Ways and Means Committee in 1795 to develop plans for new taxation and spending. Hamilton was reportedly "mortified" and resigned his post soon thereafter.[12] Hamilton's successor, Oliver Wolcott, refrained from challenging Congress. The House had won an important victory.

While the House was asserting its power of the purse, the Senate made certain to affirm its own constitutional power vis-à-vis presidential appointments. Senators understood immediately that they had an interest in seeing to it that appointments to public office should go to their friends and supporters and be denied to their enemies and political opponents. Accordingly, senators made clear to the president that nominees to executive positions would be more likely to receive favorable treatment from the upper chamber if the chief executive would listen to the "advice" of important senators before presenting his nominations. In some instances, state delegations comprising senators and House members would meet with the president to discuss appointments to offices within their own states. Neither Washington nor Adams sought to challenge the Senate's power in these matters.

The Jeffersonians in Office

During the 1790s, the Jeffersonians had developed a partisan press, using newspapers, particularly the *National Gazette,* as well as handbills, to attack their political foes, particularly Alexander Hamilton, whose illegitimate birth became grist for the mills of Jeffersonian publicists. The Federalists responded with legislation—the Alien and Sedition Acts—to outlaw criticism of the government. As these acts proved impossible to enforce, the Federalists established their own newspapers and launched vicious attacks against Thomas Jefferson.

The Jeffersonians proved to be more effective political organizers and campaigners than the Federalists and gradually expanded their political base from the South into the Middle Atlantic states. James Madison became the Democratic-Republicans' chief organizer, and from his post as chair of the Orange County, Virginia, Democratic-Republican central committee, oversaw the new party's national political efforts.[13]

In 1800, Jefferson defeated Federalist president John Adams and led his party to power, taking control of Congress as well as the White House. The presidential election revealed that the machinery of the Electoral College was seriously flawed. Under the Constitution, each elector was authorized to cast two votes, one for president and one for vice president. Each of the Democratic-Republican electors chosen by the Electoral College cast a vote for Jefferson and a vote for Aaron Burr, whom the Jeffersonians had intended to elect as vice president. Apparently the Democratic-Republicans had planned upon one of their electors abstaining from casting a second vote, thus assuring Jefferson the majority, but this scheme somehow misfired. With a tie in the Electoral College, the House of Representatives would then choose between Jefferson and Burr. House Federalists saw an opportunity to strike a blow against their political enemy, Jefferson. Many voted to elect Burr to the presidency, producing thirty-five successive votes in which neither Jefferson nor Burr won a majority. Finally, on the thirty-sixth ballot, Jefferson was elected after several Federalists decided to abstain from voting to end the impasse.[14] This flaw in the Electoral College system was corrected by the Twelfth Amendment, which stipulated separate balloting for the president and vice president.[15]

Once in office, Jefferson sought to continue Washington's policy of neutrality in the wars between England and France. In 1807 the president ordered an embargo upon all trade and shipping between America and both combatants. The 1807 Embargo Act, passed by Congress, was somewhat more damaging to England, which depended upon trade, than to France, which did not. The act, however, was economically ruinous to the American economy and was widely evaded by northeastern merchants who resorted to smuggling and subterfuge to maintain their trade routes.

Jefferson was more successful when it came to expanding America's territorial possessions. In 1803, without any specific authorization from Congress, Jefferson issued a decree—the forebear of today's executive orders—authorizing the expenditure of $15 million to purchase the Louisiana Territory from France, thus nearly doubling the size of the nation.[16] Congress later ratified the purchase despite many arguments that it was unlawful. The Louisiana Purchase was the first, but certainly not the last, case in American history when a president's capacity to act impelled Congress to follow in his wake.

To further his ambitions, Jefferson strove to make himself the master of Congress. To this end, the president recruited floor leaders—who today would be called whips—who were recognized as the president's congressional agents. These individuals were responsible for guiding the president's program through the Congress by using patronage, flattery, and deals. Jefferson also strengthened the Republican Party caucuses in both the House and Senate. Party leaders and members met on a regular basis in Albert Gallatin's home. Now Treasury secretary, Gallatin served as a direct conduit between Jefferson and his supporters in the Congress. The party caucus discussed legislation and legislative strategies. And while the Jeffersonians had opposed efforts of the Washington administration to draft bills for congressional consideration, they accepted Jefferson's drafts of important bills and, in meetings of the caucus, developed strategies to move these through the legislative process.

With Jefferson, founder and leader of the Democratic-Republicans, in the White House, the congressional party caucus served the chief executive. In 1808, however, Jefferson declined to run for a third term. At this point, the party caucus turned the tables and became an instrument through which congressional leaders could wield power. In 1808 the caucus took upon itself the task of nominating the Republican presidential candidate, selecting James Madison to succeed Jefferson as the Republican nominee and eventual president, after an easy victory in the Electoral College.

Having in effect seized the power to select the president, the Republican congressional caucus saw no particular reason to do the president's bidding. Indeed, when President Madison indicated his interest in a second term in 1812, the Republican caucus secured a number of concessions from him. These included Madison's reluctant promise to support the party's "War Hawks" and their eventually disastrous plan to invade Canada. As the congressional caucus came to be perceived as a king maker, ambitious cabinet secretaries made certain to ingratiate themselves with the leadership of the Congress, thus undercutting the authority of the chief executive. The power of the caucus, moreover, opened the possibility that some aggressive and ambitious member of Congress might come to dominate the caucus and, through it, emerge as a rival to the president for national political prominence.

Just such an individual emerged in 1811 when Henry Clay of Kentucky was elected Speaker of the House—a position he held for six terms. Clay made himself the spokesperson for westerners and with their support became the leader of the Republican caucus and Speaker of the House of Representatives. Clay dramatically increased the power of the Speaker and the influence of the House in national politics. Determined to circumvent the president and to make Congress the center of national policy initiative, Clay began by appointing his friends and allies to chair all the congressional committees. Committee chairs were discouraged from seeking advice from executive departments and were, instead, expected to cultivate their own sources of information and to use their own initiative to develop legislation for consideration by the House. To deal with legislative matters where committees did not already exist, Clay brought about the establishment of new standing committees, increasing their number to about twenty. When it came to floor debate, Clay used and enlarged the powers of the Speaker to control the proceedings, recognize participants, and cut off discussion.

Under Clay's direction, the various committees expanded oversight of the executive branch. In 1814, the House created a Standing Committee on Government Expenditures and in 1816, divided its responsibilities among six standing committees on expenditures, responsible for the State, Treasury, War, Navy, and Post Office Departments, as well as one auditing the construction of public buildings. Through these committees, Congress was able to closely monitor the operations of the federal government. The purpose of these committees was, as Clay put it, "to take control of the government." Congressional control of the government was strengthened by a host of congressional investigations of executive departments.[17] Between 1812 and 1826, congressional committees investigated the departments of the Army, Post Office, Treasury, and a number of other executive agencies with a view toward finding evidence of and punishing wrongdoing. During this period, Congress established its power to investigate executive departments and to use subpoena powers to compel testimony and the production of information.

By the mid-1820s Congress had laid full claim to its constitutional status as the first branch of American government. Through politicians like Henry Clay, Congress had identified itself with the growing and dynamic political forces of the West. The congressional caucus controlled presidential nominations; Congress had created an organizational backbone of standing congressional committees that had become the major sources of national legislation; senators wielded enormous power over appointments; and the Speaker of the House had shouldered the president aside as the nation's most important and visible political leader. Congressional power, however, came crashing down from this pinnacle when legislators encountered an opponent who could seldom be out-maneuvered, would never allow himself to be intimidated, and stood high in the popular estimation, namely President Andrew Jackson.

The Age of Jackson

His victory in the Battle of New Orleans had made General Andrew Jackson, known as "Old Hickory," America's greatest hero and an obvious presidential candidate. Like Henry Clay, Jackson spoke for the dynamic and expansionist political forces of the American West. But while Clay was merely a politician, Jackson was a living legend, "half horse and half alligator," as his campaign songs declared. And while most politicians dueled mainly if not exclusively with words, Jackson not infrequently dueled with pistols as well. The general had emerged victorious, though not unscathed, from quite a number of gunfights. In the violent America of the early nineteenth century, Jackson's notoriously bad temper and readiness to defend his honor at gunpoint only added to Old Hickory's stature as the embodiment of the nation's vigor and frontier spirit.

Standing in the way of Jackson's presidential aspirations was the fact that the general was far more popular in the nation at large than within the Democratic-Republican congressional caucus that controlled the nominating process. Leading members of the party caucus had presidential ambitions of their own and had no intention of handing the keys of the White House to the general. Matters came to a head in the 1824 presidential election. During the two years prior to the election, Jackson's followers had adopted a strategy of discrediting the caucus by securing the endorsements of state legislatures. After the Tennessee legislature voted to nominate Jackson for the presidency, several states nominated Clay, two nominated John Quincy Adams, and South Carolina nominated its favorite son, John C. Calhoun.[18] One candidate, Treasury Secretary Crawford, hoped the party caucus would give him the nomination and declined to seek state legislative endorsements.

When the party caucus convened in 1824, most members of Congress believed that the intervention of the state legislatures had effectively ended caucus control of the nominating process, and few even bothered to attend the meeting. A small group, nevertheless, nominated Crawford, and the main contenders—Crawford, Adams, Clay, and Jackson—all claiming to have been nominated by some official body, launched their presidential campaigns. By 1824, some states allowed popular election of presidential electors, while others clung to the original system in which the state legislatures chose the electors. Accordingly, the four candidates vied both for popular support and the support of the state legislatures. When the popular and legislative votes were counted, Jackson had won a plurality of the popular vote and a plurality, though not a majority, in the Electoral College. Absent an Electoral College majority, the House of Representatives was required to decide the outcome. In the House, Henry Clay threw his support to John Quincy Adams, denying Jackson the presidency. Clay received Adams's promise to be named secretary of state. Jackson's supporters called this the "corrupt bargain" of 1824 and vowed to put Old Hickory into the White House in 1828.

Between 1824 and 1828, Jackson's allies, led by Senator Martin Van Buren of New York, constructed party organizations and worked to expand the suffrage. As we shall see again in chapter 3, election rules are generally written to serve the interests of the political forces in a position to write the rules. The Jacksonians knew that the general had overwhelming support among ordinary Americans. If property restrictions on voting could be removed, and if all the states could be induced to adopt direct popular election of the presidential electors, Jackson would surely win. Accordingly, these two reforms became major goals of the Jacksonian movement, which between 1824 and 1828 succeeded on both fronts. Most property restrictions were removed, and all but two states, Delaware and South Carolina, adopted popular election of electors.

To deal with the fact that many of Jackson's supporters were poor and uneducated and had little experience of voting, the Jacksonians organized political clubs throughout the states to inform and mobilize the general's admirers and make sure they voted. Before the 1832 election, the Jacksonians also constructed a nominating system that would take advantage of the general's popularity among rank-and-file local politicians, as opposed to elites in Washington. This was the party convention mode of nomination that began with local conventions empowered to select delegates to state party conventions, which in turn chose delegates to the national party convention. Local party activists would control the nomination, and the congressional party caucus mode of nomination was gone forever. The national party conventions remained important political institutions for the next century and a half, though today the conventions are mainly ceremonial affairs, usually ratifying decisions made in the primaries.

In the 1828 election, Jackson defeated his only rival, President John Q. Adams, by a solid margin, winning nearly 57 percent of the popular vote and close to 70 percent of the electoral vote. During the administrations of Madison, Monroe, and John Q. Adams, the presidency had waned in importance. Jackson moved to change the place of the presidency in the American political structure and to relegate the Congress to a secondary position.

One of the three elements determining the political power of a legislative assembly is, as we noted earlier, the legislature's ties to groups and forces in society that see it as expressing their views and serving their interests.[19] Congress had grown in power as its most prominent leaders made themselves spokespersons for western and southern interests that in turn supported the Congress in its battles with the presidency. However, a charismatic and demagogic president may, at least briefly, convince those selfsame groups to identify with and give their support to the executive, thus weakening the Congress and compelling its members to do his bidding. This was precisely Jackson's strategy.

Jackson was already a national legend, especially in the South and West, eclipsing the comparatively lackluster Washington crowd. The democratization of the presidential selection process further increased the power of the office, as Old Hickory could call upon the support of a national electorate following in his battles with his political foes. And while Americans needed little reminding, in order to encourage citizens to view Jackson as the dominant force in American politics, Jackson's followers built a vigorous party press to promote the president's ideas and even hired a group of painters to make certain that the president's image was everywhere, including on buttons, jugs, plates, and engravings widely distributed among members of the American public.[20] Moreover, as the undisputed leader of what now called itself the Democratic Party, Jackson could usually count on the support of Democratic senators and representatives, who commanded majorities in both houses of Congress

One way in which Jackson permanently strengthened the presidency and weakened Congress was by his use of the veto power. Prior to Jackson's presidency, the veto had been seen as an extraordinary action, to be used only if the president believed that a congressional action usurped the authority of the executive branch. The president was not viewed as having the authority to veto a bill simply because of a policy disagreement. Even George Washington had only made use of two vetoes, and Adams, Jefferson, and J. Q. Adams never vetoed a piece of legislation. Jackson vetoed twelve bills and made it clear that he believed the president to possess the constitutional authority to veto bills that did not comport with his own view of the national interest. In subsequent decades the veto became a routine presidential instrument.

The prominence of the Senate had begun to increase in the 1830s as well. During that decade, the divisions over slavery and tariff policy that led to civil war in 1861 began to manifest themselves. These divisions pitted states against one another, and senators were, of course, spokespersons for states. The rules of the Senate, moreover, allowed members to speak for hours rather than the few minutes normally permitted in the House.

From the 1830s onward, the sectional issues of the day were aired in lengthy speeches and great debates in the Senate, with several senators emerging as sectional champions. Spokespersons for the southern cause included Senator Robert Y. Hayne of South Carolina, while the interests of the North were defended by one of the greatest orators in Senate history, Daniel Webster of Massachusetts. During the two-day-long Hayne-Webster debate of January 1830, Hayne assailed the North, defended the concepts of nullification and state sovereignty, and called for an alliance of southern and western states against northeastern interests. Webster replied, attacking Hayne's arguments, and ended with the famous refrain "Liberty and Union, now and forever, one and inseparable!"[21] Westerners, including President Jackson, were strong nationalists, and Webster's speech had a profound effect on them. The Senate's importance as a forum and, at times, as the institution in which sectional divisions could be discussed and compromises reached put the Senate at the center of American politics, where it would remain until the Civil War.

The prominence of the Senate, in turn, meant that senators with presidential ambitions were able to use the national political stage afforded them by their Senate seats to increase their political prominence. One way to generate publicity and to gain a reputation for courage and independence was to attack the administration, gradually making the Senate the chief locus of opposition to Jackson.

A number of Jackson's Senate opponents, most notably Henry Clay, went so far as to form a new political party. They named this party the "Whigs" to evoke the memory of British opponents of royal absolutism, and resolved to contest the Democratic Party's hold on power. The misnamed era of good feelings was at an end.

The Resurgence of Congressional Power After Jackson

After Jackson left the White House, the power of the presidency waned. Jackson had believed in a strong presidency. Ironically, however, after Jackson left office the political party that he and his followers had built, now calling itself the Democrats, weakened the presidency and strengthened not only the Congress but the states as well. The Democratic Party had been constructed as a congeries of state party organizations. Within each state, a clique of party notables reigned supreme, controlling political nominations, patronage positions, and, when the birth of the Whig Party reignited interparty competition, the armies of party workers that were charged with mobilizing voters. Each state's paramount party leaders often had themselves appointed to the U.S. Senate by the state legislatures they controlled.

After the departure of their supreme leader, Old Hickory, these state party notables saw no reason to defer to the wishes of meddlesome outsiders, such as presidents, when it came to managing the affairs of their own states or the nation as a whole. First, from their posts in the U.S. Senate, state party leaders became a logrolling coalition for state power, confining the federal government to marginal activities and limiting its revenues to customs duties and the proceeds from public land sales. Each clique of state party leaders controlled its own state and united with other state party leaders in agreeing that the federal government should refrain from bothering them. The leaders of the southern states were especially vehement members of this coalition for state power, seeing in the sovereignty of the states the best security against outside efforts to interfere with slavery. Secure in their control of the Senate, state party leaders also worked to marginalize the presidency.

Indeed, with Jackson out of the picture, the Senate was emboldened to increase its role in national affairs. To begin with, senators consolidated their power over appointments, successfully demanding to be consulted regarding the appointment of citizens of their own states and appointments to federal offices located within their states. Members of the House began to assert similar claims. President Polk wrote in his diary, "Many members of Congress assume that they have the right to make appointments, particularly in their own states, and they often . . . fly into a passion when their wishes are not gratified."[22]

In addition to appointments, Congress worked to increase its control over the administrative agencies of the executive branch. One instrument of congressional control was a reporting system instituted by Congress requiring agencies to produce complete fiscal reports covering all transactions, particularly expenditures on buildings and grounds. Agencies were also required to furnish complete data on all contracts into which they had entered as well as full personnel data. The latter were to include the names and salaries of all employees. To digest these reports and generally monitor the agencies, Congress increased the number of its standing committees. By the late 1850s, the House had established thirty-nine standing committees and the Senate, twenty-two.[23] House committee chairmen were generally appointed by the Speaker, while in the Senate the majority party caucus would usually determine which senators were to chair committees. In the 1830s, both houses authorized their standing committees to hire small numbers of full-time clerks assigned mainly to assist in overseeing executive departments.

Of particular interest to Congress were the financial activities of the executive agencies. Congress took its constitutional power of the purse quite seriously. Under rules that had been adopted in 1820, agencies had been required each year to submit general estimates of the coming year's expenditures. Beginning in 1836, however, Congress required "specific" estimates with "minute and full" explanations of all proposed expenditures. For example, the estimate submitted by the superintendent of the military academy in 1859 included such items as $45 for "brooms, brushes, tubs, pails, etc. for policing."[24] For construction estimates, the agencies were required to include detailed building plans. If any estimate differed even by a few dollars from the previous year's expenditure, the agency was required to provide full justification. For example, in 1842 the secretary of the Treasury felt compelled to justify an increased expenditure of $250, explaining that the department's senior messenger was suffering from rheumatism and needed help to bring wood and coal from the basement.[25] These estimates were reviewed by the House Ways and Means Committee and the Senate Finance Committee, and after negotiations with agency executives, revisions were made by the committees and the results incorporated into the annual appropriations bill.

Agencies resorted to a number of expedients to circumvent congressional direction. One such expedient was to transfer funds from one account to another. An agency might secure an appropriation it did not actually need and then transfer the funds to an account from which it hoped to spend more than Congress had appropriated. The Navy and War Departments were particularly adept practitioners of this ploy until Congress enacted legislation in 1842 prohibiting transfers from one account to another. Agencies also sought to escape congressional limitations on their expenditures through the simple expedient of spending more money than had been appropriated and then asking Congress to make up the deficiency. Members of Congress railed against this practice, and some suggested that administrators known to willfully overspend their appropriated funds should be sent to prison.

For the most part, Congress had the upper hand in its fiscal dealings with the executive. One president however, James K. Polk, sought with some success to strengthen presidential control over the federal budget. Polk initiated a practice that was later dropped but then revived and institutionalized during the 1920s. This practice was the idea of central budgetary clearance. Prior to Polk, every government department had submitted its budget directly to Congress. Congress regarded direct review of agency budgets as essential to the exercise of its constitutional power of the purse. The problem, however, was that the budget of the United States became simply a sum of the individual departmental budgets, with no overall mechanism for predicting annual outlays or linking expenditures to revenues. Polk required department heads to submit their budget requests to him rather than to Congress. The president then reviewed the requests and sent a consolidated budget to Capitol Hill. Polk's innovation was not only fiscally prudent but, to Congress's annoyance, it also enhanced presidential power. When Polk's term ended, Congress put an end to the consolidated budget and resumed direct negotiations with department heads. Polk's innovation, however, was not forgotten and set the stage for the creation of the Bureau of the Budget (subsequently renamed the White House Office of Management and Budget) three-quarters of a century later.[26]

With the partial exception of Polk, the presidents who followed Jackson were not inclined to challenge congressional power. This was especially true of the presidents elected by the Whig Party, which won two of the seven presidential elections that followed Jackson's retirement. The Whigs consisted of a disparate coalition of politicians who held a variety of views on economic and social matters. They were united by only one political principle, and that was opposition to Andrew Jackson. As a result, the Whigs eschewed discussion of issues, particularly the sectional differences that increasingly split the nation and, in presidential elections, nominated famous military commanders, for example, Generals William Henry Harrison and Zachary Taylor, who had no known political views.

One manifestation of party leaders' determination to protect the power of the individual states and the superordinate position of the Congress relative to the executive was the character of the presidential nominating process. The Jacksonians had introduced the idea of the party convention as a democratic political reform, albeit one designed to elect Jackson. Now the party convention became an institution designed to select presidential nominees who would not make trouble, lacked strong opinions on sectional issues, and would avoid interfering with the control that state party notables exercised within their own domains. Van Buren, Harrison, and Taylor were easy choices and posed no threat to established political interests. In 1844 the Whigs broke their own rule and nominated Henry Clay, whose proposed "American system" of internal improvements was unpopular in the South and was seen by other political notables as divisive. That same year, however, the Democrats began a practice that was to last for the next century and would, more often than not, produce mediocre nominees who might be electable but were unlikely to pose a challenge to party nabobs and potentates.

Beginning with the 1844 Democratic convention, at each party's national nominating convention, competing party factions, consisting of state delegations and coalitions of state delegations, would put forward the names of their own leaders as presidential candidates. Over the next several days or even weeks, competing party factions would fight one another to a standstill. At this point, serious negotiations would commence among the rival factions, leading to the choice of a nominee, sometimes a political unknown, dubbed a "dark horse," who seemed weak and unlikely to pose a threat to the balance of power within the party or, if eventually elected, to the power of party leaders in the nation at large.

Nominees of this era were chosen because they were inoffensive and, once in the White House, most lived up to their lack of promise. The reputations of Martin Van Buren, William Henry Harrison, John Tyler, Zachary Taylor, Millard Fillmore, Franklin Pierce, and James Buchanan have, at least thus far, remained lackluster at best, despite the heroic efforts of the usual swarm of presidential hagiographers. Ironically, of the post-Jackson presidents, the one exception to the rule of inoffensiveness was the very first of the dark horses, James K. Polk.[27] In his previous positions, Speaker of the U.S. House of Representatives and governor of Tennessee, Polk had shown little evidence of outstanding ability or ambition and was, for the most part, a Democratic "wheel horse," or loyal party lieutenant, first to Andrew Jackson and later to Martin Van Buren. As president, Polk surprised and disappointed the party and congressional leaders who had counted upon him to recede into the background.

Sectionalism and Secession

The most important role played by Congress in the Jacksonian era was its ultimately futile effort to resolve America's sectional differences. Since the founding of the nation, sectional struggles between the North and the South had threatened to undermine American unity. At the heart of the conflict was a sharp division of economic interest. The southern states were among the world's low-cost producers of several important agricultural commodities, including cotton, rice, and tobacco. The northern states, on the other hand, had developed economies based upon trade and manufacturing. As low-cost agricultural producers and importers of manufactured goods, southern interests were vehement advocates of free trade. The northerners, on the other hand, competed against lower-cost European manufacturers and advocated high tariffs to provide them with a captive national market. The tariff was the central issue of American politics in the early nineteenth century, leading, as we saw, to the Nullification Crisis of the 1830s.

Overlaying and exacerbating this economic controversy was the issue of slavery. Southern agriculture depended upon a labor force that by 1860 consisted of more than three million black slaves descended from Africans who had been enslaved and transported to North America. The debate over slavery, which roiled American politics from the founding to the Civil War, was at once a matter of economics and morality. Southerners saw slavery as the linchpin of their region's economic prosperity and political power. To some in the free states of the North, on the other hand, who called themselves abolitionists, slavery was a monstrous evil to be opposed without compromise.

At the Constitutional Convention of 1789, northern and southern delegates agreed that for purposes of representation in the House of Representatives, which was to be based upon population, three-fifths of each state's slaves would be counted toward determining its quota of representatives. The delegates also agreed that slaves could continue to be imported, but only until 1808, when the practice would be banned, and they agreed as well to a Fugitive Slave Clause stipulating that slaves who escaped to the free states would be returned to their owners.

These compromises seemed to be a satisfactory basis for union, but the issue of slavery arose again in relation to the territories acquired for the United States by Jefferson's Louisiana Purchase. The question was whether slavery would or would not be permitted in these territories. If slavery were permitted, the power of the southerners would be increased by the addition of an enormous new domain. If, on the other hand, slavery were prohibited, the new domain would likely be linked to the North, leaving the South to watch as northern commercial and political power grew. However, since expansion of slavery into the territories was at this time more a political than a moral concern, a compromise proved possible. This was the Missouri Compromise of 1820, which banned slavery in the Louisiana Territory above 36 degrees, 30 minutes north except within Missouri, which would be admitted to the Union as a slave state, while, for political balance, Maine would be admitted as a free state. Practically speaking, the compromise seemed to give the advantage to the North. Missouri and the Arkansas Territory would permit slavery, while, in addition to Maine, slavery would be prohibited in an enormous swath of territory that encompassed the future states of Kansas, Nebraska, Colorado, Wyoming, North and South Dakota, and Montana. The compromise was negotiated in the Congress, which was then, as we saw earlier, the locus of national political power. President Monroe played only a minor role in the negotiations. Many in the South were not happy with the compromise, but most seemed to accept the idea that the addition of Missouri to the southern domain was more important than the North's capture of the arid and barely populated western territories.

The issue of slavery in the territories came to the fore again with the Mexican-American War. Many abolitionists had opposed the war, fearing that its result would be the acquisition of new lands for slaveholders. Texas's agricultural economy was already becoming dependent upon slave labor, and Texas laid claim to most of the New Mexico Territory. Recall that Henry David Thoreau wrote his famous essay justifying civil disobedience in direct response to what he and other northern abolitionists viewed as a war to expand slavery. At the end of the war, northerners and southerners compromised again, with California admitted to the Union as a free state, Texas as a slave state, and the New Mexico Territory, which included modern-day Arizona and a portion of Utah, allowed to decide later when it petitioned to enter the Union as a state. Once again, the main forum for negotiations was the Congress, with Senators Henry Clay and Stephen A. Douglas acting as the chief architects of the final series of bills that embodied the agreement. President Fillmore's main role in the matter was to sign the bills with which he was presented.

This Compromise of 1850 had been more difficult to achieve than previous compromises because the issue of slavery had become partially detached from its economic roots and had come to be seen as a compelling moral question. Over time, the abolitionists had convinced many in the North that slavery was evil. And in the course of responding to abolitionist arguments, southerners had convinced themselves that many in the North wished only to steal their property, impoverish them, and deprive them of their freedom. What began as an economic dispute had become a moral issue. This meant that politicians seeking grounds for compromise were likely to be castigated by all parties concerned as lacking moral fiber.

Matters came to a head in 1854, when Senator Stephen Douglas introduced a Kansas-Nebraska bill that would create the territories of Kansas and Nebraska but, contrary to the terms of the Missouri Compromise, would permit the white residents of those territories to decide whether slavery would or would not be permitted within their borders. Douglas, who often served as a spokesperson for railroad interests in the Senate, hoped to create territorial governments in Kansas and Nebraska as a necessary first step toward the construction of a transcontinental railroad through Nebraska. The railroad would open millions of acres of excellent agricultural land for cultivation, but by the terms of the Missouri Compromise, slaveholders would not have access to it. Accordingly, southern senators blocked both the railway project and the incorporation of the two new territories. Douglas offered a new compromise. He called it "popular sovereignty," which he said meant that the settlers of the two territories could vote on whether to permit or prohibit slavery. Congress passed the bill, which was dutifully signed by President Franklin Pierce, who had played little role in the negotiations. An unanticipated result of the act, though, was that pro- and antislavery forces flooded the two territories with settlers, paramilitary forces, and weapons to attempt to control the outcome of the vote. Sporadic fighting broke out in the territory, and what reporters dubbed "bleeding Kansas" became a prelude to civil war.

One important response to these events was the formation of a new political party, calling itself the Republican Party of the United States. The party, declaring its opposition to the expansion of slavery in the territories, was formed in 1854 as a coalition of all the nation's opponents of slavery and the political power of the South. These included outright abolitionists who wanted slavery ended, "free-soilers" who opposed the expansion of slavery, commercial interests seeking higher tariffs, and a variety of others. Against the backdrop of political crisis, the new party's influence spread through the northern states, where it began to supplant the Whigs as the main opposition party. Republican presidential nominee, frontier scout, and California senator John C. Frémont carried eleven states in the 1856 presidential race, finishing second to the Democrats and well ahead of the rapidly disintegrating Whigs. The new Republican Party also took ninety seats in the House for a strong second-place finish, and twenty seats in the Senate, where staggered terms prevented the Republicans from taking even more seats.

Support in the North for the Republicans surged in the wake of the Supreme Court's 1857 Dred Scott decision, which invalidated both the Missouri Compromise and the Compromise of 1850 by declaring that the federal government had no constitutional power to regulate slavery in the territories.[28] The decision was cheered in the South but assailed in the North as a step in a southern effort to compel even the free states to accept slavery. Within a year of the Dred Scott decision, the Republicans had become the North's dominant party. Advancing under the slogan "free soil, free speech, free labor, free men," Republicans won control of the House of Representatives in the 1858 national elections, added six Senate seats, and prepared to do battle for the presidency in 1860.[29]

President Andrew Jackson had been a dominant figure in American politics. Old Hickory made the presidency a more democratic office, won the vehement support of millions of citizens, and bullied or ignored most of his opponents. As founder and leader of the major political party of his time, Jackson generally led majorities in both houses of Congress. After Jackson's retirement, however, the political coalition he assembled found it more expedient to exercise power through Congress than the White House. The party machinery built by Jackson was now taken over by state party bosses, who used it to strengthen the states and the Congress. The growth of the congressional committee system, with committees specializing in more areas of legislation, gave Congress the institutional capacity to develop legislation and the subject-matter expertise to oversee government agencies. And as sectional conflicts came to the fore, sectional spokespersons in the Senate helped make that body the nation's "great sounding board," as Massachusetts senator Charles Sumner liked to say. Led by ambitious senators, the Congress worked to enhance its power relative to the executive branch, and by the late 1850s there was little doubt that Congress was the first branch of American government. This era of congressional dominance, however, came to a temporary end in 1860.

The Civil War: An Interlude of Presidential Government

At their national party convention, held in Chicago, the Republicans nominated Abraham Lincoln for the presidency. Lincoln's political experience consisted of one term in Congress some sixteen years earlier. He had, however, become nationally famous for his speeches during a series of debates during the 1858 Senate race, when Lincoln sought to oust Senator Stephen A. Douglas from his Illinois seat. Since the Democrats carried the state legislature, Douglas was reappointed to the Senate in 1859, but Lincoln's eloquent and passionate assertion of opposition to slavery made him a hero to antislavery forces in the North. The debates were followed by other speeches, including a famous address at New York's Cooper Union, where Lincoln asserted that slavery was morally wrong and that no compromise was possible between a principle that was morally right and one that was morally wrong. By nominating Lincoln, the Republicans were throwing down the gauntlet to the South. The economic issue with moral overtones had become a moral issue that could no longer be discussed peacefully.

The 1860 election gave Lincoln a popular plurality and an Electoral College majority. All his electoral votes came from the North; he failed to carry a single

Southern state and only two counties in all the South went for Lincoln. The Republicans also won control of both houses of Congress, also on the basis of northern votes. Most Southerners believed that Lincoln and his party intended to bring a rapid end to slavery and had promised to support dissolution of the Union if Lincoln won the presidency. In preparation for this eventuality, constitutional conventions were called throughout the South. One month after the Electoral College results became official, South Carolina voted to secede from the Union. Six other states—Texas, Louisiana, Mississippi, Florida, Alabama, and Georgia—followed South Carolina out of the Union and banded together as the Confederate States of America. This new Confederacy chose Mississippi senator Jefferson Davis as its president.

The Presidency Ascendant

With the outbreak of the Civil War, President Lincoln, ignoring the Congress and, to some extent, the Constitution, issued a series of executive orders for which he had no clear legal basis. While Congress was out of session and its members dispersed to their home constituencies, Lincoln combined the state militias into a ninety-day national volunteer force, called for forty thousand new volunteers, enlarged the regular army and navy, diverted $2 million in unspent appropriations to military needs, instituted censorship of the U.S. mails, ordered a blockade of the Southern ports, suspended the writ of habeas corpus in the border states, and ordered the arrest by military police of individuals whom he deemed to be guilty of engaging in or "contemplating" treasonous actions.[30]

In almost every instance, Congress subsequently enacted legislation legitimating the president's actions. Thus, after the president ordered the expansion of the army and navy, Congress enacted legislation to that effect. Similarly, after the president instituted military conscription, Congress voted a draft law. And after the president ordered the creation of military commissions to try individuals accused of treason against the United States, Congress enacted legislation governing the organization and conduct of such commissions. Some historians have asserted that Lincoln generally left nonmilitary concerns to Congress.[31] In wartime, however, the line between military and civilian matters is sometimes so thin as to be nonexistent.

For its part, in the 1863 *Prize* cases, the Supreme Court upheld the president's power to order a blockade of the Southern ports.[32] In the 1866 case of *ex parte Milligan,* however, the Court rejected the president's suspension of habeas corpus and indiscriminate use of military tribunals in areas of the nation that were not actually theaters of military operations. The Court, however, recognized the president's power to declare martial law and to suspend civil liberties in areas actually subject to military threat.[33]

Before the war, Congress had sharply limited the federal government's resources to safeguard the primacy of the states. The war, however, created a justification for an enormous expansion of the federal government's financial base. Accordingly, Lincoln called Congress into special session in 1861 and pointed to the need for an escalation in revenues to support the war effort. One result was the enactment of the 1861 Revenue Act, which established America's first federal income tax. Subsequently, Lincoln and Treasury Secretary Salmon Chase persuaded Congress to authorize the issuance of $50 million in Treasury notes, redeemable in gold or silver specie, to meet military payrolls.

While Congress followed Lincoln's lead, it was also compelled to expand its own fiscal capabilities to comply with the president's demands. Prior to the war, the House Ways and Means and Senate Finance Committees dealt with both appropriations and revenues. To deal with the complexities of wartime and post-war funding and debt repayment, both houses created appropriations committees separate from their tax-writing committees.[34]

Reconstruction and the Republican Era: An Imperial Congress?

In the aftermath of the South's surrender and President Lincoln's assassination, the influence of the presidency was eclipsed by a resurgence of congressional power. Congress began reasserting its authority even before Lincoln's death. In 1864, when it became clear that Northern forces were gaining the upper hand, Congress passed the Wade-Davis Bill, imposing a number of severe conditions upon the Southern states before they would be allowed to return to the Union. Lincoln favored a conciliatory policy toward the South and pocket-vetoed the bill. Lincoln's action caused a furor in the Republican Party and led to the issuance of the famous Wade-Davis Manifesto asserting the primacy of Congress in national affairs. The president, declared the manifesto, "must understand that the authority of Congress is paramount, and must be respected . . . and that . . . he must confine himself to his executive duties—to obey and execute, not to make the laws."[35] Lincoln ignored these protestations. Congress made certain, however, that future presidents would pay more attention by impeaching Lincoln's successor, Andrew Johnson. The proximate cause of Johnson's impeachment was his violation of the Tenure in Office Act of 1867, which was designed to prevent the president from removing without Senate approval officials who had been confirmed by the Senate. The larger cause was a clash between the president and Congress over postwar Reconstruction policy.

Though Johnson survived impeachment to complete his term in office, Congress had demonstrated that it, not the president, determined the policies of the U.S. government. President Grant, elected to succeed Johnson, was given to understand that Congress, and particularly the Senate, governed the nation and that the president should do as he was told. "The most eminent senators," wrote Massachusetts senator George Hoar, "would have received as a personal affront a private message from the White House expressing a desire that they should adopt any course in the discharge of their legislative duties that they did not approve. If they visited the White House it was to give, not receive advice."[36] Grant, for his part, understood the president's new place in the scheme of things and, "yielded a quick deference to Republican leaders in the House and Senate, notably the latter."[37]

The Republican Era

Fifteen presidents governed America from Abraham Lincoln's election in 1860 to the inauguration of Franklin D. Roosevelt in 1932. Of these, thirteen were Republicans and only two, Grover Cleveland and Woodrow Wilson, were Democrats. Thus, it seems appropriate to call this seventy-two-year period a Republican era. In terms of the role of Congress and the presidency, however, the era should be divided into three periods. The first is the Lincoln presidency itself, when America's chief executive exercised unprecedented wartime powers. During the second period, including the presidencies of Johnson, Grant, Hayes, Garfield, Arthur, Cleveland, Harrison, and McKinley, Congress regained its position as America's chief governmental institution. In the third portion of the long Republican era, which encompassed the presidencies of Theodore Roosevelt, Taft, Wilson, Harding, Coolidge, and Hoover, the importance of the presidency began to increase once again.

Grant deferred to Congress in almost all matters. President Hayes, though, sought to restore a measure of presidential independence by ignoring the Senate when appointing the heads of the various government agencies. Congress had grown accustomed to being consulted on all appointments. Representatives exercised significant influence on all federal appointments within their districts; senators influenced appointments within their states and appointees from their states; and the Senate leadership demanded to be consulted on major executive appointments. Hayes determined to nominate cabinet officers without obtaining the prior approval of Senate leaders. The Senate refused to confirm the nominations, but, after a major public campaign, Hayes was able to secure confirmation of his appointees. One presidential historian declared that this battle marked the beginning of a decline in senatorial power.[38] Senate leaders, however, responded by strengthening the practice of senatorial courtesy, which required a president to obtain the assent of a nominee's home-state senators before the Senate would approve an appointment. In subsequent fights during the Hayes presidency and brief presidency of James Garfield, the White House sometimes succeeded in overcoming senatorial courtesy but was not able to overturn the principle.[39]

Despite occasional successes, presidents from Grant to McKinley were eclipsed by the Congress when it came to the formulation of national policy. The years from 1868 to the turn of the century included a good deal of struggle and strife in the nation. Conflicts arose over monetary policy, the role of organized labor, agricultural policy, immigration, political corruption, America's role in the world, and a host of other matters. For the most part, policies to deal with these issues were formulated by the leaders of Congress rather than the president. Even America's 1898 war with Spain was declared by Congress despite President McKinley's misgivings.[40] Henry Adams summarized the relationship between the two branches during this period by writing, "So far as the president's initiative was concerned, the president and his cabinet might equally well have departed separately or together to distant lands. Their recommendations were uniformly disregarded."[41] No less an authority on government than Woodrow Wilson wrote, ". . . unquestionably the predominant and controlling force, the centre and source of all motive and of all regulative power, is Congress."[42]

And even as Congress ignored the president's views, lawmakers made certain to impose their own views on the administration of government. According to Leonard White, members of Congress "swarmed" in and out of government offices, investigating administrative practices, addressing constituents' complaints, and generally seeking to control administrative affairs.[43] Congress also enacted numerous statutes dealing with the details of administrative procedures and ceding little discretionary authority to the executive.[44] Congress made it a routine practice to attach "riders," that is, substantive legislation, to appropriations bills, making it difficult for the president to exercise a veto unless he was prepared to strike down the entire bill.

During this period, Congress enhanced its institutional capabilities in a number of other ways as well. First, congressional committees were authorized to enlarge their staffs and, beginning in 1893, individual members of Congress were authorized to employ one or two staff members. In 1908, with the completion of the Cannon House Office Building, members were assigned offices in which to house their staffers.[45] Increased staffing and office space are no small matters. These tools gave committees and individual members greater ability to involve themselves in the details of legislation and to intervene into administrative processes. In any bureaucracy, increased staffing usually offers an opportunity for the exercise of greater power. Second, Congress extended the length of its sessions. Early Congresses had generally met only two or three months a year. After 1911, Congress was generally in session six months per year. This allowed great time to engage in legislative business and meant that presidents had less ability to act on their own while members of Congress were scattered to their own states and districts. Recall that President Lincoln issued the orders that sent the nation to war while Congress was out of session. Third, committee jurisdictions were rationalized to reduce jurisdictional overlap and to ensure that all substantive areas of governance were covered. Some committees formed standing subcommittees to address specialized legislative areas and to ensure congressional oversight in even the smallest and most arcane governmental niches.

Finally, Congress strengthened its own leadership. In the early 1920s Senate Democrats and Republicans created the positions of majority leader and minority leader to bring greater order to the deliberations of the upper chamber. In the House, the powers of the Speaker were increased through the establishment of a Rules Committee, chaired by the Speaker, to determine the agenda for floor debate and the rules under which each piece of pending legislation would be considered. This gave Speakers and their lieutenants considerable power. The most powerful of these Speakers was "Czar" Thomas B. Reed, who instituted what were called the "Reed Rules." Under these rules, the Speaker could determine the absence or presence of a quorum, block attempts by his opponents to delay action, and control the House calendar

The peak of leadership power in the Congress occurred during the late nineteenth and early twentieth centuries. The power of the leaders depended upon party discipline. The national parties controlled the process of nomination to office and the patronage machines that played critical roles in determining election outcomes. A member of Congress who opposed the leadership would find it virtually impossible to be renominated or reelected to office. Two turn-of-the-century political reforms, however, gradually reduced the authority of party leaders. These were the growing use of primary elections and the spread of civil service reform. Primary elections stripped party leaders of their control over political nominations, while civil service reform reduced the weight of the patronage armies of lower-level political appointees used by party leaders to win elections. These two reforms encouraged members of Congress to stake out more independent positions and, in 1910, led to a House "revolt" against the dictatorial Speaker, Joseph G. Cannon. The result of the revolt was limitation of the Speaker's power and the strengthening of seniority rules governing the appointment of committee leaders. These changes began an erosion of the party discipline that had been an important factor in the overall power of the Congress. Speaking for a unified House majority, the Speaker could be more than a match for the president; unable to command a majority, the authority of the Speaker was reduced, and with it the weight of the House in national politics.

While some reforms weakened Congress, one political reform of this era on balance strengthened the legislative branch. In 1913 the Seventeenth Amendment to the Constitution was ratified, bringing about direct popular election of senators. On the one hand, the senators chosen by the state legislatures were powerful state politicians and major figures in the national political parties. On the other hand, the selection of senators by the state legislatures had tended to make the Senate a somewhat parochial body except in the years leading up to the Civil War, when conflicts between the states made the Senate the nation's "great sounding board." Direct popular election gave new groups and forces access to the upper chamber and gave the Senate new vigor in the policy-making arena, particularly in the realm of foreign policy, where the Senate's constitutional power to reject treaties negotiated by the president would become an important factor in American politics.

Progressivism

When President William McKinley was assassinated by an anarchist in 1901, he was succeeded by Vice President Theodore Roosevelt. Roosevelt was an abrasive, forceful, and energetic individual. The various state party leaders saw Roosevelt as a threat to their own power and probably would never have given him the presidential nomination. Republican leader Senator Mark Hanna declared his opposition even to giving Roosevelt the vice-presidential slot. "Don't any of you realize," asked Hanna, "that there's only one life between that madman and the presidency?"[46]

Roosevelt was far more successful than his immediate predecessors in influencing the legislative process and in using executive power to convince the public that the presidency was, indeed, a center of action and initiative. In 1903 Roosevelt was able to persuade Congress to enact the Elkins Act, which sought to strengthen railroad regulation, and the Expediting Act, to speed antitrust cases against the steel, rail, oil, and meatpacking industries, and to bring about the creation of the Department of Commerce and Labor, which was to have important regulatory responsibilities. In 1906, Roosevelt pushed through the Hepburn Act, which gave the Interstate Commerce Commission rate-setting powers, as well as the Federal Meat Inspection Act and the Pure Food and Drug Act, both designed to deal with issues of food safety. This president did not yield "a quick deference" to Congress.

Roosevelt's ability to act forcefully in the legislative arena was not simply a matter of personality. Roosevelt was able to take advantage of a number of turn-of-the century changes that created a potential for greater executive power. One such change was a communications revolution. Following the Civil War, the entire nation had been linked by telegraph lines, which allowed news to travel electronically rather than by horseback, from one part of the nation to another. Taking advantage of this new innovation were the "wire services," news organizations that, for a fee, began to distribute national and international news to America's thousands of local newspapers. Calculating that the activities of the president rather than those of members of Congress were more likely to be of interest to a nationwide audience, the wire services focused on the chief executive, providing same-day coverage of presidential actions and speeches to a national audience. It was this focus that gave Roosevelt a chance to become America's first media president. He used speeches to shape public opinion and bring public pressure to bear upon members of Congress. Roosevelt said the presidency gave him a "bully pulpit" and made "going public" an important weapon of presidential power.[47]

For Roosevelt's immediate successors, Taft and Wilson, speeches and press conferences became routine instruments. In his messages to Congress and public statements, President Taft regularly promoted a "laundry list" of objectives and legislative initiatives attempting to create an agenda for legislative action and to mobilize public and press opinion in support of his initiatives.[48] Taft lacked Roosevelt's skill as a speaker, but the next president, Woodrow Wilson, combined oratorical ability with a determination to halt congressional encroachment on the powers of the executive. Wilson was determined to exert leadership in the legislative process. This he did, leading a successful effort to enact a number of major pieces of legislation, including the Federal Reserve Act, the Federal Trade Commission Act, the Clayton Antitrust Act, and a new income tax. Wilson also worked to overcome neutralist sentiment and lead America into war against Germany in 1917. Of course, at the end of the war, Wilson lost an epic battle with the Senate when he failed to obtain the two-thirds majority necessary to confirm the Treaty of Versailles ending the war and establishing the League of Nations. America agreed to make a separate peace with Germany and refused to join the league. Wilson suffered a stroke soon thereafter and was incapacitated for the remainder of his term.

While the presidents who followed Wilson are not remembered for their bold new approaches, one very important presidential innovation was introduced by Warren Harding and cultivated by Calvin Coolidge. This was the creation of the Bureau of the Budget (BOB) in 1921. In the previous century, President Polk had invented the idea of a consolidated presidential budget, but the idea soon fell into disuse in favor of a return to the practice of each agency submitting a separate budget estimate to Congress. In the aftermath of the First World War, the federal budget had grown large enough that differences between federal taxing and spending would have an impact on the economy, but the impact was difficult to predict. Economists had suggested giving the executive responsibility for estimating future government revenues and linking these to a consolidated budget estimate. Congressional leaders saw the creation of such an office as an infringement on Congress's power of the purse, but economic realities could not be ignored. The 1921 Budget and Accounting Act had placed the BOB in the Treasury Department, where it reported to the secretary and to the president but could be overseen by Congress. Both Harding and Coolidge made a point of regularly consulting Charles Dawes, the BOB's first director, and endeavoring to enhance presidential influence over its operations. Harding worked with the BOB to prepare an executive budget in 1922.[49] To keep an eye on the BOB,

Congress created an new auditing arm, the General Accounting Office (GAO), which worked directly for the legislative branch. Decades later, the GAO would be renamed the Government Accountability Office and its functions expanded to include audits, evaluations, and investigations of government agencies.

The New Deal and the Imperial President

Franklin D. Roosevelt was elected president in 1932 and proceeded when he took office to reshape the presidency and the American political process more generally. Roosevelt's successors, both Democrats and Republicans, inherited and built upon a presidency that has gradually overmatched Congress and for the most part has left the chief executive in control of the nation's government. Franklin D. Roosevelt broke the two-term tradition that had been established by George Washington and won election to four terms in office. FDR, of course, died before completing his last term but was succeeded by his vice president, Harry S. Truman, who won reelection in his own right in 1948.

With the support of overwhelming Democratic majorities in the Congress, FDR presided over an enormous expansion of the executive branch, enhancing its power and that of the nation's chief executive, and the role of the federal government more generally. Since the administration of Andrew Jackson, ambitious presidents had seen themselves as legislative leaders, and FDR lost no time in proposing new legislation to the Congress. During his first one hundred days in office, sometimes called the "First New Deal," Roosevelt and his advisers introduced some fourteen new programs, each administered by a new government agency. These included creation of the Federal Deposit Insurance Corporation, the Securities and Exchange Commission, the Agricultural Adjustment Administration, and the Civilian Conservation Corps. Between 1935 and 1938, sometimes called the "Second New Deal," Roosevelt presided over the passage of still more legislation, including the Social Security Act and the National Labor Relations Act. To administer these and hundreds of other pieces of legislation required the creation of a score of new agencies and the recruitment of hundreds of thousands of additional federal workers. Roosevelt declared that this expansion of the executive branch was necessary to deal with the crisis of the Great Depression, and soon America faced an even greater crisis—World War II.

The growth of the executive branch accelerated during the Second World War, when numerous new agencies were created to support the war effort in every area, from the mobilization of troops, to the production of supplies and munitions, to maintaining civilian morale. New agencies also meant more federal employees. In 1930, the federal government had employed 966,000 workers, many scattered throughout the nation as, for example, postal workers. By the end of the war, the national government employed more than 3 million civil servants, with many if not most working in Washington.[50] Today, if one includes the contract employees who work side by side with federal employees in most government offices, the true number may be close to 17 million.[51]

The expansion of the executive branch threatened to marginalize Congress, which responded with two important pieces of legislation. The first was the 1946 Legislative Reorganization Act, which sought to strengthen the committee system. The act was based upon a 1945 study conducted by the Joint Committee on the Organization of Congress and contained numerous provisions designed to enhance Congress's role in lawmaking and Congress's ability to oversee the huge new bureaucracies of the executive branch. First, the act reduced the number of House and Senate committees but created a number of new specialized subcommittees within the larger committees. Second, House and Senate committees were designed to parallel one another to smooth the flow of legislation. Third, the authority of the House and Senate Committees on Appropriations was increased, and specialized subcommittees were created within each committee. Finally, committee and subcommittee staffs were enlarged to give them greater oversight and legislative capacity.

A second important piece of legislation enacted by Congress in 1946 was the Administrative Procedure Act, which many hoped would further strengthen Congress's oversight capabilities. The enormous expansion of government that took place during FDR's presidency, moreover, made it impossible for Congress to continue closely monitoring the activities of executive agencies as it had in the past. Congress resorted to what political scientists Mathew McCubbins and Thomas Schwartz have called "fire alarm" management, intervening only when called and leaving the day-to-day management of the executive branch to administrators and the president.[52] To make certain that the fire alarm would be rung, the Administrative Procedure Act required agencies to publish proposed new rules and regulations and to provide an opportunity for affected interests to comment and come to Congress with complaints, in effect ringing the alarm. This procedure is called "notice and comment rulemaking."

Presidents, in turn, responded to these congressional initiatives by seeking ways of circumventing the legislative branch altogether. Roosevelt, for example, had sought, insofar as possible, to govern through executive order. An executive order is a presidential directive to a federal agency to undertake some course of action, and the expanded executive branch made executive orders more important instruments. During his time in office, FDR issued 3,522 executive orders, almost surpassing the total that had been issued by all the presidents who preceded him. Many of these orders had to do with military policy, and others with domestic policy. One very important executive order, issued in 1937, created the Executive Office of the President (EOP) and moved the Bureau of the Budget from the Treasury Department, where it had been lodged since 1921, into the EOP. Creation of the EOP gave FDR and his successors the staff and agencies with which to supervise the executive branch. Control of the BOB, later renamed the White House Office of Management and Budget (OMB), for its part, gave presidents greater control over the nation's spending priorities and Congress's legislative agenda. Presidential budgets came to be packaged and sent to Congress as agenda-setting bundles of proposals. The terms "New Deal," "Fair Deal," "New Frontier," "Great Society," and so forth, were labels for presidential budgets designed to capture media and public attention and to guide the legislative process.

In terms of foreign policy, Roosevelt eschewed treaties in favor of the use of executive agreements, which often did not involve congressional approval. FDR often pointed to Wilson's failure to obtain Senate approval for the Treaty of Versailles, a failure which the president claimed paved the way to World War II, as a reason not to involve lawmakers in foreign relations unless absolutely necessary. Executive agreements continue to be favored by presidents, who now seldom negotiate treaties that must be approved by the Senate. One of the cornerstones of postwar American international economic policy was GATT, the General Agreement on Tariffs and Trade. As the name implies, American participation was based upon an executive agreement, not a treaty. In 2015, the Obama administration signed a nuclear arms agreement with Iran that, if presented as a treaty, could not have received a two-thirds favorable vote in the Senate. Since the deal was an agreement, the tables were turned and Congress would have needed to muster a veto-proof two-thirds majority of both houses to block the president's actions.

By the time Roosevelt died in 1944, the nation, the executive branch, and the presidency had been transformed. Americans—and even the Congress—now looked to the chief executive for leadership. And presidential power continued to grow during the administrations of Roosevelt's successors, Harry Truman and Dwight David Eisenhower. Against the backdrop of economic and international crises, Congress enacted the 1947 National Security Act, which created the Department of Defense, the Central Intelligence Agency (CIA), and the National Security Council (NSC), all designed as instruments of presidential power. Historian Arthur Schlesinger Jr. called the result the "imperial presidency," and Presidents Eisenhower, Kennedy, Johnson, and Nixon made use of its power at home and abroad. The imperial presidency, though, came under attack during the Johnson and Nixon administrations.

In 1960, John F. Kennedy was elected to the presidency. In his inaugural address, Kennedy announced a series of domestic initiatives and budget priorities he labeled the "New Frontier." These included expansion of domestic social programs, investment in science and space exploration, and a "Peace Corps" that would send young American volunteers to third-world nations to promote literacy and technology. Kennedy did have some legislative successes and used executive orders to implement portions of his program, such as the Peace Corps, that encountered congressional opposition. The New Frontier, however, ended prematurely with Kennedy's November 1963 assassination.

Kennedy was succeeded by Vice President Lyndon Johnson, who seemed determined to make his mark on history and in particular to outshine Kennedy. During five years in office, Johnson led Congress in enacting a number of Great Society programs, including Medicare and Medicaid, and in declaring a "War on Poverty" by establishing an Office of Economic Opportunity (OEO) to inject federal funds into local antipoverty programs. The OEO no longer exists, but other war-on-poverty programs, such as Head Start, an educational enrichment program for poor children, continue its efforts.

Johnson, more than any president since Lincoln, promoted laws banning discrimination against black Americans. Particularly important was the 1965 Voting Rights Act, which promoted the registration of black voters throughout the South, sent federal officials to the southern states to monitor election practices, and prohibited a number of jurisdictions, found to have been guilty of a pattern of racial discrimination, from changing any of their election laws without obtaining the prior approval of the federal government. As a result of this legislation, millions of new black voters were registered throughout the South.

Unfortunately for his place in history, President Johnson's record was marred by the Vietnam War. During his five years in office, Johnson sent several hundred thousand American troops to Indochina, where they waged a bloody and inconclusive war against Vietnamese forces led by President Ho Chi Minh of what was then called North Vietnam. The war was extremely divisive within the United States and led to several years of violent demonstrations that unsettled a nation already shaken by nearly a decade of violent clashes between civil rights advocates and their foes. Congress played an important role during this period by holding hearings, chaired by Democratic senator J. William Fulbright of Arkansas, to look into Johnson's war policies. Stung by opposition within the Democratic Party, Johnson, who had won reelection in a landslide in 1964, withdrew from the 1968 race.

Johnson's withdrawal and splits in the Democratic camp gave the 1968 presidential election to former Republican vice president Richard M. Nixon. That year marked the last in which the party conventions actually selected the presidential candidates. In 1968, the liberal wing of the Democratic Party asserted that the presidential nomination had been stolen by party bosses and given to Vice President Hubert Humphrey. Prior to the 1972 presidential contest, the Democrats introduced major changes in their rules requiring most convention delegations to be chosen in primary elections. The Republicans followed suit after 1972, with the result that today's party convention acts to ratify choices made by primary voters rather than to make decisions of its own. One implication of this change is that the dark-horse candidates of yesteryear, chosen because they were seen as unambitious and deemed unlikely to make trouble, have given way to ambitious and aggressive presidential candidates who have been willing to devote years to a single-minded quest for power.

Once elected, Nixon moved to end the Vietnam War by reaching an agreement with the North Vietnamese to withdraw American forces and effectively allowed President Ho to unite Vietnam under his rule. Nixon's term included a number of foreign policy successes, such as the establishment of relations with China. Nixon is, however, chiefly remembered for the Watergate affair that drove him from office. Nixon had become involved in a major conflict with Congress over his efforts to reorganize federal agencies in a way that would increase presidential power and diminish congressional influence over their operations.[53] Angered by leaks from within the administration and convinced that the Democrats planned "dirty tricks" to win the 1972 election, Nixon authorized the clandestine employment of a group of former intelligence agents, "the plumbers squad," to conduct covert operations against Nixon's political foes. The plumbers were caught breaking into Democratic headquarters at Washington's Watergate Hotel, and in the subsequent congressional investigation, Nixon's ties to these illegal efforts were revealed. The president resigned to avoid certain impeachment.

In the aftermath of Nixon's resignation, Congress enacted several pieces of legislation designed to curb presidential power. These included the War Powers Resolution, intended to restore a measure of congressional control over presidents' use of military forces; the Case Act of 1972, designed to compel presidents to disclose all executive agreements; the Ethics in Government Act, designed to facilitate congressional inquiries into executive conduct; and the Congressional Budget and Impoundment Control Act, intended to enhance the congressional power of the purse. Congress also created a new staff agency, the Congressional Budget Office (CBO), which gives the legislature its own capacity to assess budgetary and economic issues and to prepare cost estimates of proposed legislation. Prior to the creation of the CBO, Congress was dependent upon the reports and estimates of the OMB, an agency that works for the White House. It should also be noted that even before Nixon's resignation, Congress had enacted the 1970 Legislative Reform Act, which, among other things, expanded committee staffing, provided computers for members' offices, introduced electronic voting machines to the House floor, created the Congressional Research Service (formerly the Legislative Reference Service), and otherwise strengthened Congress's operational capabilities. With the help of these legislative and organizational changes, Congress seemed to be regaining the upper hand during the presidencies of Nixon's successors Gerald Ford and Jimmy Carter. With Ronald Reagan's election in 1980, however, the onward march of presidential power resumed.

Presidential Unilateralism

President Reagan was determined to restore presidential power, which he and his advisers saw as dangerously "fettered" by the events of the preceding several years.[54] Reagan embarked upon a systematic effort to undermine the War Powers Resolution, ignored the Case Act, and sought to use the Budget Act for his own purposes. Moreover, as we shall see in chapters 6, 7, and 8, Reagan continued to make use of executive orders and executive agreements while introducing new unilateral instruments of presidential governance, such as regulatory review and signing statements. His successors, George H. W. Bush, Bill Clinton, George W. Bush, Barack Obama, and Donald Trump, followed in his footsteps, using and sharpening the weapons developed by Reagan. Clinton, even as Congress was impeaching him and refusing to consider any of his proposals, managed to implement much of his agenda through executive orders. Then, in the wake of the 9/11 terror attacks, President George W. Bush claimed new emergency powers, including the power to order surveillance of U.S. citizens without judicial approval. And in 2014, declaring that he had waited too long for Congress to act, President Obama issued executive orders designed to begin the reorganization of America's immigration policy. President Trump issued a number of executive orders seeking to limit immigration from the Middle East and Latin America. Unilateralism has become a hallmark of the contemporary presidency. As the actions of these contemporary presidents and congressional efforts to cope with executive unilateralism will provide much of the material discussed in the pages to come, let us postpone further discussion of their administrations and consider some of the lessons to be learned from our short history of the presidency.

Thoughts on Congressional History: The Onward March of Executive Power

We noted at the beginning of this chapter that the Constitution gave Congress impressive powers, but the capacity to actually wield its powers was not guaranteed. This capacity would depend upon Congress's continuing ability to maintain ties to important national constituencies, on its ability to develop strong internal governance structures, and on its capacity to oversee and compete with the executive branch. Each of these dimensions has become problematic for the Congress.

As to ties with constituencies, Congress continues to be available to groups and forces throughout American society. However, the executive branch has become a rival in this realm. One of the unanticipated consequences of the Administrative Procedure Act is that private and public interest groups throughout the nation now have direct access to the bureaucracy that effectively makes much if not most of the nation's law. APA requires agencies to consult with interested parties before promulgating new rules, and most agencies are happy to develop a cohort of "stakeholders"—private and public interest groups with whom they regularly work. Agencies are sometime said to engage in "round up the usual suspects" rulemaking. Rather than lobby Congress, these usual suspects engage in what is called "corridoring," or lobbying executive agencies. One Washington reporter noted that in September 2015, though Congress was out of session, Washington's lobbyists were busier than usual lobbying administrative agencies engaged in writing important rules. One prominent lobbyist said, "It's a bit unseemly," but was hard at work nonetheless.[55] In this way, APA has encouraged a shift of representative functions from Congress to the bureaucracy, a process that can only weaken Congress and strengthen the bureaucracy as interests look to the agencies, more than Congress, as their friends in Washington.

Second, as to its internal organization, Congress has made a valiant effort to strengthen its own institutional capabilities to produce legislation and oversee the executive branch. Congress, as we have seen, has strengthened its staff system, streamlined its committee structure, and created staff agencies—the GAO and OMB—to give the legislative branch a more powerful voice in the governmental process. These efforts are important and will be discussed in considerable detail in chapter 4, where we will examine some of Congress's most recent institutional reforms. At the end of the day, however, Congress will always be hampered by the fact that it is a representative assembly where debate, deliberation, and compromise are inherent to its operations. Can such an assembly compete effectively with a unitary president and the vast bureaucracies of the executive branch?

This third dimension of congressional power—ability to compete with the president—has become the most problematic. The executive branch is enormous, perhaps even too complex for presidents to control. Presidents, who had always possessed certain advantages in conflicts with Congress, now have developed unilateral instruments that allow them to use the bureaucracy in ways that sometimes enable them to ignore and circumvent congressional power. Presidents issue executive orders, reach executive agreements, issue signing statements intended to rewrite legislation, and expand "regulatory review" to take control of the bureaucratic rulemaking process. Each of these matters will be discussed in the pages to come.

For now, let us observe that readers who might be indifferent to the place of Congress in America's governmental framework might do well to recall that Congress is the federal government's only democratic institution. Every citizen should be concerned with its influence in the governmental system.

3

Congressional Elections

EVERY TWO YEARS, AMERICANS ELECT all 435 members of the House of Representatives to serve two-year terms, and one-third of the nation's 100 senators to serve six-year terms. An additional 6 delegates are chosen to serve in the House by the residents of the District of Columbia and the U.S. territories. These delegates participate in debates and on committees but do not have the privilege of casting ballots on the floor of the House. The Constitution imposes age, citizenship, and residency requirements for service in the Congress but no other restrictions. Senators must be thirty years of age, and House members must be at least twenty-five. To be eligible to serve in the Senate an individual must have been a U.S. citizen for nine years, while service in the House requires an individual to have been a citizen for seven years. To be eligible for election, both senators and House members must be residents of the state they serve. House members are not constitutionally required to reside in their own districts, though virtually all find it politically expedient to do so.

At a time when various states imposed race, gender, and property restrictions on voting rights, the Constitution imposed no such restrictions on the right to hold federal office. In 1866, women's suffrage activist Elizabeth Cady Stanton ran for Congress. Prior to the ratification of the Nineteenth Amendment in 1920, state laws generally prohibited women from voting. Nevertheless, Stanton's right to hold federal office could not be disputed. Stanton lost, and while women may have been eligible to serve, no woman sat in Congress until Jeannette Rankin of Montana was elected in 1916.

The Constitution's framers, as we saw in chapter 1, viewed elections as the best means of ensuring that the government would pay heed to the will of the people. The framers, nevertheless, saw electoral politics as fraught with risks. Elections, they worried, could provide an opportunity for unscrupulous politicians or demagogues to hoodwink credulous voters. Too rapid a turnover of elected representatives, which James Madison called "mutability in the public councils," could lead to incessant and ill-conceived changes in laws and policies.[1] Sudden political fads and impulses, the framers feared, might sweep the nation, leading to the selection of unqualified and inappropriate representatives before the public came to its senses.

These concerns help to explain the system of congressional elections mandated by the Constitution. Fear of demagoguery was one reason that senators were to be chosen by the state legislatures, whose members were presumed to have more political experience than ordinary citizens. This changed with the ratification of the Seventeenth Amendment in 1913, providing for popular election of senators. To prevent rapid turnover of new representatives, members of the House are chosen for two years rather than one year, as was more common in America at that time. Indeed, critics of the proposed Constitution, the so-called Anti-Federalists, thought that elections for the House should be held every year, as they had been under the Articles of Confederation and in several of the states. Anti-Federalist pamphleteers were fond of citing the maxim, "Where annual elections end, tyranny begins."

The framers, however, argued that annual elections might produce continual political tumult and would not allow representatives enough experience in office to become familiar with their duties or the needs of the nation. And to prevent transient political impulses from having an impact upon the government before the nation had sufficient time to evaluate their wisdom, senators were to be chosen to serve for six years and their terms staggered. These arrangements were designed to give the nation a chance to think about novel political ideas and to evaluate the virtues of emergent political movements before handing their spokespersons a complete set of the keys to the Capitol.

Today, we might consider all these electoral rules to be inappropriate restrictions on popular democracy. However, in the context of the late eighteenth century, when representative government was in its infancy, the framers had reason to be prudent. Indeed, more than two centuries of experience with representative institutions may have taught us that the framers were not completely wrong to worry about unscrupulous and demagogic politicians, credulous voters, and ill-considered political fads.

The framers' concerns about congressional elections underscore a basic dilemma of representative government—the trade-off between representation and effective governance. If membership in a representative assembly is fairly stable over time, representatives have an opportunity to gain experience and develop expertise in the techniques of governance as well as to increase their own commitment to the institution they serve. Members of a stable assembly can build the capacity to craft legislation, supervise the bureaucracy, and resist encroachments from the executive. A stable assembly would contribute to Congress's organizational capacity to govern, which, as we saw, is an important dimension of congressional power. All fine and good.

Unfortunately, however, such an assembly would almost certainly fall short when it came to representing the people of the United States. As society changed, such an assembly would gradually lose its representative character. It might govern well but represent badly. In the United States today, some argue that legislators should be subject to term limits, restricting them to a set number of terms. Several states, including California, have adopted term limits for state legislators. At the federal level, term limits for members of Congress would require a constitutional amendment, as in the case of the Twenty-Second Amendment, which set term limits for the president.

Ultimately, the power of a representative assembly, as we observed in chapter 2, depends upon both its organizational coherence and its representative character. If the assembly fails to adequately represent its constituency, especially as political change produces new interests, groups, and forces, it inevitably forfeits its relevance and political support despite the experience and expertise of its members. Hence, oxymoron or not, representation and government must be effectively conjoined if representative assemblies are to avoid losing their significance. Better an oxymoron than a dinosaur. Let us keep these concerns in mind as we review the congressional electoral process. We will consider, in turn, the candidates, the campaigns, the voters, and the consequences of the process.

Running for Congress

Each election year, thousands of ambitious individuals consider running for seats in the House or Senate. Their reasons vary. Some see an opportunity to serve their fellow citizens or to advance causes they deem important. Others view political office as a symbol of personal achievement or route to power and influence. These individuals come from all walks of American life. For example, in almost every congressional year, several students decide to run for Congress. Thus, in 2014, Columbia School of International and Public Affairs second-year student Estakio Beltran decided that he would mount a campaign for a seat in Congress. "I had committed myself to public service," Beltran said. "For me, [running for Congress] was like a response to that call for service."[2] Another student running for Congress, Stan Tran, a third-year medical student at Brown University's Warren Alpert Medical School, said he did not expect to win but instead hoped "to start the conversation," and force Congress to listen to the will of the people.[3] Neither Beltran nor Tran was elected.

With students running for Congress, how can professors be left behind? Every election year several professors decide to try to wow the electorate with their classroom skills. In 2014, for example, Miami University of Ohio education professor Tom Poetter launched a bid to unseat Republican House Speaker and twenty-four-year incumbent John Boehner. Though Boehner had achieved a high position in Washington, Poetter asserted that the Speaker was out of touch with his constituents in Ohio. "I've talked to a lot of people in this district who have never met him," Poetter said. "He's a very inaccessible representative."[4] For reasons unrelated to Poetter's candidacy, Boehner resigned his seat and the speakership in 2015.

Though Poetter's quest may seem a bit quixotic, another college professor, David Bratt, an economist at Randolph-Macon College in Virginia, managed to unseat House majority leader Eric Cantor in the 2014 Republican primary. In Virginia's heavily Republican Seventh Congressional District, Bratt easily won the general election. In the 2018 midterm election, though, he was defeated by Abigail Spanberger (D), a former CIA operations officer. One academic, former Duke University political science professor David Price, has represented North Carolina's Fourth Congressional District since 1987. Price was defeated in 1994 but returned to office two years later.

Incumbents

Among the many individuals who may consider running for Congress, some are in an especially favorable position. These are the *incumbents*—current officeholders running for reelection. In recent decades, incumbent representatives seeking reelection have been successful in about 90 percent of their races and incumbent senators have succeeded in about 80 percent. Most elections in which an incumbent participates are barely competitive, with incumbents displaying victory margins of about 30 percent. Indeed, many incumbents are not challenged. In 2018, forty-two congressional incumbents ran unopposed. Every election year, a small number of incumbents, to be sure, choose not to run for reelection—fifty-six chose not to seek reelection in 2018—but even taking these into account, the average rate of incumbent reelection hovers just below 90 percent in House races and about 80 percent in Senate contests.[5] Madison's fear of mutability in the public councils seems not to have been warranted.

The importance of incumbency stems from America's Constitution and party system. Under the Constitution, all members of the House and Senate are independently elected in their own districts or states. No votes cast outside their own constituencies affect them, and while regional or national trends may roil the local waters, so long as they maintain the support of the local electorate, members of Congress are secure in their own domains. The near-decisive importance of incumbency, though, is a modern phenomenon. In the earliest years, as we saw in chapter 2, most members had no interest in serving more than a term or two. During the nineteenth and early twentieth centuries, electoral politics was dominated by political parties. Party leaders selected the candidates and organized the campaigns, and voters were taught to focus on parties rather than individual contenders. Party leaders sometimes rotated members of Congress in order to give many loyal functionaries a chance at federal office. With the introduction of primary elections and civil service reforms, the power of party organizations was reduced and individual members of Congress won greater control over their own political destinies. Today, many strive to take advantage of the possibility of making congressional service a multiyear career.

Incumbents have a number of political advantages. To begin with, members of Congress and their staffs are in a position to provide many individual services to constituents. These services include answering questions, discussing concerns, helping constituents navigate the maze of rules and regulations surrounding federal benefits, and, in the case of businesses and interest groups, attempting to influence decisions by federal agencies. No service aimed at pleasing voters is too small. Congressional staffers will even help constituents visiting Washington arrange tours of the Capitol and White House.

These constituency services are called *casework,* and much of it takes place not in Washington, but in legislators' state and district offices. Every member of the House has a government-funded, full-time district office, and many have one or two satellite offices staffed on a part-time basis. Senators have more than one state office, with the senators from the larger states boasting several official addresses. Senator Ted Cruz of Texas has seven offices in the Lone Star State, while Senator Chuck Schumer of New York assigns staffers to nine offices scattered throughout the Empire State. Senators are allotted an average of forty-four staffers each (depending upon the size of their state), whom they may divide among their Washington and district offices as they wish. Representatives may do the same but are assigned, on average, only sixteen staffers. Perhaps not all constituents are grateful for the help they receive, but the opportunity to provide such help provides incumbents with a good chance to generate gratitude—and votes.

Most casework is undertaken by staffers, but all representatives and senators make certain to spend time with their constituents. No politician wants to be accused of being out of touch with the folks at home. Hence, however powerful they may be in Washington, members of Congress generally hasten home for town meetings, dedications, ribbon-cutting ceremonies, inspection tours, and, of course, fund-raisers. Most of these activities are covered by the local media, but, to leave nothing to chance, every congressional staff includes a press officer charged with maintaining good relations with local editors and reporters and circulating media releases to them to polish the incumbent's image. Press officers also tweet to thousands of "followers" in the state or district and post continually on Facebook and other social media to publicize the senator's or representative's activities. Many members of Congress maintain blogs, where they or their press officers discuss current legislation and present the member's actions in a positive light.[6] For older voters, who may still think a tweet is a birdcall, members make use of the congressional franking privilege to send postage-free mail extolling their achievements. Under a law enacted in 1789, members of Congress may send mail free of charge to their constituents informing them of governmental business and public affairs. Currently, members receive an average of $15,000 per year in free postage for mailings to voters in their own states or districts. Franked mail cannot be sent outside the state or district. Most senators and representatives send regular newsletters to all constituent households highlighting the many efforts and initiatives the incumbent has undertaken on behalf of the community.

Members of Congress lose no opportunity to garner local publicity and advertise their efforts on the constituency's behalf. Events that are ignored by the national media may, nevertheless, be of considerable significance to local voters. Senators and representatives seek to associate themselves with these events and send out press releases highlighting their involvement.

Take for example a press release issued by the office of Congressman Eric Swalwell of California's Fifteenth District honoring the managers and employees of a new sanitation facility in his district. In fact, at the ribbon-cutting ceremony for the new plant, a staffer from Swalwell's office presented the facility's general manager with a "Certificate of Special Congressional Recognition," for the facility's "commitment and dedication to renewable energy." Thousands of these certificates, suitable for framing, are awarded by members of Congress every year. Generally, the recipients are grateful and the event is covered by the local media and vigorously tweeted by all concerned.[7]

Legislation

Unlike challengers, who can only offer promises, incumbents have a chance to promote legislation favored by important groups and interests in their districts. If the constituency includes a major industry, representatives will almost always promote legislation that will please the workers and managers of that industry. The late senator Henry M. Jackson of Washington took pleasure in being known as the "Senator from Boeing." Often, representatives find it useful to strongly support essentially symbolic legislation that will please constituency groups. This is the case sometimes when a particular piece of gun-control legislation is proposed by members who know the bill will not be passed, but want to make a statement nonetheless. These symbolic gestures are one form of what is sometimes called "position taking."[8] Generally, position taking is a more effective tactic when it comes to pleasing ordinary voters. Organized interests are less likely to focus on symbols and more likely to look for tangible benefits.

One major difficulty with the use of legislation as a reelection tool is that constituencies, especially states, can be quite diverse. A bill favored by some constituency groups may be bitterly opposed by others. For example, a 2015 Senate vote on regulation of hydraulic fracturing, commonly known as "fracking," caused problems for a number of senators. The bill was strongly supported by environmentalists who claim fracking pollutes the water table, but it was strongly opposed by energy interests who say fracking is safe and lowers energy costs. Senators from states like Colorado and New Mexico, where both interests are active, found themselves able to please some constituents only by alienating others. Indeed, former senator Jeff Bingaman of New Mexico was a legislator known for calling loudly for extended study of the fracking question, presumably so that he would be able to avoid having to vote.

The Federal Pork Barrel

Incumbents also make it their business to support the interests of local companies and labor unions and of the district or state more generally when it comes to federal projects and contracts. Such efforts are known as *pork barreling* and are seen by incumbents as tangible evidence of achievements for which they can claim credit and that are crucial to their reelection chances.[9] The late senator Robert Byrd of West Virginia, longtime chair of the Senate Appropriations Committee, was sometimes called the "King of Pork," for his skill at steering federal projects to his state. During Byrd's tenure in office several billion dollars in federal funds for highways, dams, and government facilities flowed into West Virginia. Byrd disliked the title "King of Pork" but did refer to himself as "Big Daddy" when he presided over the opening of the federally funded Robert C. Byrd Biotechnology Science Center in his home state. Citizens Against Government Waste named Byrd "Emperor Palpatine of Pork" and gave the senator the group's lifetime achievement award. Other members of Congress vying for the title "King of Pork" include Mississippi senator Thad Cochran, who captured billions of dollars in federal projects for his state, and the nineteen-term late congressman John Murtha, who was able to direct hundreds of millions of dollars in federal defense contracts to companies in his rural Pennsylvania district. All three members of this porcine royal family were reelected time after time. Cochran recently retired during his seventh Senate term; Byrd served six years in the House and fifty-one years in the Senate, and Murtha served thirty-eight years in the House. Their records seem to suggest that pork pays.

Pork, of course, comes in several flavors. Chief among these are appropriations, earmarks, and tax breaks. As to the first, about $16 billion every year are appropriated for projects that particularly serve local or special interests. Members of the House and Senate appropriations committees, like the late senator Byrd, are particularly well situated to garner funding for such projects, but other senior and influential senators and representatives are often in a position to land their own federal largesse. For example, Boston's "Big Dig," a project designed to relocate several miles of interstate highways underground through Boston, was funded by an appropriation championed by then House Speaker Thomas P. ("Tip") O'Neill of Massachusetts. The project eventually cost nearly $15 billion, making it the most expensive highway project in U.S. history.

An *earmark* is a provision that some member or members of Congress are able to insert into a general appropriations bill that directs special funding to their own constituents. One of the most famous earmarks of recent years funded Alaska's Gravina Island Bridge. The project, which cost several hundred million dollars, was inserted into a federal public works bill by the late Alaska senator Ted Stevens. The bridge served fifty residents of a remote island and was called by its critics the "Bridge to Nowhere." At one time earmarks were very obvious, but today they are prohibited by party rules and most are hidden in the language of the bill and difficult to find. These so-called "zombie earmarks" will be discussed again in chapter 5. For the moment, suppose that a hospital construction bill requires that $50 million of the funds to be spent should go toward the construction of facilities for hospitals with more than 150 but fewer than 200 beds in counties with a certain demographic makeup and level of physician availability. Who but the author of the bill would know that only one such hospital existed in the entire nation—and that this fortunate hospital happened to be located in the author's district? In 2010 House Republicans declared that in the interest of economy they would no longer make use of earmarks, and both houses soon forswore earmarking. Enthusiasm for this idea, however, has waned, and earmarks are again becoming commonplace forms of pork. Indeed, when the Big Dig ran out of appropriated funds it had to be finished with a zombie earmark. President Trump actually urged Congress to formally restore earmarks in order to smooth the flow of legislative business.

A third common form of pork is the *tax expenditure,* or "loophole." In recent years, members of Congress have provided their supporters and constituents with a variety of tax breaks. These include special tax treatment for certain motorsports entertainment complexes, several utility companies, Hollywood filmmakers, and some investors in District of Columbia property development. By the way, these and a number of other examples of tax pork are drawn from a piece of legislation entitled the Investing in American Jobs and Closing Tax

Loopholes Act of 2010. What better place to hide loopholes than in an act nominally closing loopholes?

So that the recipients of federal pork do not forget the name of the senator or representative responsible for the gifts bestowed upon them, congressional benefactors like to see pork barrel projects named for themselves. Bridges, roads, dams, and buildings are named for the kings of pork—the Byrds, Murthas, and Cochrans of Capitol Hill. One huge portion of the Big Dig, for example, is named the O'Neill Tunnel. But the lesser princelings of pork are also eager to claim naming rights. Take, for example, Arizona congressman Raúl Grijalva. The congressman apparently helped the city of Tucson secure a relatively small amount of federal funding to complete an electric streetcar line through the city. Grijalva was rewarded with a plaque naming the streetcar stop on the corner of Avenida del Convento and Congress Street the "Grijalva streetcar stop." The delighted congressman exclaimed, "This is very special. Long after I'm gone people will come up to this plaque and go, who was he?"[10] A named streetcar stop may not be as impressive as a major federal building, but at least it is not a bridge to nowhere.

Another important electoral advantage generally possessed by incumbents is superior access to campaign funds. Incumbents are usually far better able than challengers to raise money. For most senators and representatives, fund-raising is a year-round activity. Incumbents hope not only to outspend challengers but to deter prospective challengers from even undertaking the race, knowing they'll probably face an insurmountable fund-raising disadvantage. Incumbents also fear the possibility that outside interests will target their own race. In recent years, national liberal and conservative "super PACs" have raised tens of millions of dollars to attempt to sway the congressional balance of power as well as presidential contests.

Thus, incumbents engage in a constant quest for money. They attend fund-raising luncheons, dinners, and special events hosted by supporters and lobbyists. Attendees are charged for admission and the opportunity to rub shoulders with a lawmaker and perhaps engage in a bit of face-to-face advocacy for their cause. The proceeds are added to the politician's campaign chest. The major donors, particularly to incumbent campaigns, include interest groups, corporate political action committees (PACs), and wealthy individuals. Most incumbents have developed direct mail lists, and increasingly members have turned to online targeted solicitations aimed at raising large numbers of small contributions from individuals whose demographic status or past political activities seem to make them good prospects.

Despite the Internet, old-fashioned fund-raising events abound in the nation's capital and around the country. In a recent and fairly typical week in Washington, donors paid $2,500 each to sit in a box seat with a member of Congress to watch a Taylor Swift concert at the Washington Nationals baseball park. Thirteen Republicans and six Democrats joined together for the fund-raising event, and seats quickly sold out. The two parties may not be able to find common ground on Capitol Hill, but apparently they can at the ballpark. During the same week, contributors forked over cash to participate in a "weekend in the Hamptons" with Representative Lee Zeldin, a Napa Valley Wine Tour to benefit the Senator Pat Roberts Victory Committee, the annual Hook 'N' Bullet event in Sun Valley with Senator Mike Crapo, and the annual Family Friendly! weekend with Representative Tom Price.[11]

Of course, some challengers are also experienced fund-raisers, and some wealthy challengers are able to spend their own funds on a congressional or senatorial bid. However, since incumbents are likely to win, interest groups, trade associations, and the like are far more eager to contribute money to the campaigns of incumbents who are likely to continue to be influential in Washington than to those of challengers. This calculation becomes a self-fulfilling prophecy, as interest-group and other contributions help to ensure incumbent success. In recent years, incumbents have, on average, outspent their challengers by wide margins in both House and Senate races, which is one factor explaining incumbents' high rates of electoral success.[12]

The success of congressional incumbents is often cast in a negative light, as though it were undeserved or a result of improper activities. It is worth noting, however, that incumbents are reelected, at least in part, because of the vigorous efforts they make on behalf of their constituents. Incumbents undertake constituency casework, try to make certain that the flow of funds from the federal pork barrel favors their own districts, and work to identify legislative responses to the constituents' concerns. These are hardly nefarious activities. Incumbents generally believe that they have a good chance of reelection if they work hard for their constituents. This belief encourages them to work hard. We should think carefully before agreeing to proposed reforms, such as a constitutional amendment, to impose term limits on members of Congress. If hard work could bring no reward, why would representatives bother? Would any student make an effort in a class that he or she was absolutely certain to fail?

We will return to issues of incumbency in relation to our general questions concerning representation and governance. For now, though, let us consider the other candidates who run for Congress.

Challengers and Open Seats

In recent election years, an average of about forty members of the House of Representatives and ten senators did not seek reelection, leaving their seats without an incumbent. These open-seat races are highly contested. At the same time, challengers generally come forward to wage political warfare in the primaries and general elections against nearly all the incumbent senators and most House members seeking reelection. Few incumbents run unopposed in both the primary and general-election contests. Challengers hoping to win a House or Senate seat can be divided into five major categories. These are the ladder climbers, the ideologues, the party recruits, the celebrities, and the speculators.

The *ladder climbers* are professional politicians who view political offices as a series of ladders whose rungs they endeavor to climb, always reaching for a higher office. Ladder climbers are politically cautious since they dread sliding down the ladder, and are usually to be found campaigning for open seats or attacking incumbents wounded by scandal or redistricting that has diluted their electoral base. Ladder climbing was well illustrated by the events that took place in the state of Maryland in 2015 when longtime Democratic Barbara Mikulski announced that she would not seek reelection in 2016. Very quickly, seven of Maryland's eight House members began considering whether to make a run for the Senate. Generally speaking, politicians consider a seat in the Senate to be a higher rung on the ladder than a position in the House. The Senate is usually deemed more prestigious; senators have six-year rather than two-year terms along with larger staffs, higher salaries, and greater visibility, and even a chance to ascend all the way to the top rung of the ladder, the White House itself.

Of the politicians interested in Mikulski's seat, the foremost candidate appeared to be Representative Chris Van Hollen, a seven-term Democratic congressman from Maryland's Eighth District, a district centered in the Washington, D.C., suburbs and one of the wealthiest districts in the nation. A member of the House Democratic leadership, Van Hollen had been climbing the political ladder for twenty-five years. He began his career in 1991 by serving for four years in the Maryland House of Delegates. Van Hollen then moved up to the Maryland State Senate, where he served for eight years. In 2002, a redistricting plan that Van Hollen supported in the state legislature added more Democratic voters to the Eighth District and left the longtime Republican incumbent vulnerable. Seeing a weakened incumbent and an opportunity to climb another rung, Van Hollen entered and won the Democratic primary and then the general election. In 2016, Van Hollen climbed another rung on the ladder, defeating his Democratic primary opponents and GOP opponent to replace Mikulski in the U.S. Senate.

When Van Hollen announced that he would run for the Senate, leaving his House seat open, a number of politicians a rung or two below him on the ladder saw their own opportunities to climb. Within days of Van Hollen's announcement, three state senators, three members of the House of Delegates, and two members of the county council whereof the bulk of the Eighth district was made up indicated that they were considering congressional races. Thus, Senator Mikulski's resignation touched off a cascade of ladder climbing in the state of Maryland. Van Hollen was ultimately elected to the Senate and is sometimes mentioned as a potential Democratic vice-presidential candidate in 2020 or 2024.

The *ideologues* are generally political amateurs drawn into politics because they hope to further some political or social cause. Ideologues typically campaign in the primary elections, with conservative ideologues seeking to wrest Republican congressional nominations from more middle-of-the-road Republicans, and liberal ideologues campaigning against Democrats whom they deem to be insufficiently attentive to environmental, feminist, gay rights, or other progressive issues. In 2018, a large number of progressive Democrats, sometimes new to politics, campaigned for federal and local office, promising that a "blue wave" would sweep the Republicans from office.

Generally, incumbents of both parties make sure to cover their ideological flanks by staking out appropriate symbolic positions on ideologically fraught issues. Nevertheless, during periods of political or social turmoil, centrists and pragmatists can find themselves having to fend off challengers in the party primaries. During the past several years conservative Republicans, backed by the "Tea Party" movement, have mounted aggressive campaigns against GOP incumbents. The Tea Party is a loosely coordinated set of conservative groups opposed to liberal social programs and high taxes, in favor of private gun ownership, concerned about immigration, opposed to abortion and same-sex marriage, and disturbed by differing aspects of Democratic foreign policy. Tea Party candidates often receive support from national groups like the Club for Growth and FreedomWorks, groups primarily focused on reducing government spending. Currently, among the most visible Tea Party–supported Republicans are Senators Ted Cruz and Rand Paul, both of whom campaigned unsuccessfully for the presidency in 2016.

Some Tea Party insurgents have managed to displace prominent mainstream Republicans. In 2012, for example, thirty-six-year Senate veteran Richard Lugar of Indiana was defeated in the Republican primary by Indiana state treasurer Richard Mourdock. Mourdock, backed by Tea Party activists, charged that Lugar had lost touch with the voters of Indiana and had backed President Obama's foreign policy initiatives and judicial nominations. In 2014, as we saw earlier, a Tea Party–backed candidate defeated House majority leader Eric Cantor in the Virginia primary. In 2014, another Tea Party–backed Republican came very close to unseating longtime Mississippi Republican senator Thad Cochran in the Republican primary. Cochran is, as we saw earlier, one of the "Kings of Pork" on Capitol Hill. Though his positions on most issues are conventionally conservative, the senator came under fire from Tea Party groups who saw him as insufficiently militant on family values, immigration, and foreign policy issues. Cochran was challenged by Republican state senator Chris McDaniel and forced into a runoff before eking out a narrow victory. During periods of ideological ferment, some voters lose interest in pork barrel politics and look instead for ideological purity.

In 2018, another year of ideological tumult, several progressive Democrats with little political experience defeated long-time Democratic incumbents in the primaries. In New York, for example, Alexandria Ocasio-Cortez, a first-time candidate, defeated ten-term incumbent Joe Crowley to win the Democratic nomination in the Tenth Congressional District.

Despite a number of successes, most ideologues have been defeated in the primaries or, if they have been able to win a party nomination, have gone down to defeat in the general election. Thus, after defeating Richard Lugar in the Indiana GOP senatorial primary, Richard Mourdock was in turn defeated by the Democratic nominee, costing the Republican Party a Senate seat it had held for thirty-six years. Party leaders usually regard ideologues with suspicion and worry that they will hurt the party's overall chances for victory.

Despite leaders' concerns, the ideologues play a very important role in congressional electoral politics. As new groups and new ideas arise in the nation, the availability of congressional elections and the Congress to serve as forums for their expression greatly strengthens the legislative branch. During the 1960s and 1970s, antiwar activists challenged mainstream Democrats in primary elections and, despite protestations of gloom and doom from party elders, reinvigorated the party and the Congress. After several decades of being marginalized by the imperial presidency, with the support of new social forces Congress found the energy to oppose Presidents Johnson and Nixon, forcing both to relinquish the presidency sooner than they'd planned.

More recently, and in a similar vein, conservative activists have mounted vigorous campaigns in the Republican primaries, unseating some incumbents and forcing others to guard their right flanks by adopting positions favored by the activists. Like liberal Democrats three decades ago, conservative Republicans have sought to use their positions in Congress to attack the president's programs and put forward proposals of their own. Conservative congressional Republicans have managed to thwart the president on such matters as immigration reform, taxes, foreign policy, domestic surveillance, social spending, defense programs, and a host of other matters. Critics of their efforts refer to the result as "gridlock," but from the perspective of conservative congressional activists, the result is better described as fighting the White House to a standstill. In this way, the ideologues have invigorated Congress, given it the support of new social forces, and enabled it to do battle with the White House. In 2018, Democratic ideologues hoped to use Congress to do battle with President Trump. Some even hoped to impeach Trump.

A third category of candidates, the *party recruits,* are, as their name implies, individuals sought out by Democratic and Republican leaders and persuaded to compete for seats in the House and Senate. For the two parties, candidate recruitment is an important matter and generally the responsibility of the Senate and House Democratic and Republican campaign committees, though interest groups associated with the two parties also attempt to identify candidates.

Occasionally, party leaders are forced to seek out recruits under exigent circumstances. For example, in 2010, a Delaware Democratic senatorial candidate, the late Beau Biden, son of the vice president, dropped out of the race at the last minute for health reasons. Democratic recruiters scrambled for a replacement and found Chris Coons, a local officeholder who won the election and has served in the Senate ever since.

For the most part, though, the party recruits are the cannon fodder of political warfare. Open-seat contests and races against incumbents wounded by scandal, redistricting, or other political misfortune generally draw large numbers of party ladder climbers, and no special effort is needed to recruit candidates. Candidates are, however, needed to compete against incumbents in the scores of races where challengers face such long odds that none are eager to enter the fray. From each political party's perspective, it is important to field candidates in as many of these races as possible, however hopeless they may seem. Occasionally, fortune smiles and last-minute scandals or national political tides suddenly make seemingly safe incumbents vulnerable. Political prudence dictates having a challenger at the ready.

Every uncontested race, moreover, allows the opposition to shift financial and other resources to more competitive parts of the battlefield. A contested race, on the other hand, even if the odds seem to strongly favor the incumbent, cannot be ignored by the incumbent party. Money must be spent, campaign consultants deployed, media attention secured, and so forth. Thus, by sending recruits even into hopeless battles against entrenched incumbents, each party hopes to tie down the opposing side's resources and prevent them from being used on other electoral battlefields. The hapless recruits are likely to lose their contests but may nevertheless succeed in their mission of drawing enemy fire away from more important political targets.

Both the Democrats and Republicans have organized ongoing recruiting efforts to identify potential candidates and persuade them to run for Congress. Even though the recruits are not told they may be cannon fodder, the job of recruitment can be difficult. One top Republican recruiter, Rob Collins, a strategist for the National Republican Senatorial Committee, compared his efforts to those of University of Alabama football coach Nick Saban. "Nick Saban is a genius recruiter because he's constantly talking to his recruits. He's in their face. He lets them know they're wanted. He lets them know they fit into the team and that they'll have a role that they would want," Collins said.[13]

Even where the probability of success is low, party recruiters try to seek out credible candidates who might have some chance if something happens to weaken the incumbent. These efforts can pay off. In 2010, for example, the national political climate shifted sharply against President Obama and the Democrats, and a number of Republican recruits defeated longtime Democratic incumbents, including Ike Skelton of Missouri, Jim Oberstar of Minnesota, and Solomon Ortiz of Texas, who had held their seats for decades.

Recruiters particularly like wealthy candidates willing to finance their own races, and celebrity candidates whose name recognition will force incumbents to expend more resources. For example, in 2014, Democrats recruited actress Ashley Judd to challenge Kentucky senator Mitch McConnell, then Senate minority leader, for his seat. Some party leaders were hesitant, but Judd was strongly backed by Stephanie Schriock, head of EMILY's List, which spends millions of dollars to recruit women candidates who back abortion rights.[14]

It turned out that Democratic leaders were right to be nervous. Republicans quickly painted Judd as an enemy of the coal industry—Kentucky's major employer. Judd was persuaded to drop out of the race and was quickly replaced by a more conventional candidate, Alison Lundergan Grimes, Kentucky's secretary of state. Grimes only polled 40 percent of the vote in the general election but played her assigned role quite well. She campaigned vigorously and forced McConnell and the Republicans to work hard and spend a good deal of money to retain Kentucky's Senate seat.

Finally, we come to the *celebrities* and the *speculators*. These two types have a good deal in common. Both are political outsiders, often novices, and both hope to translate success and prominence achieved in some other domain into successful bids for political office. The difference between the two is that the celebrities hope to make use of their fame, while the speculators seek to make use of their money to win election to Congress.

Celebrities and famous individuals of all stripes have run for Congress. John Glenn's renown as an astronaut, for example, helped him win a seat in the U.S. Senate; he was not able to launch a presidential bid from there but was later launched back into space. In recent years, a number of well-known entertainers and professional athletes have sought to parlay their celebrity status into political careers. In 2018, for example, *Sex and the City* television star Cynthia Nixon used her fame to launch an unsuccessful bid for the Democratic gubernatorial nomination in New York.

As to the speculators, wealth is always a useful political asset. Nearly half the members of the U.S. Senate and, perhaps, a third of the members of the House of Representatives are millionaires, and hardly any of the others are poor. In recent years, the political importance of personal wealth has increased. To begin with, because of increased media expenditures, the cost of political campaigns has risen sharply over the last decade. For example, the average expenditure by a winning Senate candidate in 2016 was more than $10.4 million, while the average cost of winning a seat in the U.S. House of Representatives that same year was near $1.6 million. Candidates able to at least partially finance their own campaigns are strongly preferred by party leaders and activists.

Before we leave the candidates, it is worth mentioning one residual sort of contender—the *nebbish*. A nebbish is an ever-hopeful but ineffectual individual who asks, "Why not me?" One political science professor who mounted an unsuccessful race for Congress said, "Politicians tend to have an incredible ability to delude themselves about their electoral chances."[15] In every senatorial and congressional race there are a number of candidates who collectively win less than 1 percent of the vote. Many of them are nebbishes. Indeed, in every contest there are those who felt they had excellent ideas but could not collect enough voter signatures to earn a place on the ballot—nebbishes. All we can say is that democracy is for nebbishes too.

Voters

Each political party claims the allegiance of several core constituencies. For the Democrats, African Americans, Jews, and labor union members represent a solid bedrock of support whose levels of enthusiasm and turnout are among the keys to victory and defeat. For the Republicans, rural small-town white voters, white southerners, and Evangelical Protestants are solid constituencies. The electorate, however, is a dynamic rather than a constant force. Over the past several decades, the American electorate has been undergoing a major transformation. As recently as the 1960s, the electorate was overwhelmingly white; today, Hispanic and African American voters account for nearly one-third of the voting-age population. Hispanics are the most rapidly growing group in America, particularly in states and districts in the Southwest, and are being courted by both parties. Soon, a presidential ticket without a Hispanic presence will be at a decided disadvantage. Indeed, Hispanic senators Ted Cruz and Marco Rubio were candidates for the 2016 Republican presidential nomination. Despite these prominent Hispanic Republicans, many Republicans are concerned that President Donald Trump's negative comments about Hispanic immigrants during the 2015–16 GOP presidential debates cost the party dearly and will for years to come. Each House and Senate race is a separate battleground with a unique mix of personalities, voters, problems, and possibilities. Candidates and their staffs try to understand which groups of voters are solid supporters who must be encouraged to vote, which groups are solid opponents who might be discouraged from voting, and which groups are on the fence and might be persuaded by the right messages and appeals. Incumbents have usually spent time talking to voters and have developed a good feel for these issues. Nonincumbents must learn quickly.

The Electoral Arena: States and Districts

Congressional and senatorial candidates run for office in states and districts. The boundaries of states are, for all intents and purposes, immutable. Some states are generally safe Democratic bailiwicks; some are generally safe Republican fiefdoms, and a handful, mainly in the Upper Midwest, are so-called "swing" states, where partisan outcomes can vary from election to election. Presidential contests and campaigns for control of the Senate are fought in these swing states. The fact that each state elects two senators regardless of state size gives less populous rural states an advantage over more populous urban states. Since the GOP tends to be favored in rural areas, the Republicans also derive a slight advantage in Senate races from the effects of the Constitution's Great Compromise. At the present time, America's five least-populous states are represented in the Senate by seven Republicans, two Democrats, and an Independent, Bernie Sanders of Vermont, who mounted a vigorous campaign for the Democratic presidential nomination in 2016.

Unlike states, the boundaries of House districts are subject to periodic revision. Every ten years the census reallocates congressional seats among the states, which results in a nationwide redrawing of district boundaries. America's population growth has been greatest in the South and West, resulting in a shift of congressional seats to those regions. After the 2010 census, for example, Texas gained four seats while New York lost two. Congressional district boundaries are generally drawn by each state's legislature and proposed in a bill that must be signed by the governor. If one party controls both the state legislature and the governor's mansion, it will usually seek to draw district lines in such a way as to maximize the number of congressional seats it is likely to control. This practice is called *gerrymandering*. Republicans controlled a majority of the state legislatures after the 2010 national elections and made use of their power to the party's advantage. As a result of gerrymandering, in the 2012 congressional elections the GOP retained control of the House of Representatives despite winning 1.4 million fewer congressional votes than the Democrats.[16] In 2016, Republican congressional candidates received 50 percent of the popular vote, representing a small plurality. GOP candidates, however, won 55 percent of the congressional seats, a bonus attributable to districting.

Interestingly, in 2018 the Democrats won the popular vote over Republicans in House races by a 7.1 percent margin, which is about 3.5 million more votes. This time the Democrats were able to win control of the House, but not by the number of seats that would be expected given the number of actual votes Democratic candidates received. Some analysts assert that the gains made were in no small part due to the court-ordered "re-draws" of district lines in three states, Pennsylvania, Florida, and Virginia. In Pennsylvania, for example, the congressional representation after the 2018 midterm election was evenly split between the Republicans and Democrats, with each party holding nine of the state's eighteen seats. Before the 2018 election, the Republicans had thirteen of those seats and the Democrats had the other five. With the next U.S. census to be held in 2020, the impact it could have on redistricting is being closely watched because state legislatures will rely on the new data when redistricting. Three states in 2018 passed nonpartisan redistricting measures in anticipation of this: Colorado, Missouri, and Michigan. Meanwhile, a state like Wisconsin, which is considered highly gerrymandered for Republicans, actually elected Democrats for governor and the Senate. In the end, turnout can be a significant determinant of election outcomes as well. In 2018, the midterm election set a national record because, for the first time, voter turnout exceeded 100 million people: in fact, over 113 million voted.

Where partisan control of a state is divided, the legislature often compromises by drawing boundaries to protect incumbents of both parties. This practice is called bipartisan gerrymandering. Some states do not wait for the census but proceed to redraw their congressional district lines at politically opportune moments. In 2004, for example, Texas Republicans, not waiting for the next census, redistricted the state so cleverly that the GOP was able to oust four Democratic incumbents. Ten states have established nonpartisan commissions to advise their legislatures on districting. Two states, California and Arizona, have turned over full responsibility for districting to bipartisan commissions to avoid periodic partisan struggles and ensure some measure of fairness in districting. The Arizona plan was adopted by a voter referendum, over the legislature's objections.

Generally speaking, the party that controls the state legislature can attempt to draw boundaries in such a way that the supporters of the opposite party are all crammed into as few districts as possible, a practice called "packing," or are scattered across many districts where their votes will be diluted, a tactic called "cracking." Computer models help legislators, especially in the larger states, employ a mix of packing and cracking strategies to maximize their own party's chances while minimizing those of the opposition. The courts, though, have placed some general limits on the fine art of gerrymandering by declaring that districts must be compact and contiguous. In other words, no part of a district may be geographically disconnected from the remainder of the district, and the entire district must occupy a relatively compressed space. Courts have also held that district boundaries may take account of "communities of interest," allowing individuals who share similar histories and backgrounds to be included in the same district. A number of states require communities of interest to be considered in districting plans. Finally, courts have encouraged states to take account of political boundaries such as county or township lines. Several states require congressional district boundaries to follow such political jurisdictions. Districts must also contain reasonably equal numbers of individuals.

The courts have also taken an interest in the racial composition of congressional districts. The 1982 amendments to the Voting Rights Act encouraged states to create congressional districts in which racial minorities would have decisive majorities. It was hoped that this would increase the number of minority representatives in Congress, and, indeed, after the 1991–1992 round of redistricting, the number of predominately minority districts increased from twenty-six to fifty-two. Some white Republicans cheered this development because it meant that minority voters, who are overwhelmingly Democrats, would be packed into a small number of districts. The number of minority representatives might increase, but the number of Democrats would be reduced. In the 1992 case of *Miller v. Johnson,* the Supreme Court placed limits on racial redistricting by asserting that race could be taken into account in redistricting but could not be the "predominant" factor in creating electoral districts.[17]

Voting Rules and Apportionment

The drawing of district boundaries is only one form of electoral engineering that can affect the outcomes of congressional elections. A second instrument that can be employed by competing political forces is state law governing who may vote. Before the civil rights revolution, some states required prospective voters to pay poll taxes and pass literacy tests, aiming to deny voting rights to African Americans. These practices have since been outlawed. In recent years, though, a number of Republican state legislatures have implemented rules that Democrats allege are designed to keep minorities, young people, and recent immigrants from the polls. These include voter identification requirements, time restrictions on early voting, and rules that would nullify ballots cast in the wrong precinct. Democrats say that voter identification laws, in particular, disfranchise poor, young, and minority voters—key Democratic constituencies—who may not have driver's licenses, the chief form of government-issued photo ID. Republicans retort that voter identification laws are necessary to stop voting fraud, a practice they say is widespread. Liberal billionaire George Soros has pledged $5 million to the legal battle against restrictive voting laws, and unsuccessful Democratic presidential candidate Hillary Rodham Clinton made the effort a centerpiece of her 2016 campaign.[18]

Generally speaking, restrictive voting rules do have their greatest effect upon minority and immigrant voters and so help Republican congressional and presidential candidates. Whether this consequence is a function of fraud reduction or because of the disfranchisement of legitimate voters is a matter of debate. It is worth noting, however, that debates about voting rights in the United States are generally lost by advocates of more restrictive practices. In the 2018 midterm election, there were accusations of voter suppression in Georgia, and it led to a recount of the governor's race there. Recounts also occurred in Florida and Arizona. Florida, which had disenfranchised more possible voters than any other state, did pass a ballot initiative that restored voting rights to more than one million ex-felons in the state. Meanwhile, Maryland, Michigan, and Nevada approved ballot measures that allow for same-day voter registration or enacted automatic voter registration, which are largely seen as effective countermeasures to restrictive voting laws.

The Campaign

Districting creates the political arena. It is up to the candidates and their supporters to do battle in that arena. Though they are affected by external forces, each state and district is a battleground of its own. Congressional incumbents go into campaign mode almost from the first day they take office, raising money,

cultivating supporters, and securing media attention. Their congressional staffers form the nucleus of the next campaign staff. Challengers and candidates for
open seats generally begin their campaigns several months prior to the primaries.
Prospective candidates start with informal visits to influential individuals and
important groups in their constituency. If informal consultations, requests for
pledges of support, and so on seem promising, the next step is the formation of
an "exploratory committee" which must be registered with the Federal Election
Commission (FEC), and "staffing up," that is, retaining consultants, attorneys,
media experts, and data analysts to organize primary and general-election campaigns. All this must be accomplished during a period of a few months. One
political consultant called campaigns "the fastest start-ups in the world."

In the nineteenth century, campaigns were planned and directed by party
bosses employing the services of hundreds of thousands of patronage workers
whose government jobs depended upon their willingness to engage in political
activity on the party's behalf. Contemporary congressional campaigns, particularly Senate campaigns, are led by political consultants utilizing activist volunteers, paid campaign workers, lawyers, and sophisticated communications
technology. Most consultants began their careers in the world of advertising
or marketing. A small number actually have degrees in campaigning from such
programs as George Washington University's Graduate School of Political Management. Consultants generally develop the campaign's overall strategy, frame
issues, commission focus groups and opinion polls, recruit campaign workers,
raise money, maintain useful relationships with the mass media, plan direct mail
campaigns, seek damaging information about the opposition, and, in short, undertake all the activities needed for political success.

Some consultants have become political celebrities in their own right. Barack
Obama's senior political advisor was Chicago media consultant David Axelrod.
In the consulting world, Axelrod was known for his ability to help black candidates overcome the suspicions of white voters and had worked for a number of
African American politicians before signing on with Obama. Axelrod is widely
credited with developing the theme of "change" that helped carry Obama to the
presidency in 2008. Axelrod is currently a very visible media commentator and
has advised candidates in England and Italy. Another important Obama consultant, Jim Messina, is hardly known outside Washington political circles. Messina
crafted Obama's successful social media campaign and is credited with giving
Obama a million Twitter followers. George Bush's chief strategist, Karl Rove,

was a powerful figure in Washington for eight years and now heads a conservative "super PAC" (see "Money and Politics" section), aimed at promoting the interests of Republican congressional candidates. Of course, one well-known politician does not place much faith in consultants and strategists. Donald Trump mainly consults himself.

Campaign Workers

With the disappearance of patronage employees, campaigns turned to volunteers and paid employees to work as staffers and fund-raisers. Some congressional candidates are better able to attract grassroots volunteers than others. Candidates supported by the Tea Party, religious right, organized labor, environmental groups, feminists, gay rights groups, or senior citizens' groups like the AARP can rely upon their allies to provide foot soldiers for the political trenches. Candidates who are not so fortunate must often rely upon paid fund-raisers and campaign workers. Prior to the 1980s, Democratic candidates were far better able than their Republican rivals to recruit volunteers. Organized labor provided the Democrats with workers, as did environmental and peace groups. During the 1980s, the balance of infantry power shifted. During the Reagan era the GOP forged an alliance with the Christian right and mobilized regiments of Christian soldiers for political warfare. Democrats countered by increasing their efforts to recruit volunteers from politically progressive groups. These volunteers can be found in most congressional campaigns, handing out leaflets, posting lawn signs, staffing phone banks, and so forth.

Lawyers

No contemporary campaign would be complete without the services of a phalanx of legal specialists. Fifty years ago, the courts seldom became involved in electoral processes and few attorneys knew much about election law. Today, election law is a major legal specialty and some large Washington law firms have created election law groups to deal with an ever-growing caseload. An important set of campaign-related legal issues concerns the accuracy of vote counts. Since the 2000 Florida presidential election, which was, of course, decided in the courts after a statewide recount, every serious campaign has placed lawyers on retainer ready to challenge an unfavorable election outcome, especially if the election was close, or to defend against such a challenge. Hundreds of attorneys were waiting in the wings, ready to attack or defend close outcomes in every state during the 2004, 2008, and 2012 national elections as well as during the off-year congressional races. Issues that can be raised to attack an election result include the eligibility of voters, the validity of ballots, the accuracy of counting procedures, the propriety of the instructions given to voters, and whether or not illegal incentives might have been offered to voters. For example, Arizona's Second Congressional District race in 2014 between Democratic incumbent Ron Barber and Republican challenger Martha McSally generated a number of lawsuits challenging the outcome. On the basis of the official vote tally, McSally seemed to have won by 161 votes. Barber's attorneys, however, charged that the vote count had included a number of improprieties, including the improper disqualification of 133 votes. After a complete recount, McSally's victory was confirmed. Several years ago, President Bush's attorney Benjamin L. Ginsberg called the 2000 Florida election struggle the "greatest peacetime mobilization of lawyers in American history." If so, the lawyers have never been fully demobilized. In 2016, attorneys representing Green Party candidate Jill Stein challenged the presidential tallies in three states—Michigan, Ohio, and Pennsylvania—but were unable to overturn the results.

The Primaries

Before candidates can compete in the general election they must earn a place on the ballot. For those hoping to run as independents or as minor-party candidates, this can mean the collection of many petition signatures from registered voters. Since voters are usually unwilling to cast ballots for candidates they perceive as having no chance to win, most political aspirants opt to seek the nomination of the Democratic or Republican Party. At one time, party leaders controlled these nominations, but since about 1900, voters in primary elections have decided the matter.

Primary elections are governed by state law and political party rules. The fifty states and two parties have devised four main types of primaries (see box 1).

Generally speaking, party leaders prefer closed primaries to prevent members of the opposite party from affecting the nomination. Thus, where parties are strong enough to write the law, they will choose the closed contests. Open primaries are generally employed by states whose parties are so weak that leaders were not able to secure their preferred voting rules. Semi-closed primaries represent a compromise position. Most of the nation's primaries are closed, open, or semi-closed. The top-two primaries, currently used only in California, in

Box 1. Types of Primaries

Open Primary

In an open primary, voters of any affiliation may vote in the primary of any party they choose. They cannot vote in more than one party's primary, although that prohibition can be difficult to enforce in the event that a party has a runoff election. In many open-primary states voters do not indicate partisan affiliation when they register to vote. One area of contention in open primaries is "crossover" voting, which may change who wins a party nomination. It most often involves voters registered with Party B (either in an area dominated by Party A or in a year when Party B's nominee is a foregone conclusion) voting in the primary for the Party A candidate whose views are closer to their own. Occasionally, there are also concerns about sabotage, or "party crashing," which involves partisans strategically voting for a weaker candidate in another party's primary in the hope that the opposition party will nominate a candidate who is easier to defeat in the general election.

Closed Primary

In a closed primary, only voters registered with a given party can vote in that party's primary. Parties may have the option to invite unaffiliated voters to participate, but such independent voters usually are left out of the primary unless they decide to give up their independent status. Closed primaries preserve a party's freedom of association, but critics claim that closed primaries can exacerbate the radicalization that often occurs at the primary stage, when candidates must cater to their party's "base" rather than the political center. In a few states, independent voters may register with a party on Election Day. However, they must remain registered with that party until they change their affiliation again. A handful of states even allow voters registered with one party to switch their registration at the polls to vote in another party's primary. In these rare instances, a closed primary can more closely resemble open or semi-closed primaries than the closed primaries of other states.

Semi-Closed Primary

In a semi-closed primary, unaffiliated voters may choose which party primary to vote in, while voters registered with a party may only vote in that party's primary. Representing a middle ground between the exclusion of independent voters in a closed primary and the free-for-all of open primaries, the semi-closed primary eliminates concerns about voters registered in other parties from "raiding" another party's nominating contest. People who align with a given party may theoretically still vote in another party's primary if they are registered as independent. The potential for such tactical party registration is also present in the strictest of closed primaries.

Top-Two Primary

The top-two primary system puts all candidates, regardless of party affiliation, on the same ballot. The top two vote-getters then face off in the general election. The top-two system is used in California and Washington, as well as in Nebraska for its nonpartisan elections to the state's legislature. Louisiana uses a variation of top-two in which a second-round runoff only takes place if a candidate fails to win more than 50 percent of the vote in the first round. Top-two primaries are sometimes referred to as "open primaries," but that term refers to party primaries in which all voters may choose to participate in a given party's primary. By contrast, the top-two system eliminates party primaries altogether, with the field winnowed regardless of candidates' party affiliation. In 2016, California's top-two system produced a Senate race between two Democratic candidates, Loretta Sanchez and Kamala Harris, the top two finishers in the primary.

Source: The Center for Voting and Democracy, "Primaries," http://www.fairvote.org/research-and-analysis/presidential-elections/congressional-and-presidential-primaries-open-closed-semi-closed-and-top-two/.

Washington, and in Louisiana congressional races, generally reflect one-party systems whose leaders want to be certain that both general-election candidates in most districts will be drawn from their own party.

Primaries are typically fought for open seats. Most incumbents do not face primary challenges, and those who do are generally victorious. Occasionally, however, a wounded incumbent will be ousted in the primaries, and, as we have seen, during periods of ideological ferment, candidates with a cause may be able to mobilize groups of like-minded voters. Ideologically motivated candidates can present a threat in primary elections because voter turnout in these contests is low and candidates who can mobilize supporters driven by a cause can, as in the case of Tea Party activists, surprise an unwary incumbent.

Primaries differ in one important respect from general-election contests— that is in the matter of the electorate's ideological diversity. Democratic Party primary voters tend to be more liberal than the general electorate, while Republican Party primary voters tend to be more conservative than the electorate at large. Party leaders constantly worry that the primaries will produce more liberal candidates (in the case of the Democrats) or more conservative candidates (in the case of the Republicans) than would be preferred by the general electorate. This matter of ideology is probably not important in solidly Democratic or Republican states and congressional districts, where strong liberal or conservative credentials can be a plus. It is difficult to be too liberal for Massachusetts or too conservative for South Carolina. Both, however, can be handicaps in more politically diverse settings.

The General Election

For the fortunate candidates who survive the primaries and the even more fortunate candidates who faced no opposition in the primaries, the next step is the general election. As we observed earlier, nineteenth-century presidential campaigns relied upon the hundreds of thousands of workers, usually patronage employees, whom each party could field like infantry armies on Election Day. These infantry armies still count in the primaries and in the general election. Many thousands of volunteers ring doorbells, hand out leaflets, and place signs in yards and posters on walls. In modern campaigns, however, a new array of weapons—perhaps we should label it "air power"—has joined, if not entirely supplanted, the infantry armies of the past.

Polling

Virtually all campaigns make extensive use of opinion polling. Campaigns collect data to assess the electorate's needs, hopes, and fears. Polls, conducted throughout the campaign, provide the basic information used to craft strategies, select issues, and check voter responses to candidate appeals. Only a decade ago, polling was associated mainly with presidential politics. Today, all senatorial campaigns and most House campaigns rely upon poll data. The theses, issues, and messages that candidates present are generally based upon polls and small face-to-face sessions with voters called "focus groups." Pollsters have become important campaign consultants and often continue to work with incumbent members of Congress long after the election to help secure the enactment of legislation that will advance their careers.

The Broadcast Media

Extensive use of the broadcast media, television in particular, is the hallmark of the modern presidential campaign. Candidates endeavor to secure as much positive news and feature coverage as possible. This type of coverage is called *free media* because candidate do not pay for airtime. Candidates can secure free media coverage by participating in newsworthy events. Sitting public officials, especially incumbent members of Congress, can call for new legislation, sponsor hearings, undertake inspection tours of fires and floods, and meet with foreign dignitaries to capture the attention of the television cameras. Challengers can announce new proposals or launch attacks against the incumbents. In addition to seeking free media coverage, primary and general-election candidates, parties, and political advocacy groups collectively spend tens of millions of dollars to purchase television ads, most running for sixty, thirty, or even fifteen seconds. These so-called "spot ads" allow a candidate's message to be delivered to an audience before indifferent or hostile viewers can reach their dials to tune them out. Some of the more memorable recent ads include one run in 2014 on behalf of Joni Ernst, running for the Senate in Iowa. In the ad, Ernst makes the argument that she's uniquely qualified to cut spending in Washington. "I grew up castrating hogs on an Iowa farm, so when I get to Washington, I'll know how to cut pork," says Ernst, smiling as video footage of pigs is played. "Washington's full of big spenders. Let's make 'em squeal," Ernst declares.[19] This ad, which went viral nationally, helped Ernst defeat Democrat Bruce Braley.

In one amusing 2018 ad, the wife of a Travis County, Texas, commissioner is pleading in an online campaign video for voters to reelect her husband so he'll get out of the house and relieve her of his nonstop prattling about county issues. The ad posted to YouTube shows Charlyn Daugherty rolling her eyes at the camera as Gerald Daugherty drones on about tax rates, light rail, and other issues while doing household chores. "Please reelect Gerald," she says at the end. "Please."[20]

Perhaps the most tasteless spot ad of recent years was run by J. D. Winteregg, who ran in the 2014 Ohio Republican primary against House Speaker John Boehner. The ad charged Boehner with suffering from "electile dysfunction" in a spot styled after commercials for drugs like Cialis. "Your electile dysfunction?" the narrator intones. "It could be a question of blood flow. Sometimes when a politician has been in D.C. too long, it goes to his head and he just can't seem to get the job done." The narrator adds, "If you have a Boehner lasting more than twenty-three years, seek immediate medical attention." Not only did Winteregg lose the primary, he also lost his teaching position at a Christian college.[21]

Ads generally do not present coherent arguments or evidence. They are designed to establish candidate name recognition, to create a favorable image of the candidate and a negative image of the opponent, to link the candidate with desirable groups in the community, and to signal the candidate's stand on salient issues. Generally, negative ads, excoriating the opponents, have a greater impact upon voters than positive ads praising the candidates. Voters profess to dislike negative ad campaigns, but they are more likely to remember negative images and be influenced by them, particularly when the targets of negative ads issue denials and defend themselves, providing extended free coverage of the accusation.

The Internet and Social Media

Since the 1990s, the Internet has become an increasingly important tool in political campaigns. Many congressional incumbents and candidates have developed an Internet strategy for fund-raising, mobilizing support, and getting out the vote. Almost as a matter of course, politicians create social networking sites that allow them to post information about themselves and give supporters an opportunity to chat with one another to build enthusiasm for their candidate. Twitter has become the preferred medium for candidates to send a constant stream of news to supporters and voters. According to several studies, hundreds if not thousands of politicians have opened Twitter accounts.[22]

Through the Internet, messages transmitted by the campaign to its supporters are often retransmitted to ever-growing groups of Facebook friends and Twitter followers and so forth in a process known as *crowdsourcing*. Crowdsourcing amplifies the power of political messages, bringing them to millions of individuals in a short period of time. And individuals are more likely to trust messages that come from friends than those they receive directly from campaigns. Many candidates have also found that blogs are quite effective instruments for attacking the opposition. Often voters are unaware of the partisan leanings of particular blogs and are inclined to take at face value information that amounts to little more than partisan propaganda. Often too, accounts presented by bloggers are picked up by the mainstream press and widely disseminated. Because of its growing importance, the two parties have been fighting vigorously for control of the "blogosphere."

In recent years too, each party has developed a database containing hundreds of pieces of information on every registered voter. The information is acquired from census reports; credit, banking, and store purchase records; warranty cards; magazine subscription lists; memberships; travel records; answers to opinion poll questions; and a myriad of other sources. Using this information and a number of sophisticated computer programs, consultants can infer a good deal about the attitudes, preferences, concerns, and likely political behavior of each voter. These inferences in turn allow campaigns to develop individualized advertising and fund-raising messages that can be sent to voters via phone calls, mail, social media, and e-mail, a practice called "microtargeting." This tactic not only reaches the right voters with the right messages but also increases the efficiency of fund-raising. Of course, this same technology has left campaigns vulnerable to hacking. In the 2016 election, hackers, some based in Russia, sought to influence election results by manipulating Facebook and other social media sites. In July 2018, before the midterm elections, Facebook took action to eliminate what it said were thirty-two fake pages and accounts it detected that were intended to "disrupt" the elections. The company continues to expand its security efforts and has hired counterterrorism experts as part of that.

Campaign Themes and Tactics

In principle, democratic elections permit voters to make any choices they please. In practice, voters' choices are constrained by the options offered to them. The late V. O. Key Jr. once called electoral choices "echoes in an echo chamber."[23] The options offered to voters include not only the candidates themselves but also the policy choices or other alternatives they present to the electorate. If the competing candidates mainly discuss foreign policy, voters would be hard-pressed to base their decisions on their own concerns about Social Security. And similarly, if candidates devote their energies to attacking one another's personal integrity, voters are likely to try to choose the more honest of the two.

Media accounts of battles over political issues seem to assume that these arise more or less spontaneously from popular needs and citizen demands. Yet the truth is that most political issues are developed by intellectuals, political consultants, academics, and staffers in Washington's partisan "think tanks," like the Brookings Institution, Heritage Foundation, American Enterprise Institute,

Progressive Policy Institute, Cato Institute, and dozens of others. Indeed, "issues consulting" is a major Washington industry, with hundreds of experienced and would-be issue entrepreneurs peddling their ideas to public officials, political candidates, and interest groups. Sometimes these entrepreneurs create issues from whole cloth. That is, they offer a politician a potentially useful issue in which the public has exhibited no prior interest. For example, former Tennessee senator Al Gore's campaign against suggestive lyrics in rock music seems to have been the brainchild of a musically challenged consultant.

More often, however, rather than invent issues based upon problems in which the public has exhibited no prior interest, issue entrepreneurs usually seek to identify potentially useful issues from among the many matters with which the public already has some concern. For example, issue specialists did not invent segregation or abortion. Instead, they found a vocabulary through which to frame and dramatize these matters, painting as moral evils needing to be rectified what some might have simply accepted as facts of life. An example is Dr. Martin Luther King Jr.'s strategy of leading groups of peaceful marchers into southern towns like Selma, Alabama, where they were sure to be attacked by the police. By so doing, Dr. King demonstrated to millions of northern whites, watching on television, that what they had previously ignored or downplayed as peculiar southern "folkways" (to use President Eisenhower's characterization of the Jim Crow system) was a state of affairs fundamentally inconsistent with American values. Dr. King took a fact and created an issue. In a similar vein, with the help of issues consultants, candidates have been able to redefine individuals once called illegal immigrants as "DREAMers," whose rights should be defended, and the once widely accepted fact that women are paid less than men has been defined as the civil rights issue of equal pay for equal work.

Candidates can propose a seemingly infinite variety of choices to the electorate. In recent years, campaigns have focused on war and peace, public morality, candidates' personal integrity, social issues, the economy, and a host of other concerns. But while the possibilities may seem endless, there are essentially only four major themes that can be presented to the electorate individually or in some combination. These are *salutary* issues, *solidary* issues, *moral* issues, and *character* issues. Salutary issues are those focused on general social or economic benefits and solutions to national problems. Solidary issues involve questions of political, social, cultural, or ethnic identity to remind designated blocs of voters of their political loyalties and allegiances or to signal to them that people like themselves have a stake in a particular political outcome. Moral issues address matters of personal and public rectitude. Finally, campaigns address questions of candidates' character. Character issues are designed to undermine the enthusiasm of the opposing side's normal supporters and to discourage them from coming to the polls by showing that their candidate lacks the moral stature required of an important public official. This is the chief purpose of "opposition research," or dirt digging, designed to secure information that will discredit a candidate in the minds of all but his or her most vehement supporters.

Partisanship

Usually more important than issues in congressional races is partisanship. Most Americans identify with either the Democratic or Republican Party and will usually support that party's candidates. Partisanship is not unrelated to issues and identities. Typically, particular groups develop ties to one or another party on the basis of its stands on important issues or its efforts to cultivate the group's allegiance during some period of economic or political crisis. In the 1930s, for example, Franklin D. Roosevelt and the Democrats used labor and social programs to win the support of unionized workers and members of urban ethnic groups whose prior partisan allegiances had been shaken by the Great Depression. Many African Americans and Jews, in particular, were drawn to the Democratic Party because it provided them with political opportunities that they had been previously denied. Once established, though, partisan identification, like a brand preference in the marketplace, can become "sticky" and take on a life of its own. For many Americans, partisan loyalty is a lifelong commitment, which they even seek to pass along to their children.

An individual's partisan identification can change. Most white southerners were staunch Democrats until the 1960s. But the Democratic Party's support for the civil rights movement weakened their Democratic allegiances and opened the way for the GOP to create Republican majorities in most states of the old Confederacy. Nevertheless, partisan ties can be quite resilient once established. Most Jews, for example, continue to loyally support the Democrats even though, as a generally wealthy group, Jews tend to benefit from Republican economic policies. One prominent Jewish GOP activist told me that the first time he voted for a Republican candidate he felt as though he had abandoned his religious faith and converted to Christianity.

Identity

Campaigns also appeal to voters on the basis of their social or political identities. Politicians typically make such appeals by emphasizing that they share or at least sympathize with some salient trait of the voters whose support they are seeking. Such traits include gender, ethnicity, race, religion, and various other physical or social characteristics voters deem to be important. One well-known example of identity politics is the ethnically balanced ticket. In the nineteenth century, urban political machines typically enrolled voters from a variety of immigrant groups. To maintain voter loyalty, machine leaders always made certain that the party's slate of candidates included representatives from all the major groups. Even as recently as the 1960s, the Democratic Party's slate in New York City was led by candidates named Lefkowitz, Fino, and Gilhooley, which presumably reminded the city's numerous Jewish, Italian, and Irish voters that they had reason to support the Democrats.

In addition to balancing the ticket, contemporary politicians endeavor to balance their appeal by vigorously expressing their sympathy and admiration for groups to which they do not actually belong. Almost every New York politician, for example, is certain to make a political pilgrimage to Jerusalem, the Vatican, and Dublin, stopping en route at numerous senior citizens centers, African Methodist Episcopal churches, and mosques. Many politicians have learned to speak a few words of Spanish or, like Florida's governor Jeb Bush, happily publicize their ties by marriage to America's rapidly growing Hispanic community. The Republican Party, attempting to broaden its ethnic base, has encouraged the political aspirations of Senators Ted Cruz and Marco Rubio as well as those of Nikki Haley, who is of Indian descent and has served as governor of South Carolina and U.S. ambassador to the United Nations. And of course, a variety of politicians hope to benefit from supporting affirmative action, women's rights, subsidized health care for seniors, and other programs aimed at cultivating the sympathy of one or another racial, social, or ethnic group.

Character Issues

Many Americans view good character as an essential attribute of political leaders. Character is a term that includes a number of attributes, and most presidential candidates present themselves as honest, courageous, intelligent, and possessing good moral values. If they can, they will endeavor to suggest that their opponents manifest the opposite qualities. Sometimes these charges and counter-charges will degenerate into what politicians call a mudslinging contest.

Mudslinging usually begins with opposition research, known as "oppo research" in Washington, to identify salient facts or rumors that can be used to attack an opposition candidate's character and fitness for public office. One of the GOP's best-known opposition researchers is Barbara Comstock, who became a member of Congress from Virginia's Tenth District but was defeated in the 2018 midterm election. During the 1990s, Comstock headed the Republican National Committee's war room, where she ran the party's opposition research operation against Vice President Al Gore. Comstock called her unit "Chicks with Attitude"—a dig at the Gore campaign, whose own oppo research group called itself the "Men of Zeal." Comstock sought, with some success, to portray Gore as a "serial exaggerator."[24]

In 2014, Comstock ran for Congress, hoping to replace the retiring Representative Frank Wolf. During a televised debate among GOP primary candidates, Comstock found herself the target of a rival's oppo research. One of her primary opponents, Rob Wasinger, told the audience that Comstock had been a lobbyist for Carnival Cruise Lines, a company that allegedly had overcharged the government for providing emergency housing for Hurricane Katrina evacuees. "How can we possibly trust her to cut government spending when she's been first in line at the trough?" Wasinger asked.[25] Other candidates joined in the attacks on Comstock with their own bits of oppo research. Comstock, without a hint of irony, dismissed her critics as "bullies." She went on to win the nomination and the seat.

Money and Politics

All political campaigns require money. In 2014, congressional candidates and interest groups spent just over $4 billion on House and Senate races. Super PACs controlled by the Koch Brothers—"FreedomWorks" and "Americans for Prosperity"—alone spent nearly $500 million on congressional races, primarily on behalf of GOP candidates. Campaign spending in 2016 and 2018 exceeded these numbers.

In some instances, to be sure, candidates who spend lavishly come out on the short end. But even when this happens, they are usually defeated by opponents who spent almost as extravagantly. Though superior financial resources do not guarantee success, generally the candidate who raises and spends the most money wins. A study conducted by the Center for Responsive Politics found that 92 percent of the House races and 88 percent of the Senate races were won by the candidate who spent the most money.[26] The candidate without money, like Machiavelli's unarmed prophet, is usually doomed to failure. Generally speaking, challengers must spend a great deal of money in order to have any chance of winning office against the inherent advantages usually possessed by congressional incumbents.

Some campaign dollars are donated by individuals who, under the law, may give up to $2,700 to each candidate as well as make contributions to party committees and political action committees. Before 2014, individuals were subject to a limit of slightly more than $100,000 in total contributions to all races per election cycle. This aggregate limit was, however, struck down by the Supreme Court in the 2014 case of *McCutcheon v. FEC* as representing a limit on free speech.[27] Usually more important than individual donations are contributions from corporate and labor political action committees. A PAC is an entity established by a corporation or interest group to channel the contributions of its members into political campaigns. Under the terms of the 1971 Federal Election Campaign Act, PACs are permitted to make larger contributions to any given candidate than may be made by individuals. While individuals are limited to $2,700, PACs may give up to $5,000 per candidate. Some forty-five hundred PACs have been organized by corporations, trade associations, unions, and professional groups. In addition, many party leaders have established their own PACs, known as leadership PACs, to provide funding for their political allies. The impact of both individual and PAC contributions is often enhanced by a tactic known as "bundling." The "bundler," usually a lobbyist or political activist, raises money from a variety of groups and individuals and presents it to the campaign in a single package, or "bundle." The contributors hope to leverage the importance of their gifts, the campaign benefits financially, and the bundlers increase their own political clout. In recent years, bundlers have brought hundreds of millions of dollars to presidential and congressional campaigns.

In recent years, hundreds of millions more were spent in support of congressional and presidential candidates by nominally independent nonprofit groups— the so-called 527s and 501(c)(4)s—which are not covered by federal campaign spending restrictions. These groups, named for the sections of the tax code under which they are organized, can raise and spend unlimited amounts on political advocacy so long as their efforts are not coordinated with those of any candidate's campaign. A 527 is a group established specifically for the purpose of political advocacy, while a 501(c)(4) is a nonprofit group established for some other purpose that also engages in advocacy. A 501(c)(4) may not spend more than half its revenues for political purposes, but many political activists favor this mode of organization because, unlike a 527, a 501(c)(4) is not required to disclose where it gets its funds or exactly what it does with them. As a result, it has become a common practice for wealthy and corporate donors to route campaign contributions through 501(c)s. The donor makes a contribution to the 501(c), which keeps a cut and donates the remainder of the money to a designated "grass-roots" campaign on behalf of the politician.

A third form of independent group, the independent expenditure–only committee, or "super PAC," came about as a result of an FEC interpretation of the Supreme Court's 2010 decision in the case of *Citizens United v. FEC*. The FEC ruled that the Supreme Court's decision permitted individuals and organizations to form committees that could raise and spend unlimited amounts of money to run political advertising so long as their efforts were not coordinated with those of the candidates.[28] Super PACs are also 527 organizations, but in common political usage, a 527 does not *expressly* advocate on behalf of a particular candidate, while a super PAC does engage in express advocacy. Because of this difference, super PACs have become popular vehicles for wealthy donors.

In addition to these sources of funding, candidates may receive contributions from the relevant party committees and from other members of Congress. (See box 2.) Some candidates are, moreover, sufficiently wealthy to play a major role in financing their own campaigns. Party contributions usually amount to a small percentage of any candidate's war chest, though direct spending by the parties on behalf of candidates can be very substantial. Under the terms of the Federal Election Campaign Act, party committees can only give candidates $5,000 per race, but can spend far more—currently between $94,000 and $2.7 million for each Senate race, and $47,000 for each House race ($94,000 in states that have only one House member). Unlike spending by super PACs, this spending can be coordinated with the candidate's own spending. The parties, moreover, can be very helpful, especially to inexperienced candidates, in providing training and guidance in every aspect of campaigning and fund-raising.[29] In addition to party money, candidates often receive donations from members of their own party in Congress. Usually, congressional leaders contribute to other races in order to

---

Box 2. Where the Money Comes From

Individuals—May contribute up to $2,700 per candidate, $5,000 per PAC, and an unlimited amount to 527s and 501(c)(4)s. No limit on total contributions.
PACs—up to $5,000 per candidate.
Bundlers—No overall limit, but individuals within bundles are subject to the individual limit. Subject to record-keeping and disclosure requirements.
527 Committee—No limit on issue advocacy, but may not coordinate with any campaign. Subject to record-keeping and disclosure requirements.
527 Super PAC—No limit on express candidate advocacy, but may not coordinate with any campaign. Subject to record-keeping and disclosure requirements.
501(c)(4)—May spend up to half its revenue for campaign activity, including express candidate advocacy, but may not coordinate with any campaign. Not required to disclose donors.
National Party Committees—Up to $5,000 per candidate, but in conjunction with its senatorial campaign committee may give up to $47,400 per campaign to each Senate candidate.
State and Local Party Committees—Up to $5,000 per candidate. Note that party committees can spend much more on behalf of candidates and that this spending can be coordinated with candidates' own campaigns.

Source: Center for Responsive Politics, OpenSecrets.org, "2018 Campaign Contribution Limits," 2018, https://www.opensecrets.org/overview/limits.php.

---

increase the chances that their party will win control of Congress and to earn the gratitude of their fellow members. Current democratic leader Nancy Pelosi (D-CA), for example, used campaign contributions to achieve and retain her position in the House.[30]

Voters and Donors

In principle, there are two reasons to think that elections might allow citizens some measure of control over the government's conduct. These are, to put it simply, choice and accountability. Elections permit citizens an opportunity to choose representatives who share their own interests and preferences. They also give citizens a chance to hold officials accountable for their actions by threatening to depose those whose conduct in office is inconsistent with popular wishes. These ideas certainly seem plausible. The problem, though, is that the behavioral presumptions underlying the choice-and-accountability model apply more aptly to the relationships among politicians and interest group donors than to the connections between politicians and ordinary voters.

Most voters have relatively little information upon which to base their choices. To a considerable extent, voters rely upon candidates to supply them with information about themselves and allow their preferences to be formed during the campaign by the marketing efforts of politicians, often by negative campaign ads. Organized groups, on the other hand, are typically not very interested in candidates' campaign commercials. Corporate, labor, and ideological groups have well-defined interests and preferences and often employ staffers and lobbyists to identify the strategies through which these are most likely to be advanced.

Corporate interests also endeavor to be strategic in their choice of lobbyists. Many of Washington's lobbyists also serve as campaign treasurers and major fund-raisers for political candidates. Individuals like Peter Hart, Tommy Boggs, Peter Knight, Ken Duberstein, and Vin Weber are influential, in part, because of their ability to raise money for politicians. Interest groups will often hire lobbyists whom they know to be key fund-raisers for the politicians they hope to influence. In so doing, they are not making a campaign contribution that would have to be reported to the Federal Election Commission, but they are nevertheless seeking to make use of the fact that the lobbyist promoting their interests will be seen by the targeted politician as an important source of campaign money. For example, in 2003, a coalition of television networks seeking to loosen rules governing their ownership of local TV stations hired Gregg Hartley as their lobbyist. Hartley, formerly a top aid to the powerful House majority whip Roy Blunt, now a senator, is one of Blunt's top fund-raisers. Companies hiring Harley to lobby for them are almost certain to receive a positive reception from Blunt. Seventy-one members of Congress list lobbyists as treasurers of their reelection committees. Seven members of the powerful House Appropriations Committee, five Republicans and two Democrats, have political action committees headed by lobbyists with business before the committee.

Interest groups are not only in a better position than mere voters or even small donors to employ a strategic calculus in doling out their support, they also are far better able than voters to hold politicians accountable for their actions in office. As David Mayhew has observed, the average voter has only the "haziest awareness" of what a member of the House or Senate is actually doing in office.[31] Most voters pay no attention, and even many of those who do pay attention have little understanding of the complexities of the legislative process. Even attentive voters who read the newspapers and watch televised discussions would be hard-pressed to distinguish between a member of Congress who actually works hard to promote a particular cause and one who merely makes speeches or who issues press releases.[32] Interest groups are in a much better position to make such judgments. Their lobbyists and staffers attend hearings, meet with legislators and members of their staffs, and prowl the corridors of Capitol Hill exchanging information with one another.

Of course, even interest groups can be duped. Nevertheless, Washington's more savvy interest groups know precisely what legislators are doing and can react furiously if they feel betrayed. Take, for example, the AARP, which employs twenty-two full-time lobbyists, a thirty-two-scholar think tank, and more than two thousand volunteer organizers. AARP lobbyists monitor congressional activity on a daily basis and meet with members of Congress to present the organization's views and complaints. AARP organizers are prepared to touch off furious phone and letter campaigns in the districts of members whose attentiveness to senior issues is deemed lacking. In Washington, AARP is nicknamed "Darth Vader," and members of Congress know they will definitely see the dark side of the force if they take the organization's money and fail to follow through on their commitments.[33]

It is sometimes said that money and lobbying do not buy legislation; they are said merely to buy "access" to lawmakers. This is a naive perspective. Unlike some starstruck voters, organized groups are not much interested in being photographed with famous politicians. Their goal is to secure the enactment of legislation that serves their interests. And from all indications, they accomplish this on a regular basis. Consider the following recent news stories: Over the past several years, a coalition of sixty corporations, including Pfizer, Hewlett-Packard, and Altria, spent close to $2 million in lobbying fees and campaign contributions to persuade Congress to lower the tax rate on earnings from their foreign operations. The result was legislation signed by the president in 2004 that has already saved the companies about $100 billion in taxes.[34]

Can anything be done to address this problem? In 1971 and 2002, Congress enacted campaign finance legislation nominally designed to reduce the role of money in politics by limiting campaign spending and contributions, prohibiting certain forms of campaign spending, and creating a voluntary form of public funding for presidential campaigns. Much of this legislation lies in shambles as a result of three Supreme Court decisions and a decision made by then Senator Obama. In 2008 Democratic candidate Obama decided not to accept public funding, while his Republican rival, Senator John McCain, agreed to accept such funding. By accepting public finding, McCain became legally ineligible to solicit private donations. In the ensuing campaign, Obama was able to outspend McCain by a wide margin. It seems unlikely that any future presidential candidate will make McCain's mistake.

As to court decisions, the Supreme Court's 1976 *Buckley v. Valeo* decision struck down a provision of the 1971 Federal Election Campaign Act that limited candidate spending.[35] And, as we saw earlier, overall limits on campaign contributions were struck down by the Supreme Court's *McCutcheon* decision, while the High Court's *Citizens United* decision ended most restrictions on campaign spending by outside groups. The result is a campaign environment in which bundlers and wealthy donors have a great deal of influence.

Consider, however, the implications of restricting campaign spending. The 2002 Bipartisan Campaign Reform Act (BCRA) contained a provision prohibiting interest groups and organizations from airing ads advocating the victory or defeat of any federal candidate within thirty days of a primary or caucus, or sixty days of a general election. The nominal purpose of this restriction was to prevent "attack ads" from being aired just before an election, leaving little time for the target to respond. But what might seem to most Americans as an effort to ensure fair play was generally understood in Washington as "incumbent relief legislation," that is, a law designed to make it more difficult to unseat political incumbents who are well aware of the fact that limits on spending help them stave off challengers. One of the central principles of campaign finance rules is that those writing the rules are unlikely to overlook their own interests. Hence, we should be wary of proposed campaign finance reforms. If you and I are vying for office and I write the rules, you might do well to begin planning your concession speech. In this, as in so many areas of political life, there are no easy answers.

Putting It All Together: The View from the Top

To congressional candidates, an election is about local matters—the variables they can control. As we have seen, these include such primal and fundamental factors as partisan loyalty money, pork, mud, and local issues. The precise mix of these elements will vary from election to election, district to district. Usually, incumbents will prevail, but a bit of extra mud clinging to them, or an inopportune shortage of funds, can send enough incumbents home to make the others wary.

In addition to local factors, though, elections are also influenced by national factors beyond the control of congressional candidates. In 2016, congressional candidates viewed the outsize personality of the GOP presidential candidate with a mixture of hope and fear, knowing that his provocative remarks might swing thousands of congressional votes one way or the other. In presidential election years, national issues and personalities leave a mark on almost every local contest, sometimes enough to decide the outcome. In off-year elections, voter turnout tends to be low, with only a relatively small group of core voters participating. These tend to be older, more partisan, and more inclined to vote for incumbents with whom they are familiar. During presidential years, on the other hand, local elections are more heavily influenced by the national issues and personalities voters see every day on their television screens. Presidential elections attract a surge of more peripheral voters, not so closely tied to local interests and more likely to be influenced by the presidential contest and associated issues.

Often, the party that wins the presidential race adds to its congressional seats, as the "surge" voters also support congressional candidates from the winning candidate's party. In the following off-year election, the party that controls the presidency loses some of these seats, a phenomenon often noted by the media, as the surge voters stay home and the partisan balance within each district returns to its underlying level. This cycle of surge and decline affects congressional elections at the margins: most incumbents are returned to office, but the margins can make a difference in determining which party will control Congress.

In recent years, national groups, often with ideological agendas, have formed super PACs in an effort to influence congressional races around the nation. On the conservative side, groups such as FreedomWorks and American Crossroads invest tens of millions of dollars in congressional races, while on the liberal side America's Families First Action Fund provides millions to Democratic candidates. The effect of this outside spending is to partially nationalize congressional elections and make their outcomes a bit less dependent upon local factors and a bit more a function of national political factors. Heavy spending by conservative super PACs played a role in the GOP's ability to take control of the

House of Representatives in 2010 and the Senate in 2012 and to retain control of both houses of Congress in 2014. When asked what factors affected their voting decisions in congressional races, a sizable number of voters say that national issues and national events are more important than local matters. If this is true, the day of the entrenched congressional incumbent may be drawing to a close.

Looked at from an institutional rather than individual perspective, the most important fact about the outcome of any congressional election is whether it results in a Congress controlled by the president's party or not. As we will see in chapter 6, in contemporary America the executive is the center of policy initiative. For reasons we shall discuss, relatively few programs and policies originate from the Congress. The question then becomes whether or not Congress will serve as a check on the White House. Generally, the president can count upon the support of his own party and is likely to be opposed by members of the other party. Hence, whatever else might occur during a presidential contest, the race will determine whether the next two years are marked by conflict or cooperation between the White House and Capitol Hill.

Representation and Governance

When the dust settles and a new Congress is elected, the first question we might wish to ask is how well the 435 representatives and 100 senators reflect the views and priorities of the American people. The answer is complicated but generally affirmative. Empirical studies have suggested that on a district-by-district basis members of Congress do tend to pay attention to constituency opinion. And, on an aggregate basis, at least one new study indicates that congressional priorities, as manifested in bills introduced, reflect the general priorities of the American people.[36]

But before we leave the topic of congressional elections, let us return to the question with which we began this chapter. The framers of the Constitution were concerned that election results might produce too much turnover—mutability in the public councils—to permit the legislature to govern effectively. Today, on the other hand, critics point to the power of incumbency in congressional races and fear that we have too little turnover to permit Congress to constantly speak for new groups and forces in American society and to function effectively as a representative institution. If this were true, as we have observed, Congress would have failed to have effectively linked itself to its rightful constituency and would lose its ability to govern. It would seem that both the fears of the framers and those expressed by Congress's current critics are a bit misplaced. The power of incumbency seems to ensure that the problem of mutability is kept in check. At the same time, while incumbents are reasonably secure from election to election, over time they tend to circulate out of the House and Senate. In recent years, the combination of electoral defeat, retirement, and death has meant that members of the House have an average tenure of about eight years, and members of the Senate about nine years.[37] On average, congressional terms are not trivial in length but are also no longer than those of presidents and certainly far shorter than those of judges and most government bureaucrats.

Looked at another way, Congress is likely to experience substantial turnover in membership every eight years or so. Of those House members sworn in in 2007, only about one-third took the oath of office in 2015. Two-thirds had been replaced by new members. Midterms often lead to significant turnover in the House. In 2010, Republicans won sixty-three seats and regained the House that year, which was midway through President Obama's first term. In 2018, the Democrats won control of the House again, bringing in thirty-five newly elected members midway through President Trump's first term. This is the biggest Democratic gain in the House since 1974, when forty-nine new members were elected post-Watergate. In all, over one hundred current members of the 115th Congress will not be part of the 116th Congress due to retirement, losing an election, or other reasons (for example, resignations due to scandals). A historic number of women, over one hundred, were elected, and this included forty women of color and a number of "firsts"—the first Muslim woman, the first Native American woman, and the youngest woman ever elected to Congress (twenty-nine-year-old Alexandria Ocasio-Cortez, D-NY). There are over two dozen new members who are under forty, and at least fifteen veterans were elected. Is the turnover rate of Congress too little, too great, or, like Goldilocks's porridge, just right? Does the composition of the institution allow it to adequately represent the nation as a whole? Let us continue thinking about these questions as we take a look at Congress in action.

4

Political Parties and the
Organization of Congress

THE CONGRESS OF THE UNITED STATES, as we observed in chapter 1, is a unique political institution. It is a representative assembly that actually governs. Most of the world's representative bodies play only a limited role in the governmental process. European parliaments select a prime minister and approve laws but do little to actually write statutes or shape policies. This is the job of the executive. Authoritarian regimes, for their part, use representative assemblies to create the impression that citizens' views are taken into account in the governmental process, but such bodies as, say, North Korea's "Supreme People's Assembly" have little or no actual influence over legislation. These assemblies are sometimes called "rubber-stamp legislatures" because they exist mainly to give a stamp of approval to the actions of the nation's actual leaders.

From the earliest days of the American republic, the Congress has developed policies, enacted laws, and played a major, sometimes dominant role in the governmental process. In order to actually govern, Congress has been forced to develop an elaborate internal structure consisting of leadership positions, committees, subcommittees, and other entities. Without this organizational structure Congress could not play much of a role in government, no matter how representative an institution it might be.

The Constitution creates two congressional leadership posts—Speaker of the House of Representatives and president pro tempore of the Senate. Every other element of congressional organization and leadership, including the committee system, was established by the Congress itself. The key actors in building and maintaining Congress's organizational structure are America's political parties. America's first political parties, the Jeffersonian Republicans and the Hamiltonian Federalists, arose in the Congress as a result of factional clashes over economic and foreign policy during President George Washington's second administration. The Constitution did not anticipate political parties and nowhere says that party leaders should become congressional leaders. However, with the emergence of political parties, their leaders quite naturally sought to build congressional structures that would allow them to control the Congress and to use its legislative powers for their own political purposes.

Thus, during Thomas Jefferson's first administration, the chairs of several of the newly created House and Senate committees served as floor leaders for the president's program. The president met with them for dinner three times a week to formulate ideas and policies. These humble beginnings of party structure and the practice of voting along party lines were denounced by the Federalists. Roger Griswold of Connecticut complained that the Jeffersonians "have adopted the plan of meeting in divan and agreeing on measures to be pursued and passed in the House and they vote in mass without admitting any alteration to the plan proposed."[1]

By long-standing practice, the top leadership positions in each chamber of Congress are filled by that house's majority party. Over time, moreover, the organizational structure of Congress has reflected the needs and views of shifting partisan majorities. Organization of Congress by the political parties has advantages and disadvantages. On the minus side, partisan struggles can sometimes produce congressional gridlock, as we have been seeing in recent years. On the plus side, however, organization by the parties enhances Congress's role as a representative institution by ensuring that Congress's internal governance structure mirrors political tides and the balance of political power in the nation as a whole.

Party Leadership and Congressional Organization in the House and Senate

Every two years, at the beginning of a new Congress, the members of each party meet to elect their leaders. Let us begin with the House of Representatives. In the House, Republicans call their meeting the *conference*. Democrats call their gathering the *caucus.* The elected leader of the majority party is later proposed to the whole House and is elected to the position of *Speaker of the House* on a straight party-line vote. The House majority conference or caucus then selects a *majority leader.* The minority party goes through the same process and selects a *minority leader.* Each party also elects a *whip* to line up party members on important votes and to relay voting information to the leaders. These party leaders then appoint deputies and assistants (see table 4.1).

Next in order of importance for each party after the Speaker and majority or minority leader is what the Democrats call the Steering and Policy Committee (Republicans have separate steering and policy committees), which assigns new legislators to committees and deals with the requests of incumbent members for transfers from one committee to another. At one time, party leaders strictly controlled committee assignments, using them to enforce party discipline. Today, representatives may request whatever assignments they want, but party leaders still exert influence by resolving competing requests.

Generally, representatives seek assignments that will allow them to influence matters of special importance to their districts. Seats on powerful committees, such as House Ways and Means, which is responsible for tax legislation, and the appropriations committees, which control the nation's spending, are especially popular.

Under the Constitution, the vice president of the United States is the Senate's presiding officer. The vice president is entitled to vote only in the event of a tie. Vice presidents rarely have the opportunity to break ties. In 2017, Vice President Pence's tiebreaking vote to confirm Betsy DeVos as secretary of education was the first time in American history that the vice president had cast the tiebreaking vote on an appointment, and the first time since 2007 that the vice president had cast any vote in the Senate.

In actuality, the vice president seldom even attends sessions of the Senate. Instead, the majority party designates a member, usually the individual with the greatest seniority, to serve as *president pro tempore,* a position of primarily ceremonial leadership. Real leadership power in the Senate is in the hands of the *majority leader* and *minority leader,* each elected by a party conference. Together the majority and minority leaders control the Senate's calendar, or agenda, for legislation. Each party also elects a *policy committee,* which advises the leadership on legislative priorities. Let us look in more detail at the House and Senate leadership structures and how they operate in practice.

Table 4.1. Leadership of the 116th Congress (2019–2021), 1st Session

U.S. Senate	U.S. House of Representatives
Constitutionally Mandated Officers	**Constitutionally Mandated Officers**
Vice President	**Speaker of the House**
Michael Pence (R)	*Nancy Pelosi (D-CA)*
President Pro Tempore	
Chuck Grassley (R-IO)	**Political Party Leaders**
	Democratic Leadership:
Political Party Leaders	**Majority Leader**
Republican Leadership:	*Steny H. Hoyer (D-MD)*
Republican Leader	**Democratic Whip**
Mitch McConnell (R-KY)	*James E. Clyburn (D-SC)*
Assistant Republican Leader	**Assistant Democratic Leader**
John Tune (R-SD)	*Ben Ray Luján (D-NM)*
Republican Conference Chairman	**Democratic Caucus Chairman**
John Barasso (R-WY)	*Cheri Bustos (D-IL)*
Vice Chairman of the Senate Republican Conference	**Republican Leadership:**
	Minority Leader
Joni Ernst (R-IA)	*Kevin McCarthy (R-CA)*
Republican Policy Committee Chairman	**Minority Whip**
Roy Blunt (R-MO)	*Steve Scalise (R-LA)*
Republican Senatorial Committee Chairman	**Republican Conference Chair**
Todd Young (R-IN)	*Liz Cheney (R-WY)*
Democratic Leadership:	**Republican Policy Committee Chair**
Democratic Leader, Chairman of the Conference	*Gary Palmer (R-AL)*
Charles Schumer (D-NY)	
Whip	
Richard Durbin (D-IL)	
Assistant Democratic Leader	
Patty Murray (D-WA)	
Chair of Policy and Communications Committee	
Debbie Stabenow (D-MI)	
Vice Chair of the Conference	
Elizabeth Warren (D-MA)	
Vice Chair of the Conference	
Mark Warner (D-VA)	
Chair of Steering Committee	
Amy Klobuchar (D-MN)	
Chair of Outreach	
Bernard Sanders (I-VT)	

Source: "Leadership and Officers, U.S. Senate" 2019, senate.gov; McPherson, Lindsey, 2018 (December 4), "House Democrats' New Elected Leadership Team Is More Progressive and Diverse," *Roll Call;* "Here's the List of House Republican Leaders for the Next Congress," 2018 (November 14), *Roll Call.*

The House of Representatives: The Speaker

The most important office in the House of Representatives is that of the Speaker. Indeed, the Speaker of the House is the first federal official identified in the Constitution. Article I, Section 2, states that the House of Representatives shall "chuse their Speaker and other Officers." Even though it is not specified that the Speaker must be a member of Congress, they all have been. According to the Presidential Succession Act of 1947 (Pub. L. 80-199), the Speaker is next in the presidential line of succession after the vice president of the United States and before the president pro tempore of the Senate. The Speaker, as noted earlier, is elected by the majority vote of the House, which usually means by the unanimous vote of the majority party.

The Speaker is the presiding officer of the House and has the power to refer measures to committee, to make rulings on points of order, to direct floor debate, and, in consultation with other members of the House leadership, to set the agenda for the chamber. In addition, the Speaker appoints members to committees and to commissions, task forces, and conference committees. The Speaker is also in charge of support functions (for example, the food services and office support for members). Of course, the Speaker typically delegates some of these administrative duties to others in the majority party.

The legislative and administrative powers of the Speaker make this office a powerful leadership position. Nevertheless, the power of the Speaker has waxed and waned over time. Over the first hundred years of the Congress, power within the House became centralized in the office of the Speaker, culminating in the years between 1890 and 1910, which are frequently referred to as the era of "czar rule." Speakers like Joseph Cannon and Thomas ("Czar") Reed epitomized czar rule in the house. These Speakers appointed committees and committee chairs, chaired the House Committee on Rules, and had great discretion over the legislative calendars and all the business of the House. The Speaker's power came "not simply in his prerogatives under rules, nor in his positions as party chief, but rather in the manner in which these two sources reinforced each other."[2]

The Speaker also directed the legislative agenda and could determine when a bill would get moved out of committee, could have a project inserted into a bill, or could bring a measure to the floor by granting a rule or using unanimous consent and suspending the rules. At the same time, Speakers could use these same procedures to block measures they did not favor. In the nineteenth century, America's strong party system gave Speakers the power to threaten rebellious members with the loss of federal patronage and, ultimately, with the loss of their seats in Congress. By the end of the nineteenth century, however, party strength in the nation began to decline and Speakers were forced to bargain and cajole more than threaten. Members demanded more democratic rules in the House, and committee leadership was determined by seniority rather than the whims of the Speaker. Today, Speakers must attempt to balance the views of various cliques and factions within their party caucus. Where Czar Reed would have given orders, Speaker Paul Ryan (R-WI) led by seeking to forge compromises and consensus among his members. This process can be extremely difficult. Ryan's predecessor, Republican House Speaker John Boehner of Ohio, resigned in 2015 when he lost the confidence of conservative Republicans and found it increasingly frustrating to maintain even a semblance of cohesion among House Republicans.

The difficulties faced by Boehner and Ryan illustrate the difference between the strong political parties of the nineteenth century and strong partisanship today. Nineteenth-century American political parties were organizational powerhouses, capable of mobilizing millions of voters and controlling the electoral process. This meant that the Speaker exercised enormous influence over the political careers of rank-and-file members. Today's political parties are more ideologically coherent than organizationally strong. Most of today's House Democrats are quite liberal, and most House Republicans quite conservative in their political views. Each group is inclined to vote together against the other and to follow its leaders into battle. However, since party unity today is a matter of choice rather than organizational discipline, it can more easily be undermined by factionalism. Within the Democratic coalition are many types of liberals, while the Republican coalition includes many shades of conservatism. This potential for factionalism constantly poses a challenge to party leaders. If the Speaker cannot forge some measure of consensus in the majority caucus, congressional business can grind to a halt. Thus, for example, in April 2016 a bill aimed at providing emergency funding to combat the Zika virus stalled in the House when fiscal conservatives in the GOP caucus questioned the need for an emergency appropriation to fight the virus.[3] Later, the party's social conservatives demanded language in the bill to prevent money being spent on family planning related to the effects of the virus, which attacks pregnant women.

It was interesting to see that after the 2018 midterm election victory for the Democrats, Nancy Pelosi was reelected by her party to be Speaker once again. She overcame opposition by a coalition of incumbents and newly elected progressive Democrats. In just days after the election, over two hundred people calling for a "Green New Deal" were protesting outside of Pelosi's congressional office. There were some arrests, and newly elected representative Alexandria Ocasio-Cortez spoke to the group and noted her opposition to Pelosi serving as Speaker. Pelosi said she welcomes the activists as she continues to strive for balancing the diverse interests within her own party.

House Party Leadership

While the position of Speaker was established by the Constitution, other House leadership positions were created over time by the political parties. Party leadership in the House consists of the majority leader, majority whip, minority leader, minority whip, Assistant Democratic Leader, Democratic Caucus Chairman, Republican Conference Chair, and Republican Policy Committee Chair.

The *majority leader* is elected by the caucus or conference of the majority party and is the second-most senior official in the House. The majority leader is responsible for managing the business of the floor on a daily basis and works with the other members of the majority party leadership to form the party's consensus on legislative action. The *majority whip* builds support for his or her party's positions on votes and is elected by his or her party caucus or conference. To assist the whips, party leaders appoint a number of deputy, assistant, regional, and at-large whips to help in the process of persuading members to follow their leaders. The term "whip" originates from British parliamentary practice and is based on the "whipper in" term from fox hunting, referring to the person "responsible for keeping the fox hounds from leaving the pack."[4]

The *minority leader* is elected by the caucus or conference of the minority party and is that party's senior official. The minority leader's primary role is to work with his or her party to set its agenda and legislative strategy and also to appoint minority party members to task forces or commissions that the Speaker may form. The Democrats also appoint an assistant who works with Democratic leaders to shape the message of the party and focus on communication and research for it as well. The *minority whip* is elected by the party caucus or conference and is assisted by a network of deputy, assistant, regional, and at-large whips. The whip organization works to build support for the minority party's positions, to secure needed votes, and to determine members' positions on future bills.

The *Democratic Caucus* and *Republican Conference* each serve as the organizational structure for their party's members and are led by a chair and a vice chair for each. The Republican Conference also elects a secretary. The main function of these organizations is to foster consultation and communication among party members. Other House party structures include the *Republican Policy Committee,* elected by the Republican Conference to develop policy ideas for the party, as well as the *Democratic Congressional Campaign Committee* and *National Republican Congressional Committee,* which focus on fund-raising and electoral strategy and particularly work to assist the reelection efforts of party members.

In recent years, a number of informal caucuses have developed both within and across party lines to promote particular issues. The Congressional Black Caucus, for example, mainly enrolls Democrats, though it is open to Republicans. On the other hand, most members of the Tea Party Caucus and the Freedom Caucus are conservative Republicans. These two Republican groups have exercised considerable power and often effectively challenged their own party's leadership. In 2015, the Freedom Caucus played an important role in deciding who would replace retiring Representative John Boehner as Speaker. The caucus had been bitterly critical of Boehner, whom it viewed as insufficiently conservative to lead House Republicans. When it appeared that Boehner might be replaced by the majority leader, Kevin McCarthy (R-CA), the caucus refused to support the move and forced McCarthy to withdraw his candidacy. Eventually, members of the Freedom Caucus agreed to the selection of Paul Ryan as Speaker. In 2016, the Freedom Caucus ignored Speaker Ryan to seek the impeachment of the Internal Revenue Service commissioner John Koskinen. Members of the caucus accused Koskinen of complicity in arranging IRS audits that allegedly targeted conservative groups. And in 2017 the Freedom Caucus refused to support the Speaker's efforts to enact President Trump's proposed revision of Obamacare, threatening one of the president's major campaign promises.

It is also important to note that in recent years, the Republican Conference has become increasingly conservative and the Democratic caucus increasingly liberal. This reflects the ideological polarization of the electorate and mass media, as well as being an unanticipated consequence of the 1976 Government in the Sunshine Act. This piece of legislation, as well as subsequent House rules changes, requires most congressional activities to take place in public. The glare of television cameras encourages lawmakers to posture and take extreme positions in order to satisfy organized liberal and conservative constituency groups that equate compromise with betrayal. Also contributing to polarization is an ongoing process of gerrymandering, which, as we saw in chapter 3, has produced more safe partisan seats and fewer moderate "swing" districts.

The impact on Congress of these factors has been ideological division and "hyperpartisanship." This means members of each party craft laws only in consultation with their fellow partisans and vote as a unified block against the other party, whose members are "equally united in opposition."[5] Citizens often lament this highly divisive level of partisanship. As one citizen tweeted during President Obama's State of the Union address in 2016 when the president called for a massive campaign to cure cancer, "Republicans can't even clap for curing cancer because it involved a Democrat. Let's get over the party lines and work together!"[6] This "hyperpartisanship" can make it difficult to enact legislation and helps to explain why recent Congresses have been among the least productive in American history.

Senate Leadership

The Senate is not as hierarchical in its structure as the House. The Senate's smaller size, moreover, means that senators can discuss policy agendas and ideas in more informal settings, such as each party's weekly Tuesday lunches. The Tuesday lunch is a long-standing tradition in the Senate, dating back to the 1940s. Senators of each party relish this tradition because it builds camaraderie and gives them a "closed door" place away from staff and the press, where they can engage in frank exchanges and "air their differences."[7] Each party's lunch begins with a leadership report that might include discussion of policy priorities, current topics, and some "fund-raising chatter." Subsequently, committee chairs or others may be recognized to speak. According to former senator Judd Gregg (R-NH), the discussions are usually "very animated, very free flowing," and "what happens at lunch stays at lunch."[8] Of course, what happens at lunch usually leaks to the press within hours, if not minutes. Thus, it was immediately after a Republican lunch in February 2016 that the press learned that all Senate Judiciary Committee Republicans had agreed to block any attempt by President

Obama to name a successor to Supreme Court Justice Antonin Scalia, who had just died. This tactic worked, and in 2017 President Trump was able to nominate a conservative justice, Neil Gorsuch, to take Scalia's place.

Press conferences are held afterward, and even though each party holds its own Tuesday lunch, this mechanism provides some space out of the public eye to help build friendships that facilitate the chamber's lawmaking capacity. During his first week as House Speaker, Paul Ryan accepted an invitation to attend the Republican Tuesday lunch. Even President Obama was invited and attended Tuesday lunches for both political parties. The Senate Tuesday lunches are likely to provide a forum where at least some of the important groundwork for legislation is laid. While meetings closed to the press may seem undemocratic to some readers, such meetings allow senators to speak frankly to one another without the ideological posturing required during public debates. The Tuesday lunch helps to make the Senate a less polarized body than the House.

Under the Constitution, as we noted earlier, the vice president of the United States is the president, or presiding officer, of the Senate, but may only vote in the event of a tie among the members (Article I, Section 3, Clauses 4 and 5). The Constitution further declares that a *president pro tempore* will be elected by the Senate to preside if the vice president is absent from the chamber—as is usually the case. Senate rules give the president pro tempore few powers. Hence, the position is largely ceremonial and by tradition is usually held by the longest-serving member of the Senate's majority party. It may seem odd that the Senate, unlike the House, has entrusted little power to its presiding officer, but there is a good reason for this. The Speaker of the House is chosen by the House and is always the leader of the chamber's majority party. The president of the Senate, on the other hand, is the running mate of the candidate who happens to have won the national presidential election and is often a member of the Senate's minority party. Senate majorities have been unwilling to cede power to an office that may often be held by their political foes.

The Senate's most important officer is the *majority leader.* In the House, the majority leader ranks behind the Speaker, who is both the presiding officer and the actual leader of the majority party. In the Senate, though, the majority leader is the leader of the chamber's majority party, while the presiding officer, be it the vice president or president pro tempore, has little influence over deliberations. Unlike the Speaker of the House, the position of majority leader was not created by the Constitution but was, instead, established by Senate rules just under a century ago. The first Democratic leader was chosen in 1920, and the first Republican leader was elected in 1925. The majority leader and an *assistant majority leader* (*majority whip*) are elected by the party caucus or conference. The assistant majority leader is, in turn, assisted by an appointed *chief deputy whip,* who works to persuade members to support the party's positions on all legislative matters and duties.

SENATE MAJORITY LEADER The majority leader's primary responsibility is management of the legislative agenda and floor activity of the Senate. The leader works closely with the committee chairs and consults with the leaders of the minority party to bring measures to the floor for debate. Generally, measures come to the Senate floor by the *unanimous consent* (see chapter 5) of all the senators, usually the result of prior bargaining and agreements, so the majority and minority parties have some stake in working together. The majority leader exercises several important powers. For example, the leader helps to shape the Senate's agenda and exercises the prerogative of "first recognition" to determine the order in which proposed amendments will be considered.

By history and tradition, however, the Senate is a more individualistic body than the House, and the Senate's rules give each member a considerable amount of power. Any senator may block debate on a bill using a tactic known as the *filibuster.* Ending a filibuster, a process called *cloture* (prescribed by Senate Rule XXII), requires the agreement of a three-fifths "super-majority" of sixty senators (two-thirds if the issue is a change in Senate rules). One important type of legislation that cannot be filibustered is a budget reconciliation bill (see chapter 5). Leaders of the majority will sometimes seek to package controversial proposals with the budget reconciliation to prevent it from being blocked by a filibuster. This tactic was used by Democratic leaders to guide Obamacare through the Senate in 2010 when Republicans promised to filibuster the bill. The question of what legislation can be included in a budget reconciliation bill is not easy to answer. House Speaker Paul Ryan once quipped that the most important person in the Senate was "Elizabeth." When asked if he meant Senator Elizabeth Warren (D-MA), he said no, he was referring to Elizabeth MacDonough, the Senate parliamentarian, who decides whether a proposal can or cannot be included in a budget reconciliation bill.[9]

Individual senators may also place *holds* on nominations or block consideration of a bill. Like filibusters, holds can be overturned by the votes of sixty senators, but this is often difficult to achieve because senators will defer to their colleagues in the expectation that these selfsame colleagues will someday reciprocate by deferring to them. In 2016, for example, Republican senators placed holds on a number of President Obama's judicial nominees, sometimes for partisan reasons and sometimes because a senator was using the hold as a form of leverage with the administration on other matters. The result was that more than 10 percent of the seats on the nation's district and circuit courts remained unfilled as the president's term came to an end. This backlog occurred despite a 2013 rules change that allowed the Senate's presiding officer to rule that a hold or filibuster applied to any given appointee, except a Supreme Court justice, could be overcome by a simple majority vote. Then Democratic leader senator Harry Reid called this rules change his "nuclear option" to overcome Republican obstructionism. Soon thereafter, however, the GOP took control of the Senate. Republican leaders were not about to rule against Republican holds on President Obama's nominees. The tables had been turned, and so long as Republicans controlled the Senate, only Democratic holds were vulnerable to the nuclear option. As we saw in chapter 1, Republicans in 2017 applied the nuclear option to Supreme Court nominees as well, in order to secure the confirmation of Neil Gorsuch to the High Court.

The power of individual senators generally means that the majority leader must rely more on persuasion than coercion to lead the chamber. Generally, leaders will focus on the need to act as a "team" in support of or in opposition to the president's program (depending upon whether their party controls the White House) and will seek to find positions that unite the senators of their party. Senate majority leader Mitch McConnell (R-KY) is well known for his strong belief that to reclaim and then retain control of the Senate, the Republican senators needed to "stick together" and oppose anything Democratic President Obama supported. This view, as some Republican senators put it, was that "when you have multi-voices, you have no voice," and "If [President] Obama was for it, we had to be against it."[10]

This position made sense in terms of preserving the cohesion of the Senate Republican conference. In practice, however, this meant that McConnell frequently found himself defending the very conservative positions advocated by Senate libertarians and Tea Party advocates and eschewing any form of compromise with the Democrats. Even some Republicans lamented this state of affairs.

As one Republican commentator noted in dismay over the extreme level the uncompromising stance of party leaders had reached, even the "'constitutional conservatives' began to speak of compromise as a synonym for capitulation, which is odd given that the Constitution itself was the result of a whole series of accommodations and [President Ronald] Reagan, a hero to many conservatives, was a gifted compromiser."[11] In fact, as this commentator goes on to remind readers, the "Great Compromise" of the Constitutional Convention established that every state would have two U.S. senators to offset the proportional representation in the House of Representatives.[12] The entire structure of Congress is the result of compromise.

The stance of the Senate majority leader can be extremely important to a president's agenda. Both the domestic and foreign policy objectives of the administration can be promoted or frustrated by a majority leader who supports or opposes a president's nominations to the cabinet and federal courts or with respect to treaties. These approval powers are unique to the Senate. The significance of these powers was underscored by the events of 2016 when, following the death of Supreme Court Justice Antonin Scalia, majority leader Mitch McConnell quickly announced that the Senate would not allow the seat on the Court to be filled until after the next presidential election, which was then nine months away. Democrats charged that this move by the majority leader flagrantly shirked the constitutional duty of the Senate to consider a nomination by the president and to work to fill rather than continue to leave open the vacant seat on the highest court of the land for at least a year. Most Republicans, however, thought delay might be a good idea, at least until the GOP's presidential nomination struggle was resolved and the party's chances to retake the White House in 2016 could be assessed. With Donald Trump's victory and promise to appoint a conservative justice, McConnell's decision to delay consideration of Obama's nominee turned out favorably for the Republicans. When President Trump nominated Judge Neil Gorsuch to fill the Supreme Court vacancy, Republicans were delighted and McConnell declared that he would do whatever was necessary to secure Gorsuch's confirmation.

SENATE MINORITY LEADERSHIP The Senate *minority leader* is elected by his or her party caucus or conference and serves as the senior official for that political party. The second-ranking minority party leader is the *assistant floor leader* (*minority whip*) who is assisted by a *chief deputy whip* and primarily focuses on counting votes on measures of importance to the minority party and "whipping up" support for them.

The leaders of the minority party face the same dilemmas and choices as their majority colleagues. Maintaining the cohesion of the party in the Senate may entail strong opposition to the majority's programs. On the other hand, if it is to achieve any legislative goals, it must work with the majority even at the risk of being accused of compromising the party's principles. This dilemma becomes especially acute if the Senate minority is drawn from the same political party as the president and sees working with the majority as the only route to implementing at least some elements of the president's program. Thus, Senate minority leader Harry Reid, who lamented that the Senate was "the most unproductive in the history of the country" under Republican leadership, did work to make the Democrats a "constructive minority" to ensure that legislation supported by President Obama did move in the realms of transportation, taxes, energy, and opioid laws, as well as at least some of the twelve annual spending bills at the heart of passing the national budget.[13]

SENATE PARTY CONFERENCES AND PARTY COMMITTEES The *Democratic caucus* is the party's organizational body for the Democratic senators. It is chaired by the majority or minority leader depending on whether the Democratic Party controls the Senate or not. The caucus also elects a vice chair and secretary who work to advance the party's agenda. The *Republican Conference* operates in much the same way, though without a secretary. The Senate Tuesday lunches discussed earlier are held by each party's conference or caucus.

Each Senate party has also established policy committees, campaign committees, and steering committees. Specifically, there is the *Democratic Policy Committee* and the *Republican Policy Committee,* and each works with its party's leadership to develop policy proposals. The *Democratic Senatorial Campaign Committee* and the *National Republican Senatorial Committee* serve as the political, that is, electoral, units for their respective parties. The *Democratic Steering and Outreach Committee* and the *Republican Steering Committee* operate somewhat differently. The Democratic Steering and Outreach Committee focuses on building coalitions, while the Republican Steering Committee is primarily responsible for making committee assignments. In addition, there is the *Democratic Committee on Committee Outreach,* which serves to maintain communication among the party's committee leaders.

Table 4.2. The Congressional Committee System

	House	Senate
Standing Committees	Agriculture	Agriculture, Nutrition, and Forestry
	Appropriations	Appropriations
	Armed Services	Armed Services
	Budget	Banking, Housing, and Urban Affairs
	Education and the Workforce	Budget
	Energy and Commerce	Commerce, Science, and Transportation
	Ethics	Energy and Natural Resources
	Financial Services	Environment and Public Works
	Foreign Affairs	Finance
	Homeland Security	Foreign Relations
	House Administration	Health, Education, Labor, and Pensions
	Judiciary	Homeland Security and Governmental Affairs
	Natural Resources	Judiciary
	Oversight and Government Reform	Rules and Administration
	Rules	Small Business and Entrepreneurship
	Science, Space, and Technology	Veterans' Affairs
	Small Business	
	Transportation and Infrastructure	
	Veterans' Affairs	
	Ways and Means	
Special, Select, and Other Committees	Permanent Select Committee on Intelligence	Aging (Special Committee)
		Indian Affairs (Other Committee)
		Intelligence (Select Committee)
Joint Committees	Select Committee on Budget and Appropriations Process Reform	
	Economic	
	Library	
	Select Committee on Solvency of Multiemployer Pension Plans	
	Printing	
	Taxation	

	House	Senate
Commissions and Caucuses	Commission on Security and Cooperation in Europe (U.S. Helsinki Commission) Tom Lantos Human Rights Commission	Caucus on International Narcotics Control

Source: U.S. Library of Congress, 2016, https://www.congress.gov/committees.

The Committee System: Committees and Subcommittees of the House and Senate

Much of the work of Congress is accomplished in committees. Three types of committees organize the business of Congress: standing, select (also called special), and joint committees. A fourth type of committee, the *conference committee,* is created on an ad hoc basis to reconcile House and Senate versions of bills. As we shall see in chapter 5, the conference committee is being increasingly replaced by what is sometimes called the "ping-pong" procedure, in which House and Senate committees negotiate directly and reconcile their bills without requiring the creation of a conference committee. Generally speaking, members of the House may serve on two standing committees and four subcommittees.[14] Senators may serve on three standing committees, and there are no limits for subcommittee assignments.[15] Representatives and senators may additionally serve on special committees, joint committees, and conference committees.

Standing committees in both chambers are permanent entities whose jurisdiction is laid out in House Rule X or Senate Rule XXV; such committees generally exercise much of primary legislative authority in Congress.[16] Today, there are twenty standing committees in the House and sixteen standing committees in the Senate (see table 4.2). The committees are organized around subject-matter jurisdictions, such as agriculture or energy, and, in general, House and Senate committees parallel one another, facilitating legislative work. As we shall see in chapter 5, it is in committees that problems are investigated and legislation is crafted. Generally, before a bill can be brought to the floor of either house for a vote, committees hold hearings, deliberate, and draft the proposed law. House and Senate rules determine the jurisdiction of each committee, and before sending a bill to committee, the chamber's leaders will determine which committee is most appropriate for the matter at hand. Sometimes a complex bill will cross jurisdictional boundaries and may be referred to more than one committee, a process called *multiple referral*. As we shall see in chapter 5, multiple referral may also be used as a leadership tactic to dilute the power of committee chairs. Committee sizes and the party ratios of the committees are set at the beginning of each new Congress through negotiations between party leaders in each chamber. Generally, the ratios aim to secure a "working majority" on each committee for the majority party.[17]

Most standing committees are broken into subcommittees that specialize in particular aspects of each committee's work. For example, the Senate Committee on Foreign Relations has seven subcommittees, each specializing in a different geographic region. When a bill is referred to committee, the committee leadership will determine which subcommittee is most appropriate for the matter in question. Subcommittee jurisdictions are poorly defined, and committee chairs have considerable discretion in assigning bills. Much of the hard work of deliberating, holding hearings, and "marking up"—as the process of amending or rewriting a bill is called (see chapter 5)—takes place in the subcommittees, though further markup may occur in the full committee after the amended bill leaves the subcommittee.

The number of subcommittees and their jurisdictions changes over time. Current House rules limit most committees to five subcommittees. Senate rules do not specify limits. One House committee not subject to the five-subcommittee limit is the one for appropriations. The House Appropriations Committee is divided into twelve subcommittees. These subcommittees are paralleled in the Senate, whose own appropriations committee is divided into the same twelve subcommittees. Each House and Senate subcommittee is responsible for a defined legislative area, such as agriculture, defense, labor, homeland security, and so forth within its house of Congress. In principle, after Congress votes on a budget resolution determining the total amount of federal spending for the year, the House and Senate appropriations committees will divide that total among each chamber's twelve subcommittees. Based on funds available, each subcommittee will then determine the level of funding for particular programs within its jurisdiction. As we will see in chapter 5, this process often does not work smoothly.

The relative importance of many committees tends to vary with the nation's political agenda and with the character of the committee's leadership. During the Vietnam War, for example, the Senate Foreign Relations Committee chaired by Senator J. William Fulbright (D-AR) became the visible center of congressional opposition to President Lyndon Johnson's war policies. Several committees, however, are almost always important. These include the House Ways and Means Committee, charged with writing tax legislation; the House and Senate Budget Committees, which jointly develop Congress's overall annual spending plan; the House and Senate appropriations committees, charged with the allocation of funds to particular categories of government spending; and the House and Senate Rules Committees, which determine the procedures under which bills will be considered by their respective bodies.

The House Rules Committee is Congress's oldest standing committee, having been created in 1789. As we shall see in chapter 5, the Rules Committee determines the procedures that will be used for the consideration of any given bill. This includes the bill's precedence on the House calendar and the extent to which members may suggest amendments to the bill. The Rules Committee is sometimes called the "Speaker's Committee." Until 1910, the Rules Committee was actually chaired by the Speaker, but even today the committee's composition and actions are strongly influenced by the Speaker's preferences. Whatever the balance of power in the House, the Rules Committee is dominated by the majority party, which is assigned nine of its twelve seats. The majority party is assigned a majority on every committee (with the exception of the House Ethics Committee), but for all other committees, that majority tends to be much smaller and closer to the majority's percentage of seats in the chamber as a whole. The precise party ratio on each committee is a matter of negotiation among party leaders. The Rules Committee, however, is too important to the Speaker to allow the minority party any influence over its proceedings.

Both in the House and the Senate, as we saw in chapter 2, the first standing committees were established quite early in the chambers' histories: in the 1790s for the House and in 1807 for the Senate. As the country matured and the purview and workload of the federal government expanded, Congress created more committees to strengthen its capacity both to legislate and to oversee the executive branch.[18] In 1885, Woodrow Wilson (D), who later became president, wrote in his doctoral dissertation, *Congressional Government,* that Congress was "a government of the chairmen of standing committees."[19] Congress was still at the center of government at this time, and committees were at the core of the institution's power.

The chairman of every committee is nominated by the Democratic Caucus or Republican Conference, depending, of course, on which party holds a majority in that congressional chamber. Generally, this nomination is heavily influenced if not completely controlled by party leaders. The nominees are then formally named to their posts by a vote of the full chamber. A similar procedure is followed in the selection of the ranking minority member of each committee. This ranking member is a shadow committee chairman and will often be named to chair the committee if control of the chamber changes hands. Current House rules stipulate that no member may chair the same committee for more than six years. This term limits rule has resulted in a frequent game of "musical chairs" as committee leaders trade places with one another.

Often, each committee is chaired by the member of the majority party with the most years of continuous service on that committee. This is known as the principle of *seniority*. The seniority principle, however, is not absolute. When Republicans took over control of the House in 1995, they violated seniority principles in the selection of a number of key committee chairs. House Speaker Newt Gingrich (R-GA) said, "You've got to carry the moral responsibility of fielding the team that can win or you cheat the whole conference." Since then, Republicans have frequently departed from the seniority principle, choosing chairs on the basis of loyalty, competence, or fund-raising ability rather than strict seniority. Democratic Speakers have been more likely to rely on seniority in their choice of committee chairs but have also ignored seniority when it served their purposes. In recent years both parties have circumvented the seniority principle on numerous occasions. In the House, Speakers have used the Steering and Policy Committee to make choices based upon "moral responsibility" rather than seniority.

For example, in 2003 when President George W. Bush's (R) administration made enactment of a Medicare reform bill a major priority, Speaker Dennis Hastert (R-IL) nominated Bill Thomas (R-CA), instead of the most senior member, to chair the House Ways and Means Committee. Hastert saw Representative Thomas as more aggressive, more conservative, and a stronger dealmaker than the other member.[20] Speaker Nancy Pelosi (D-CA) also violated the seniority rule when she appointed Representative Alcee Hastings (D-FL) to chair the House Committee on Intelligence rather than Jane Harman (D-CA), even though Representative Harman had been the ranking minority member of the Intelligence Committee. Pelosi believed Hastings would be more aggressive in his opposition to President Bush's "War on Terror." Similarly, Representative Henry Waxman (D), also from California, was chosen in 2007 to chair the Energy and Commerce Committee over Representative John Dingell (D-MI), who was the most senior member of the House, because the Speaker believed he would be a stronger negotiator and dealmaker when important environmental legislation was considered later that year.[21]

Generally, subcommittee chairs are chosen by the committee chairs, though the choice may be overturned by committee members. In the House, subcommittee chairs, like committee chairs, are generally limited to six-year terms.

Select or special committees are usually created to address a particular problem or investigate wrongdoing and may be disestablished once that problem loses its salience. In 2014, for example, the House created a select committee to investigate the events surrounding a terrorist attack in Benghazi, Libya, that resulted in the death of a number of Americans including America's ambassador to Libya. Republicans hoped the investigation would embarrass former secretary of state Hillary Clinton. *Joint committees* are permanent and consist of members of both the House and the Senate. These are established by law or concurrent resolution.[22] There are presently four joint committees addressing broad issues requiring study by both chambers, such as the Joint Economic Committee and the Joint Committee on Taxation, or possessing administrative authority such as the Joint Committee on the Library or the Joint Committee on Printing.

The rules and procedures that House committees follow are found in a volume entitled *Constitution, Jefferson's Manual, and Rules of the House of Representatives,* published by the Government Printing Office.[23] The volume includes the currently relevant portions of *Jefferson's Manual of Parliamentary Practice* and also includes part of the Congressional Budget Act and other statutory provisions that operate as procedural rules for the House. This and two other volumes, *House Practice: A Guide to the Rules, Precedents, and Procedures of the House* and *Procedure in the U.S. House of Representatives* (also called *Deschler's Procedure,* after a former parliamentarian of the House), are the primary reference sources used in the House regarding rules and procedures.[24]

For the Senate, the *Senate Manual* is prepared by the Senate Committee on

Rules and Administration, usually during the second session of each Congress. It contains the standing rules, orders, laws, and resolutions affecting the Senate, as well as other historical documents and some statistical data on the Senate and other government entities.[25] Along with two other books, *Riddick's Senate Procedure: Precedents and Practices* and *Senate Cloture Rule,* these are the main references for Senate rules and procedures.[26] These volumes for the House and Senate are distributed to members of each of the respective houses of Congress.

Over the course of American history, the number of congressional committees and subcommittees has increased and decreased following changes in society and in the balance of political forces within the Congress. The growing size of the federal government and the complexity of legislative solutions for the nation's problems have exerted an inflationary pressure on the committee system. At the same time, however, there are other important political considerations affecting the committee system. Generally speaking, party leaders prefer fewer committees and subcommittees since they fear dispersion of their own power to the committees and view a more streamlined and compact committee system as enhancing Congress's power vis-à-vis the executive. Rank-and-file members, on the other hand, prefer more committees and subcommittees since this creates more leadership positions and, hence, more opportunities for people like themselves to exercise power.

Since World War II, and the growing challenge of executive power, congressional leaders have been able to rein in the growth of the committee system despite the pressure from the rank and file to give leadership opportunities to more members. One major example of this effort is the Legislative Reorganization Act of 1946 (60 Stat. 812). This act represented a bicameral and bipartisan effort to ensure that the organization and operations of Congress could be reformed to adapt "to the complexities of modern society and the commensurate growth in the executive branch bureaucracy and powers of the presidency."[27] The resulting effort was led by Robert M. La Follette Jr. (PROG/R-WI), who cochaired the joint committee with A. S. "Mike" Monroney (D-OK) and produced a piece of legislation that passed with large margins in both chambers.

The act primarily focused on streamlining the committee system and did so by reducing the number of standing committees and redefining committee jurisdictions, although it did not completely eliminate overlap between them. The number of committees in the House was reduced from forty-eight to nineteen and in the Senate from thirty-three to fifteen. Committee jurisdictions were codified, and for the first time committees were assigned professional and clerical staffs. The Legislative Reference Service (now known as the *Congressional Research Service*) was expanded. In addition, the process for overseeing executive agencies was strengthened and a joint budget committee created to strengthen Congress's role in the budget process. Lobbyists were also required to register with Congress for the first time and to file reports of their activities periodically.[28]

The 1946 act produced mixed results largely because the reduction in the number of standing committees was offset by a proliferation of subcommittees for which the act had established no limits. Legislative oversight did improve, however, and the creation of committee staff positions bolstered the legislative capacity of the institution.

There have been more than a dozen congressional reform efforts since 1946. In the 1970s, for example, an era when Congress was usually controlled by Democrats, leaders bowed to pressure from the rank and file by increasing the number of subcommittees and giving greater autonomy to subcommittee chairs. Traditionally, committee chairs had determined hearing schedules, selected subcommittee members, appointed committee staff, and used their power to block consideration of bills they opposed.

By enhancing subcommittee power and allowing more members to chair subcommittees and appoint subcommittee staffs, the reforms undercut the power of committee chairs. This seemed open and democratic but fragmented power, making it harder to reach agreement on legislation and vie with the growing power of the executive. In 1995, incoming Republican House Speaker Newt Gingrich sought to reverse this fragmentation of congressional power and to concentrate more authority in the top congressional leaders. Hoping to centralize power and, in particular, to empower the Speaker, Gingrich reduced the number of subcommittees and limited the time committee chairs could serve to three terms. In 2001, Republicans replaced thirteen committee chairs who had reached their term limits. When Democrats took control of Congress in 2007, they repealed the term limits on committee chairs, but Republicans reinstated them in 2010.

One effect of the Gingrich reforms was to somewhat reduce the power of committees. Today, legislation backed by the party leadership will sometimes go directly to the floor from the Steering and Policy Committee, bypassing the system of standing committees altogether. As we will see in chapter 5, this shift in power from committee chairs to party leaders has had important consequences for the legislative process. Significantly, today party leadership and loyalty are based on ideology more than committee organization in Congress. As we will see in the next chapter, two aspects of the "new order" in Congress reflect this, and these are "follow-the-leader" lawmaking and "DIY" legislating, which typify congressional policy making today.

Rule changes are always possible, however, to rebalance the power between party leadership and rank-and-file members. The current trend, though, is to continue what is sometimes referred to as "outcome-oriented leadership," in which the party leaders use their procedural power to control the legislative process to ensure their desired outcome. This is in contrast to the more deliberative "service-oriented leadership" of the past, which Senate leaders such as Mike Mansfield (D-MT) and Robert Byrd (D-WV) typified. The service-oriented leadership used floor leaders more, and this involved a broader number of rank-and-file members in the legislative process. Wallner argues that senators could reassert their power if in the Republican Conference they vote to reform the chamber's "hotline" system, which notifies Republican senators of significant floor developments by phone or e-mail.[29] This is one way that the relationship between party leaders and their members could be rebalanced.

Building Legislative Capacity: Congressional Agencies and Staff

One important factor behind congressional reform in 1946 and since was a perception by congressional leaders that Congress must make efforts to strengthen its institutional capabilities if it was to cope with the growing power of the executive branch. As part of the same effort, Congress sought to bolster its own staff and agencies. Member and committee staff and congressional agencies, as was noted in chapter 3, provide the legislative branch with information and a capacity for action. Without its staff and agencies, Congress would simply be an audience for the actions of the executive.

During the 1970s, Congress created two new agencies working directly for the House and Senate and staffed by congressional employees, and strengthened the three existing congressional agencies. The new congressional agencies were the *Office of Technology Assessment* (OTA), created in 1972 (and later eliminated in 1999), and the *Congressional Budget Office* (CBO), created in 1974. The purpose of these two agencies was to provide Congress with expertise on technical and budgetary issues previously available only to the executive branch.

These agencies joined the two existing staff agencies, the Congressional Research Service (CRS) and the General Accounting Office (GAO, now the Government Accountability Office), to provide Congress with a heightened technical capability. Today, concern is expressed both inside and outside of Congress that there is a "lack of basic technological literacy" in the institution, and the capacity that was building in the 1970s has eroded, with serious consequences for congressional policy making in this century. When Mark Zuckerberg, CEO of Facebook, testified before Congress in 2018 regarding his company's mishandling of Facebook users' data during the 2016 election season, the lack of technical expertise within Congress and among the members was painfully evident. It helped fuel momentum for calls to revive the Office of Technology Assessment or some agency like it and to increase staff for the existing congressional agencies that have seen steady reduction in staff size since the mid-1990s.[30]

Congressional Budget Office

The CBO was created as a result of the Congressional Budget and Impoundment Control Act of 1974 (Pub. L. 93-344) to provide strictly nonpartisan and objective analysis of budgetary and economic issues for the legislature to support the congressional budget-making process. The CBO consists of about 248 employees, most of them economists hired solely on the basis of their academic credentials and experience rather than political connections. Each CBO report or cost estimate summarizes the methodology used and all the underlying assumptions of the analysis, and no policy recommendations are given. The agency is just over forty years old and has solidified its reputation as "one of the most influential and well-regarded institutions in Washington."[31]

Despite the impartial and credible reputation of the CBO's work, members of Congress often complain about the agency, particularly if their own legislative proposals do not fare well when scrutinized and reported on by CBO analysts. CBO criticisms usually fall into three categories: (1) the budget and cost estimates are "wrong"; (2) the emphasis is only on costs in the analyses and not benefits, including less quantifiable ones for society; and (3) the cost estimates are biased.[32] In fact, budget and cost estimates are rarely "right" no matter who conducts them, and how economic or cost analyses are done are important parameters for understanding the limitations of any such analyses.

Nevertheless, the CBO has been an important asset for the Congress. As former Treasury Secretary Jack Lew said in 2004 based on his experience in both the legislative and executive branches, "In terms of the relationship between Congress and the White House on budget issues, CBO has empowered Congress in a way that is very significant . . . just the fact that it's a check on the White House empowers Congress."[33]

Congressional Research Service

The congressional Legislative Reference Service was created in 1914 when President Woodrow Wilson signed legislation that included a provision offered by Senator Robert La Follette Sr. (PROG/R-WI) and Representative John M. Nelson (R-WI) to establish it as a separate part of the Library of Congress. It seemed a fitting extension of the Library of Congress given that in 1815 former president Thomas Jefferson (D-R), when selling his private collection to the Library of Congress to reestablish its collection after its destruction from fire during the War of 1812, remarked, "There is, in fact, no subject to which a member of Congress may not have occasion to refer."[34] This remains the guiding principle for acquisitions for the library, but establishing the Legislative Reference Service was also clearly a product of the Progressive Era.

Progressives firmly believed that science and technology in the industrial age could be employed in a variety of ways for the benefit of humankind, including the promotion of "good governance." Progressives believed that trained and impartial minds could learn how to harness the nation's natural resources and address economic and social problems. Through education and good government, progress could be made in the greater public interest. Establishing an agency to assist Congress in researching and applying the latest thinking to legislating on the issues confronting the nation was in keeping with the mentality of the Progressive Era.

The 1970 Legislative Reorganization Act, as noted earlier, renamed the Legislative Reference Service the Congressional Research Service (CRS) and greatly expanded its size and statutory obligations. The main motivation then was to help ensure that Congress could build its capacity to keep pace with the expanding national agenda and growing expertise of the executive agencies. The CRS today is often referred to as Congress's "think tank" and employs about 660 individuals, many of whom are policy analysts, reference librarians, and attorneys. The agency receives tens of thousands of requests each year from individual members of Congress as well as from congressional committee staffs. The CRS produces over seven hundred reports a year, and its work is seen as authoritative, impartial, and influential. The agency's specialty is rapid turn-around, with most requests for information or issues briefs completed within hours, days, or a few weeks. Particularly complex CRS reports may take several months to complete. CRS analysts sometimes provide confidential memorandums or briefings on particular topics and can be called to testify before Congress.

Congressional staffs on behalf of their members and committees use the CRS at all stages of the legislative process. CRS analysts may be consulted even before a bill is drafted, to assess different aspects of or approaches to addressing an issue, particularly in light of how Congress may have done so previously. Throughout the committee hearing and floor debate stages of the legislative process, the CRS can be used. In addition, the CRS performs oversight analysis of enacted laws and sometimes agency activities. Occasionally, members have criticized findings of particular CRS reports with which they disagreed—often for partisan reasons.[35] Generally speaking, however, members and their staffs recognize the importance of CRS services.

Government Accountability Office

The General Accounting Office was established at the end of the Progressive Era in 1921 and was renamed the Government Accountability Office (GAO) in 2004. It has over 3,100 employees. The GAO was traditionally defined as the "fiscal watchdog" for Congress, monitoring agency expenditures and conducting financial audits to uncover waste, fraud, and abuse in executive agencies. Over time, the GAO has come to play a significant role in broader oversight for Congress and is usually referred to as the "congressional watchdog." The referential change reflects the evolving mission of the agency. Today, the GAO is tasked with undertaking performance audits in addition to financial audits. GAO auditors look into agency compliance with congressional mandates and the quality of the work done by the agencies. GAO employees will sometimes even act as "secret shoppers" to see how well an agency performs its mission. The GAO produces over nine hundred audits and investigative reports a year with the goals of improving the performance of government and ensuring accountability for the public.

The GAO produces the annual *Financial Report of the United States Government* for the country and releases other studies under its own initiative, but primarily does its investigations at the requests of members or because of a stat-

utory mandate directing it to do so. GAO reports are frequently covered exten-
sively by the press, and GAO staff members testify often about them before
Congress. The head of GAO is the comptroller general of the United States,
who is appointed for a fifteen-year, nonrenewable term from a list of three individuals recommended by an eight-member bipartisan, bicameral congressional
commission. There have been only eight controllers general since 1921, and this
congressional agency too is seen as a nonpartisan source of information for the
legislative body.

Congressional Committee and Personal Staff

The three existing congressional agencies employ just over 4,000 staffers.
Approximately 19,600 congressional staffers on Capitol Hill work for individual
members, committees, or elsewhere (for example, with the Architect of the Capitol or U.S. Capitol Police) within the legislative branch.[36] Approximately 7,700
staffers work in the House. Of these, 1,664 are committee staffers and 6,000 are
personal staffers. In the Senate, committee staffers number about 900 individuals, personal staffers number about 4,000, and leadership and other staffers
number approximately 1,000, for a total of roughly 6,000 staffers for the chamber. Along with the congressional agency staffs (about 3,800) and the Capitol
Police and other building and maintenance staffs (about 2,000), the total of
congressional professionals and nonprofessionals is under 20,000 employees.

Representatives may employ a total of eighteen full-time and four part-time
staffers. In the Senate, there is no restriction on staff size, and it varies from
fewer than twenty to over sixty. The chief of staff runs the entire office, usually
consisting of the policy staff, communications staff, office staff, and district
staff. The chief of staff, legislative director, and scheduler positions are usually
the most prestigious and best-paid positions, and the average age of these staffers is thirty-one. The average age of a legislative assistant is under twenty-nine,
and the average pay has remained unchanged in the last two decades at about
$30,000 a year.[37] Legislative correspondents and staff assistants are typically
recent college graduates. The turnover on the Hill is high given the relatively
low pay and long hours, with most staffers leaving their first position within
one to two years and leaving the Hill altogether within five years.

The Hill remains a popular place for young civic-minded individuals to
work, but given shifts within the institution, the nature of work on the Hill has

changed in recent years. One of the noteworthy shifts is that in 1976, nearly 75 percent of personal staff was based in Washington, D.C. By 2005, however, about only about 50 percent of personal staff was left in D.C. This shifts means that a greater focus is placed on electoral and constituent functions of the office than legislative ones. As a study on the issue by the Sunlight Foundation concluded, "this 30-year tectonic shift likely diminished the House's policymaking capabilities."[38]

Committee staff members tends to be a bit more experienced than personal staff members and are consequently a bit older and better compensated, and often include attorneys, with a salary range of roughly $60,000 to $80,000 a year. Over the past three decades, Congress has responded to budgetary concerns by reducing the number of committee staff positions by nearly one-third. This reduction in staff size has resulted in greater reliance on lobbyists to provide analysis and even legislative language to members and their staffs. Currently, there are 12,500 registered federal lobbyists. There is a well-known "revolving door" through which congressional staffers leave the Hill and sharply increase their salaries by taking positions with lobbying firms.[39] In addition, some staffers move to positions in the executive branch or in consulting firms. Some staffers run for office and become elected officials themselves.

In 1891, there were just over one hundred staff members for both houses of Congress, and it is reported that most members did their own work at their desks on the floors of their respective chambers.[40] By 1950, the staff size had more than doubled but was primarily committee staff with very few personal staff. Today, as Congress has grown and become more complex institutionally, its staff has as well, but how staff is used, namely less on lawmaking and more on personal member needs, reflects the changing focus of Congress as well.

Ad Hoc Groups in Congress: Caucuses, Informal Groups, and Congressional Membership Organizations (CMOs)

There are a number of ad hoc groups in Congress that operate outside of the committee structure or political party leadership and have a limited number of members, but can have a strong influence on the policy-making process. This is especially true in recent years, when both the Tea Party Caucus and Freedom Caucus, as discussed briefly earlier and further in chapter 5, have exerted great influence over the House in particular. Some of these groups are ad hoc and informal. Others register with the House Committee on Administration as Congressional Member Organizations (CMOs). All are known simply as "caucuses." There are currently some three hundred CMOs, but the numbers fluctuate over time. Caucuses and other types of informal groups are typically bicameral and bipartisan and can be focused on policy issues that are regional, such as the Congressional Western Caucus, or have a national constituency, such as the Congressional Black Caucus or the Congressional Caucus for Women's Issues. Others are focused on the party issues or a range of other issues, such as the arts, rural health, or steel. There is even a Congressional Bourbon Caucus to promote the interests of that industry.

Political scientists who study these caucuses find that a "powerful caucus system now operates in the U.S. Congress," which is "an important adjunct to the formal committee system and the political party system within Congress."[41] One study found that "[m]embers of moderate factions do not simply assert their ideological differences; they vote those differences when possible on roll-call votes. Likewise, members of ideologically polarized caucuses vote their ideological and partisan preferences in the House."[42] Even so, a recent study found "no statistically significant evidence that amendments offered that were supported by new conservatives caucuses [that is, the Tea Party, Liberty Caucus, and Freedom Caucus] were more conservative than other amendments offered by conservative members."[43] Political parties and committee structure are still the key congressional institutions, but caucuses can matter as well.

Commissions and Boards

Congress has also created many commissions and boards, such as the commission convened to help appoint the comptroller general of the U.S. who directs the GAO. Some commissions address particular issues, such as the Congressional-Executive Commission on China, which was created when China was being considered for membership in the World Trade Organization. It consists of nine senators appointed by the president pro tempore of the Senate, nine representatives of the House chosen by the Speaker, and five executive officials named by the president.[44] Boards are generally established by statute to oversee governmental or quasi-governmental agencies. For example, members of Congress serve on the boards of the Smithsonian Institution, the John F. Kennedy Center for the Performing Arts, and the U.S. Air Force Academy.[45]

Organizational Complexity and Governance

Congress is organizationally complex, and some critics profess to see in its complexity a source of gridlock. One pundit recently declared that the problem with Congress was that it was based upon a 227-year-old organizational prototype that diffuses responsibility, creates too many centers of power, and impedes sound financial management.[46] Yet, consider an alternative perspective. Congress is organizationally complex because it actually governs. The committee system and every other element of congressional organization was an outgrowth of efforts by America's elected representatives to play a primary role in the process of government. We can, of course, find many representative bodies around the world that lack any organizational elaboration. They consist of an assembly that meets as a body according to some schedule, listens to speeches, casts votes, and returns home. These representative assemblies are never gridlocked, never engage in rancorous and uncivil debate, never fail to pass legislation that the president or prime minister thinks is necessary. How different from the Congress! There is, of course, one other small difference. These assemblies do not govern.

To be fair, despite their relative lack of organizational complexity, democratically elected parliamentary bodies do influence the governmental process by choosing the prime minister, voting on proposed legislation, preparing reports, and so forth. Parliamentary opposition parties quite often voice severe criticisms of the prime minister's handling of governmental affairs and work to replace the current prime minister with one of their own choosing. Is parliamentary government a better and more efficient system than America's regime of separated powers? Well, it depends. Parliamentary systems tend to operate smoothly so long as the parliament is controlled by one party. If, however, no single party is able to build a parliamentary majority, a coalition of parties must be assembled, leading to—you guessed it—instability and gridlock. In politics, there are no perfect answers.

5

The Legislative Process:
The Rise of the New Order in Congress

ARTICLE I, SECTION I, OF THE U.S. CONSTITUTION assigns the legislative power, the power to make the law, to the Congress of the United States. The framers viewed the legislative power as the fundamental power of government and believed that it should belong to a representative assembly, not to the executive or the courts. Any member of the House or Senate may propose a law. These legislative proposals are usually called "bills" and must be passed by a majority vote in both houses of Congress and signed by the president before they can become law. Members of Congress may also propose "resolutions," which, with one exception, are essentially expressions of congressional opinion and do not have the force of law. The exception is the "joint resolution," most often used for emergency appropriations, to propose constitutional amendments, or to declare war.

Each year many bills are introduced in Congress, but very few are actually enacted into law. In fact, only 2–3 percent of the total number of bills introduced each year become laws. Some call recent Congresses unproductive, but the difference between current and prior Congresses is not as great as the national media seem to believe. Even during some of Congress's most productive legislative periods, such as the 1970s when a large number of new regulatory laws were passed, the average proportion of enacted laws each year was only about 4 percent.[1] This reflects the strong legacy of institutional design. The framers feared constant change in the law and, hence, thought it should not be easy to enact laws. This is one reason they devised a legislative process that requires many steps.

152

In high school civics classes students are usually taught a version of the congressional process that, on Capitol Hill, is known as "regular order." As explained in more detail to come, regular order is the basic "textbook" version of how a bill becomes a law. Under the terms of regular order in the House of Representatives, a member introduces legislation and the Speaker, in consultation with the House parliamentarian, refers the bill to the appropriate subject-matter committee. In the committee, the bill is debated and hearings are held before a final draft of the proposed legislation is reported out and then voted on by the full chamber.

The congressional process, though, has changed in recent decades, and many, both inside and outside the Congress, consider the process and, indeed, the entire institution "broken" because of what some describe as the "unorthodox" and seemingly haphazard nature of contemporary lawmaking.[2] But contemporary lawmaking is not as disorderly as some scholars and pundits suggest. In actuality, a "new order" has evolved in Congress. This new order, supplanting regular order, is a peculiar mix of partisanship and factionalism. As Walter Oleszek argues in his book *Congressional Procedures and the Policy Process,* "deviations from the regular order have increased because Congress is less insular, more partisan, more ideological, and more permeable to outside forces than ever before."[3]

The new order reduces the power of the congressional committees and undermines deliberation, but it can still produce legislation, especially when Congress and the president are of the same party. The new order consists of three key elements, which will be discussed in this chapter: (1) "follow-the-leader" lawmaking; (2) "do-it-yourself" (DIY) legislating; (3) and "catching-the-omnibus" budgeting. This chapter examines the legislative process, paying particular attention to the role of congressional leaders and the changing impact of party and partisanship. We shall also look in detail at one very important part of the legislative process—the budget and appropriations process through which Congress exercises its constitutional "power of the purse."

"Regular Order" and "Textbook" Lawmaking

Regular order has certainly not disappeared in the Congress, and elements of regular order can be found throughout the legislative process even as members complain about its demise. So let us review the "regular" process through which a bill becomes a law as a backdrop for our discussion of Congress's new order. Table 5.1 outlines the basic actions in the legislative process.[4]

Introducing a Bill

Any member of the House or Senate can introduce a bill. The legislative proposal for a bill is usually drafted by the member and his or her staff, sometimes with the help of interest groups and outside experts. The actual language of a bill is drafted by lawyers in the House or Senate Office of Legislative Counsel. In the House, a bill is formally introduced by the member who drops the bill into a special box called the "hopper" at the Speaker's rostrum. In the upper chamber, a senator introduces a bill by placing it on the presiding officer's desk or by formally presenting it on the Senate floor. The member of Congress who introduces a bill becomes the bill's *sponsor*. Members usually sponsor bills of interest to themselves and their constituents. In some cases, members do not expect their bill to be passed. They introduce legislation to satisfy important constituencies or to make symbolic points. This is known as position taking. Often enough, though, members are prepared to fight hard to see their bill enacted. Sponsors will often seek cosponsors to broaden the base of support for their bill. Cosponsors will be able to claim credit with relevant constituencies as though the bill was their own idea. For example, in 2015, when Senator Diane Feinstein (D-CA) introduced legislation in the Senate nominally aimed at preventing terrorists from obtaining firearms, she was able to recruit more than thirty cosponsors even though the legislation had little chance of passage. For many Democrats, the bill was an opportunity to make a symbolic point about gun control that could be used against GOP rivals in future political campaigns.

In the House a bill clerk will assign the bill a number that begins with "H.R." (resolutions begin with "H.Res.," "H.Con.Res.," or "H.J. Res."). In the Senate, a bill clerk assigns a bill number that begins with "S." Once this happens the bill's title will be read on the floor. This is called the "first reading of the bill." After the first reading, the bill is referred by the majority party leadership to a committee for the next stage of legislative action. Once the bill is introduced, an electronic copy is sent to the Library of Congress and its status will be entered on Congress.gov, a public website. In the House, as noted in chapter 4, the Rules Committee will determine the rules under which the bill will be considered by the committee and on the floor if and when the chamber votes on it. The

Table 5.1. The Legislative Process

Legislation can begin in either chamber; often bills are introduced in both chambers.

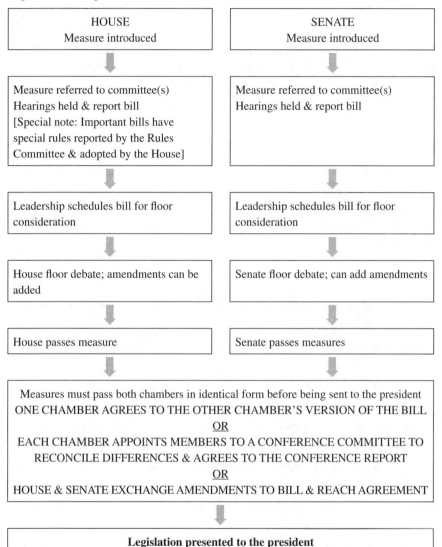

HOUSE	SENATE
Measure introduced	Measure introduced

HOUSE	SENATE
Measure referred to committee(s) Hearings held & report bill [Special note: Important bills have special rules reported by the Rules Committee & adopted by the House]	Measure referred to committee(s) Hearings held & report bill
Leadership schedules bill for floor consideration	Leadership schedules bill for floor consideration
House floor debate; amendments can be added	Senate floor debate; can add amendments
House passes measure	Senate passes measures

Measures must pass both chambers in identical form before being sent to the president
ONE CHAMBER AGREES TO THE OTHER CHAMBER'S VERSION OF THE BILL
OR
EACH CHAMBER APPOINTS MEMBERS TO A CONFERENCE COMMITTEE TO
RECONCILE DIFFERENCES & AGREES TO THE CONFERENCE REPORT
OR
HOUSE & SENATE EXCHANGE AMENDMENTS TO BILL & REACH AGREEMENT

Legislation presented to the president
President signs bill into law OR president does not sign within 10 days*
OR president vetoes bill**

*If Congress is in session, the bill becomes law; If Congress is not in session, it is a "pocket veto" and bill does not become law.
**Bill only becomes law if both chambers override the veto by 2/3 majority votes.
Source: Adapted from "Legislative Process Flowchart" in *Congressional Deskbook* (2012), https://hobnob-blog.com/legislative-process-flowchart-from-the-congressional-deskbook/. Copyright © by TheCapitol.Net.

Senate has a tradition of open debate, and its Rules Committee does not have the power to set the terms under which a bill will be considered.

In the House, the majority party controls the Rules Committee. The committee's makeup is heavily weighted in its favor, with nine majority and four minority party members. The House Speaker will almost always appoint his or her most trusted allies to the Rules Committee. Accordingly, the Rules Committee is known as "the Speaker's Committee," and the House majority leadership works through the committee to advance the party's legislative agenda.

There are generally four types of rules:

1. *Open rules* allow any member to offer an amendment that complies with the standing parliamentary rules of the House (and also the Budget Act, as we will discuss).[5]
2. *Modified open rules* allow only amendments that have been preprinted in the *Congressional Record,* or may put a time limit on consideration of amendments, or may put both of these types of restrictions in place.
3. *Structured rules* limit amendments offered to a bill to only those designated in a special rule.
4. *Closed rules* prohibit any amendments being offered.

The choice of rules by the leadership of the House is extremely important. Closed and structured rules reflect and reinforce the power of the majority party leadership and will be applied to important pieces of legislation when the leadership is fairly confident of being able to enforce its will. Closed rules also limit the influence of the minority party. Open rules, on the other hand, allow members an opportunity to voice their views. Open rules also allow members of the minority party to exert some influence over legislation. In recent years, party polarization combined with efforts by GOP leaders to maintain discipline within their ranks have led to the frequent use of closed rules for the consideration of bills before the House. Structured rules are also commonly used when coalitions of members insist on having some say in the legislative process and refuse to follow the leader unless their views are acknowledged. In recent years, to maintain Republican unity, the Speaker has felt compelled to allow the GOP's conservative Freedom Caucus an opportunity to propose amendments but has, at the same time, worked to limit the number and character of the amendments that could be offered. Structured rules became the best available leadership tool.

Committee Action and Markup

When a bill is referred to a committee, the chair of each committee (often in consultation with the majority party leadership) determines the next step. In truth, for most bills, there is no next step. They are "tabled" and never heard from again. Such bills are said to have died in committee. Any bill that is not enacted by the Congress in which it was introduced "dies" at the end of that Congress's two-year period and must be reintroduced in the next Congress if it is to be reconsidered. Rarely, a *discharge petition* is adopted by the House. This requires an absolute majority (that is, 218 members in the House) to sign a petition to force a chair to put a bill or resolution on the committee's calendar to report it out. In October 2015, for example, a discharge was used to bring the renewal of the Export-Import Bank charter to a vote. While some criticize the bank, a quasi-governmental corporation that provides credit to foreign purchasers of U.S. goods, it enjoys bipartisan support in Congress and its charter was renewed until 2019.

If the chair of the committee to which the bill is referred decides to move a bill forward, the bill will be referred to the subcommittee that deals with the bill's particular subject matter for fuller consideration. Once a bill is referred to a subcommittee, it is reviewed and studied by subcommittee members and staffers. If subcommittee leaders favor the proposal, they will schedule *hearings*. At these hearings, witnesses will be called to speak for and against the bill and testimony will be heard from interested parties. Among those testifying will be experts, supporters, and opponents, who can present information and views about the proposed legislation. Representatives of interest groups favoring or opposing the bill, private citizens, academics, and agency experts with experience in the matter at hand are the types of individuals who are called to testify at congressional hearings.

Some of the hearings are televised by C-SPAN and may attract broader media attention, while others receive little or no coverage. In any given week, hearings are held on a wide range of topics, such as a week in July 2016 when the Senate held hearings on global economic issues, counterterrorism efforts, and appropriations for the Department of Veterans Affairs. The Senate Committee on Banking, Housing, and Urban Affairs held a hearing about financial risks posed by China; the Homeland Security and Governmental Affairs Permanent Subcommittee on Investigations held a hearing to examine how ISIS operates online and how to counter terrorist radicalization and recruitment on the Internet and social media; and the Appropriations Subcommittee on Military Construction, Veterans Affairs, and Related Agencies held a hearing to review the Department of Veterans Affairs' electronic health-record system and its interoperability with the Department of Defense's electronic health-record system. On any given day when the House is in session, as many as a dozen or more hearings may be scheduled.

Even at this point, a subcommittee can also table a bill it decides it does not want to advance. If, however, the subcommittee wishes to move the bill forward, hearings are followed by "subcommittee markup" in which both majority and minority members participate, and members then vote to accept or reject the changes. If a marked-up version of the bill is approved, it is sent back to the full committee for approval or rejection. At this point, the full committee may table the bill or hold additional hearings and undertake its own markup. If the full committee passes the bill, it is *"reported out,"* which means it is released along with a report explaining the provisions of the bill. *Committee reports* become part of the legislative history of the bill. If the bill becomes a law, the committee report can be important if there are any legal challenges to it and the courts need to determine *"legislative intent."* The bill is now put on the chamber's calendar.

The next stage of the legislative process is the full committee's markup of the bill. In the past, members of the committee would literally sit together around a conference table and mark up the bill with handwritten strike-through edits. Typically, the majority committee members reach agreement on changes before even showing the committee's minority party members the proposed legislative text. This pre-markup is called the "chairman's mark." Once the markup is complete, the committee votes to accept or reject changes made to the bill during the markup session. Any amendments offered by the minority are usually rejected, although sometimes token amendments are accepted if they are considered harmless, such as calling for research on the topic at hand. Sometimes the committee decides to introduce a new, "clean bill," with a new number, if many changes or amendments to the bill have been made. Throughout the legislative process, committee chairs exercise considerable power. Chairs generally control the committee's staff and may instruct staffers to give priority to a bill or to ignore it. The chair influences the selection of witnesses and can instruct the staff to stack the witness list with individuals who will support a particular point of view. The chair wields enormous influence over the bill's markup.

Floor Debate and Vote

A bill that has survived the previous steps will be brought to the floor for a vote by the chamber as a whole, but this can happen in a variety of ways. The usual way for important bills to come to a vote in the House is through a parliamentary device known as the *Committee of the Whole,* in which the House is considered a single large committee. The rules of the Committee of the Whole speed up floor action and debate and require a smaller quorum (one hundred members) than is normally required for floor action in the House. The rules of the House require that all revenue and appropriations bills be considered first by the Committee of the Whole and then by the House itself. This requirement is intended to ensure appropriate deliberation. Other bills are not required to follow this process, but most do.

As noted earlier, the members debate bills according to rules set by the Rules Committee, that is, under an open, modified open, structured, or closed rule or some other form of special rules. The House majority leader determines the order in which bills will be brought to the floor. If the majority party leadership favors a bill, it may give it precedence over the House's regular order of business. At the beginning of each week, the majority leader makes public by posting on his or her website and e-mailing to members the floor schedule for that week. For minor pieces of legislation, the House leadership may move to suspend the rules and quickly pass the bill. Suspension requires approval of two-thirds of those present and so is not likely to be allowed in the cases of important bills. After the *floor debate,* if the bill is being considered under an open rule, amendments can be offered by members at this time. If a closed rule is in effect, only amendments recommended by the reporting committee can be considered. In the House, proposed amendments must be "germane" to the subject matter of the bill. In the Senate, amendments may be proposed that seem unrelated to the matter at hand. Such unrelated amendments are known as "riders." Senators will seek to attach riders to bills likely to pass, such as military appropriations bills.

In the Senate, as noted in chapter 4, the majority leader directs the floor activity for a bill in coordination with the committee chairs and minority party lead-ers. The majority and minority parties have some incentive to work together to bring legislation to the floor because this is typically done by a procedure called *unanimous consent,* a process used to expedite proceedings. Unanimous con-sent means all senators present agree that the bill may be discussed. If even one senator objects, the request is rejected and a time-consuming vote must be taken on a "motion to proceed." A request for unanimous consent to vote on a bill is generally not made until the senators supporting the proposed legislation have negotiated with their colleagues and can inform the majority leader and minority leader that the Senate is ready to proceed.

In the Senate, as required by the Constitution, a quorum is needed for the body to act. A quorum is defined as a majority, currently fifty-one senators. A quorum is presumed to be in place unless a senator requests a *quorum call* by "suggesting the absence of a quorum," which triggers the Senate clerk calling the roll of the senators and noting which are present. In most cases, senators request quorum calls to delay action without having to call for the adjournment of a session. Typically, a senator may be seeking a delay to gain more time for a compromise to be worked out with colleagues off the floor or to give col-leagues time to return to the chamber to make speeches.

During the debate on a bill the first senator to stand up to speak must be recognized by the presiding officer (although the majority leader and minority leader are given priority even if another senator rises first). Senators must begin their speeches by addressing the presiding officer by saying, "Mr. President," referring to the president pro tempore of the Senate. The third person, rather than personal names, is used to refer to other senators. The form of speech is to recognize "the senior senator from New York State," or "the junior senator from Kentucky." According to the *Standing Rules of the Senate,* speeches can be of any length, although only two can be given by the same senator on the same legislative day.[6] Time limits for speeches are sometimes adopted through unanimous consent agreements, or in the case of the budget they are imposed by statute.

Other times the *filibuster* is used to prolong debate on a bill or motion or defeat it. As noted in chapter 4, a filibuster is a parliamentary procedure that allows debate over legislation to be extended and is an obstructionist tactic in which one or more senators speak to "talk out a bill" or "talk it to death."[7] The filibuster may involve offering amendments or additional motions along with long speeches. The late senator Strom Thurmond (D-SC, later R-SC) holds the record for the longest filibuster. Thurmond held the floor for more than twenty-four hours when he tried unsuccessfully to block passage of the Civil Rights Act of 1957 (Pub. L. 83-315). *Cloture* is the procedure that can be used to end a filibuster. In the past, it was rarely used because it requires bipartisan support to achieve a three-fifths supermajority of sixty senators to stop the filibuster.[8] As filibusters increased in use, however, so did the use of cloture to stop them. Very rarely, as might be the case regarding a sensitive national security issue or possibly impeachment proceedings, the Senate may hold a closed session. In a closed session only senators are present in the chamber and are sworn to secrecy.

A third reading of the bill takes place after debate on the amendments has ended. The floor debate is recorded for the *Congressional Record* and also sent to the Congress.gov website, which is updated based on the latest actions on the bill. The bill is then put to a *vote,* and members in attendance vote electronically to pass or not to pass the bill in the House and cast votes nonelectronically in the Senate. In the House, voting is generally held open for only fifteen minutes to discourage last-minute dealmaking. In the Senate, the presiding officer has the discretion to decide when to close the voting, but the voting must be open for at least fifteen minutes.

In the House, many bills are decided upon by *voice vote.* This means that a tally is taken, but the identities of voters are not recorded—the equivalent of a secret ballot. In the Senate, a voice vote is a bit different. No tally is taken. Instead, senators shout "yea" (for a "yes" vote) or "no" (when against a measure) and the chair renders a judgment on the outcome. Any senator, however, can challenge the chair's judgment and demand a recorded vote. *Roll call votes,* in which members' individual votes are actually recorded, can occur in either chamber.[9] The Constitution requires that a roll call vote be held if it is demanded by one-fifth of a quorum. Since a quorum is defined in the Senate as 51 senators, one-fifth of a quorum equals eleven senators. In the House, a minimum of 144 members is necessary to require a roll call vote. Members will call for a roll call vote whenever they want to create a public record of how each member voted on the measure. Constituents or any members of the public can find out a member's voting record for all roll call, that is, recorded, votes. Members cast a vote of "yea" for approval, "nay" for disapproval, or "present" to record that they are present for the vote but do not choose to vote on the bill. If

the majority of the members in the chamber pass the bill, then it is recorded as
passed legislation and is referred to the other chamber to go through a similar
process of approval. A bill passed in one house of Congress is said to be "engrossed." A bill passed by both houses and sent to the president is said to be
"enrolled."

Bill Referral to the Other Chamber and the Conference Committee

When it receives an engrossed bill, the other chamber may send the bill to
committee for study or mark up . . . or it may ignore the bill passed by its colleagues and instead work on its own bill dealing with the same issue. When the
matter is one that party leaders deem to be of national importance, the House
and Senate will typically be working on legislation simultaneously. If a bill or
similar bill is passed by the other chamber, a *conference committee* is convened
to consider and reconcile differences between the bills. According to the Constitution, before a bill can be sent to the president it must be passed in identical language by both houses of Congress. The conference committee consists
of members of both the House and the Senate. Once differences are worked
through and the bill is agreed upon by the conference committee, then the conference report is voted on by each chamber. After that vote it is deemed "enrolled" and is sent to the president for signature.

Presidential Action: Law, No Law, and Veto Override

The president may sign the bill and it becomes law. Or the president can decide to veto or reject the bill. The president may also employ what is called a
"pocket veto." A pocket veto occurs when the president does nothing and Congress adjourns while the bill remains in the president's "pocket." If this happens,
the bill dies and does not become a law. If, however, the president does nothing
and Congress remains in session, the bill automatically becomes law after ten
days. If the bill becomes a law, it is given a public law (Pub. L.) number by the
Office of the Federal Register (OFR), which is part of the National Archives
and Records Administration. The Congress.gov website will list the public law
number, which consists of the number of the congressional session and a hyphen
before the numerical order assigned, for example, Pub. L. 114-150 is the public
law number given to the 150th bill passed in the 114th session of Congress. If
the president vetoes the bill, he or she will issue a veto statement noting the
reasons for objecting to the bill. When a bill is vetoed it returns to the chamber

from which it originated. The presidential veto can be debated on the floor of each chamber and a vote taken to override it, if there are the votes for that, otherwise the bill does not become a law. A two-thirds vote is needed in both chambers to override the president's veto. On the rare occasions when the president's veto is overridden, the bill becomes a law without the approval of the chief executive.

In 2017, ninety-seven laws (seventy-four bills and twenty-three joint resolutions) passed Congress, which, along with a low number passing in 2018, means the 115th Congress is on pace for passing the lowest number of laws in forty years. Many of the laws passed in any given year are of symbolic rather than substantive importance. Some name post offices or other federal buildings to honor noteworthy citizens. Others are commemorative, such as the Fallen Heroes Flag Act of 2016 (Pub. L. 114-156) and the Breast Cancer Awareness Commemorative Coin Act (Pub. L. 114-148). Some laws reauthorize existing statutes, for example, the Global Food Security Reauthorization Act of 2017 (Pub. L. 115-266); the Older Americans Act Reauthorization Act of 2016 (Pub. L. 114-144); and the Foreclosure Relief and Extension for Servicemembers Act of 2015 (Pub. L. 114-142). Each year, however, laws are enacted to also address new issues. For the 115th Congress these included the Weather Research and Forecasting Innovation Act of 2017 (Pub. L. 115-25) to upgrade the national weather system to better forecast large weather events; the Save Our Seas Act of 2018 (Pub. L. 115-265) to help reduce plastic waste in the oceans; and the Patient Right to Know Drug Prices Act (Pub. L. 115-263).

Is Regular Order Still Regular?

The foregoing discussion summarizes regular order in Congress. Regular order guarantees that a bill's journey to become a law will be long and arduous. Indeed, the process can be maddeningly slow for a bill's proponents. Most bills are not enacted into law, and even those that do become law are seldom enacted during the first or even second congressional session in which they are considered. The process is slow and cumbersome. Regular order, however, ensures a deliberative process in which many voices are heard and both the majority and minority parties play a role. In short, regular order exemplifies deliberative democracy at its best. For better or worse, however, there is no longer anything regular about regular order. In modern times, regular order is usually, albeit not always, abandoned in favor of procedures designed to move bills along more quickly or with fewer layers of review, trading deliberation for what the framers of the Constitution dismissed as "promptitude." Today, most bills are promptly rejected and only a handful promptly passed.

In recent years, instead of regular order, bills have tended to follow a set of paths that collectively might be called the "new order." Regular order enhanced the power of committees and subcommittees. The new order generally reflects the contemporary strengthening of partisanship and the power of party leaders, in particular the Speaker and the majority leader, but it also leaves room for individual action by the members of Congress. One thing the new order does not emphasize is deliberation. The new order allows party leaders to push the president's agenda if the president is of their own party, or to do battle with the president if the president is of the opposite party. This is primarily why Congress was prone to deadlock during the Obama era of high levels of partisan division. It is likely with a newly elected Democratic-controlled House that there will be increased checking by that chamber on President Trump and his administration. Some in Congress call for a return to regular order, but it is not clear how realistic that is.[10] As we shall see, the forces that led to the new order were set in motion by institutional reforms of the 1970s and other factors that are not likely to be reversed.[11] In Donald Wolfensberger's analysis, *Changing Cultures in Congress: From Fair Play to Power Plays,* whichever party is in the majority now games what in the past was intended as an impartial set of rules to a system that favors the majority and marginalizes the minority party members.[12]

"The New Order" and Contemporary Lawmaking

There are three distinct aspects of the new order: (1) *follow-the-leader* lawmaking, a process in which party leaders rather than committees orchestrate and control the legislative process; (2) *do-it-yourself* ("DIY") legislating, wherein members rather than committees function as the main legislative actors; and (3) *catching-the-omnibus* budgeting, as increasingly party leadership takes control of the budget process and packages enormous appropriations bills for the chamber to consider. As the bill is crafted, members fight for "seats" on the omnibus for their own projects. Let us review each of these elements of the new order.

Follow the Leader

The chief point of departure from regular order to new order occurs when party leaders are impatient to enact legislation and are willing to bend the rules and strong-arm opponents to achieve their legislative purposes. For example, Newt Gingrich (R-GA), Republican House Speaker from 1995 to 1999, frequently deviated from regular order during the first hundred days of his leadership to ensure swift action on the agenda of the Republican Party's "Contract with America." This package of bills included tax cuts, welfare reform, and a constitutional amendment for a balanced budget. During the period from January 4 through April 7, 1995, the House held about twelve hundred hearings and markups and was in session more than double the number of hours of the previous Congress. Generally, the hearings were brief, the markups perfunctory, and little time was devoted to deliberating. Several years later, Democratic Speaker Nancy Pelosi (D-CA) also ignored regular order to drive legislation implementing President Obama's priorities through the House in the first hundred days of the 110th Congress (2007–2009). Legislation included raising the minimum wage and addressing ethics and lobbying reform.[13]

CLOSED RULES The first element of follow-the-leader lawmaking is the frequent use of closed rules to prevent rank-and-file members—and the minority party—from amending legislation approved by the leadership. Closed rules, which some critics call "gag rules," prohibit most floor amendments and often limit debate to a short period of time. Debate on a complex measure may be limited to one hour. This is hardly enough time to begin to read, much less debate, a bill that may be more than one thousand pages long.

For many years, tax bills have been considered under closed rules because most members have agreed that tax provisions were too complex and the provisions too intertwined to be amended from the floor.[14] What once was limited mainly to tax bills has now become what Walter Oleszek calls the "new normal."[15] Whether Congress is controlled by the Democrats or the Republicans, party leaders find closed rules and strict time limits on debate to be instruments that enhance their own power and compel the rank and file to follow the leader.

In 2009, for example, Speaker Nancy Pelosi imposed closed rules to limit discussion of several major pieces of legislation high on President Barack Obama's (D) agenda, including the American Recovery and Reinvestment Act of 2009

(Pub. L. 111-5), also known as the "stimulus bill." This generated enough concern among even Democratic members, including the majority leader Steny Hoyer (D-MD), that fifty-five members sent a letter to Speaker Pelosi asking for a return to regular order, reflecting the fact that "many committee and subcommittee chairs resented being shut out of [the] decision-making."[16]

In the case of the stimulus bill, Speaker Pelosi pushed for passage on the floor within forty-eight hours of the bill being reported out by the committees, demanding that all Democrats support the new president. This meant there would be no time for deliberation on a $787 billion spending measure. Hundreds of billions of dollars were being spent with little thought. As *The New York Times* reported at the time, the stroke of a pen changing the number "4" to the number "1" for an appropriation for energy and water development meant that $3.1 billion rather than $3.4 billion would be appropriated, that is, $300 million less for those state programs.[17] Just like that.

During the reign of Republican House Speaker John Boehner (R-OH), who led the House from 2011 to 2015, open rules made a bit of a comeback. During Boehner's speakership, ultraconservative Tea Party Republicans demanded a voice in the legislative process and Boehner was forced to accommodate them. Boehner's successor, Paul Ryan (R-WI), had frequently asserted his opposition to closed rules. Once elected to the speakership, however, Ryan saw many advantages to more closed processes and "walked back" his previous position, especially in the case of spending bills. In the appropriations realm, in particular, Ryan sought structured rules that accommodated dissident GOP members but blocked certain amendments (especially those seen as "poison pills" that could derail legislation) and tightened the leadership's grip on the process.[18]

MULTIPLE REFERRAL A second element of follow-the-leader lawmaking is "multiple referral." In the House multiple referral was introduced by a rules change in 1975 and has since become commonplace. In the Senate, multiple referral is allowed by unanimous consent but is infrequently used because it clashes with other Senate procedures. Multiple referral means that bills are sent to several committees rather than to just one for consideration and markup.

There are three types of multiple referrals: joint, split, and sequential. Joint referral means that the leadership assigns the same bill to more than one committee. Sequential referral means that the leadership assigns a bill to a second committee if it does not like the actions of the first committee. Split referral means that different sections of a bill will be assigned to different committees. In 1995, House rules were modified so that even if the leadership made a joint referral, one committee was designated as the primary committee on the bill.

Multiple referral might seem to allow more participation in the deliberative process, and sometimes it does. At the same time, however, multiple referral works to expand the power of party leaders and reduce the power of committees by preventing any one committee from blocking a piece of legislation. The power of multiple referral was first demonstrated by Jim Wright (D-TX), who served as House Speaker from 1987 to 1989, when a scandal forced him from office. Wright assigned bills to several committees, chose his preferred results, and used the Rules Committee to draft rules blocking amendments on the House floor.[19]

Speaker Pelosi made extensive use of multiple referral. The Affordable Care Act (also known as Obamacare) is a prime example of this in that three committees wrote the law, but the committee chairs all followed the Speaker's direction on the details of moving the bill through the legislative process. The three committees were Ways and Means, Education and Workforce, and Energy and Commerce. Speaker Pelosi dubbed the committee chairs the "three tenors" and was indisputably in charge of the entire legislative process. She and majority leader Steny Hoyer met often—daily at times—with the committee chairs working on the details of the legislation and shepherding it through the process. Pelosi and Hoyer crafted special rules to ensure quick and smooth passage without amendments in the House and worked to educate other members about the legislation to garner the support needed for its passage.[20]

PING-PONGING A third element of follow-the-leader lawmaking is the declining use of the conference committee. Conference committees can expand the number of voices heard in discussions of a piece of legislation. However, the effort to create a conference committee, particularly in the case of a controversial bill, gives the Senate minority, in particular, many opportunities to block enactment of the bill. Under Senate rules, the minority party has opportunities to filibuster several steps in the process, to propose amendments, and to move to instruct its conferees to insist upon provisions known to be unacceptable to the House. The House minority also has procedural weapons with which it might derail a conference.

To deal with these problems, House and Senate leaders (if they are of the same party) have developed procedures for "ping-ponging" amendments back and forth between the relevant House and Senate committees to reconcile differences between bills or major measures without convening a conference committee at all. House Speaker Nancy Pelosi made extensive use of the ping-pong procedure in the 111th Congress (2009–2011). In general the ping-pong approach to legislating strengthens the House and Senate leadership. In addition, it further marginalizes the role of the minority party in the legislative process.[21]

Taken together, closed rules, multiple referrals, and ping-ponging are designed to strengthen party leaders in the Congress, reduce the power of the committees and subcommittees, and compel members to follow the party leader. While it is widely acknowledged that today's party leaders in Congress are more powerful than ever and control the legislative process, some scholars point out ways in which rank-and-file members can exert some checks on their leadership. Ruth Bloch Rubin, in her book *Building the Bloc: Intraparty Organization in the U.S. Congress,* finds that "party dissidents" who form such coalitions as the House Freedom Caucus carefully construct intraparty blocs designed to shift the balance of power between party leaders and rank-and-file members to favor their own legislative agenda.[22] In fact, there is evidence that through roll-call-vote analysis, party leaders may sometimes cajole or outright pressure members to vote the party's preference, but other times they are allowed to "defect," especially if it is known it will enhance a member's chances for reelection. This is what political scientists refer to as either "responsible party" representation or "belief sharing" representation. In the latter, a member is voting based on the preference of his or her constituents.[23] Let us now consider the other two elements of the new order.

Do It Yourself (DIY): Legislating by Activist Lawmakers

A second aspect of the new order is DIY legislating. As just noted, members of Congress sometimes find it advantageous to distance themselves from their own party and to "run against Washington" in their reelection campaigns even while they are actively part of the selfsame Washington. Sometimes a DIY legislator is obstructionist, for example, using the filibuster to delay or derail legislation she or he does not support. Other times, the DIY members will proactively use tactics such as the new soft or "zombie" earmarks (see that section) to advance programs or policies they or their constituents desire. Whichever tactic is used, individual activists or small groups of activists can be important because (as noted in chapter 4) party discipline today is based on ideology—which is a choice—rather than organization, which involved hierarchy and gave party leaders the power to punish dissidents. This is why follow the leader and DIY, which seem to be polar opposites, are both elements of the new order.

THE NEW FILIBUSTER The use of the *filibuster* in the Senate is one example of the individualistic style that typifies the do-it-yourself legislative path of the new order. A filibuster, as noted earlier, is a parliamentary procedure in which a senator can extend debate over a proposed piece of legislation to delay or prevent a vote on it by the chamber. Often it is referred to as "talking a bill to death."

Prior to 1960, filibusters were rare, and typically one or none might occur during a session of Congress.[24] By the 111th Congress (2009–2010), the number of filibusters per Congress had risen to fifty-four, with many more threatened.[25] What makes the new filibuster new is that members now use or threaten to use the filibuster on a routine basis, whereas at one time the filibuster was a tool rarely used and then only on issues of great national importance. Until recent years, a senator who frivolously or frequently threatened to filibuster bills would be marked by his or her colleagues as an obstreperous and uncooperative individual and would be threatened with ostracism. Today, the threat to filibuster is a routine part of senatorial business. Congressional scholar Richard Fenno attributed this change to the more general shift from the Senate's collegial politics of yesteryear to the individualistic politics of today. This shift was, in turn, encouraged by heightened media coverage, which gave outspoken senators a political advantage while penalizing their quiet and genteel colleagues.[26] The filibuster and cloture motions to limit or end them are useful strategies for the DIY senators. Until the rules were changed in 1975, two-thirds of the Senate needed to agree to a *cloture motion* to break a filibuster. Since that time, three-fifths of the Senate, that is, sixty votes if all one hundred senators are present, are needed for a successful cloture motion. Ironically, the greater ease of ending filibusters seems to have contributed to the increased frequency of their use, as members can filibuster to make a point without actually bringing the business of the Senate to a close for very long. Filibusters began to increase in use from the time of President Clinton and soared after President Obama took office.[27] The new filibuster is a tool for individual members, sometimes encouraged by interest groups or lobbyists for special interests, to use—or some would say to exploit—their procedural rights to force consideration of issues of interest to them and their constituencies or block those they oppose.[28]

An example of the new filibuster used to bring attention to a current public issue was Senator Chris Murphy's (D-CT) filibuster on gun-control issues in the aftermath of the mass shooting in Orlando, Florida, in June 2016. His colleagues Senator Richard Blumenthal (D-CT) and Senator Cory Booker (D-NJ) joined him in a filibuster that lasted about fifteen hours and was widely covered by traditional news sources and social media. Senator Murphy's filibuster can be deemed successful, since Senate leaders agreed to consider two amendments addressing gun control, one that would prevent suspected terrorists from purchasing guns, and one to expand background checks on gun purchases. Though the Senate did not adopt either amendment, Senator Murphy received enormous press coverage for the filibuster.

Of course, filibusters can sometimes actually block legislation. In 2010, the DREAM Act, which had passed the House and was a bill President Obama championed to provide a "path to citizenship" for the children of illegal immigrants, was first delayed and then defeated by the Republican senators who were then in the minority. In 2014, the Paycheck Fairness Act, which sought to toughen penalties for discrimination and unequal pay for male and female employees, was blocked four times by Senate Republican filibusters and ultimately failed.[29]

The filibuster is used by members of both parties. When Senator Jefferson Sessions (R-AL) accused Democrats of "always do[ing] what is convenient at the time," Democrats countered that they do not "filibuster every bill regardless of merit," which they contend the Senate Republicans did to block any laws supported by President Obama.[30]

MEMBERSHIP PROTESTS   The House version of the Senate filibuster is the membership protest, used to block or influence the chamber's business. In response to the Orlando terror attack of 2016, Representative John Lewis (D-GA) led a sit-in protest on the House floor to push for a vote on gun-control measures. Democrats had decided they needed a more dramatic effort than a symbolic "moment of silence" in the chamber for the latest victims of gun violence in the country, and they settled on the sit-in tactic. As an icon of the civil rights movement, Representative Lewis, who marched with Martin Luther King Jr. as a young man, was the logical choice to lead this effort. Initially about 40 members of the House of Representatives entered the chamber to "occupy" the House floor, but within an hour more than 120 members joined the protest. When

C-SPAN stopped televising the sit-in during the night because the Republican leadership recessed the House, the protesting members used their cell phones to live-stream the sit-in.[31] The membership protest allowed a group of representatives to draw national attention to their efforts on a highly salient public issue. In the end, the membership sit-in forced an adjournment of the House rather than a vote, but from the perspective of their constituencies, the members achieved a political victory.

"ZOMBIE," OR SOFT, EARMARKS *Earmarks* are legislative directives by Congress that money be spent on particular programs or projects, often in the district or state of the sponsoring member. The origin of the term is the notch once used to mark the ears of cattle or swine to indicate ownership. Offering members the opportunity to insert earmarks into bills was one of the traditional ways that support was built for important pieces of legislation. Without earmarks, members have less reason to agree to the enactment of bills in which they see no personal stake.

Though earmarks never accounted for more than 1 percent of the nation's budget, to many Americans they symbolize "pork" and were perceived to be a major way in which Americans were being "fleeced" by members of Congress and the special interests that stood to benefit from the earmarked measures. In 2011, Speaker Boehner led efforts to eliminate earmarks to restore the public's trust in the institution. Although the number of earmarks was reduced, they were not eliminated.[32] Instead, what Representative Jim Cooper (D-TN) dubbed "zombie" earmarks, or others call "soft" earmarks, are on the rise. The zombie earmark does not mention a specific beneficiary. Instead, the creator of the zombie will seek to include language in a bill that seems neutral but will inexorably direct federal funds to a particular set of interests, often located in the author's district. For example, a famous zombie earmark requires the Defense Department to heat American military bases in Germany with a particular form of anthracite coal. This coal just happens to be mined only in one part of Pennsylvania. The language of the law seems to promote U.S. energy exports generally, but the specific provisions, examined carefully, benefit a small group of mining interests.

In 2007, the Honest Leadership and Open Government Act (Pub. L. 110-81) was enacted with the goal of increasing transparency, or "sunshine," with respect to earmark provisions. The most significant change was that House committees are required to keep a record of earmark requests. What this has done, though, is drive the earmark process even further underground, as both legislators and lobbyists find ways to circumvent this new restriction. For example, if an executive agency makes a request for a particular program as part of the budget process, it is not an earmark, but if a congressional committee does so, then it violates the ban on earmarks. Not surprisingly, lobbyists now focus much more of their attention on the executive agencies.[33]

Today, some members use another alternative to earmarking through a practice called "letter marking." Letter marking occurs when a member directly contacts agency officials to request how appropriated funds be spent for a particular project in his or her district.[34] In 2010, congressional bills contained an estimated seventeen hundred earmarks, mandating a total of $10.3 billion in expenditures. By 2015, the total number of earmarks had declined, but defense spending bills alone were estimated to contain fifty-six zombie earmarks costing about $2.3 billion. As the Citizens Against Government Waste annual tracking of earmark spending shows, even though the number of earmarks continues to be low, the spending level is on a sharp rise again and is approaching the 2010 pre-ban level.[35] Members view earmarks as electorally advantageous sources of benefits to their states and districts. Those members with the most influence with respect to the appropriations process tend to benefit the most.[36] In fact, a recent study confirms that the earmark ban has had little impact on the actual distribution of federal grant dollars across congressional districts.[37]

It seems rather unlikely that the zombies will ever be sent to their final resting place. Not only have Republicans and President Trump discussed lifting the ban on earmarks, but House minority whip Hoyer speculated in 2018 that if the Democrats win back the House (which they did) they too should bring back some earmarks. This is because those on both sides of the aisle believe that the old earmarks were more transparent than today's zombie earmarks. Some analysts argue that earmarks keep spending more directly in the hands of elected officials rather than empowering unelected executive branch bureaucrats. As Steven Gordon puts it, "Earmarks or no earmarks, the power of the purse belongs in the hands of those who are incentivized to represent constituent concerns."[38]

Catching the Omnibus: "Power of the Purse," the New Order, and the Budget Process

The third element of the new order is the omnibus budget. The U.S. Congress is one of few legislatures in the world to have the primary role in its government's budgetary process. This "power of the purse" derives directly from Article I, Section 8, of the Constitution, which asserts that Congress "shall have Power To lay and collect Taxes, Duties, Imposts and Excises . . . [and] To borrow money on the credit of the United States." According to Article 1, Section 9, moreover, "No Money shall be drawn from the Treasury, but in Consequence of Appropriations made by Law." The Constitution also specifies that revenue measures must originate in the House so that taxation is levied by the body closest to the people. By tradition, appropriations bills also originate in the House.

While giving Congress the power of the purse, the Constitution does not prescribe the procedures to be used for actually drafting the government's budget. Over the years Congress has enacted legislation specifying budgetary procedures and has developed a "regular order" for appropriations bills. Every federal program requires both an authorization and an appropriation. Appropriations bills are the funding mechanisms that specify how much money will be given to different government agencies and programs. Authorization bills, which might cover multiple years, must be passed by Congress to grant the actual legal authority for government agencies to spend the budget money. If a program is authorized but no money is appropriated, the program cannot be implemented. In principle, authorizing bills asserts policies and appropriating bills pays for them. In practice, the line is sometimes not so sharp. Appropriations committees sometimes attach "limitation riders" to an appropriations bill, prohibiting funds from being spent for particular purposes. Republicans, for example, have sought to use limitation riders to prevent federal dollars from being spent on abortions.

Under law, funds must be appropriated for the category of expenditure known as direct or mandatory spending. This includes such programs as Social Security and Medicare benefits, which are not part of the appropriations process since the government is required by law to pay statutory benefits to all eligible citizens. For fiscal year (FY) 2016, 53 percent of the federal budget consisted of these mandatory spending obligations. In 2018, about 62 percent of the federal budget consisted of these mandatory spending obligations. Of the discretionary spending dollars, national defense expenditures were 15 percent of the overall budget and represented the largest non-mandatory portion. The remaining approximately 24 percent of the budget was for education, welfare, transportation, general government operating expenses, interest on our national debt, and all other government spending.[39]

Section 300 of the 1974 Congressional Budget and Impoundment Control Act (Pub. L. 93-344) gives the timetable for the budget process. It follows five basic steps:

1. Each year, before the first Monday in February, the president is required to submit a budget request to Congress based on agency budget proposals reviewed by the Office of Management and Budget and its preparation of the president's budget.
2. The House and Senate Committees on the Budget each prepare and pass budget resolutions, with the House initiating the process.
3. The twelve House and Senate appropriations subcommittees "mark up" the appropriations bills to determine the exact funding levels for all discretionary funding.
4. The House and the Senate debate and vote on the appropriations bills and reconcile the differences from each of the twelve subcommittees involved. Each chamber adopts a reconciliation instruction directing the appropriate standing committees to recommend legislation changing existing law to bring spending into accord with the budget resolution. Committee action is followed by a reconciliation bill containing the various changes. Debate on the bill is limited to twenty hours. Following the so-called "Byrd rule," named for the late senator Robert Byrd of West Virginia, reconciliation provisions may not deviate from the goals established by each chamber in its budget resolution. However, because under Senate rules a reconciliation bill cannot be filibustered, Senate leaders sometimes succumb to the temptation to include extraneous matters in the reconciliation bill.
5. The president signs each of the twelve appropriations bills, and the budget becomes law.[40]
   If this blueprint is not followed, continuing resolutions (CRs) must be passed to keep the government operating, or nonessential federal agencies will be forced to close their doors, as happened on October 1, 2013 (and lasted for over two weeks).

As is true for much of the rest of contemporary congressional policy making, the "regular order" of the budget process is not typically followed in the Congress. Partisan division and struggles between Congress and the White House have made it difficult to secure the enactment of the twelve separate appropriations bills reported by the twelve House and Senate appropriations subcommittees. In 2016, for example, congressional Republicans and Democrats agreed in January to cooperate in passing the twelve regular spending bills. By midyear, though, failed appropriations bills had "piled up in the Senate like a multicar crash on the highway."[41] Republicans were especially outraged that Senate Democrats filibustered the defense appropriations bill. Republicans said Democrats were willing to compromise national security for partisan reasons. Democrats said it was the GOP that demonstrated indifference to the nation's real security needs. Given the parties' stark disagreements over spending priorities, regular order seems generally unlikely to prevail. Indeed, since 1999, the "regular" budget process has failed to produce a budget more often than it has succeeded.

Departing from regular order, Congress has come to rely on the omnibus appropriations bill crafted by party leaders. The omnibus bill combines all or many of the smaller appropriations bills into a single package that can be passed with one vote in each house of Congress. The omnibus bill allows party leaders to establish their own spending priorities and to offer opportunities—"seats on the omnibus"—to individuals or groups of legislators to add their own favored programs to the omnibus in order to ensure their support for the overall bill.

Thus, the proposed 2016 omnibus spending bill contained a number of provisions dear to the heart of the Senate Appropriations Committee chairman, Thad Cochran (R-MS), whose support for the bill was vital. Cochran's state would benefit from hundreds of millions of dollars of defense spending, flood-control projects, and energy projects. At the same time, members of Congress supporting such interests as the wind-power industry were able to secure an extension of the wind-production tax credit for their industry, members supporting the solar-power industry were able to secure an extension of the solar-investment tax credit, and so forth.

For the most part, the legislative minority is excluded from the process, though in some instances the support of minority party members can be garnered by giving their interests seats on the omnibus. In 2015, for example, Democratic senator Diane Feinstein agreed to support the GOP's omnibus spending bill after the Republican leadership agreed to include several of her pet projects, including a cybersecurity bill that would have been unlikely to pass on its own. Generally, some members of the Senate minority must be given seats on the omnibus to reduce the threat of filibusters.

Interestingly, Senator Richard Shelby (R-AL) in 2018 did achieve the rare feat of securing bipartisan support and passage of all twelve annual spending bills. One strategy used to achieve this was to package the spending bills into smaller "minibus" packages to secure their passage more quickly. For example, this was done for the three spending bills for military construction and veterans affairs, energy and water development, and the legislative branch. House Speaker Ryan noted that passing this "minibus" not only would keep the government funded through the 2018 midterm elections and avoid a government shutdown, but it was "the first time since 2007 that 'multiple appropriation measures' were finished on time."[42]

In sum, the omnibus bill, and the minibus version of it, are the budgetary components of the new order. The omnibus bill combines elements of follow-the-leader lawmaking and do-it-yourself legislating. The omnibus bill is generally constructed by the House and Senate leadership. Omnibus bills discourage deliberation because of their sheer size. Members may only have a couple of days to digest a bill that can be one thousand pages long and includes a host of complex funding provisions. Rather than read it, members seek to make sure that their own favored programs are included in the omnibus spending bill. Like harried commuters throughout the nation's capital, members must run to "catch the omnibus."

The New Order and Lobbying

The rise of the new order has affected the tactics and role of lobbyists. The term "lobbying" refers to an effort by a group to influence policy by persuading government officials, in this case members of Congress, to act in a manner consistent with the interests of the lobbyists' employers. Lobbying is a constitutional right. The Constitution's First Amendment provides for the right to "petition the government for the redress of grievances." Since petitioning is not permitted on the floors of the House or Senate, petitioners must address members of Congress in the lobbies of the legislative chamber—hence the term "lobbying."

The 1946 Federal Regulation of Lobbying Act defines a lobbyist as "[a]ny person who shall engage himself for pay or any consideration for the purpose of attempting to influence the passage or defeat of any legislation of the Congress of the United States." The 1995 Lobbying Disclosure Act requires all lobbyists to register with Congress and to disclose whom they represent, whom they lobby, what they are looking for, and how much they are paid. More than twelve thousand lobbyists are currently registered. During the opening weeks of the 115th Congress, scores of new lobbyists descended upon Washington. The new administration's promise to bring major change to the Capitol excited some interests and alarmed others. Corporations, seeing a business-friendly administration, mobilized lobbyists to seek new opportunities. Consumer and environmental groups, sensing danger, mobilized lobbyists to protect their hard-won legislative gains.

Lobbyists attempt to influence the legislative process in a variety of ways. They provide information to lawmakers and congressional staffers about their interests and pending legislation. They often testify on behalf of their clients at committee and subcommittee hearings. Lobbyists talk to reporters, place ads in newspapers, and organize letter-writing, phone-call, and e-mail campaigns designed to influence members of Congress. These faux grassroots campaigns are sometimes called *AstroTurf* lobbying. Lobbyists, as we noted in chapter 3, also play a major role in fund-raising, helping to direct clients' contributions to members of Congress whose support they seek to win. Lobbyists often work as "bundlers," combining large numbers of smaller contributions into large bundles of cash for representatives' campaign treasuries.

Effective lobbyists also wield influence by providing information about policies to busy members of Congress while providing their clients with an opportunity to receive a friendly hearing from key senators and representatives when legislation is being discussed. Lobbyists also provide ideas and information likely to steer members of Congress in the desired direction, showing them how they and their constituents are more likely to benefit from one course of action than another.

The influence of lobbyists, as we saw in chapter 3, is often related to the networks of personal relationships they have formed with lawmakers. Many of Washington's top lobbyists have close ties to important members of Congress or were themselves important political figures, thus virtually guaranteeing that clients will have direct access to congressional leaders. For example, according to the Capitol Hill newspaper *The Hill,* Jim Blanchard of DLA Piper was governor of Michigan; Chuck Brain of Capitol Hill Strategies worked in the White House Office of Legislative Affairs under President Clinton; Al D'Amato of Park Strategies was a senator from New York; Mitchell Feuer of Rich Feuer Anderson was counsel to the Senate Banking Committee; Broderick Johnson of Bryan Cave Leighton Paisner was a senior aide at the Clinton White House;

Kenneth Kies of The Federal Policy Group was an important congressional staffer on tax issues; Lisa Kountoupes of Kountoupes Denham Carr & Reid was an aide to Representative John Dingell; Robert Van Heuvelen of Van Heuvelen Strategies was chief of staff to the chairman of the Senate Budget Committee. The list goes on. Some important lobbyists have more than a business relationship to lawmakers. Quite a few are married to prominent political figures. For example, Linda Daschle of LHD & Associates is the wife of former Senate majority leader Tom Daschle, and Hadassah Lieberman, wife of Senator Joseph Lieberman, was for many years a lobbyist for the pharmaceutical industry.

Corporate interests always endeavor to be strategic in their choice of lobbyists. Many of Washington's lobbyists also serve as campaign treasurers, bundlers, and major fund-raisers for political candidates. Lobbyists like Peter Hart, Tommy Boggs, Peter Knight, Ken Duberstein, and Vin Weber are influential in part because of the ability to raise money for politicians. Interest groups will often hire lobbyists whom they know to be key fund-raisers for the politicians they hope to influence. In so doing, they are not making a campaign contribution that would have to be reported to the Federal Election Commission, but they are nevertheless seeking to make use of the fact that the lobbyist promoting their interests will be seen by the targeted politician as an important source of campaign money. For example, a coalition of television networks seeking to loosen rules governing their ownership of local TV stations hired Gregg Hartley as their lobbyist. Hartley, formerly a top aide to former House majority whip Roy Blunt, whose support the coalition sought, was one of Blunt's top fund-raisers. Companies hiring Hartley to lobby for them were almost certain of receiving a positive reception from Blunt. Many members of Congress list lobbyists as treasurers of their reelection committees. Several members of the powerful House Appropriations Committee sponsor political action committees headed by lobbyists with business before the committee.

The importance of insider lobbying became evident during one of the most hotly contested struggles on Capitol Hill in recent decades—the battle over Obamacare. President Obama had made health care his main legislative priority, and congressional Democrats promised to craft legislation that would increase the availability and affordability of health care for all Americans. The health care industry is among America's largest and includes insurance companies, hospitals, physicians, pharmaceutical companies, medical device manufacturers, and a host of others. Each of these interests was, of course, determined to make certain that it would not be hurt by and indeed would benefit from the law that might eventually be enacted. To promote their interests, more than three hundred industry groups deployed hundreds of lobbyists and spent nearly $1 billion on lobbying and campaign contributions. Many of the lobbyists employed by health care groups were former members of Congress and former congressional staffers with close ties to key lawmakers. Indeed, 166 individuals who had previously worked in the congressional leadership offices or for key members of committees involved in writing health legislation, along with 13 former members of Congress, represented health care clients in 2008 and 2009.

One important consequence of this lobbying effort was that the health insurance industry was able to secure language in the Senate's 2009 health care bill that would require 30 million Americans to buy health insurance while blocking a public option or expansion of Medicare that might compete with the private insurance companies. Polls suggested that most Americans favored a publicly financed health care option or an expansion of Medicare, but, of course, most Americans do not employ armies of lobbyists.

Lobbying by special interest groups has always been an important force in the Congress, as it had been in the colonial legislatures and the British Parliament. Indeed, James Madison, the principal author of America's Constitution, considered the problem of interest groups in a democracy and famously suggested in *Federalist* 10 that the existence of a large variety of interests would tend to reduce the power of any given interest. Today, we refer to this idea as the theory of pluralism, which holds that interest and lobby groups check one another and prevent any one group from undermining the public interest. Critics of pluralist theory correctly note that the idea is somewhat problematic since not all interests are equally represented. Nevertheless, clashes among competing groups at least increase the likelihood that no one set of interests will dominate the legislative arena and that the eventual policy outcome will represent a compromise among competing views.

The pluralist ideal is reinforced by the New Order. Traditionally, lobbyists focused their activities on congressional committees and their staffs. Lobbyists relied for influence upon their policy expertise and connections to committee members and their staffs as well as generous campaign contributions to committee members (see chapter 3). Lobbyists specialized in "schmoozing" with the members and gaining information of importance to their clients.[43] Schmoozing might involve going to dinner or a ball game with a legislator or simply "talking politics" with staffers. Any information a lobbyist gains that provides insight on policy issues of interest to his or her organization can be as valuable as actually influencing a particular piece of legislation. Often former members and former congressional staffers are hired by lobbying firms on K Street NW, in Washington, D.C., to use their special knowledge of the political process to lobby the very institution for which they worked. Relative to the huge number of interests in Washington, the number lobbying a particular committee or subcommittee is small, and often one or two lobbyists have the inside track for their clients. The pluralist idea of competing forces fighting one another to a standstill does not represent political reality.

The new order, however, breathes new life into pluralist doctrine. The increased importance of party leaders in the legislative process means that schmoozing a small number of subcommittee members is less likely to be effective. Lobbyists must focus their efforts on party leaders. Here, dozens, if not hundreds, of lobbyists must compete directly with one another, thus diluting the influence of any one special interest. One recent study reports that from 1978 to 2014 party leaders received an increasing share of political action committee (PAC) donations to their electoral campaigns "at the expense of committee leaders and the rank-and-file" members.[44] The concentration of power in the hands of party leaders, Oleszek observes, means that "no single [group] is likely to exercise dominant influence over policy formation as sometimes occurred in the past."[45] Perhaps the rise of the new order helps to explain why an increasing number of recent studies have questioned the effectiveness of lobbying. One major study observed that at best the results of lobbying are mixed, and at least half the time "interest organizations" have no effect on congressional action.[46] The new order also enhances the effectiveness of grassroots and public interest lobbying as a tactic. Grassroots and public interest lobbies can affect the interests of parties as a whole and force party leaders to listen.

The New Order and the Theory of the "Broken Congress"

Many critics today charge that Congress is "broken."[47] Its new order has certainly changed Congress, but different does not mean broken. In the Obama years, the goal for the Republican leaders of Congress was to block presidential policy initiatives and to reduce federal spending. In this context, then, it can be argued that recent "unproductive" Congresses have actually been highly effective. The Congress between 2011 and 2016 under Republican leadership reduced discretionary spending by a larger fraction than President Ronald Reagan (R) and the 97th Congress did in 1981. In a highly partisan era, many may not agree with the actions or inactions of Congress, but if the measure of legislative achievement is the attainment of the highest priority goals of the majority party, then the low productivity of recent Congresses cannot be judged as a "failure" of the institution. Rather, like it or not, it reflects the will of the legislative body's majority. Some congressional scholars note that even in recent times, Congress has been "enormously productive" if one focuses on the number of "important" or major laws that are passed.[48] With the White House also in the hands of a Republican, by the end of its first session, the 115th Congress had enacted forty-six major measures, including fourteen whose chief purpose was to repeal various rules adopted by the Obama administration.[49]

In one respect, however, the new order is clearly inferior to regular order. That is the matter of deliberation. Regular order ensured that bills would be read and reread by the subcommittees and committees of both houses of Congress. The new order sacrifices deliberation for leadership control and speed. In the new order, committees and their deliberative processes are increasingly bypassed in favor of a centralized process controlled by the leadership. Members are asked to vote on bills that they and their staffers have never read. And when it comes to voting, especially in the House, the leadership continually imposes increasingly restrictive and special rules on measures that reach the floor, limiting the actual choices members have when considering legislation. As table 5.2

Table 5.2. Restrictive Rules on Major Legislation, Selected Congresses (95th–113th)

Congress	Years	Percentage of Rules Structured, Modified Closed, or Closed
95th	1979–1980	21
97th	1981–1982	18
100th	1987–1988	42
101st	1989–1990	42
103rd–107th	1993–2002	67*
108th–113th	2003–2014	95*

*Mean percentage for these Congresses.
Source: Based on table 6.3 in Barbara Sinclair, *Unorthodox Lawmaking: New Legislative Processes in the U.S. Congress,* 5th ed. (Washington, DC: SAGE/CQ Press, 2017), 155.

shows, Barbara Sinclair found that beginning with the 103rd Congress (1993–1994), nearly 70 percent of the special rules for legislation reaching the floor restricted amendments to some degree. The trend is even stronger after the 111th Congress (2009–2010), with 99 percent of the major legislation considered with restricted rules.[50]

Has this trade of deliberation for "promptitude" always been desirable? Perhaps not always. But perhaps this trade is the necessary price for ensuring that a legislature designed in the eighteenth century can continue to function in the twenty-first.

6

Congress, the President, and Domestic Policy: Who Governs?

CONGRESS IS THE NATION'S LEGISLATURE, responsible for formulating and making the law. Members of Congress can and do act as "policy entrepreneurs," promoting legislation dealing with domestic or foreign policy.[1] Such pieces of legislation as the Dodd-Frank Wall Street Reform and Consumer Protection Act for regulating financial services, the McCain-Feingold Bipartisan Campaign Reform Act, and the Kennedy-Kassebaum Act (the Health Insurance Portability and Accountability Act of 1996) were primarily congressional in origin and are known by their sponsors' names.

As we saw in chapter 2, however, initiative in lawmaking has gradually passed from the Congress to the president. In the early decades of the Republic, congressional leaders were often offended by what they saw as importunate efforts by presidents to promote their own legislative agendas. Today, however, most major pieces of legislation emanate from the White House.[2] The president's role, in principle, is to execute the laws enacted by Congress. Nowhere does the Constitution suggest that the president is expected to take a lead role in lawmaking. Yet, many presidents have taken a broad view of their responsibilities, and, since the 1930s and Franklin D. Roosevelt's New Deal, every president has proposed packages of programs and policies to the Congress. Like his predecessors, upon assuming office in January 2017, President Trump presented Congress with a package of priorities and proposals. These included repeal of Obamacare, infrastructure investment, increased military spending, and school choice. Congress was receptive to these ideas but not to another Trump suggestion—congressional term limits. Senate majority leader Mitch McConnell said term limits would not be on the congressional agenda. He declared that congressional term limits had already been mandated by the Constitution. These were called elections.

Let us examine the patterns of conflict and cooperation between the president and Congress in the realm of domestic policy. As we observed in chapter 2, congressional power depends upon constituency, organization, and Congress's relationship to the executive. In the realm of domestic policy, its inability to solve this third problem has gradually pushed Congress into a subordinate role.

Presidential Initiative and Congressional Opposition: The Presidential Blunderbuss Meets "Dr. No"

Though enacted by Congress, arguably the two most important sets of government programs introduced during the past century—Franklin D. Roosevelt's New Deal and Lyndon Johnson's Great Society—were developed by these two presidents and their advisers, albeit with some modifications made by Congress. For a number of reasons, Congress has been eclipsed by the president in the realm of policy making, especially policy innovation. First, the president is a unitary actor, while Congress consists of 535 individuals in two houses. It is difficult for Congress to act in a unified or coordinated manner and to agree on an agenda for action. Congress depends upon the president to provide the agenda, and contemporary presidents are happy to oblige. The grueling presidential electoral process generally produces ambitious Presidents who hope to make a mark on history through their leadership and policy innovation. Presidents, moreover, have developed an institutional capacity for policy innovation, through the White House staff, the Executive Office of the President, and connections to America's universities and "think tanks," which provide every administration with plans and proposals. All presidents know they are graded on the new policies they develop, and those who merely do no harm are not likely to join the pantheon of the greats.

President Obama was no exception. While Obama's name is inextricably linked to one major piece of legislation, the 2010 Affordable Care Act, also known as Obamacare, the president can claim credit for quite a number of other programs, though none as extensive in scope and reach as his signature health care initiative. Presidential initiatives played a role in Congress's enactment of a major economic stimulus package, a bail-out of troubled banks and auto companies, the passage of a new pay-equity law, new tobacco regulation, a new free-trade treaty, policies that wound down the wars in Iraq and Afghanistan, and a variety of other programs. President Trump has begun to make his mark in the realms of economic policy, trade policy, immigration policy, and foreign policy, and by rescinding many rules and regulations, especially in the area of climate change, which he views as diminishing the competitiveness of American industry.

As we shall see, when presented with presidential initiatives, members of Congress often have strong reason to oppose the chief executive. Though many congressional Republicans, as we saw in chapter 3, were reluctant to support candidate Trump, almost all pledged to support President Trump after the election. Members of the president's own party, to be sure, are usually, albeit not invariably, supportive. The president's fellow partisans are more likely to share the president's views, to be responsive to similar interest groups and social forces, and to believe that the president's success or failure may affect their own electoral fortunes. Even so, partisan loyalty is no guarantee of congressional support for a president. A number of conservative House Republicans refused to support President Trump's effort to revise Obamacare in 2017, demanding that the legislation be repealed altogether.

Converse reasons will usually, though not always, lead members of the other party to oppose the president.[3] Hence, presidents have their best chance of policy success when their own party controls Congress, and they work at a serious disadvantage when even one house of Congress is controlled by the opposition. Occasionally, of course, peculiar circumstances will find the president allied with the opposing party against his own. In 2015, for example, Republicans supported President Obama's trade policies while Democrats, under pressure from labor unions, opposed the president.

Political scientist Stephen Skowronek once characterized the president as a "blunderbuss," a muzzle-loading firearm with considerable power, if poor aim.[4] If the president is a blunderbuss, Congress is often "Dr. No," refusing to accede to presidential demands. Often the ability to say no is Congress's most important weapon, though in using its weapon it risks being called obstructionist by the White House and its allies. Nevertheless, unlike the president, members of Congress are seldom personally blamed or credited for their legislative accomplishments.[5] Some, however, do seem to be especially adept at claiming credit.[6]

While voters may disparage the Congress collectively as a bunch of do-nothings, they generally like their own representative and, as we saw, are usually inclined to return that worthy individual to office.[7] For many members, especially those not of the president's party, being a do-nothing, a Dr. No, is the only form of power available. So why not say an emphatic *no!* to the importunities of the White House?

The Constitution: Separated Institutions Sharing Power

Article I of the Constitution vests legislative power in the Congress, while Article II assigns executive power to the president. Yet under the principle of checks and balances, each is assigned an important role in the activities of the other. The Congress can refuse to pass legislation requested by the president or decline to provide funding for programs sought by the president. Congress can reject presidential appointments or refuse to ratify treaties negotiated by the president. Congress can override presidential vetoes and impeach and remove the president from office. Congress can declare war and order the president to take charge of the war effort. And, though not specified in the Constitution, Congress has claimed the implied power to conduct investigations into the president's conduct and to oversee the activities of executive agencies.

Presidents, for their part, can veto acts of Congress, call Congress into special session, and adjourn Congress if the two houses cannot agree on a time of adjournment. The president is charged with executing the laws enacted by Congress and with commanding the nation's military forces in wars declared by Congress. The president, according to Article II, Section 2, of the Constitution, must inform Congress "from time to time" on the state of the Union and recommend to Congress "such Measures as he shall judge necessary and expedient." The vice president serves as the presiding officer of the Senate and can cast a deciding vote in the case of ties in that body. The most recent vice president to do so was Mike Pence, who cast a tie-breaking vote in 2017 to confirm Betsy DeVos as secretary of education. Presidential scholar Richard Neustadt correctly observed that the constitutional separation between the presidency and the Congress is not a case of separation of powers but is, rather, an example of separated institutions sharing powers.

In principle, the president and Congress might cooperate and the constitutional system might operate smoothly to produce and implement legislation. The president might suggest necessary and expedient measures to Congress, which might then develop and enact legislation. The president might, without further ado, sign the legislation and go about the business of implementing and executing it. All this could happen and sometimes does, especially in the event of some national emergency such as the 9/11 terror attacks, when President Bush and congressional leaders worked swiftly to craft and implement a response.[8]

Even in more mundane areas, the president and the Congress sometimes act together in an expeditious manner. Take, for example, the 2009 Lilly Ledbetter Fair Pay Act (the current fashion is to give a human face to legislation by naming laws for the person who nominally inspired it). Ledbetter, a supervisor for Goodyear Tire & Rubber Company, discovered that she had been paid far less than her male counterparts. She filed a discrimination suit, which went all the way to the U.S. Supreme Court but was ultimately dismissed in 2007 because Ledbetter had not filed suit within 180 days of her first paycheck, which was then the statutory requirement. A bill to change the law to allow a suit to be brought within 180 days of *any* paycheck died in the Senate in 2007.

The Ledbetter bill became an issue in the 2008 presidential campaign, with Republican candidate John McCain expressing opposition to the bill and then Democratic candidate Barack Obama saying he would make enactment of the Ledbetter bill a legislative priority. After the election, Democrats controlled not only the presidency but both houses of Congress as well. Obama had no difficulty in prompting House Democrats to reintroduce the proposal, which was strongly supported by a host of labor, women's, and other groups in the Democratic constituency. The bill passed the House and Senate on party-line votes. President Obama signed the bill, which went into effect on January 29, 2009. President and Congress had cooperated, and within one month a new law had been enacted.

Yet this sort of cooperation is more the exception than the norm. Even when the result is eventually successful, the road is usually long and difficult. In the case of Obamacare, the White House was initially stymied by congressional opposition, with even some Democrats expressing skepticism, but found that the key to success was to craft the proposal in a way that served the interests of major health insurance companies and the pharmaceutical industry. Health insurers hoped to sell millions of new policies to individuals who would be compelled to purchase insurance, and the pharmaceutical industry envisioned $35 billion in additional profits by selling drugs to these newly insured consumers.[9]

Yet despite the support of these powerful industries and their lobbyists, the bill passed the House and Senate on straight party votes, with complex procedural maneuvers required to prevail in the Senate. After Democrats lost control of the House of Representatives in the 2010 national elections, most other elements of the president's agenda, especially immigration reform, were blocked by Republican leaders. After the 2016 national elections, the GOP controlled both houses of Congress as well as the White House, and congressional leaders agreed with the president on a number of major matters, including the appointment of two conservative Supreme Court justices, immigration reform, and the need to repeal or modify Obamacare. Both Republicans and Democrats agreed with the new president's plan to spend more money on the nation's decaying infrastructure, though there was disagreement on spending priorities. Thus, at least at the outset, Congress seemed happy to cooperate with President Trump. Experience tells us, however, that such honeymoons are short and the subsequent marriage filled with arguments.

Electoral Complexity

When it comes to policy issues, the relationship between the Congress and the president is more often antagonistic than cooperative. To begin with, the electoral process guarantees that the president and many members of Congress will disagree, often strongly, on national priorities and directions. The president is independently elected in a set of fifty-one separate contests across the nation— fifty states plus the District of Columbia—taking place on the same day. Senators are elected in states, one-third on the same day the president is chosen, and two-thirds elected in previous years, following the constitutional principle of staggered terms. House members are elected in districts, which are subdivisions of states. The framers of the Constitution believed that subjecting the principal officers of the government to separate elections, even at different times, would serve as a precaution against mass movements or unwise policies in response to some sudden shift in the public's mood. As Alexander Hamilton explained in *Federalist* 71, the complexity of the electoral system would prevent "an unqualified complaisance to every sudden breeze of passion, or to every transient impulse which the people may receive."[10]

Electoral complexity means that the president is likely to have different priorities than many members of Congress, subscribe to political beliefs that differ from those of many members of Congress, and often, since the president's electoral coattails are generally short, to have a different party affiliation than the majority in one or both houses of Congress. Presidents are far more likely to receive support from members of their own party than from members of the partisan opposition and are often frustrated when one or both houses of Congress are controlled by their partisan opponents. Divided government has become quite common in recent years in part because demographic changes have given the Democrats an advantage in presidential elections while the redrawing and gerrymandering of congressional district boundaries have given the GOP an advantage in House races.[11] Since 1995, Republicans have held majorities in the House during eight of ten elections, while the Democrats have won three of five presidential contests. For only two brief, two-year periods in this time did one party control the White House and both houses of Congress. The Democrats between 2009 and 2011 and the Republicans from 2017 to 2019.

The difficulties caused by electoral complexity have been exacerbated in recent years because in several states each party has sought to create safe congressional seats for itself by drawing congressional district lines in such a way as to create heavily Democratic and heavily Republican districts with few "swing" districts inhabited by voters with differing points of view.[12] As a result of this strategy, members of Congress have less incentive to moderate their stands to appeal to a broad range of voters in their districts. To the contrary, Democratic members have become more liberal while Republican members have become more conservative.[13] Elected by an ideologically diverse national constituency, Republican presidents may have difficulty pleasing their more conservative copartisans in the House, while Democratic presidents are likely to be criticized by their more liberal Democratic House colleagues. During the Obama years, for example, many House Democrats found the president insufficiently attentive to liberal causes, while most House Republicans saw the president as a committed leftist.[14]

Policy Ambition

A second factor producing conflict between the president and Congress is presidential ambition. During the early decades of the Republic and even into the early twentieth century, presidential nominees were chosen by party leaders who preferred to see unassuming and deferential figures in the White House. Accordingly, most presidents were content to leave the work of governance to the Congress and harbored little desire to direct the affairs of the nation. Perhaps the extreme case was James Buchanan, elected in 1856, who defended his inactivity as the nation disintegrated by saying that he had "called the attention of Congress to the subject" of impending southern secession and war, but believed that "it was the imperative duty of Congress," not the president, to determine what, if any, action needed to be taken.[15]

Complementing presidential diffidence was the much more aggressive conduct shown by the leaders of the House and Senate during this era. Because of party discipline, the Speaker of the House, in particular, led an institution of government then more powerful than the presidency. House leaders and Senate leaders, as well, were anxious to defend their institutional prerogatives, to manage the affairs of the nation, and to keep meddlesome presidents in their place.

Around 1900, as a result of Progressive Era reforms, party discipline in Congress began to wane and, at the same time, new communications technologies allowed presidents to mobilize popular support on behalf of their own legislative objectives. These two changes provided an opportunity for presidents like Teddy Roosevelt, William Howard Taft, and Woodrow Wilson to present legislative programs to Congress, taking advantage of the constitutional admonition to present to Congress, from time to time, measures the president deems to be "necessary and expedient." In 1933, President Franklin D. Roosevelt called the Congress into special session to deal with the nation's economic crisis and presented it with proposed banking legislation that passed both houses within a few hours. Throughout his twelve years in office, FDR seized the legislative initiative, and presented Congress with dozens of major proposals that collectively became the New Deal.

According to political scientist Andrew Rudalevige, Roosevelt's practice became institutionalized under Harry Truman.[16] President Truman and his advisers used the Bureau of the Budget, which an FDR executive order had moved into the Executive Office of the President (also created by executive order), to develop legislative ideas. BOB staffers solicited ideas from the executive agencies, from the White House staff, and from universities and research institutes like the Brookings Institution. These ideas were sifted, packaged, and sent to Congress in presidential messages asserting the nation's legislative needs. FDR had generally bullied Congress and, by force of will and against the backdrop of national emergencies, had compelled legislators to accede to many of his demands. During the Truman administration, presidential efforts to set the legislative agenda became institutionalized.

Roosevelt was an aggressive and extremely ambitious individual, and Truman did not share FDR's personality. However, Roosevelt advisers like Dean Acheson and George C. Marshall, inherited by Truman, expected the new president to proceed in what they regarded as an appropriately presidential (Rooseveltian) manner and sought to create institutions that would compensate for FDR's absence. The presidents who followed Truman, though, were cut more from the FDR mold. Changes in the presidential nominating process meant that the role of party leaders was all but eliminated, and the selection process came to favor ambitious politicians willing to devote years to the single-minded pursuit of the nation's highest office. When elected, such individuals generally claimed to have a popular mandate and a plan and were quick to present Congress with a presidential agenda. Some presidents, like Reagan, brought new ideas with them. Others shopped for ideas. Kennedy and Johnson, for example, made extensive use of the growing network of think tanks and university-based policy "wonks" to create task forces that would recommend innovative proposals. All post–New Deal presidents relied upon experts in the Bureau of the Budget (later called the White House Office of Management and Budget, or OMB), the Council of Economic Advisers, the National Security Council staff, and other advisory groups within the Executive Office of the President (EOP) to propose new ideas and initiatives.

Since the 1921 Budget Act, presidents have been required to provide Congress with a consolidated annual budget that reconciled agency budget requests with expected revenues. Before FDR the annual budget was more an accounting exercise than an effort to set the nation's agenda. Roosevelt, Truman, and their successors, on the other hand, have used the annual budget message to introduce new packages of programs and initiatives. George W. Bush and Barack Obama essentially consolidated the budget message and the State of the Union address in order to highlight presidential budget requests.

The public and even Congress have come to rely upon the president to set a legislative agenda. A president who failed to present Congress with a package of new programs and initiatives would be widely castigated for lacking imagination and initiative. At the same time, however, the president's agenda is sure to create conflicts with the members of Congress who have partisan, ideological, or programmatic differences with the president. Thus, presidential ambition is certain to produce clashes between the executive and the legislative branches.

Presidents are often gauged on their ability to steer legislation through the Congress, but unless the electorate has been kind enough to fill both houses with members of the president's own party who also share his or her agenda and beliefs, and the nation's enemies helpfully provide a crisis, this process can be quite problematic. Presidents vary in their personal ability to bargain with Congress. Lyndon Johnson was reportedly extremely adept at the arts of persuasion, intimidation, and greasing the wheels of government with special favors. Other presidents have been less adept, and most have developed staff resources to smooth the way for their legislative requests. The EOP includes a number of staff members whose chief task is legislative liaison, in other words lobbying on behalf of the president's program. Like all good lobbyists, presidential staffers develop friends and contacts on Capitol Hill, provide information to congressional offices that supports the president's views, and seek to frame issues in a way that will increase presidential support in Congress.[17] Yet the bottom line is that presidents will generally receive the support of members of their own party and will generally not receive the support of members of the opposing party. At one time, presidents could change a few votes by offering special legislative favors and so forth to members of the other party, but today presidents must concentrate on making sure their own coalition remains intact. In recent, ideologically polarized Congresses, party-line voting on major issues has become the norm and presidents have little room to pick up votes from the other side if their own party is in the minority.

Principal-Agent Disputes

A third source of conflict between the president and Congress derives from what might be called their principal-agent relationship. When Congress enacts a law, the executive is required to execute it. One might say that the president is serving as an agent for the Congress. Conflicts almost inevitably arise in any relationship of this sort. Whether the agent is a president or a plumbing contractor, the principal is likely to find instances in which the agent did not follow the precise terms of the contract or, perhaps, failed altogether to fulfill the contract.

Unlike most plumbing contractors, presidents are agents with their own agendas and their own ideas about the public interest. Presidents may decide to reject a congressional initiative, to nominally agree but not to do exactly what

Congress mandated, or perhaps to accept Congress's mandate but take no action at all if they believe that Congress wants to take the nation in the wrong direction. As to outright rejection of a legislative initiative, the Constitution gives the president a conditional veto power—conditional because Congress may override the president's veto. As we saw in chapter 2, America's early presidents seldom vetoed laws, believing that the veto could only properly be used to protect the institution of the presidency from legislative encroachments. When Andrew Jackson vetoed a bank bill expressly because of a policy disagreement, he was censured by the Senate, and when John Tyler vetoed a bank bill, he was threatened with impeachment. Today, the veto or threat of a presidential veto is fairly common—FDR vetoed 372 bills—but during the Bush and Obama administrations, because of partisan gridlock, so few bills were passed that presidential veto pens grew rusty. In 2013, Congress passed only 57 bills, the fewest in its history. None were vetoed by the president. The media noted in 2014 that there was so little legislative activity that even the number of demonstrations and protests on Capitol Hill had dropped sharply. There seemed to be little point to demonstrating when so little legislative activity was taking place.[18]

The presidential veto is not as powerful a weapon as the veto power possessed by many state governors. Governors usually have "line-item vetoes," that is, they may veto portions of bills without having to veto the entire bill. The president possesses no such ability. Presidents must accept or reject bills in their entirety, which gives Congress a chance to include measures the president opposes with measures the president would be hard-pressed to veto, such as defense appropriations bills. In 1996, Congress enacted legislation giving the president a line-item veto power, which President Clinton used a number of times. In 1998, however, the Supreme Court found that the line-item veto was not consistent with the Constitution's Presentment Clause, because it improperly gave the president the power to amend legislation.[19] Recent presidents, as we shall see, have sought to use signing statements for just this purpose.

The veto is a presidential power expressed by the Constitution. The two other ways in which presidents and the executive branch more generally can thwart Congress are not. The first of these is through the execution of a law in a manner inconsistent with congressional intent. This practice is associated with the agencies of the executive branch as well as directly with the president. A recent case that has caused a great deal of controversy involves a 2014 decision by the IRS to effectively rewrite a portion of the Affordable Care Act. The act states that individuals who purchase health insurance through state exchanges are eligible for tax credits. These credits were intended to encourage individuals to purchase insurance through this mechanism and to encourage the states to establish such exchanges. By 2014, however, thirty-six states had declined to establish exchanges. In consultation with other agencies and the White House, the IRS decided to reinterpret the law to allow individuals who had not purchased their insurance in this manner to also receive tax credits. This seemingly minor change involved hundreds of millions in potential benefits and costs to businesses, individuals, and the national treasury and pointed to problems in the underlying statute. Initially, federal courts split on the question of whether the IRS acted properly or not, but in June 2015, the U.S. Supreme Court upheld the agency's actions in the case of *King v. Burwell.*[20]

When presidents themselves plan to execute the law in a manner inconsistent with statutory language, they often make their intent clear so that federal agencies will know what is expected of them by the chief executive. Signing statements are one vehicle presidents have used for this purpose. Thus, for example, when President George H. W. Bush signed a bill that included a provision requiring contractors on a particular federal project to pursue affirmative action in their hiring practices, his signing statement directed the secretary of energy to ignore the requirement.[21] Similarly, when President George W. Bush signed legislation creating an inspector general to oversee U.S. operations in Iraq, he issued a signing statement asserting that this official should refrain from audits and investigations into matters involving intelligence and counterintelligence.[22] The legislation contained no such provision. As a presidential candidate in 2008, Barack Obama deplored this type of signing statement. As president, however, Obama followed the trail blazed by his predecessors, issuing some thirty signing statements indicating his intention to disregard potions of laws enacted by Congress and signed by the president. For example, according to one provision of the 2014 National Defense Authorization Act, the president is obligated to give Congress thirty days' notice before releasing any prisoners from the Guantánamo Bay Naval Base military prison. When President Obama signed the law, he indicated that he would not be bound by this provision and later released five Taliban prisoners in exchange for an American soldier, Bowe Bergdahl, then held by the Taliban.

It hardly seems necessary to point out that when presidents plan to directly violate a prohibition or a criminal statute, they usually seek to avoid public disclosure of that fact. Thus, only through a determined congressional investigation was it learned that the Reagan White House had decided to directly violate a statutory prohibition, known as the Boland Amendment, forbidding further government funding of the Nicaraguan Contras, whom the president had strongly supported.

Another way in which presidents can use their executive powers to thwart Congress is by failing or refusing to execute the law. President Nixon, for example, several times refused to spend, or "impounded," funds appropriated by Congress. This practice was later severely restricted by the 1974 Congressional Budget and Impoundment Control Act. Presidential refusals to execute laws are not altogether uncommon and tend to be associated with presidential efforts to win favor with important constituency groups. President Clinton, for example, declared that a section of a defense appropriations bill requiring the discharge of military personnel found to be HIV-positive was unconstitutional and would not be enforced. President Obama, long before the Supreme Court struck down many of its provisions, found reason not to enforce major portions of the Defense of Marriage Act, which barred the government from recognizing same-sex marriage.

The Obama administration also refused to enforce the Unlawful Internet Gambling Enforcement Act, aimed at blocking Internet gambling, and granted waivers to ten states freeing them from provisions of the No Child Left Behind Act. The statute, as enacted by Congress, makes no provision for such waivers. The administration also announced that it would refuse to deport undocumented immigrants who came to the United States as children. Congress had considered and refused to enact legislation that would have adopted this policy. According to a White House official, "Often times, Congress has blocked efforts and we look to pursue other appropriate means of achieving our policy goals. . . . the president isn't going to be stonewalled by politics, he will pursue whatever means are available to do business on behalf of the American people."[23]

When the president refuses to enforce a statute or reinterprets a statute, there is little Congress can do, at least in the short run. In 2014, Republican House Speaker John Boehner announced plans to sue the president in federal court for, among other matters, failing in his constitutional responsibility to see to it that the laws are faithfully executed. As we shall see in chapter 9, however, the courts have generally been unwilling to intervene in disputes between Congress and the president, in effect, telling Congress to fight its own battles.

How Congress Can Do Battle with the Executive: How Can I Say No? Let Me Count the Ways

In fights with the executive, Congress is not without power. Actually, Congress has at least six major weapons at its disposal. These are its legislative powers, its quasi-executive powers, the congressional power of the purse, legislative oversight, legislative hearings and investigations, and, Congress's ultimate constitutional weapon, impeachment.

Legislative Powers

The simplest manner in which Congress can oppose the president is by enacting laws aimed at blocking presidential actions, or refusing to enact laws favored by the president. On a routine basis, Congress often declines to enact legislation sought by the president. In some instances the president has little recourse but to denounce congressional obstructionists. In other cases, the president may seek to circumvent Congress by using executive tools to achieve the desired effect. Two of the most important of these tools are executive orders (sometimes called presidential memoranda) and regulatory review. An executive order or memorandum is a presidential decree directing some federal agency to undertake (or refrain from undertaking) some course of action. President Obama sought through executive action to implement various pieces of immigration legislation that Congress declined to enact, including the so-called DREAM Act, which would have provided various rights and a route to citizenship for several million undocumented immigrants. Obama issued orders, currently being challenged in the federal courts (see chapter 9), to federal agencies halting the deportation process. Executive orders and memoranda must be linked to the president's statutory or constitutional authority, cannot supersede existing law, and can be contravened by a subsequent president.

This latter point can be significant. President Obama issued orders in 2013 via executive memoranda introducing a "Climate Action Plan." In addition to several executive orders, the plan called for the Environmental Protection Agency (EPA) to develop new rules—which it did—to strengthen carbon pollution standards for energy plants, essentially forcing the closure of all or most coal-fired plants. Obama's orders and the new EPA rules were challenged in the federal courts and were still on hold when Obama left office. President Trump sought to bring an end to the Climate Action Plan by rescinding Obama's orders, appointing new EPA administrators to rewrite the rules, and, in the meantime, refusing to fund implementation of the rules. Despite their limitations, presidential orders can be very important—Jefferson's Louisiana Purchase was, after all, an executive order. An executive order can hypothetically be overturned by Congress, but this would require mustering a veto-proof majority, something seldom possible in today's closely balanced and polarized national legislature.

The federal courts may overturn an executive order, but, as we shall see in chapter 9, they seldom seem willing to confront the president. In June 2016, however, the Supreme Court handed an unusual setback to the president when, on a 4–4 vote, it left in place a lower-court ruling striking down a presidential order shielding several million undocumented immigrants from deportation and making them eligible for work permits. This issue is likely to be heard again by the Supreme Court now that a ninth justice has been appointed.

Another tool through which presidents may try to circumvent the Congress is regulatory review. Recent presidents have developed mechanisms through which to use the bureaucratic rulemaking process to write regulations to achieve goals that Congress would not approve via legislation. For example, when Congress refused to enact the various environmental bills sought by President Clinton, the president used regulatory review to implement a good deal of his environmental agenda.[24] We shall return to regulatory review in chapter 8.

Despite executive orders and regulatory review, Congress's legislative powers give the nation's legislature considerable power vis-à-vis the White House. Two examples of lawmaking aimed at thwarting the president were mentioned earlier—the 1974 Congressional Budget and Impoundment Control Act and the 1982 Boland Amendment. The first of these was enacted in the wake of the Watergate battle between Congress and President Nixon (to be more fully discussed). Since the administration of Thomas Jefferson, presidents had engaged in the practice of sequestering, or "impounding," funds appropriated by Congress for programs they opposed. Jefferson refused to spend $50,000 appropriated by Congress for the construction of new gunboats to be used by the navy to patrol the Mississippi River. Jefferson said that the gunboats were not needed.

Impoundment became a major issue during the Nixon administration. President Nixon made extensive use of impoundment both to block programs he opposed and to increase his leverage over executive agencies. In 1973–1974 alone, Nixon refused to disburse nearly $12 billion in funds that had been appropriated by the Congress. Following Nixon's resignation, Congress enacted legislation that provided detailed rules governing the president's impoundment authority. Subsequently, in the case of *Train v. City of New York*, the Supreme Court declared that the president had no authority to impound appropriated funds unless the appropriating legislation specifically granted such power.[25]

Quasi-Executive Powers: Overriding Presidential Vetoes

Reinforcing its legislative powers and consistent with Neustadt's notion of separated institutions sharing powers, the Constitution assigns Congress several powers that might be considered quasi-executive. Congress can override executive vetoes, and the Senate must confirm presidential appointees and must confirm treaties, the latter by a two-thirds majority. Each of these powers can bolster Congress's position vis-à-vis the executive. We examined the confirmation power in chapter 1 and will consider the treaty power in chapter 7. Here, let us discuss the veto override.

The veto override is often attempted but seldom successful.[26] A two-thirds majority of both houses is required to overturn the president's veto and, often enough, two-thirds of the members of both houses would fail to agree on the proposition that the marigold is a pretty flower. Generally speaking, presidential vetoes are most likely to be overridden when both houses of Congress are firmly controlled by the president's partisan and ideological foes. Thus, not surprisingly, the presidents who saw their vetoes overridden most frequently were Andrew Johnson, Harry Truman, and Gerald Ford. Nine of Franklin Roosevelt's vetoes were also overridden, but FDR was extravagant in his use of the veto power, turning back 372 bills. The most recent veto override came in 2016 when Congress overwhelmingly voted to override President Obama's veto of legislation allowing victims of the September 11, 2001, terror attacks to sue the government of Saudi Arabia (see table 6.1).

Congressional Power of the Purse

As to Congress's third set of weapons, its spending powers, the framers of the Constitution conceived the "power of the purse" to be Congress's most fundamental prerogative, and for more than a century this power was jealously guarded by powerful congressional leaders like Taft-era House Speaker "Uncle Joe" Cannon, who saw congressional control of the budget as a fundamental safeguard against "Prussian-style" militarism and autocracy.[27] In the nineteenth

Table 6.1. Presidential Vetoes 1789–2016

President	Vetoes	Overridden
Washington	2	—
J. Adams	—	—
Jefferson	—	—
Madison	5	—
Monroe	1	—
J. Q. Adams	—	—
Jackson	5	—
Van Buren	—	—
W. H. Harrison	—	—
Tyler	6	1
Polk	2	—
Taylor	—	—
Fillmore	—	—
Pierce	9	5
Buchanan	4	—
Lincoln	2	—
A. Johnson	21	15
Grant	45	4
Hayes	12	1
Garfield	—	—
Arthur	4	1
Cleveland	304	2
B. Harrison	19	1
Cleveland	42	5
McKinley	6	—
T. Roosevelt	42	1
Taft	30	1
Wilson	33	6
Harding	5	—
Coolidge	20	4
Hoover	21	3
F. D. Roosevelt	372	9
Truman	180	12
Eisenhower	73	2
Kennedy	12	—
L. B. Johnson	16	—
Nixon	26	7

continued

Table 6.1. *continued*

President	Vetoes	Overridden
Ford	48	12
Carter	13	2
Reagan	39	9
G. H. W. Bush	29	1
Clinton	36	2
G. W. Bush	12	4
Obama	12	1
Trump	0	0
Total	1,508	111

Source: History, Art & Archives, United States House of Representatives, "Presidential Vetoes," August 16, 2017, http://history.house.gov/Institution/Presidential-Vetoes/Presidential-Vetoes/.

century, Congress frequently itemized appropriations for executive branch agencies down to the last dollar, leaving no discretion in expenditures. An 1871 appropriation of $58,280 for one office was divided as follows: $3,000 for the first auditor, $2,000 for the chief clerk, and $720 for each of the other clerks.[28]

Today, when it appropriates funds for particular purposes, Congress generally allows administrators considerable discretion in their use. However, Congress continues to take appropriations very seriously. As we saw, the House and Senate have each established twelve matching appropriations subcommittees based upon subject-matter jurisdictions. Each subcommittee holds hearings in which it considers the president's budget, congressional revenue, and expenditure targets, and hears testimony from agency officials and other parties it deems relevant before developing an appropriations bill funding the agencies within its jurisdiction. The bill is subject to amendment by the entire chamber. Eventually, both houses must pass appropriations bills in precisely the same language.

When Congress is pleased with a program and its administrators, it can reward them by approving their budgets without subjecting them to much review or criticism. This gives administrators an incentive to seek good relations with their congressional appropriators. If, on the other hand, Congress is displeased with a federal program or agency, it can react by reducing or even eliminating the money appropriated for that function.[29] Congress may also attach riders to bills, forbidding agencies to spend money for particular purposes.[30] In 2014 the House of Representatives voted to cut more than $1 billion from the IRS budget to punish the agency for allegedly targeting conservative political groups for special tax scrutiny. A variety of other cuts were also approved, including the elimination of funding for renovating the White House bowling alley. Absent a congressional appropriation, no funds can be spent, and it appears that the president might be forced to find some other bowling venue. Most federal programs operate on an annual budget, with the exception of entitlement programs like Social Security and Medicare, whose spending and appropriation levels are set by legal formulae that remain in force unless changed by law, as well as agencies like the Federal Reserve, which are self-funded. Social Security and Medicare are also partially self-funded. Under the Constitution, government spending must be approved by bills initiated in the House of Representatives, agreed to by the Senate, and signed by the president. If Congress and the president are unable to enact a budget, the 1984 Antideficiency Act requires that government activities begin shutting down so as to avoid violating the constitutional authority of Congress over spending. Usually, to avoid shutdowns, Congress and the president will agree on a continuing resolution (CR) to keep spending at or near existing levels. Indeed, the U.S. government operated on a series of CRs from 2009 until 2015 because Congress and the president were unable to reach an overall budget agreement. Congress may also appropriate funds for particular purposes even without an overall budget agreement.

Historically, congressional committees reviewed individual budgetary requests from every office and agency. These were made directly from the agencies to the Congress, and the federal budget consisted of the sum total of agreements between the agencies and congressional committees. The president was mainly out of the loop. The 1921 Budget Act, creating the BOB, however, ushered in a period of enhanced presidential influence over federal spending. Claiming powers not precisely specified by the act, President Harding introduced the principle of central legislative clearance.[31] Federal agencies were required to obtain BOB clearance for all requests and recommendations submitted to Congress. The agencies resisted, but Harding's successor, Calvin Coolidge, mandated a central clearance procedure for all agency requests and recommendations with budgetary implications—a procedure that with modifications is still used today.

Since the New Deal, successive Congresses have yielded to steadily increasing presidential influence over the budget process. In 1939, Congress allowed Franklin D. Roosevelt to take a giant step toward presidential control of the nation's purse strings when it permitted FDR to bring the Bureau of the Budget into the newly created Executive Office of the President. Roosevelt and his successors have used the BOB (now called the White House Office of Management and Budget, or OMB) to influence the nation's legislative and budgetary agenda by assembling a more or less coherent package of legislative proposals for the Congress to consider. Using the BOB/OMB as a presidential agenda setter rather than as a mere clearinghouse for agency requests, successive presidents made their budgetary proposals the starting points for congressional action on taxing and spending, often relegating the Congress to the subsidiary role of reacting to presidential initiatives rather than developing programs of its own.

In 1974, Congress responded to Richard Nixon's efforts to further enhance presidential control of spending when it enacted the Congressional Budget and Impoundment Control Act. The budget provisions of this piece of legislation centralized Congress's own budgetary process and established the Congressional Budget Office (CBO) to rival the president's OMB.[32] Under the terms of the 1974 act, Congress undertook an independent budgetary process, leading to the creation of a unified congressional budget resolution that rivaled the president's budget. Many members of Congress hoped the 1974 act would limit presidential power by restoring congressional control over the nation's taxing and spending agenda.

Legislative Oversight

A fourth arrow in Congress's quiver is legislative oversight. Oversight refers to congressional review and supervision of the activities of executive agencies. Through oversight, the Congress has an opportunity to determine whether the actions of the executive in administering programs are consistent with legislative intent, as well as to investigate the effectiveness and efficiency of government agencies. Charges of waste, illegal conduct, and abuse of citizens' rights are also topics for legislative inquiry.

As we observed in chapter 1, the Constitution makes no mention of oversight, but it seems implied by several of the enumerated powers of Congress, including the power to appropriate funds, to raise and support armies and navies, and even to impeach judges and members of the executive branch. Article I also gives Congress the power to makes laws necessary and proper for carrying out its enumerated powers. It seems reasonable to assume that Congress is thereby empowered to hold hearings and conduct investigations into the conduct of executive branch agencies

By statute, Congress has authorized House and Senate standing committees to oversee executive programs under their jurisdiction. And among the various provisions of the 1974 Budget Act was one authorizing congressional committees to conduct performance evaluations of executive agencies. By statute too, agencies are required to furnish a variety of reports to Congress, and each agency's inspector general is required to inform Congress of serious management and performance problems within his or her agency.

If Congress determines that an agency is not properly performing its tasks or is not acting in a manner consistent with its authority, legislators have a number of options. They may cut the agency's budget, as exemplified by the House's decision to slash the IRS budget in 2014. Legislators may restrict an agency's regulatory authority, as occurred in the 1980s when Congress reduced the EPA's rulemaking discretion. Congress may also write new legislation to narrow the agency's jurisdiction or, in some instances, may recommend that the Justice Department look into misconduct by agency executives

Since the early days of the Republic, Congress has held hearings and conducted investigations to examine the activities of executive branch agencies. In 1792, the House of Representatives launched an investigation into the failure of a military expedition against a tribal confederation ordered by President Washington and led by General Arthur St. Clair. The House called for "such persons, papers and records as may be necessary to assist their inquiries," and justified its investigation by declaring that inquiries into the expenditure of all public money were the indispensable duty of the House.[33] President Washington was surprised by the congressional request for records and papers and was not certain that it was appropriate. After considering the matter carefully, though, Washington concluded that the House could appropriately institute such inquiries and was entitled to receive papers and records unless their disclosure "would injure the public."[34] This principle was repeated by Washington when he resisted congressional demands for papers relating to the Jay Treaty, negotiated with Great Britain in 1794.

As in many other instances, President Washington's decision set lasting precedents. He determined that Congress was entitled to conduct inquiries into the activities of the executive branch but that the president should exercise discretion in deciding what to disclose. This discretion came to be called "executive privilege" and was formally recognized by the Supreme Court in its Watergate tapes decision nearly two centuries later.[35] After investigating the causes of St. Clair's defeat, Congress concluded that much of the fault lay with the mismanagement of the army supply services. Accordingly, Congress enacted legislation transferring management of the supply services from the War Department to the Treasury Department. This was the first, but not the last, time that oversight of the executive branch led to an attempted legislative remedy.

In subsequent decades, Congress came to be recognized as the "grand inquest of the nation," and began to require regular reports from executive agencies on all their activities and expenditures.[36] In 1808, for example, Congress required detailed statements of all contracts made by Departments of the Treasury, War, Navy, and Post Office, and by collectors of customs. The next year Congress demanded full reports of all claims and expenses of the War and Navy Departments, which were suspected of profligate spending.[37] In 1816, Congress created six standing committees on public expenditures, one each for the State, Treasury, War, Navy, and Post Office Departments, and one on public buildings. These committees were established by House Speaker Henry Clay for the express purpose of overseeing the executive departments within their jurisdictions. They were responsible for "watching the conduct of business, criticizing laxness, and for the use of funds."[38]

Today, Congress exercises legislative oversight through a variety of tools and mechanisms.[39] Among the most important is the Government Accountability Office (GAO), originally called the General Accounting Office, and established by the same 1921 Budget and Accounting Act that created the Bureau of the Budget. The GAO is headed by the comptroller general of the United States, appointed by the president, subject to senatorial confirmation, for a fifteen-year term. The GAO's original mission was to audit and report to Congress on executive agencies' use of appropriated funds. Over the years, however, the GAO has gone beyond financial audits to undertake performance audits of executive departments and agencies on Congress's behalf. During the past year alone the GAO has reported widespread waste in government software spending, deficiencies in the operations of Department of Veterans Affairs hospitals, faulty practices on the part of the Transportation Security Administration (TSA), problems with the Federal Aviation Administration (FAA) pilot certification, and poor reporting practices by the Federal Reserve. In 2014, a GAO "secret shopper" found that the contractors employed to staff federal insurance exchanges made no effort to verify the identities of supposed clients and allowed individuals with false identifications and no documents to enroll for federally sponsored health insurance under the Affordable Care Act.[40]

In both the House and Senate, oversight is conducted by authorizing committees, appropriations committees, and various subcommittees, as well as the House Committee on Oversight and Government Reform and the Senate Homeland Security and Governmental Affairs Committee, which have broad oversight powers. To facilitate oversight, Congress has adopted several "whistleblower" statutes to encourage federal employees, who may have inside information on agency operations, to come forward if they are aware of abuses or misconduct. These whistleblowers are an important part of the oversight process. In 2014, for example, whistleblower testimony before the House Committee on Veterans Affairs led to the resignation of the VA secretary and other top officials as well as legislation designed to reform VA practices.

One oversight tool that has not been very effective is the Congressional Review Act (CRA) procedure for disallowing new rules proposed by executive agencies. Under the provisions of the 1996 CRA, enacted as part of the Small Business Regulatory Enforcement Fairness Act, all major new rules must be submitted for review to both houses of Congress and to the GAO before they can be adopted. If the OMB has previously determined that the rule is "major" in terms of its potential economic impact, it cannot take effect for at least sixty days, nominally giving Congress time to disallow the rule if it wishes to do so. By 2011, the GAO had reviewed 1,029 major rules, and 72 joint resolutions of disapproval were introduced relating to 49 rules.[41] In only one case was a joint resolution of disapproval actually adopted and signed by the president. This involved an Occupational Health and Safety Administration (OSHA) ergonomic rule enacted in the final month of the Clinton administration. The newly elected Republican Congress lost no time in disallowing the rule, and President Bush was only too happy to sign the resolution.[42] Since 2012, federal agencies have avoided the CRA procedure by the simple expedient of neglecting to report new rules to Congress.[43] Since Congress has no reliable capacity to monitor the thousands of rules promulgated by the agencies, it has no idea which, if any, it might like to disallow.

Many critics claim that despite nominally possessing various oversight tools, Congress is not especially adept at the routine supervision of federal agencies.[44]

Reading the thousands of reports filed by the agencies and inquiring into their day-to-day activities, as was common in the nineteenth century, is seen today as a tedious activity that does not contribute to congressional career or electoral interests. Political scientists Mathew McCubbins and Thomas Schwartz call this routine form of oversight "police patrol" oversight and agree that members of Congress shun this activity. McCubbins and Schwartz, however, assert that Congress is much better at what they call "fire alarm" oversight.[45] Fire alarm oversight takes place when a whistleblower, the media, a GAO report, or other event brings a problem to Congress's attention. When the alarm rings, Congress may jump into action, schedule hearings, summon executive branch officials, and discuss possible legislation.[46]

For example, in 2013, when a whistleblower, National Security Agency (NSA) contractor Edward Snowden, revealed the existence of a massive NSA eaves-dropping program that routinely intercepted U.S. citizens' electronic communications, a variety of congressional committees scheduled hearings to look into the matter, identify potentially illegal activity, and consider what, if any, legislative steps should be taken. The hearings, many of which were held behind closed doors, included testimony from top officials of the U.S. intelligence community, who, not surprisingly, reassured Congress and the public that all their actions were monitored by the courts and were needed to protect America from terrorist threats. Several pieces of legislation to reform intelligence collection practices were introduced, but none were enacted. The ringing of the fire alarm became somewhat muted but has not quite disappeared, as new allegations of improper activities on the part of the NSA and other agencies continue to surface.

More recently, the Senate Commerce Committee conducted hearings when cruise-ship passengers complained that they had been mistreated and even criminally assaulted by employees of cruise lines while the ships were at sea and outside U.S. jurisdiction. Senator Jay Rockefeller (D-WV), the committee chairman, said the passenger testimony pointed to the need for legislation regulating the cruise industry and providing greater protection for Americans at sea.[47]

Legislative Hearings and Investigations

As these examples suggest, legislative hearings can be important oversight tools. Hearings may be launched by standing committees or by specially created committees. There are two types of legislative hearings. In the most common variety of oversight hearing, Congress listens to testimony, quizzes executive branch officials, and hears complaints from members of the public in order to better fulfill its legislative responsibilities. In the example given in the previous paragraph, Congress looked into complaints from cruise-line passengers to see if some legislative remedy for the problems adduced might be needed. In recent years, Congress has held hearings and conducted inquiries into a variety of matters, including the actions of the national intelligence community and the Internal Revenue Service, problems surrounding the launch of Obamacare, and a host of other matters. In each case, the nominal purpose was to identify problems and possible legislative remedies. In 2014, members of the Senate Select Committee on Intelligence, which had been looking into allegations of misconduct by the CIA and the possible need for legislative remedies, discovered evidence that the CIA had hacked into Senate computer systems to spy on the committee. CIA director John Brennan first denied the allegations but then was forced to acknowledge their validity and apologize to the committee

A second type of hearing, called an investigative hearing or ethics probe, has no immediate legislative intent, though it may eventually result in legislation. The chief purpose of such a hearing is to look into allegations of misconduct on the part of one or more public officials, possibly culminating in a recommendation that the officials in question be dismissed or even subjected to criminal prosecutions.[48] Such hearings have a long history in the United States. In 1800, for example, a House committee held hearings to investigate charges that Mississippi territorial governor Winthrop Sargent had exceeded his authority, and two years later a second House committee investigated complaints that Sargent had caused one of his political opponents to be falsely arrested. As in Sargent's case, these hearings tend to be hostile in intent.[49] In the 1990s, ethics probes led to the resignations of Agriculture Secretary Mike Espy and Housing and Urban Development Secretary Henry Cisneros.

Often, in conducting such hearings, Congress has difficulty compelling executive branch officials, particularly members of the president's staff, to appear. In 2014, for example, the House Oversight and Government Reform Committee issued a subpoena to compel testimony from White House political adviser David Simas. The committee was looking into allegations that the White House Office of Political Strategy and Outreach, led by Simas, was illegally engaged in political fund-raising. The president did not wish Simas to testify, and the White House counsel sent then committee chairman Darrell Issa (R-CA) a letter stating that the subpoena posed a threat to executive branch interests as well as the president's ability to obtain candid advice and counsel. Issa pointed out that a similar claim, made by the Bush administration when then White House counsel Harriet Miers had been subpoenaed to testify before a congressional committee, had been rejected by a federal judge. The White House replied that it disagreed with the judge's opinion in the Miers case and would continue to resist the subpoena.[50] The stage appeared to be set for a long legal battle, though often in such cases Congress and the White House will negotiate an agreement allowing the subpoenaed official to testify but limiting the questions that can be asked.[51]

In 2015, the new chairman of the House Oversight and Government Reform Committee, Jason Chaffetz (R-UT), issued a new subpoena to outgoing Attorney General Eric Holder to compel his testimony in the so-called "Fast and Furious" case, involving an apparently poorly conceived scheme by federal law enforcement agents to sell weapons to drug cartels and then follow the trail of weapons to the cartels' leaders. The plan failed and the weapons were used in a number of crimes, including the murder of a U.S. Customs and Border Protection agent. Holder had ignored a 2012 subpoena and was held in criminal contempt by the committee. The Justice Department, however, declined to prosecute Holder, leaving Congress with little recourse.

Also in 2015, congressional committees looked into allegations that former secretary of state Hillary Clinton had improperly handled classified materials. The hearings were inconclusive. The investigation, however, damaged Clinton's 2016 presidential campaign, as had been their intent.

Impeachment

Congress's ultimate weapon against the executive is impeachment.[52] President Nixon would certainly have been impeached and very likely convicted if he had not resigned, and some members of Congress had hoped to present President Reagan with a similar choice in 1987. Impeachment is a two-step process. Article I, Section 2, of the Constitution gives the House of Representatives the power to impeach the president, vice president, and all other civil officers of the United States. To *impeach* means to charge an official with having committed "Treason, Bribery, or other high Crimes and Misdemeanors." An official who is impeached by a majority vote in the House then, by the terms of Article I, Section 3, stands trial in the Senate, with the chief justice of the United States presiding. In the trial, each and every article of impeachment forwarded by the House is considered, and a separate vote is taken on each. A two-thirds vote is needed for conviction on each separate article. The defendant need only be convicted on one article to be removed from office. The question of what constitutes an impeachable offense is a political question. When he was House minority leader, future President Gerald Ford said, "An impeachable offense is whatever a majority of the House of Representatives considers it to be at a given moment in history."[53]

The impeachment process is seldom used and has historically been viewed as a power to be employed only in cases involving the most egregious forms of official misconduct. Since the nation's founding, resolutions calling for the impeachment of various officials have been introduced in the House many times. Quite a number of President Obama's foes claimed that he committed impeachable offenses, though Republican House leaders were leery of the idea.[54] Some Democrats have called for the impeachment of President Trump, but since conviction would require a two-thirds vote in the Senate, the prospect seems unlikely. The House, however, has actually initiated impeachment proceedings on sixty-four occasions. Articles of impeachment have been voted nineteen times, and seven individuals, all federal judges, have been convicted by the Senate. One judge, Alcee Hastings, was convicted and removed from the bench for taking bribes but was subsequently elected to Congress from the state of Florida. The most recent judge to be convicted in the Senate was Thomas Porteous of the Eastern District of Louisiana, convicted of official corruption in 2010.

Twice, presidents of the United States have been impeached. The first, Andrew Johnson, was impeached in 1868. Johnson was charged with violating the new Tenure of Office Act, which prohibited the president from unilaterally dismissing officials whose appointments had required Senate confirmation, as well as a number of other crimes. The Senate fell one vote short of the two-thirds majority that would have convicted Johnson and removed him from office. In 1998, Bill Clinton was impeached by the House on charges of perjury and obstruction of justice relating to Clinton's sexual relationship with a White House intern.

Of course, just as his violation of the Tenure of Office Act was only the proximate cause of Johnson's impeachment, so the issue of sex in the Oval Office was hardly the full reason for Clinton's impeachment. In 1993 and 1994, Republicans had laid down a barrage of charges against Clinton and his wife, mainly related to their involvement in the failed Whitewater real estate development in Arkansas. While they were able to embarrass and harass the Clintons, Republicans were unable to disable the administration. In 1994, however, the GOP won control of both houses of Congress, gaining in the process control of the congressional authority to investigate and to secure appointment of independent counsels to investigate on its behalf. Some Republicans saw an opportunity to retaliate against the Democrats for the Watergate and Iran-Contra probes. Now headed by Republicans, congressional committees immediately launched wide-ranging investigations of Clinton's conduct during his years as governor of Arkansas.

At the same time, congressional Republicans launched several independent counsel probes to search for wrongdoing by Clinton and his associates. The most important of these prosecutors, Kenneth Starr, was able to extend the scope of his investigation to include sensational allegations that the president had an affair with a White House intern Monica Lewinsky and that he later both perjured himself and suborned perjury on the part of the intern and others to prevent disclosure of his conduct. A month after Clinton was forced to appear before Starr's grand jury and acknowledge his affair with Lewinsky, the GOP-controlled House Judiciary Committee began impeachment proceedings. Clinton's impeachment was approved by the full House on a near-party-line vote. By another near-party-line vote, the Senate declined to convict. But Clinton's presidency had been damaged.

While the process spiraled to its conclusion, the Clinton administration was preoccupied with the president's defense. Clinton and his allies responded aggressively to every accusation and innuendo, leveling countercharges against his accusers and the special counsel's office, sometimes employing private detectives to collect damaging information about the president's adversaries.[55] Throughout the long struggle between Clinton and his enemies, the president was vigorously defended by the Democratic Party. In January 1998, the Democratic National Committee (DNC) established a damage-control center to coordinate strategies, disseminate information, respond to charges, and generally seek to protect the president from new revelations and accusations.[56]

Until Clinton's admissions of sexual misconduct compelled several prominent Democrats to distance themselves from him, not a single significant Democratic politician or interest group spoke against the president. Whatever their personal feelings about him, most Democrats believed that the destruction of

the Clinton administration would bring a renewed Republican effort to undermine the domestic social institutions fashioned by the Democratic Party. Even
the women's movement, which might have been expected to turn against a president who admitted having a sexual relationship with a young intern, decided
that Clinton's support for abortion rights and federal funding for childcare, as
well as his record of appointing women to high office, outweighed his sexual
indiscretions.

The lesson to be learned from the Clinton impeachment is that so long as a
president is vigorously defended by his or her own political party and retains
strong support in the nation, impeachment is rather unlikely to succeed. The
process may disrupt an administration for a time, but barring cataclysmic revelations that completely strip a president of congressional and public support,
when the smoke of political battle clears, the same president will still occupy
the Oval Office.

Thoughts on Congress and the President: Power against Power

The Constitution's framers knew that the president and Congress would vie
for power. They saw this competition as necessary to prevent a concentration of
power that might threaten citizens' liberties. The government's "several constituent parts," said Madison, must be designed to check and balance one another.
"Ambition must be made to counteract ambition."[57] What we sometimes call
gridlock, the framers might have viewed as the proper operation of the federal
machinery.

The framers thought that in the competition between the president and the
Congress, it would be the Congress that would generally have the upper hand.
After all, the Congress would be close to the people, directly elected from small
constituencies; and in a republic, would not popular support be the decisive
factor? "In republican government," said Madison, "the legislative authority
necessarily predominates."[58] On this matter, however, Madison proved to be a
poor prophet. First, Madison did not anticipate a day when presidents themselves would be popularly elected, sharing Congress's electoral connection with
the American people. Second, Madison did not foresee the advent of media and
communications technology that would focus on the White House and give
the president more public visibility than any member of Congress. How could
Madison have predicted that a president would have tens of millions of Twitter

followers while most Americans would be unable to name their own congressional representatives?

But if Madison cannot be faulted for failing to predict these matters, he can be faulted for failing to understand the essentially asymmetric relationship between legislative power and executive power. Congress may make the laws, but it cannot execute the laws it makes. It must turn to the president and grant funding and authority to the executive branch. This is Congress's great dilemma. To accomplish any goal, other than maintaining stalemate and gridlock by saying no, it must enhance the power of the president. This is why Congress may indeed use the powers discussed in this chapter to win battles against the White House. Nevertheless, for more than two centuries, Congress has been losing the war against executive power. And in the meantime, as we saw earlier, the executive has been developing new tools to circumvent even Congress's power to say no. Dr. No could blunt the presidential blunderbuss but perhaps not the new arsenal of presidential powers.

7

Congress and Foreign Policy

THE CONSTITUTION ASSIGNS BOTH Congress and the president important powers in the realm of foreign and military policy. Article I of the Constitution gives Congress the power to declare war, to raise armies, to regulate commerce with foreign nations, and, in the case of the Senate, the power to ratify treaties and concur in the appointment of ambassadors. It is Congress, moreover, that must appropriate the funds to pay for military and foreign policy initiatives. Over the decades, however, Congress's ability to contend with the executive in the foreign policy realm has gradually declined as presidents have used their power of initiative to marginalize the legislative branch.

Presidential power in the realm of foreign relations is derived from Article II of the Constitution. This article makes the president commander in chief of the nation's military forces and gives the chief executive the power to negotiate treaties, to recognize foreign emissaries, and to appoint ambassadors and consular officials.

In many instances, congressional and presidential powers seem to overlap. Where, for example, do the congressional powers to declare war and raise armies end and the president's powers as commander in chief begin? The Constitution, as legal historian Edward Corwin once observed, proffered to the Congress and the president "an invitation to struggle" for the power to control American foreign policy.[1]

One of America's first diplomats, John Jay, wrote in *Federalist* 64 that the president has a number of advantages in this struggle. The president, he noted, is a unitary actor, with better access to information and a greater capacity for secrecy and action than the Congress has. Over the course of more than two centuries, moreover, successive American presidents, beginning with George Washington, have labored diligently to make their office the dominant force in American foreign and security policy and to subordinate Congress's role in this realm. From the perspective of 2019, it seems they have succeeded.

Already in 1793, President Washington initially accepted and several months later demanded the recall of the French ambassador, Edmond-Charles "Citizen" Genêt. In both instances, Washington deliberately refrained from consulting Congress.[2] During the same year, Washington issued a proclamation of American neutrality when war broke out between Great Britain and France, again without congressional authorization.[3] In 1796, Washington refused to accede to congressional demands for documents relating to the negotiation of the Jay Treaty. Washington declared that in his judgment, the papers were "of a nature that did not permit disclosure at this time."[4] Indeed, Washington was so determined to establish the primacy of the presidency in the realm of foreign policy that he objected vigorously to something as minor as a 1792 House resolution congratulating the French on their new constitution. Though the resolution was no more than a rhetorical gesture, Washington complained to his secretary of state, Thomas Jefferson, that Congress was seeking to "invade the executive."[5]

As we saw earlier, in his Pacificus letters, Alexander Hamilton declared that making foreign policy was inherently an executive function. The Constitution, said Hamilton, granted presidents the power to take the initiative in the foreign policy realm[6] and to undertake actions based upon their own judgments of the national interest.[7]

The actions of subsequent presidents, from John Adams and Thomas Jefferson to George W. Bush and Barack Obama, have been consistent with Hamilton's vision of executive power. Thus, America's second president, John Adams, dispatched a peace commission to France in 1799 despite the opposition of Congress and even the disapproval of most his own cabinet members.[8] In a similar vein, America's third president, Thomas Jefferson, negotiated with France for the purchase of Louisiana and issued what today would be called an executive order consummating the bargain. Though Jefferson had previously condemned Hamilton's assertions of executive primacy in foreign affairs, as president Jefferson presented the Congress with a Hamiltonian fait accompli to which it gave its sullen acquiescence.[9]

Nearly two centuries later, in 1994, America's forty-second president, Bill

Clinton, issued executive orders that provided Mexico with a $43 billion package of loans, including support from the International Monetary Fund and the Bank for International Settlements, to prevent the total collapse of the Mexican peso.[10] Congress had already rejected Clinton's request for a Mexican loan package. The president, however, believed that a Mexican economic crash would be disastrous for American economic interests and acted accordingly. In the wake of terrorist attacks in New York and Washington, America's forty-third president, George W. Bush, issued executive orders in 2001 that unleashed America's military might against the Taliban regime in Afghanistan and Saddam Hussein's regime in Iraq, created secret military tribunals for the prosecution of suspected foreign terrorists, established a program of international and domestic surveillance by the National Security Agency, and froze billions of dollars in foreign assets in the United States. Congress was barely consulted regarding any of these matters. The Obama administration, while withdrawing American forces from Iraq and Afghanistan, continued using special operations forces and unmanned aerial vehicles (UAV), popularly known as drones, to attack suspected terrorists, and killed Al-Qaeda leader Osama bin Laden, among others.

For its part, as we shall see in chapter 9, the U.S. Supreme Court has generally supported presidents' Hamiltonian view of their role in foreign policy. Justice George Sutherland, citing John Marshall, declared in the landmark 1936 *Curtiss-Wright* case that the president was the "sole organ of the federal government in the field of international relations."[11] But while Congress nowadays usually defers to the president on foreign policy matters, it does not always give in to the chief executive. In 2015, for example, over President Obama's opposition, Congress invited Israeli Prime Minister Benjamin Netanyahu, a vehement foe of Obama's efforts to forge a nuclear arms treaty with Iran, to address a joint congressional session. Later, forty-seven Republican senators signed an open letter to the Iranian government designed to undercut Obama's negotiating stance.

A majority of the members of both houses of Congress opposed the agreement that President Obama eventually signed with the Iranian government. However, since the accord was an agreement rather than a treaty, Congress would have needed to muster a veto-proof two-thirds vote of both houses to override a certain presidential veto of a congressional resolution disapproving the agreement. This was an impossible hurdle. Had the Iran deal been presented as a treaty, it would have been defeated in the Senate, where it could not have won a two-thirds vote of approval. Soon after he took office, President Trump withdrew from the Iran agreement and renewed the sanctions that Obama had ended.

The Treaty Power

As these observations suggest, one of the constitutional pillars of congressional power in the realm of foreign policy is the *treaty power*. Article II, Section 2, of the Constitution provides that the president "shall have Power, by and with the advice and consent of the Senate, to make Treaties, provided two thirds of the senators present concur." The two-thirds requirement was designed to curb presidential power and to ensure that relations between the United States and other nations had broad support, not just the support of a plurality. Formally, the Senate votes on a resolution of ratification. If the resolution passes, actual ratification takes place when the United States and the other nation exchange instruments of ratification.

Since 1789, the Senate has approved more than fifteen hundred treaties while rejecting only twenty-one. Another eighty-five treaties were withdrawn because the Senate took no action on them. Of course, it is impossible to know how many potential agreements were never submitted by the president because Senate approval seemed unlikely. The most famous treaty rejected by the Senate was the Treaty of Versailles, rejected twice, in 1919 and 1920. The Versailles treaty was a multilateral agreement negotiated by President Wilson between the United States and a number of other nations, ending World War I and establishing the League of Nations. Senate isolationists opposed the league, and the administration was compelled to negotiate a number of separate treaties with the former belligerents, bringing a formal end to America's state of war with them. In 1999, the Senate also rejected a comprehensive nuclear test ban treaty negotiated by President Clinton.

Franklin Roosevelt regarded the treaty power as a constitutional error and often told his aides that the Senate's rejection of the Treaty of Versailles was one of the factors that led to World War II. Roosevelt seldom brought treaties to the Senate but relied instead on executive agreements. Some executive agreements are brought to Congress as though they were ordinary legislation requiring a majority in both houses, but many executive agreements, especially those involving national security, are simply signed by the president without congressional approval.

For obvious reasons, presidents would prefer never to bring international agreements to Congress but are limited by the fact that without congressional assent no executive agreement can supersede existing legislation. Executive agreements are enforceable by the courts but were traditionally seen as having less international authority and longevity than treaties, since they could be abrogated by the next president. This distinction, however, seems no longer valid, since the federal courts held in 1978 that the president could unilaterally abrogate even a treaty—in this case America's 1954 mutual defense treaty with Taiwan. Since presidents seem free to use executive agreements as they see fit, the importance of the Senate's constitutional treaty power has sharply diminished. Between 1947 and 2006, the United States has entered into more than seventeen thousand different agreements with other nations and international entities. Of these, only 6 percent were submitted to the Senate for approval. Many of these treaties concerned minor matters, presented to the Senate in the form of treaties precisely because presidents knew the matter at hand was too unimportant to spark Senate opposition—such as an international treaty protecting stolen art objects.[12]

Clearly, the presidential practice of negotiating agreements rather than treaties reduces congressional power in the diplomatic realm. Congress can easily refuse to ratify a treaty but finds it more difficult, albeit not impossible, to block an agreement. To stop the ongoing erosion of its constitutional treaty power, Congress might, of course, decide that it would not acquiesce in the use of agreements as a substitute for treaties. Such a course of action, which would enhance the power of Congress as an institution, would, however, also mean that a minority in the Senate could prevent actions that many members of Congress approved. To most members, abstract questions of institutional power and prerogative are usually less significant than concrete policy matters. To the president, of course, the two are one and the same. This is just one more example of the advantage that presidents derive from being unitary actors who do not suffer from collective-action problems.

Congress's General Legislative Powers as Tools of Foreign Relations

Despite continuing presidential efforts to monopolize foreign and security policy, from the time of the nation's founding, the Congress has also sought to play a major role in both areas. Indeed, writing in response to Hamilton's Pacificus letters, James Madison, using the pseudonym Helvidius, argued that the president's powers in foreign affairs were instrumental only. That is, it was Congress's constitutional role to determine the substance and direction of American foreign policy, while the task of the president was limited to implementing the will of the legislature.[13] The Constitution, as noted earlier, assigns the Congress specific powers in the realm of foreign affairs, including the power to declare war, the power to raise armies, and the power to regulate foreign commerce. On the basis of this constitutional authority, Congress has enacted numerous pieces of trade legislation; authorized the recruitment, training, and equipment of military forces; and, on at least one occasion—the War of 1812—declared war over the objections of the president. Not unlike presidents, Congress has occasionally sought to use its constitutionally mandated powers to claim additional powers as well. For example, when Congress declared war against Spain in 1897, it included recognition of the independence of Cuba in its resolution, even though President McKinley was opposed to recognition of the Cuban insurgent government.[14]

Through its general legislative powers, moreover, Congress can exercise broad influence over foreign policy. Congress may, for example, refuse to appropriate funds for presidential actions it deems to be unwise or inappropriate. Thus, in 1796, the House of Representatives was asked to appropriate funds to implement the Jay Treaty. Opponents of the treaty demanded that the House be given all papers and records pertaining to the negotiating process—a demand rejected by President Washington. The House narrowly approved funding but accompanied its acquiescence with a resolution affirming its right to refuse appropriations for the implementation of any treaty to which a majority of its members objected.[15] And on several occasions over the years, the House has indeed refused to appropriate funds needed to implement treaties negotiated by the president and ratified by the Senate.[16]

Congressional Committees in the Foreign Policy Realm

Presidents control several enormous bureaucracies through which to develop and implement foreign and security policies. These include the State and Defense Departments and a host of other agencies. Congress has far less bureaucratic capacity of its own but is not entirely without assets that can help it influence the nation's international and military programs. Chief among these are the House and Senate committees charged with overseeing foreign policy, military affairs, and the collection and analysis of intelligence.

The Senate Committee on Foreign Relations and
House Committee on Foreign Affairs

On the Senate side, the first, oldest, and most influential of these is the U.S. Senate Committee on Foreign Relations. The committee oversees the State Department, other foreign policy agencies, and executive branch compliance with several statutes, including the War Powers Resolution. The committee consists of eighteen members and was established in 1816 as one of the original ten standing committees of the Senate. The committee includes seven subcommittees, each with a regional or subject-matter jurisdiction.

Throughout its history, the Foreign Relations Committee has viewed its role as the guardian of congressional power in the foreign policy realm. The committee's official history notes, on the one hand, its close cooperation with successive secretaries of state. Indeed, twenty secretaries, from Henry Clay to John Kerry, had formerly served as committee members.[17]

At the same, time however, the committee's official history points with pride to its refusal to act as a "rubber stamp" for the programs of the executive branch. The power of the Foreign Relations Committee stems from its responsibility to confirm State Department officials and the fact that treaties proposed by the executive branch must be reviewed by the committee before they can be referred to the full Senate for a vote on ratification. In the nineteenth century, the committee so often turned back treaties negotiated by the president that it came to be known as the "graveyard of treaties." In 1919, as we saw earlier, President Woodrow Wilson submitted the proposed Treaty of Versailles to the Senate for ratification. The Foreign Relations Committee chairman, Senator Henry Cabot Lodge of Massachusetts, viewed the league as a threat to American sovereignty and insisted on adding a number of modifications to the treaty before reporting it to the Senate. Lodge added fourteen modifications to mock the "14 Points" Wilson had touted as America's war aims. Wilson declared, "Never, never! I'll never consent to adopt any policy with which that impossible man is so prominently identified."[18] The treaty was subsequently rejected by the Senate, and Wilson, who had made ratification the centerpiece of his postwar presidency, suffered a debilitating stroke.

Following this struggle, the committee's influence waned. During the 1930s, as the world moved toward another war, the committee was dominated by isolationists whose views were increasingly out of step with American interests. President Franklin D. Roosevelt usually ignored the committee and the Senate, endeavoring insofar as possible to conduct America's foreign relations via executive orders and executive agreements rather than formal treaties. FDR often pointed to the Senate's rejection of the Versailles treaty as a reason to avoid that body whenever possible. Years later, one of the leaders of the 1930s isolationists, Republican senator Arthur Vandenberg of Michigan, admitted his mistake when he declared, "I do not believe that any nation hereafter can immunize itself by its own executive action."[19] By 1947, Vandenberg, now chairman of the committee, had become a staunch advocate of a bipartisan and internationalist foreign policy and supported the Marshall Plan, the Truman Doctrine, and other elements of the Truman administration's foreign policy.

The committee's influence was at least briefly restored during the 1960s under the leadership of Senator J. William Fulbright of Arkansas. Fulbright was a prominent critic of American intervention in the Vietnam War, and, through well-publicized hearings, made the committee a center of opposition to President Johnson's war policies. In recent years, the committee's efforts to influence presidential foreign policy initiatives have been somewhat less successful, as presidents have followed the Roosevelt example and made use of executive agreements rather than treaties that would require senatorial approval. Thus, while members of the committee were sharply critical of the Obama administration's negotiations with Iran in 2015, the president generally ignored their comments. Nevertheless, the committee occasionally flexes its muscles. One example is its refusal for a number of years to report the proposed Law of the Sea Treaty to the full Senate for ratification. Eventually, the treaty, appropriately known as LOST, was reported to the Senate but lacked the two-thirds vote needed for ratification.

In addition to its role in the treaty process, the Foreign Relations Committee also considers presidential nominees for important foreign policy posts, including the position of secretary of state. In 2017, the committee held contentious hearings on President Trump's nomination of ExxonMobil executive Rex Tillerson for the post. Senate Democrats charged that Tillerson's business ties, especially with Russia, would represent conflicts of interest—a charge denied by the nominee. Eventually, Tillerson received the committee's endorsement and was confirmed by the full Senate.

As we saw in chapter 2, during the 1940s, congressional leaders were concerned that the enormous growth of the executive branch was outpacing Congress's ability to oversee the actions of the executive. Indeed, Congress itself was becoming increasingly dependent upon executive agencies to carry out its own work. The Foreign Relations Committee had come to rely upon the State Department for information, analyses, reports, and even members' speeches. The committee had little independent ability to intervene in the nation's foreign affairs.

The 1946 Legislative Reorganization Act provided professional staffs for the Senate's standing committees, including Foreign Relations. Today, the committee employs forty-five staffers, many experts in various aspects of international affairs. Its staff along with individual members' staffs gives the committee some capacity to independently assess the claims of the executive branch and to allow members to ask informed questions during hearings. In the case of the Iran nuclear negotiations, for example, committee members seemed well briefed on the details of uranium enrichment, balance-of-power politics, relevant statutes, and other pertinent matters. Armed with information, the committee could harass the president, though not necessarily affect the outcome.

Paralleling the jurisdiction of the Senate Foreign Relations Committee is the House Committee on Foreign Affairs. The House committee is considerably less influential than its Senate counterpart because it is involved neither in appointments nor in the ratification of treaties. For the most part, the House committee's hearings focus on symbolic questions. In 2015, for example, after holding hearings, the House committee adopted a nonbinding resolution condemning the mass killings of Armenian civilians by Turkish forces in 1915. The committee had adopted similar resolutions in the past, but none had ever reached the House floor. In the face of Turkish lobbying, the 2015 resolution was not brought before the full House.

In both houses of Congress, standing subcommittees of the appropriations committees are responsible for funding the State Department, foreign aid programs, and other matters in the foreign policy realm. Through these subcommittees as well as the Foreign Relations and Foreign Affairs Committees, the Senate and House can indicate their displeasure with presidential programs by cutting or withholding funds. In 2012, for example, Representative Kay Granger of Texas, who then chaired the House appropriations subcommittee dealing with foreign aid, used her position to block $450 million in aid to Egypt that had been requested by the Obama administration.[20]

Armed Services

A number of standing committees of the House and Senate deal with defense matters. The House and Senate Armed Services Committees oversee the Department of Defense and the Department of Energy (which houses America's nuclear weapons programs). The Armed Services Committees were created in 1946 from a merger between the Military and Naval Affairs committees that had been established in 1822. In both houses of Congress, other standing committees are responsible for such matters as veterans affairs, while defense appropriations are the domains of the House and Senate Appropriations Subcommittees on Defense.

Generally, the House and Senate Armed Services Committees are friendly to the military and to the legions of defense contractors who provide support and equipment for America's military services. Frequently, these committees are chaired by former military officers—John McCain chaired the Senate committee—and attract members whose states and districts are homes to defense industries and military bases. Both committees have generally viewed their missions as protecting military budgets from spending cuts and from rival budgetary claims from nondefense programs. Republican members, in particular, have come to view themselves as "the last line of defense," when it comes to protecting the Pentagon budget.[21] Members have been known to promote defense programs likely to result in contracts for corporations located in their home states and districts. The armed forces, understanding the political context, will usually rely on the subcontracting system to make certain that major weapons systems benefit the appropriate states and districts.

The two committees do not always limit themselves to supporting the military brass. However, when they are critical, the committees often express their criticism in the form of demanding more spending on one or another effort than is currently planned by the military. Thus, the committees will make use of their staff resources and contacts in the military community to advocate for military programs not currently in the Pentagon's plans. In 2015, for example, both committees released reports calling for the armed services to focus on the growing threat of cyber attacks against U.S. weapons and communications software and authorized the expenditure of $200 million for this purpose.[22]

House and Senate Intelligence Committees

The Foreign Relations Committees view themselves as both cooperating and competing with the executive branch, and the Armed Services committees have very cozy relations with their bureaucratic counterparts. The House Intelligence Committee and the Senate Select Committee on Intelligence, though, were born during an acrimonious struggle between Congress and the bureaucracies of the intelligence community, and the events that have taken place since that birth have only worsened the relationship.

In 1974, in the aftermath of the Watergate affair, the various surveillance activities conducted by the FBI, CIA, NSA, and other federal agencies came under the scrutiny of a number of congressional committees. Perhaps the most important of these was the Senate Select Committee to Study Governmental Operations with Respect to Intelligence Activities, chaired by the late senator Frank Church of Idaho. The Church committee identified a number of abuses associated with shadowy operations, code named COINTELPRO, Operation CHAOS, Project MINARET, and various other federal surveillance programs. The committee noted, moreover, that every president from Franklin Roosevelt to Richard Nixon had used illegal surveillance to secure information about his political opponents.

In its report, the committee found that numerous individuals had been subjected to surveillance and subsequent action based solely upon their political beliefs. The report declared, "Too many people have been spied upon by too many government agencies, and too much information has been collected. The government has often undertaken the secret surveillance of citizens on the basis of their political beliefs even when those beliefs posed no threat of violence or illegal acts on behalf of a hostile or foreign power."[23] Senator Church added: "Th[e National Security Agency's] capability at any time could be turned around on the American people and no American would have any privacy left, such [is] the capability to monitor everything: telephone conversations, telegrams, it doesn't matter. There would be no place to hide. . . . [I]f a dictator ever took [over, the NSA] . . . could enable it to impose total tyranny, and there would be no way to fight back."[24]

It is worth noting that when Senator Church expressed these fears in 1975,

NSA could read telegrams and listen to phone calls. Along with other security agencies, it might also open mail, but, in practice, only a tiny fraction of the hundreds of millions of letters sent each year could be examined. Thus Church's remarks embodied a bit of exaggeration at the time. The advent of e-mail and social media, however, greatly enhanced the volume of information available to federal agencies and made the senator's comments more prescient.

In response to the Church committee's report, Congress enacted the Foreign Intelligence Surveillance Act (FISA) and established select committees on intelligence in both houses. A select committee is a permanent committee but one in which membership is temporary and rotated among members of the chamber. This process is, among other things, designed to spread a workload that is not seen as contributing to members' personal political needs. Rotation, moreover, is seen as preventing the development of cozy relationships between committee members and government officials. The committees review the president's intelligence budget and the performance of the several civilian and military agencies that make up the intelligence community. These include the Central Intelligence Agency, National Security Agency, Defense Intelligence Agency (DIA), and so forth. The committees also monitor compliance with FISA and several other pieces of legislation.

The FISA Act stipulated that in order to undertake electronic surveillance of Americans, the government would be required to apply for a warrant from a special court created by the statute. This was called the Foreign Intelligence Surveillance Court and initially consisted of seven federal district court judges appointed for seven-year terms by the chief justice of the United States. In 2001, the FISA Court was expanded to eleven judges. A second court created by the act, the FISA Court of Review, consisted of a three-judge panel empowered to hear appeals by the government from negative decisions by the FISA Court. In practice, the Court of Review has been relatively quiescent since the government has had reason to appeal only a handful of the FISA Court's decisions. Both the FISA Court and Court of Review deliberate in secret, and the content of their decisions is not made public.

In 2008 Congress placed restrictions on the power of the NSA and other intelligence agencies to target Americans. Between 2008 and 2013, the government insisted that it was not engaged in spying on Americans either at home or abroad. In March 2013, for example, James Clapper, the director of national intelligence, testifying before the Senate, indignantly denied reports that the government was collecting data on millions of Americans. Similarly, the NSA director, General Keith Alexander, denied charges by a former NSA official that the agency was secretly obtaining warrantless access to billions of records of Americans' phone calls and storing the information in its data centers. General Alexander declared that doing such a thing would be against the law.[25] Later, leaked documents suggested that both Clapper and Alexander had attempted to mislead Congress in their testimony.

As this example suggests, the two intelligence committees have had a great deal of difficulty obtaining accurate and truthful information from the intelligence community. In the Intelligence Oversight Act of 1980, Congress explicitly required the president to keep congressional intelligence committees fully and currently informed of all intelligence activities. The act also requires the director of national intelligence to provide any information required by these committees, "consistent with the protection of sources and methods." Congress has taken this phrase to mean that classified information will be given only to members of the intelligence committees and that staff members of those committees must possess requisite security clearances to receive classified information.

Since 1980, intelligence agencies have briefed the congressional intelligence committees on many of their undertakings. There is, however, reason to be concerned about the accuracy of the information given to Congress. For example, in March 2013, while testifying before the Senate Intelligence Committee, national intelligence director James Clapper responded to a question by saying that the NSA was not "wittingly" collecting information on millions of Americans. Subsequent revelations revealed that Clapper's testimony was disingenuous. To this, Clapper replied, "I responded in what I thought was the most truthful or least untruthful manner by saying, No."[26]

Leaving aside the question of veracity, some members of Congress have complained that intelligence briefings are usually filled with jargon and designed to be confusing. Because of security restrictions, moreover, members are usually barred from consulting expert advisers who might challenge or at least more fully explain the programs being discussed. And by failing to disclose significant information in the first place, intelligence agencies make it difficult for members of Congress to ask questions or request briefings. President Obama, for example, averred that any member of Congress could have asked for a briefing on a top-secret program code-named PRISM. This claim, however, seems a bit dubious. "How can you ask when you don't know the program exists?" asked Senator Susan Collins of Maine, speaking on National Public Radio.[27]

In 2015, Congress enacted legislation to end some NSA data-collection activities. Many members, however, were concerned that the legislation would be ineffective and that, as Senator Collins feared, Congress and its intelligence committees would continue to be unable to secure information about programs whose existence they were unaware of.

Congressional versus Presidential War Powers

American foreign policy has many facets, including trade policy and diplomacy. In these realms, Congress, particularly working through the Senate Foreign Relations Committee, the House Foreign Affairs Committee, and the relevant appropriations subcommittees, can exercise considerable influence. Unfortunately, however, throughout the nation's history, war and military affairs have been central foci of American foreign policy. Though the United States has fought only five formally declared wars, American armed forces have been involved in hundreds of military actions and "small wars" in every corner of the world.[28] One of America's first small wars, the 1801 naval campaign against the Barbary States, involved a handful of ships and generated few casualties. Other so-called small wars have been quite large. American military action in Korea and Vietnam required the mobilization of hundreds of thousands of troops and resulted in tens of thousands of casualties.

Whether declared or undeclared, large or small, war has been the crucible of presidential power. In wartime, Congress has generally deferred to the president's leadership. Indeed, Congress has often granted presidents significant emergency powers and acceded to presidential claims of authority under the Constitution's Commander in Chief Clause which seemed to be justified by urgent wartime conditions.

Presidential Power, Congressional Power, and the Cold War

The Cold War had an enormous impact upon the balance of power between the president and Congress. For more than forty years, the United States faced a dire military threat requiring the creation and permanent maintenance of powerful military forces ready to respond to attack almost literally at a moment's notice. Indeed, the Cold War blurred the distinction between wartime and peace-time. Against the backdrop of the dangers facing the nation, successive Cold War and post–Cold War presidents were able to expand the power of the exec-utive branch and affirm their own preeminence in security and foreign affairs. For the most part, in the face of what it perceived to be an existential threat from the Soviet Union, Congress acceded to presidential demands, as it always had during wartime. Senator J. William Fulbright, who was later to become a major critic of presidential war power, said in 1961, "As Commander-in-Chief of the armed forces, the president has full responsibility, which cannot be shared, for military decisions in a world in which the difference between safety and cataclysm can be a matter of hours or even minutes."[29] Despite congressional deference, successive presidents did not place much trust in Congress or the democratic political process. Instead, they sought to use the dangers facing the nation as a justification for building a set of institutions and procedures that would insulate presidential decision-making in the realm of security and foreign policy from public scrutiny and congressional intervention.

More than any other single factor, the construction of a national security bu-reaucracy within the Executive Office of the President made possible the enor-mous postwar expansion of presidential unilateralism in the realm of security and foreign policy. Beginning with Truman, presidents would conduct foreign and security policy through executive agreements and executive orders and sel-dom negotiate formal treaties requiring Senate ratification. Presidents before Truman—even Franklin D. Roosevelt—had generally submitted important ac-cords between the United States and foreign powers to the Senate for ratifica-tion and had sometimes seen their goals stymied by senatorial opposition. Not only did the Constitution require senatorial confirmation of treaties, but before Truman presidents had lacked the administrative resources to systematically conduct an independent foreign policy. It was not by accident that most of the agreements—particularly the secret agreements—negotiated by FDR concerned military matters for which the president could rely upon the administrative ca-pacities of the War and Navy Departments.[30]

The State Department's policy-planning staff and, especially, the NSC staff created the institutional foundations and capabilities upon which Truman and his successors could rely to conduct and administer the nation's foreign and secu-rity policies directly from the Oval Office. For example, American participation in the International Trade Organization (ITO), one of the cornerstones of U.S.

postwar trade policy, was based on a sole executive agreement, the GATT Protocol of Provisional Application (PPA), signed by President Truman after Congress delayed action and ultimately failed to approve the ITO charter.[31] Truman signed some thirteen hundred executive agreements, and Eisenhower another eighteen hundred, in some cases requesting congressional approval and in other instances ignoring the Congress. Executive agreements take two forms: congressional-executive agreements and sole executive agreements. In the former case, the president submits the agreement to both houses of Congress as he would any other piece of legislation, with a majority vote in both houses required for passage. This is a lower hurdle than the two-thirds vote required for Senate ratification of a treaty.

A sole executive agreement is not sent to the Congress at all. The president generally has discretion over which avenue to pursue. All treaties and executive agreements have the power of law, though a sole executive agreement cannot contravene an existing statute, which somewhat limits its value to the White House.[32] Since the Truman and Eisenhower presidencies, few treaties have been submitted to the Senate, as stipulated by Article II of the Constitution.[33] Indeed, two of the most important recent international agreements entered into by the United States—the North American Free Trade Agreement (NAFTA) and the World Trade Organization agreements—were confirmed by congressional executive agreement, not by treaty.[34] As discussed earlier, the potentially very important presidential deal with Iran in 2015 was sent to Congress as an agreement rather than a treaty, as the latter would have had no chance of ratification. In 2018, President Trump renegotiated NAFTA to obtain more favorable terms from Mexico and Canada and submitted the new agreement, the United States–Mexico–Canada Agreement (USMCA), to Congress.

In a similar vein, the policy-planning staff and NSC opened the way for policy-making by executive order in the areas of security and foreign policy. Executive orders issued to implement presidents' security policy goals have been variously called National Security Presidential Directives (NSPD) and National Security Decision Directives (NSDD) but are most commonly known as National Security Directives, or NSDs. These, like other executive orders, are commands from the president to an executive agency.[35] Most NSDs are classified, and presidents have consistently refused even to inform Congress of their existence, much less their content. Generally, NSDs are drafted by the NSC staff at the president's behest. Some NSDs have involved mundane matters, but others have established America's most significant foreign policies and security postures. NSC 68, developed by the State Department's policy- planning staff prior to the creation of an NSC staff, set forward the basic principles of containment upon which American Cold War policy came to be based. A series of Kennedy NSDs established the basic principles of American policy toward a number of world trouble spots.[36] Ronald Reagan's NSD 12 launched the president's massive military buildup and force-modernization program, while his NSD 172 began the development of antimissile programs. Thus, the creation of new administrative capabilities gave presidents the tools through which to dominate foreign and security policy and to dispense with Congress and what President Roosevelt had called its "incompetent obstructionists."[37]

Vietnam

The decline of congressional power in the realm of foreign and security policy, however, seemed for a time to be halted and even reversed by the clash between Congress and President Lyndon Johnson over the Vietnam War and, later, the Watergate struggle between Congress and President Richard Nixon. Unlike the war in Korea, the Vietnam War sparked enormous opposition in the American public and in the Congress. While this opposition had a number of sources, one aspect of the problem was economic. By the late 1960s, America no longer possessed the dominant position in the world economy that it had enjoyed during the previous decade. It would not be so easy for a president to produce both guns and butter. America's allies had no interest in helping to defray the costs of the war. And, to make matters worse, a powerful domestic constituency, the liberal wing of the president's own political party, was deeply committed to a set of enormously expensive social programs that President Johnson had himself defined as the nation's top priority. Diversion of funds from the president's Great Society programs to pay for the war generated enormous opposition. Later, changes in draft rules made politically potent constituencies more vulnerable to conscription and intensified their opposition to the war. The result was to drive Johnson from office and to compel his successor, Richard Nixon, to withdraw American forces under circumstances that made the victory of Communist forces, led by Ho Chi Minh, all but inevitable.

The end of the Vietnam War represented not only a military defeat for the United States but also a defeat for the presidency. In the aftermath of the war and, in particular, after the disintegration and eventual collapse of the Nixon administration, Congress seized the opportunity to enact a number of pieces of legislation designed to curb presidential power in the foreign policy and security domains. These included the 1972 Case-Zablocki Act, requiring that Congress be informed of all executive agreements; the 1973 War Powers Resolution, to limit presidential control over the deployment of American military forces; the 1974 Hughes-Ryan Amendment, to regulate foreign military assistance; the 1976 National Emergencies Act, to regulate the exercise of presidential emergency power; the Foreign Intelligence Surveillance Act of 1978 and the Intelligence Oversight Act of 1980, to provide for congressional oversight of intelligence operations; and the 1976 Arms Export Control Act, to limit presidential use of proxy forces. Congress also created intelligence oversight committees to monitor the president's use of the nation's intelligence agencies. It appeared that the classic pattern of presidential politics had reasserted itself. Political mobilization induced by war had strengthened the Congress and weakened the presidency.

The post-Vietnam retrogression of presidential power, however, proved to be short-lived. Johnson's successors took a number of steps that, within less than two decades after the last American troops were evacuated from Saigon, had more than restored presidential power in war and foreign relations. The most important of these steps involved the recruitment and internal structure of the military and its relationship to American society. For two centuries, America had relied upon citizen soldiers to fill the ranks of its armed forces and spurned the idea of a professional army as being inconsistent with democratic values. In the wake of the Vietnam War, however, presidents and military planners realized that dependence upon citizen soldiers could impose serious constraints upon the use of military forces. The risks facing citizen soldiers provided opponents of the use of military force on any given occasion with a potent issue to use against the government. The casualties and hardships borne by citizen soldiers, moreover, reverberated through society and might, as the Vietnam case illustrated, fuel antiwar movements and resistance to military conscription. University of Chicago economist Milton Friedman, who served as a member of the Gates Commission, created by President Nixon to examine the elimination of military conscription, argued that three-fourths of the opposition to the Vietnam War was generated by the draft.[38] Citizen soldiers might be appropriate for a national war in which America was attacked and domestic opposition driven to the margins. Anti–Vietnam War protests, however, convinced President Richard Nixon and his successors that an army composed of professional soldiers would give them greater flexibility to use military power when they deemed it necessary.[39] Accordingly, Nixon ended the draft in 1973 and began conversion of the military into an all-volunteer force of professional soldiers. The presumption was that sending military professionals into battle would spawn less popular and political resistance than deploying reluctant conscripts, and this supposition seems to have been borne out. Indeed, in 2002, some opponents of President George W. Bush's buildup of American forces for an attack against Iraq argued for a renewal of conscription precisely because they believed that the president would be constrained from going to war if the military consisted of draftees.[40] Members of a professional force, moreover, especially those recruited for its elite combat units, receive extensive training and indoctrination designed to separate them from civilian society, to imbue them with a warrior ethic emphasizing loyalty to the group and organization as primary values, and to reduce their level of integration into the larger society.[41] This training is designed to immunize the military against possible contagion from antiwar and defeatist sentiments that may spring up in civilian America and appears to have produced a military, especially an officer corps, that views itself as a distinct caste.[42]

In the aftermath of Vietnam, the military was not only professionalized, it was also further centralized. The 1986 Goldwater-Nichols Department of Defense Reorganization Act significantly increased the power of the Joint Chiefs of Staff (JCS) chairman, the defense secretary, and the president to determine military missions and set procurement policies.[43] This change not only promised to improve military effectiveness but also further reduced the opportunity for the individual services to publicly air their squabbles and open the way for congressional intervention. This had been a continuing, albeit muted, problem since the struggles of the Truman era and had broken out anew during the Vietnam War when the army publicly accused the air force of failing to provide adequate close air support for its ground combat troops.[44]

From Vietnam to Afghanistan and Beyond

Subsequent presidents, most notably Ronald Reagan and George H. W. Bush, worked to break the legal fetters through which Congress had sought to constrain presidential war-making. Some of these fetters proved illusory. For example, the 1980 Intelligence Oversight Act lacked sanctions or penalties and seemed to assume that the president would cooperate with Congress.[45] No subsequent president, however, showed any intention of cooperating, and, indeed, beginning with President Reagan, the White House interpreted the act as authorizing the executive to conduct covert operations.[46]

Other fetters were removed by the courts. For example, Congress had drafted the 1976 National Emergencies Act to narrow the president's emergency powers and attached a legislative veto provision to ensure its ability to control presidential actions under the act. The legislative veto is a procedure allowing Congress to overturn a president's specific use of a power that has been granted by Congress. The U.S. Supreme Court, however, in the 1981 case of *Dames & Moore v. Regan,* stemming from President Carter's handling of the Iranian hostage crisis, construed the president's emergency powers broadly.[47] And in the 1983 case of *INS* [Immigration and Naturalization Service] *v. Chadha,* the Court invalidated legislative veto provisions.[48] The result was to leave the president with broader emergency powers and less congressional control than Congress had hoped, though Congress can still end a presidentially declared emergency by a congressional joint resolution, which, of course, is still subject to presidential veto.[49]

A third presidential fetter was broken by aggressive presidential action beginning in the early Reagan years. The 1973 War Powers Resolution provided that presidents could not use military forces for more than ninety days without securing congressional authorization. Many in Congress saw this time limit as a restraint on presidential action, though, as has often been observed, it gave the president more discretion than had been provided by the framers of the Constitution. President Gerald Ford had carefully followed the letter of the law when organizing a military effort to rescue American sailors held by North Korea. But this was the first and last time that the War Powers Resolution was fully observed.[50] The demise of the act began during the Reagan administration. President Reagan and his advisers were determined to eliminate this restriction, however negligible, on presidential war power.[51] Accordingly, between 1982 and 1986, Reagan presented Congress with a set of military faits accomplis that undermined the War Powers Resolution and, in effect, asserted a doctrine of sole presidential authority in the security realm. In August 1982, Reagan sent U.S. forces to Lebanon, claiming a constitutional authority to do so.[52] After terrorist attacks killed a number of marines, Congress pressed Reagan to withdraw American forces. To underscore its displeasure, Congress activated the sixty-day War Powers Resolution clock, but after the administration accused lawmakers of undermining America's military efforts, Congress extended the president's authority to deploy troops to Lebanon for another eighteen months.

The president essentially ignored Congress but withdrew American forces in February after further casualties and no prospect for success. In October 1983, while American forces were still in Lebanon, President Reagan ordered an invasion of the Caribbean island of Grenada after a coup had led to the installation of a pro-Cuban government on the island. Once again, the president claimed that his position as commander in chief gave him the power to initiate military action on a unilateral basis. Congress threatened to invoke the War Powers Resolution, but Reagan withdrew American troops before the Senate acted. The invasion of Grenada was quick, virtually without casualties, and quite popular, especially after the president claimed to have rescued a group of American medical students attending classes on the island. Also generating considerable popular approval was the 1986 bombing of Libya in response to a terrorist attack in Berlin, which the administration blamed on Libyan agents. Again, Reagan acted without consulting Congress and claimed that his authority had come directly from the Constitution.

President Reagan was thus able to use American military forces on three separate occasions while denying that he was required to seek congressional authorization for his actions. Congress threatened and grumbled, but in each instance was outmaneuvered by the president. Of course, in 1987 several of the president's aides were prosecuted for violations of federal law when it was revealed that the administration had transferred arms to Nicaraguan Contra guerrillas then fighting against the Sandinista regime in that nation, despite specific congressional prohibitions. Nevertheless, Reagan's successor, George H. W. Bush, resumed using American military forces on his authority as commander in chief. In December 1989, Bush ordered an invasion of Panama designed to oust Panamanian strongman General Manuel Noriega. Bush claimed that American citizens living in the Canal Zone were in danger and charged that Noriega had become involved in drug trafficking. Since drugs are shipped to the United States from many nations, often with the connivance of high-ranking officials, this seemed a rather flimsy pretext. Congress, nevertheless, made no official response to the invasion. A nonbinding House resolution expressed its approval of the president's actions but urged Bush not to use drug smuggling as a reason to invade Mexico or the remainder of Latin America.[53]

In 1990–1991, of course, the Bush administration sent a huge American military force into the Persian Gulf in response to Iraq's invasion and occupation of Kuwait, actions that posed a substantial threat to American economic and political interests. Consistent with the tactics devised by Harry Truman, the administration quickly secured a UN Security Council resolution authorizing member states to use "all necessary means," that is, military force, to compel Iraq to restore Kuwaiti independence. The president's spokespersons, defense secretary Richard Cheney, in particular, asserted that the UN resolution was a sufficient legal basis for American military action against Iraq. Given the UN resolution, said Cheney, no congressional authorization was required.[54] After House Democrats expressed strong opposition to unilateral action by the president, Bush asked Congress for legislation supporting the UN resolution. Both houses of Congress voted to authorize military action against Iraq—the Senate by the narrowest of margins—but the president made it clear that he did not feel bound by any congressional declaration and was prepared to go to war with or without Congress's assent. Indeed, the president later pointed out that he had specifically avoided asking Capitol Hill for "authorization" since such a request might improperly imply that Congress, "had the final say in . . . an executive decision.[55]

President Clinton continued the Truman and Bush practice of securing authorization to use military force from a compliant international body and then presenting Congress with a fait accompli. Thus in 1994 he planned an invasion of Haiti under the cover of a UN Security Council resolution. The president hoped to oust the military dictatorship that had seized power in a coup and to reinstall President Jean-Bertrand Aristide. Congress expressed strong opposition to Clinton's plans, but he pressed forward nonetheless, claiming that he did not need congressional approval. The invasion was called off when the Haitian junta stepped down, but Clinton sent ten thousand American troops to occupy the island and help Aristide secure power. Congress was not consulted about the matter. In a similar vein, between 1994 and 1998, claiming to act under UN and NATO auspices, the administration undertook a variety of military actions in the former Yugoslavia, including an intensive bombing campaign directed against Serbian forces and installations, without formal congressional authorization. The air campaign lasted some seventy-nine days, involved more than thirty thousand American troops and more than eight hundred aircraft, and was conducted exclusively on the president's own authority.[56] The War Powers Resolution seemed to have entered the same legal limbo as state laws prohibiting lascivious carriage.

By the end of the Clinton administration, it was no longer clear what war powers, if any, remained in the hands of the Congress. Ronald Reagan, George H. W. Bush, and Bill Clinton had all ordered American forces into combat on their own authority; outmaneuvered, bullied, or ignored the Congress; and repeatedly asserted the principle that the president controlled security policy and, especially, the use of military force. Early in the administration of President George W. Bush, Islamic terrorists destroyed the World Trade Center and damaged the Pentagon. The president organized a major military campaign designed to eliminate terrorist bases in Afghanistan and to depose the Taliban regime that sheltered the terrorists. Congress, for its part, quickly passed a joint resolution authorizing the president to use all necessary and appropriate force to prevent future acts of terrorism. This resolution continues to be cited by presidents as the legal basis for their various military actions. For example, the Obama administration launched hundreds of drone attacks against suspected terrorists without ever consulting Congress about the propriety of the missions. When pressed, the administration pointed to the 2001 resolution as the legal basis for its power. The Trump administration has continued drone attacks, but this has become so commonplace that the policy is hardly questioned by Congress.

The 2001 congressional resolution was little more than a blank check, barely mentioned by the press and ignored by the public. Both were by then fully aware that whatever its rhetoric, Congress had very little real control over the use of American military might. Subsequently, President Bush issued a variety of executive orders establishing military tribunals to try suspected terrorists, freezing the assets of those suspected of assisting terrorists, and expanding the authority of the CIA and other intelligence agencies.

Congress was not completely quiescent. Within a month of the terrorist attacks, the White House had drafted and Congress had quickly enacted the USA PATRIOT Act, expanding the power of government agencies to engage in domestic surveillance activities, including electronic surveillance, and restricted judicial review of such efforts. The act also gave the attorney general greater authority to detain and deport aliens suspected of having terrorist affiliations.[57] The following year, Congress created the Department of Homeland Security, combining offices from twenty-two federal agencies into one huge new cabinet department that would be responsible for protecting the nation from further acts of terrorism. The new agency, with a tentative budget of $40 billion, was to include the U.S. Coast Guard, Transportation Security Administration, Federal Emergency Management Agency, Immigration and Naturalization Service (renamed Immigration and Customs Enforcement, or ICE), and offices from the Departments of Agriculture, Energy, Transportation, Justice, Health and Human Services, and Commerce, and the General Services Administration. The actual reorganization plan was drafted by the White House, but Congress weighed in to make certain that the new agency's workers would enjoy civil service and union protections.

It should also be mentioned that in October 2002, Congress voted to authorize the president to attack Iraq, which the administration accused of supporting terrorism and constructing weapons of mass destruction. As had become customary, the congressional resolution gave the president complete discretion, and the president, while welcoming congressional support, asserted that he had full power to use force with or without Congress's blessing. Only the late senator Byrd, who took congressional power seriously, even bothered to object to the now obvious political if not constitutional truth of Bush's claim. In a reversal of the usual pattern, however, the president used his congressional resolution to pressure the United Nations Security Council to approve the use of force. Without such a resolution, an attack on Iraq would appear politically less legitimate, and, more important, some of the nations expected to bankroll the war might well refuse, fearing their own domestic political repercussions.

The Security Council, though, stopped short of the authorization sought by President Bush, agreeing only to return UN weapons inspectors who had been ousted from Iraq some years earlier. Members of the council, especially France and Russia, argued that Iraq should be given an opportunity to disarm before being attacked. While the inspectors shuffled rather aimlessly around the suburbs of Baghdad, the president mobilized land, sea, and air forces in preparation for a military assault. And once again American diplomats worked to build a coalition. The president called it a "coalition of the willing," and said different nations would play different roles in it according to their abilities. Presumably, this meant that the British were expected to provide military support, while Kuwait and Qatar, among others, were expected to provide bases for American forces.

After his election in 2008, President Obama brought an end to the wars in Iraq and Afghanistan, but not to the president's power to wage war. The administration authorized scores of special operations and drone strikes against suspected terrorists. Some of these strikes have involved the execution of U.S. citizens suspected of terrorist activities. In 2011, for example, a drone strike in Yemen killed Anwar al-Awlaki, a U.S. citizen and imam of a Virginia mosque suspected of being a senior Al-Qaeda recruiter. The administration had allegedly placed al-Awlaki's name on a CIA "target list" and obtained a Justice Department memorandum authorizing the killing. Several months later, another drone strike killed al-Awlaki's sixteen-year-old son, also a U.S. citizen born in Denver. The CIA and military have also been authorized to launch what are sometimes called "signature strikes." These are drone attacks against groups or individuals whose identities are unknown but whose activities seem suspicious to the drone operator. These strikes inevitably cause civilian casualties because it is often impossible to distinguish terrorist actions from innocent civilian activities. A group of persons loading fertilizer onto a pickup truck may be terrorists building bombs or farmers planting crops. Like its predecessors, the Obama administration resisted congressional efforts to look into its uses of military power.

Where Do Presidential War Powers End and Those of Congress Begin?

Franklin D. Roosevelt is often credited with the creation of the modern presidency. And, indeed, during the Great Depression and the Second World War, FDR greatly expanded the executive branch and increased the powers of the Oval Office. In the realm of foreign and security policy, however, it was Harry S. Truman who laid the foundations for presidential supremacy. Roosevelt had been a wartime president who made use of his personal dynamism and political skill to fashion a series of ad hoc arrangements to control the national security arena. Truman, however, built the institutions and invented the procedures that allowed a rather inexperienced legislator from Missouri and his successors of varying abilities, backgrounds, and political persuasions to manage the foreign and security policies of what became a great imperial power. Through the mix of military and civil institutions developed during the Truman era, the United States contained the Soviet Union and ultimately prevailed in the Cold War. Through these same institutions, though, the presidency came to dominate the realm of national security, while the Congress was gradually pushed into the background.

Increased presidential control of security policy has had implications for presidential power in domestic affairs as well. Since the Civil War, presidents have demanded and received the power to regulate civilian production in wartime. Since the early years of the Cold War, moreover, military contracts have been a major factor shaping domestic industrial production and priorities. But presidential national security powers unavoidably impinge upon domestic matters, going far beyond the economic realm.

This has become especially evident since the initiation of President Bush's War on Terror. The PATRIOT Act and the Homeland Security Department have suddenly brought the president's national security powers home, much as the loyalty and security classification systems of the Cold War era once did.[58] As we saw, the PATRIOT Act, coupled with executive orders, has given the NSA the power to eavesdrop on every American and has enhanced the authority of the Justice Department to launch investigations, to obtain warrants for wiretaps, and to seize tainted assets. These powers have already been employed in a number of cases having no relationship whatsoever to terrorism.[59] And since the threat of terror is not likely to end in the foreseeable future, the War on Terror promises to become as permanent a part of American political life as the Cold War was for so many years. As the distinction between foreign policy and domestic policy diminishes, the president's growing foreign policy powers are certain to take on ever greater domestic importance while those of Congress are likely to wane.

8

Congress and the Bureaucracy:
Who Makes the Law?

FOR MUCH OF ITS HISTORY, AMERICA was known as a "stateless society." That is, the federal government was relatively small, most governmental activity was in the hands of states and localities, and Americans were governed more by the laws of the marketplace than by those of the Congress. The power of the federal government grew, mainly as a result of international threats and economic crises that required collective responses. The end of a crisis usually led to a reduction in the size of government, but never back to its pre-crisis level. Crisis has a ratcheting-up effect on government.[1] Moreover, once established, government agencies tend to sink their taproots into the political economy, providing services and benefits for some set of interests, who will then mobilize to defend "their" agency.[2] This is especially true in the case of the clientele agencies, whose benefits are concentrated but whose costs are diffused throughout the economy. For example, the Commerce Department is viewed by many in Washington as a do-nothing agency, but its friends in the business community are willing to protect it from attack to preserve the bit of largesse the agency is able to distribute. Individual programs, to be sure, are sometimes less durable.[3] Its vast organizational structure gives the executive branch much of its advantage over Congress when it comes to governance.

Ronald Reagan and George H. W. Bush both proclaimed their dedication to cutting the size of government, but neither was able to eliminate even one agency or bureau in their combined twelve years in office. During the 2012 Republican presidential debates, all the prospective presidential candidates proclaimed their desire to cut the size of the government. One candidate, Texas governor Rick

Perry, said he would eliminate three federal agencies. When pressed, however, Perry was unable to recall which agencies would be closed. Many Americans say they hate government but appear to want its services. In 2016, President-elect Trump promised to "drain the swamp" and rid America of as many as 20 percent of its bureaucrats. While some cheered this idea, many were not so certain. During the 1995 and 2013 "government shutdowns" prompted by struggles between Congress and the president over taxes and deficits, most Americans were concerned that government services would not be delivered. Few cheered the end of government.

As they carry out their assigned tasks, executive agencies engage in a host of activities, from the most mundane to the most dangerous and controversial. Agencies conduct studies, publish reports, grant contracts, audit transactions, and identify violations of the law. Some agencies operate spy satellites, intercept communications, and send military forces against those who have been declared by the president to pose threats to the United States.

Congressional Oversight

Since the first years of the Republic, Congress has viewed oversight of the executive branch to be among its chief functions. Oversight is not mentioned in the Constitution but is an implied power of Congress. Congress, at least, believes that the power to make the law implies the power to oversee its implementation. In the earliest years, members of Congress conducted oversight on an individual basis, visiting agencies in which they had an interest and demanding to speak to officials. Often, these visits involved efforts to secure jobs for constituents or to voice constituent complaints about the performance of the agency. Today, members of Congress do not barge into federal offices, but they do send letters to executive branch officials making complaints and comments and seeking information.

Contemporary oversight is conducted by congressional committees rather than individuals. In both the House and Senate, oversight is conducted by authorizing committees, appropriations committees, and various subcommittees as well as the House Oversight and Government Reform Committee and the Senate Homeland Security and Governmental Affairs Committee, which have broad oversight powers. At these hearings, almost always open to the public, agency executives are called to testify along with representatives of interest groups, trade associations, consumer groups, and others with a stake in the matter at hand. Members of the committee or subcommittee pose questions and sometimes engage in prolonged discussions with witnesses and agency officials. Wednesday, June 17, 2015, was a typical day on Capitol Hill, with several oversight hearings scheduled in addition to confirmation hearings and a variety of legislative hearings:

Oversight Hearings, Wednesday, June 17, 2015
Senate Committee on Environment and Public Works
An oversight hearing to examine the Environmental Protection Agency's final rule to regulate disposal of coal combustion residuals from electric utilities.
Location: Dirksen Senate Office Building, Room 406
9:30 a.m.

Senate Committee on Commerce, Science, and Transportation: Subcommittee on Consumer Protection, Product Safety, Insurance, and Data Security
An oversight hearing to examine the Consumer Product Safety Commission.
Location: Russell Senate Office Building, Room 253
10:00 a.m.

Senate Committee on Indian Affairs
An oversight hearing to examine accessing capital in Indian Country.
Location: Dirksen Senate Office Building, Room 638
10:00 a.m.

House Committee on Science, Space, and Technology
Subcommittee on Energy meets regarding Department of Energy Oversight: Energy Innovation Hubs
Location: Rayburn House Office Building, Room 2318
11:00 a.m.[4]

Typically, hearings are called when members hear concerns from constituent groups about the practices of one or another federal agency. As we observed in chapter 6, this is sometimes called "fire alarm" oversight. As a result of oversight hearings, Congress may recommend changes to agency executives or develop legislation to change an agency's statutory obligations. After securing the

House in the 2018 midterm election, Democrats in the new Congress are expected to greatly increase the number of oversight hearings. Many see this as the appropriate checking between the branches intended by the Founding Fathers and a benefit of divided government. As we saw in chapter 4, Congress also relies heavily on its watchdog agency, the GAO, to bring issues to its attention and to conduct audits and investigations into problematic agency practices.

In addition to oversight hearings, as was also discussed in chapter 6, committees may schedule investigative hearings. The difference between the two is that investigative hearings are organized to look into charges of potentially criminal wrongdoing by executive officials. For these types of hearings, witnesses may be subpoenaed and a criminal proceeding may accompany or follow from the congressional inquiry. Investigative hearings are often outgrowths of intense partisan battles or struggles between Congress and the White House. For example, during the postwar period, conservatives in both houses of Congress launched major attacks on the executive branch in the form of investigations designed to demonstrate that executive agencies had been penetrated by Communist agents. Joseph McCarthy's Senate investigative committee as well as the House Un-American Activities Committee (HUAC) charged that Communist spies had penetrated federal agencies. ranging from sensitive positions in the State Department through mundane posts in the Commerce Department. The ultimate target of these investigations was the presidency itself. Some radical critics of the White House asserted that Roosevelt had "sold out" to the Communists during the Yalta Conference and that Truman had acquiesced in the appointment of "one-worlders" and Communist sympathizers to high government positions. McCarthy implied that these presidents had been part of an immense conspiracy—"an infamy so black as to dwarf any previous such venture in the history of man"—to undermine the nation.[5]

In later decades, Democrats and Republicans traded blows with the Watergate, Iran-Contra, and Whitewater investigations, as well as, more recently, the special counsel probe of possible collusion between the Trump campaign and the Russians during the 2016 campaign. Legislative investigations place the White House on the defensive, forcing it to devote energy and resources to answer a constantly expanding array of charges. The McCarthy investigations, for example, led, according to political scientist Wilfred Binkley, to a "gravitation of power into the hands of Congress, at the expense of the executive."[6] Such a "gravitation" often tends to be evanescent unless Congress follows up with statutory changes calculated to take advantage of the executive's discomfiture to institutionalize the temporary gravitation of power. Following the Watergate investigations, Congress did enact several pieces of legislation, including the War Powers Resolution and the Congressional Budget and Impoundment Control Act, aimed at reducing the power of the executive and enhancing congressional authority. The other investigations mentioned earlier produced few if any permanent changes. When the dust settled, the relationship between Congress and the executive had barely changed. In some instances, indeed, agencies have been known to fight back against congressional investigators. In 2015, the House Oversight and Government Reform Committee, in the wake of several scandals relating to the U.S. Secret Service, launched a set of hearings into the agency's leadership and organization. When the committee chairman, Jason Chaffetz (R-UT), criticized the actions of agency executives, the agency threatened to release embarrassing information about Chaffetz from its personnel files. Apparently Chaffetz had applied for a position as a Secret Service agent in 2003 and had been rejected.

In 2015 and 2016 the House conducted hearings into the 2012 terrorist attack on the U.S. consulate in Benghazi, Libya, that resulted in the deaths of several Americans, including Ambassador J. Christopher Stevens. Congressional Republicans hoped to link former secretary of state Hillary Clinton, the presumptive Democratic presidential candidate, to the debacle. The hearings were inconclusive, though they did lead to further hearings on Clinton's use of a personal e-mail server for official, sometimes classified government business.

Senate committees conduct a third type of legislative proceeding—the confirmation hearing. The Constitution's Appointments Clause (Article II, Section 2) declares that federal judges, ambassadors and "officers of the United States," are to be appointed by the president but also require approval by the Senate. The Constitution does not say which officers of the United States require Senate confirmation. This was left to Congress to decide. Currently, between twelve hundred and fourteen hundred presidential appointees require Senate approval. This includes major officials, such as cabinet secretaries, and a slew of minor officials, such as all fifteen members of the National Council on Disability. When the president nominates a candidate for one of these positions, the Senate committee with jurisdiction over the agency in which the appointee is to serve schedules hearings at which the nominee is called to testify, and witnesses have an opportunity to voice their views—pro or con.

In some instances, confirmation hearings can be quite rancorous. At the beginning of the Trump administration, for example, congressional Democrats
used confirmation hearings to attack several of Trump's nominees and, by extension, the new president's viewpoints and likely policies. Democrats were
particularly critical of Senator Jeff Sessions, Trump's nominee for attorney general, and ExxonMobil chief executive Rex Tillerson, Trump's choice for secretary of state. At the Sessions hearings, some witnesses charged that the Alabama
senator was insufficiently attentive to civil rights issues. At the Tillerson hearings, Democratic senators questioned the business executive about his dealings
with Russia.

Since Republicans held a majority in the Senate, it seemed unlikely that any
of the nominees could actually be defeated or even delayed. Ironically, Senate
rules changes championed by the Democrats in 2013 to prevent the GOP from
stalling Obama appointees (see chapter 4) now made it virtually impossible for
the Democrats to block Trump appointees unless they could find a way to persuade several Republican senators to join them—a chancy prospect in today's
polarized Congress. The hearings, nevertheless, gave Democrats an opportunity
to attack the new Republican administration and to show Democratic constituency groups that their views would be heard on Capitol Hill. During the last
two years of the Obama administration, Senate Republicans used their control
of the upper chamber to prevent action on more than one hundred presidential
nominees, including a Supreme Court nomination. If Democrats had regained
control of the Senate in 2018, they would have undoubtedly turned the tables
and declined to act on Republican nominees. In October 2018, Democrats
fought to prevent Judge Brett Kavanaugh from being named to the Supreme
Court. Democrats hoped that if they could block Kavanaugh they might be able
to prevent any Trump nominee from being seated if they succeeded in taking
control of the Senate in 2018. After a bitter struggle that included charges of
sexual misconduct and concern over his judicial temperament, Kavanaugh was
confirmed.

Does Congress Still Make the Law?

Among the most important tasks undertaken by executive agencies is rulemaking. Civics texts tell us that the law consists of statutes enacted by the Congress and signed by the president. This idea may have been correct in the early

days of the American republic. Today, however, federal law is augmented by hundreds of thousands of rules and regulations possessing the force of law, which are promulgated by a host of federal agencies staffed by officials whose names and job titles are unknown to the general public.

After a statute is passed by the Congress and signed into law by the president, the various federal agencies charged with administering and enforcing the act will usually spend months and sometimes years writing rules and regulations to implement the new law and will continue to write rules for decades thereafter. Typically, a statute will assert a set of goals and establish some framework for achieving them but leave much to the discretion of administrators. In some instances, members of Congress are themselves uncertain of just what a law will do and depend upon administrators to tell them.

In the case of the 2011 Affordable Care Act, widely known as Obamacare, for example, several members admitted that they did not fully understand how the act would work and were depending upon the Department of Health and Human Services (HHS), the agency with primary administrative responsibility for the act, to explain it to them. Sometimes Congress is surprised by agency rules that seem inconsistent with congressional presumptions. Thus, in 2012 the Internal Revenue Service (IRS) proposed rules to determine eligibility under the Affordable Care Act that excluded millions of working-class Americans who Congress thought would be covered by the act. Several congressional Democrats who had helped to secure the enactment of the legislation complained that the IRS interpretation would frustrate the intent of Congress.[7] The case of the Affordable Care Act is fairly typical. As administrative scholar Jerry L. Mashaw has observed, "Most public law is legislative in origin but administrative in content."[8]

The roots of bureaucratic power in the United States are complex and date to the earliest decades of the Republic.[9] Much of today's federal bureaucracy, however, can trace its origins to Franklin D. Roosevelt's New Deal. Under FDR's leadership, the federal government began to take responsibility for management of the economy, provision of social services, protection of the public's health, maintenance of employment opportunities, promotion of social equality, protection of the environment, and a host of other tasks. As the government's responsibilities and ambitions grew, Congress assigned more and more complex tasks to the agencies of the executive branch, which sometimes were only too happy to expand their own power and autonomy.[10] Executive agencies

came to be tasked with the responsibility for analyzing and acting upon economic data; assessing the environmental impact of programs and projects; responding to fluctuations in the labor market; safeguarding the food supply; regulating the stock market; supervising telecommunications and air, sea, and land
transport; and, in recent years, protecting the nation from terrorist plots.

When Congress writes legislation addressing these and a host of other complex issues, legislators cannot anticipate every question or problem that might
arise under the law over the coming decades. Congress cannot establish detailed
air-quality standards or draw up rules for drug testing or legislate the ballistic
properties of artillery rounds for a new army tank. Inevitably, as its goals become more ambitious, more complex, and broader in scope, Congress must delegate considerable discretionary authority to the agencies charged with giving
effect to the law.

Just the sheer number of programs it has created in recent decades forces
Congress to delegate authority. Congress can hardly administer the thousands
of programs it has enacted and must delegate power to the president and to the
bureaucracy to achieve its purposes. To be sure, if Congress delegates broad
and discretionary authority to the executive, it risks seeing its goals subordinated
to and subverted by those of the executive branch.[11] But, on the other hand, if
Congress attempts to limit executive discretion by enacting very precise rules
and standards to govern the conduct of the president and the executive branch,
it risks writing laws that do not conform to real-world conditions and that are
too rigid to be adapted to changing circumstances.[12] As the Supreme Court said
in a 1989 case, "In our increasingly complex society, replete with ever changing and more technical problems, Congress simply cannot do its job absent an
ability to delegate power under broad general directives."[13]

The increased scope and complexity of governmental activities promote
congressional delegation of power to the bureaucracy in another way as well.
When Congress addresses broad and complex issues, it typically has less difficulty reaching agreement on broad principles than on details. For example,
every member of Congress might agree that enhancing air quality is a desirable
goal. However, when it comes to the particular approach to be taken to achieve
this noble goal, many differences of opinion are certain to manifest themselves.
Members from auto-producing states are likely to resist stiffer auto-emission
standards and to insist that the real problem lies with coal-fired utilities. Members from districts that contain coal-fired utilities might argue that auto emis-

sions are the problem. Members from districts that are economically dependent upon heavy industry would demand exemptions for their constituents. Agreement on the principle of clean air would quickly dissipate as members struggled to achieve agreement on the all-important details. Delegation of power to an executive agency, on the other hand, allows members to enact complex legislation without having to reach detailed agreement. Congress can respond to pressure from constituents and the media to "do something" about a perceived problem while leaving the difficult details to administrators to hammer out.[14]

As a result of these and other factors, when Congress enacts major pieces of legislation, legislators inevitably delegate considerable authority to administrators to write rules and regulations designed to articulate and implement the legislative will. Of course, in some instances, Congress attempts to set standards and guidelines designed to govern administrative conduct. For example, the 1970 Clean Air Act specified the pollutants that the Environmental Protection Agency would be charged with eliminating from the atmosphere, as well as a number of the procedures that the EPA was obligated to undertake.[15] The act, however, left many other matters, including enforcement procedures, who should bear the burden of cleaning the air, and even how clean the air should ultimately be, to EPA administrators.

Many other statutes give administrators virtually unfettered discretion to decide how to achieve goals that are only vaguely articulated by the Congress. For example, the statute establishing the Federal Trade Commission (FTC) outlaws, without expressly defining, "unfair methods of competition." Precisely what these methods might be is largely left to the agency to determine. Similarly, the statute creating the Occupational Safety and Health Administration (OSHA) calls upon the agency "to protect health to the extent feasible." What that extent might be is for the agency to determine. In its enabling act, the EPA is told to protect human health and the environment "to an adequate degree of safety."[16] As Congress continues to enact statutes setting out general objectives without specifying how the government is supposed to achieve them, the federal bureaucracy is left to fill in the ever-growing blanks.

In some instances, to be sure, Congress does write detailed standards into the law, only to see these rewritten by administrators. For example, in 2006, the Securities and Exchange Commission (SEC) announced that it was issuing new rules that would significantly change key provisions of the 2002 Sarbanes-Oxley Act (Public Company Accounting Reform and Investor Protection Act). The act had been passed in the wake of the Enron scandal to reform corporate governance and prevent fraud. As enacted by Congress, Sarbanes-Oxley contains very specific standards. However, in response to industry lobbying, the SEC announced that it would issue new standards to ease corporate obligations under Section 404 of the act, which covers the financial statements issued by public corporations.[17] The agency determined that the law, as written by Congress, had forced corporations to engage in "overly conservative" practices.

Simply comparing the total volume of congressional output with the gross bureaucratic product provides a rough indication of where lawmaking now occurs in the federal government. The 106th Congress (1999–2000) was among the most active in recent years. It passed 580 pieces of legislation, 200 more than the 105th Congress and nearly twice as many as the 104th. Some, like campaign finance reform, seemed quite significant, but many pieces of legislation were minor. During the same two years, executive agencies produced 157,173 pages of new rules and regulations in the official *Federal Register*.[18] The Occupational Safety and Health Administration, for example, introduced new regulations affecting millions of workers and thousands of businesses; the Environmental Protection Agency drafted new air-quality standards, and the Securities and Exchange Commission and Commodities Futures Trading Commission (CFTC) were announcing significant revisions of futures trading rules affecting billions of dollars in transactions. In principle, agency rules and regulations are designed merely to implement the will of Congress as expressed in statutes. In fact, agencies are often drafting regulations based upon broad statutory authority granted years or even decades earlier by Congresses whose actual intent has become a matter of political interpretation.

Most of the laws enacted by Congress have little substance until federal agencies write the rules that give them effect. Take, for example, the Food Safety Modernization Act written by Congress and signed into law by President Obama in 2010. Four years later, the act still had little reality because the Food and Drug Administration (FDA), charged with administering its provisions, had not yet finished writing the necessary rules and regulations that would give actual substance to the legislation conceived by the Congress.

Americans are often chided by the media and by academics for their lack of knowledge of current public issues and priorities. Many of the issues considered and policies promulgated by government agencies, however, are not only unknown to the public; they are also far below the radar of media and academic scrutiny. Each year, government agencies issue thousands of rules and regulations that have the force of law, along with orders, advisories, guidelines, and policy circulars that are fully enforceable by the courts. This mass of government edicts seldom receives much attention outside the small circle of stakeholders who are in continual and close consultation with rulemaking agencies.

Who outside a narrow segment of the investment community was aware of the debate surrounding a new rule adopted by the Commodity Futures Trading Commission in 2012 entitled "Business Conduct Standards for Swap Dealers and Major Swap Participants with Counterparties"? Similarly, who outside the trucking and agriculture industries was aware of the controversy over another 2012 rule adopted by the Environmental Protection Agency entitled "Regulation of Fuels and Fuel Additives: 2013 Biomass-Based Diesel Renewable Fuel Volume"?

As it happens, these two rules promise to have a large impact on the American economy. The CFTC's new rule, part of the lengthy and complex process of implementing the 2010 Dodd-Frank Wall Street Reform and Consumer Protection Act, imposes new standards for the "swaps" market, an over-the-counter market in which various financial instruments are traded by investors, usually as a means of hedging risks. The new rules, many of which were not specifically required by Dodd-Frank, establish antifraud, disclosure, and other standards for swaps dealers. The estimated annual cost to investors of compliance with the rules is approximately $10 billion. The new EPA rule, for its part, sets standards for the use of biomass-based diesel fuel used mainly by truckers and by farmers. The cost to these groups of implementing the new standards is estimated at $1 billion initially and perhaps $288 million per year thereafter.

According to one study, 131 major (generally defined as having a likely impact of $100 million or more) rules and regulations adopted by federal agencies between 2009 and 2012 imposed $70 billion in new costs on the American public.[19] The various federal agencies writing these rules, on the other hand, assert that these costs were more than offset by the benefits derived by Americans from the rules in question.[20] Agencies are required by executive order to produce cost-benefit analyses of major new rules, and, under the 2000 Right to Know Act, the Office of Management and Budget is required to submit an annual report to Congress summarizing the agencies' findings. Since many benefits are nonpecuniary, such as protection of homeland security, agencies are often creative in their accounting practices, monetizing presumptive benefits to justify actual costs. Or, as OMB puts it politely, "Some rules produce benefits that can-not be adequately captured in monetary equivalents. In fulfilling their statutory mandates, agencies must sometimes act in the face of substantial uncertainty about the likely consequences."[21]

Thus, while these rules and regulations written by federal agencies usually do not capture the attention of the public or even the news media, they can have a substantial impact. They produce costs that are ultimately paid by the public in the form of higher prices and taxes, as well as benefits that may include safer products, cleaner air and water, a safer transportation system, and so forth.

Occasionally, of course, a proposed rule comes to the general public's atten-tion. In June 2014, at President Obama's behest, the EPA proposed new rules that would force coal-fired power plants to sharply reduce carbon dioxide emis-sions. The standards threatened to increase the costs of energy produced from coal and led to howls of protest from coal producers and from politicians in states dependent upon coal as an energy source. Lawsuits were filed that de-layed implementation of the new rules, and in 2016 it was widely assumed that President-elect Trump would seek ways of preventing implementation of the rules. Typically, however, debates over the costs and benefits of proposed rules take place in obscure buildings in Washington and involve small groups of bu-reaucrats, interest group "stakeholders," and congressional staffers and do not come to the attention of the news media or the more general public.

Congress generally pays a great deal of attention to agency rulemaking when it comes to new legislation, sometimes giving agencies very precise directions and timetables and occasionally reviewing agency efforts. Congress has also adopted the use of *deadlines* and *"hammers"* embedded in legislation, to com-pel agencies to expedite rulemaking. Political scientists Cornelius Kerwin and Scott Furlong point to the example of the Resource Conservation and Recovery Act of 1976, which contained a hammer mandating a total ban on land disposal of wastes, a disastrous outcome, if the EPA failed to develop rules that articu-lated an alternative policy.[22] In this way, Congress sought to force timely agency action.

More than 80 percent of the new rules promulgated in a typical year, how-ever, involve existing rather than new programs.[23] Congress and the president certainly can become involved in this arena of rulemaking.[24] Major new rules are reviewed by OMB and by GAO. However, the rulemaking agenda for exist-ing programs, which includes statutes that have been in place for years or even decades, is largely based upon the views and priorities of the agencies them-selves.[25] Congress is only occasionally likely to become involved, and then only if some important constituency interest makes a loud complaint.[26]

The Courts, the Agencies, and Congressional Power

Generally speaking, the federal courts have reduced congressional power and contributed to bureaucratic autonomy by their decisions on the delegation of powers and agency discretion. The first of these issues, delegation of power, has led to a number of court decisions over the past two centuries generally revolv-ing around the question of the scope of the delegation. As a legal principle, the power delegated to Congress by the people through the Constitution cannot be redelegated by the Congress. This "nondelegation doctrine" implies that di-rectives from Congress to the executive should be narrowly defined and give the latter little or no discretionary power. A broad delegation of congressional authority to the executive branch could be construed as an impermissible re-delegation of constitutional power. A second and related question sometimes brought before the courts is whether the rules and regulations adopted by admin-istrators are consistent with Congress's express or implied intent. This question is closely related to the first because the broader the delegation to the executive, the more difficult it is to determine whether the actions of the executive com-port with the intent of Congress.

With the exception of three New Deal–era cases, the Supreme Court has consistently refused to enforce the nondelegation doctrine.[27] In the nineteenth century, for the most part, Congress itself enforced the principle of nondelega-tion by writing laws that contained fairly clear standards to guide executive implementation.[28] Congressional delegation tended to be either contingent or interstitial.[29] Contingent delegation meant that Congress had established a prin-ciple defining alternative courses of action. The executive was merely autho-rized to determine which of the contingencies defined by Congress applied to the circumstances at hand and to act accordingly. For example, the Tariff Act of 1890 authorized the president to suspend favorable tariff treatment for coun-tries that imposed unreasonable duties on American products. In *Field v. Clark,* the High Court held that this delegation was permissible because it limited the president's authority to ascertaining the facts of a situation. Congress had not delegated its lawmaking authority to him.[30]

The Supreme Court also accepted what might be called interstitial rulemaking by the executive. This meant filling in the details of legislation where Congress had established the major principles. In the 1825 case of *Wayman v. Southard,* Chief Justice Marshall said Congress might lawfully "give power to those who are to act under such general provisions to fill up the details."[31] In 1928, the Court articulated a standard that, in effect, incorporated both these doctrines. In the case of *J. W. Hampton & Co. v. U.S.,* the Court developed the "intelligible principles" standard. A delegation of power was permissible "If Congress shall lay down by legislative act an intelligible principle to which [the executive] is directed to conform. . . ."[32]

As Congress and the president worked together to expand governmental power during the New Deal era, Congress enacted legislation, often at the president's behest, that gave the executive virtually unfettered authority to address a particular concern. For example, the Emergency Price Control Act of 1942 authorized the executive to set "fair and equitable" prices without offering any indication of what these terms might mean.[33] The Court's initial encounters with these new forms of delegation led to three major decisions in which the justices applied the "intelligible principles" standard to strike down delegations of power to the executive. In the 1935 *Panama* case,[34] the Court held that Congress had failed to define the standards governing the authority it had granted the president to exclude oil from interstate commerce. In the *Schechter* case, also decided in 1935, the Court found that the Congress failed to define the "fair competition" that the president was to promote under the National Industrial Recovery Act (NIRA). Justice Cardozo called the NIRA an example of "delegation running riot."[35] In a third case, *Carter v. Carter Coal Co.,* decided in 1936, the Court concluded that a delegation to the coal industry itself, to establish a code of regulations, was impermissibly vague.[36]

These decisions were seen as a judicial assault on the New Deal and helped spark President Roosevelt's "court packing" plan. The Court retreated from its confrontation with the president, and, perhaps as a result, no congressional delegation of power to the president has been struck down as impermissibly broad in the more than eight decades since *Carter.* Over the ensuing years, though, the nondelegation doctrine gradually fell into disuse as federal judges came to accept the notion that professional administrators in the agencies were more competent than politicians in the Congress to identify solutions to the nation's problems. While Congress might, via statute, identify broad policy directions, federal courts increasingly found that it was perfectly appropriate to leave the search for solutions in the hands of administrators. Thus, so long as the statute offered some vague indication of Congress's general intent, it was likely to pass muster. Indeed, the Supreme Court has said that a delegation can be valid if it "sufficiently marks the field within which the administrator is to act."[37]

Take, for example, the case of *Mistretta v. U.S.*[38] This case concerned the federal sentencing guidelines promulgated by the U.S. Sentencing Commission established by Congress in 1984 in response to concern that some judges were too lenient when meting out sentences to convicted criminals. The commission was charged with the task of developing a set of mandatory "guidelines" that would remove judicial discretion in this realm. In creating the commission, Congress offered few guidelines of its own. The language of the statute was vague, mandating that the commission should develop rules that would guarantee such things as "certainty and fairness" in sentencing. On this basis, the commission promulgated hundreds of pages of rules and regulations specifying how sentences were to be calculated given the severity of the crime and the criminal history of the defendant. In *Mistretta,* the Supreme Court found that the statute's vague standards were entirely sufficient to guide the commission's work and upheld the congressional delegation of power to the agency. In 2005, the Supreme Court decided that the use of mandatory sentencing guidelines was prohibited by the Sixth Amendment but did not readdress the issue of delegation.[39]

Also signaling the Court's acceptance of expanded administrative exercise of legislative power is the so-called *Chevron* standard, or *Chevron* doctrine. This standard emerged from a 1984 case called *Chevron USA v. Natural Resources Defense Council.*[40] An environmental group had challenged an Environmental Protection Agency regulation as contrary to the intent of the statute it was nominally written to implement. While a federal district court sided with the environmentalists against the agency, the lower court's decision was reversed by the Supreme Court. In its decision, the Supreme Court declared that so long as the executive developed rules and regulations "based upon a permissible construction" or "reasonable interpretation" of the statute," the judiciary would accept the views of the executive branch. This standard implies that considerable judicial deference should be given to the executive rather than to the Congress. Indeed the courts now look to the agencies to develop clear standards for statutory implementation, rather than to the Congress to develop standards for the executive branch to follow.[41] In the 2001 case of *U.S. v. Mead Corp.,* the Court partially qualified the *Chevron* holding by ruling that agencies were entitled to *Chevron* deference only where they were making rules carrying the force of law and not when they were merely issuing opinion letters or undertaking other informal actions.[42] Despite this qualification, *Chevron* still applies to the most important category of administrative activity.

Generally speaking, the courts are satisfied if an agency's rulemaking process has complied with the provisions of the 1946 Administrative Procedure Act (APA). This legislation requires agencies to give public notice of proposed rules (usually by publishing them in the *Federal Register*), to invite public comment, and to hold public hearings. The APA does *not* require agencies to amend their proposals after receiving public comments.

An important recent decision that further enhanced administrative discretion came in the 2013 case of *City of Arlington v. FCC*.[43] The case concerned a provision of the Federal Communications Act that requires state and local governments to act on zoning applications for building wireless towers and antennas "within a reasonable period of time." The Federal Communications Commission (FCC) issued a ruling defining "reasonable period of time" as 90 days for modifications of existing facilities and 150 days for new ones. This may seem a mundane ruling, but it has important implications. The plaintiff was arguing that the statute contained no provision authorizing the FCC to set rules defining "reasonable period of time." Hence, according to the plaintiff, the FCC was asserting power that Congress never intended to grant. The Supreme Court's response, consistent with the *Chevron* doctrine, was that agencies were to be afforded considerable deference even when interpreting the scope of their own power. In other words, federal agencies should be seen as the best judges of their own power.

Occasionally, of course, the Supreme Court does rule against an agency's interpretation of its statutory authority, Thus, in July 2015, the High Court ruled that the Environmental Protection Agency had failed to comply with the Clean Air Act's requirement that regulatory costs be taken into account when rules are promulgated.[44] This decision forced the EPA to reconsider new rules requiring power plants to reduce mercury emissions. Such decisions are, however, quite rare.

What Is to Be Done?

Can Congress play a larger role in setting America's regulatory agenda? In recent years, Congress has taken small steps in this direction, enacting several pieces of legislation that require agencies to more fully report their actions and to affirm that their rulemaking efforts comport with a number of congressional priorities. As we saw earlier, for example, the Regulatory Flexibility Act mandates that agencies demonstrate concrete steps to reduce the regulatory burdens imposed on small business. The National Environmental Policy Act requires agencies to develop environmental impact statements for proposed rules. Other pieces of legislation seek to expand the scope of public involvement in rulemaking. As we noted, however, most statutory requirements apply only to major pieces of legislation and leave agencies with ample opportunity to decide that statutory provisions are not applicable to the circumstances at hand.

Somewhat more ambitious have been congressional efforts to develop legislative tools to control rulemaking. The most obvious of these has been some return to the idea of nondelegation. When an agency promulgates a rule, it does so with authority delegated to it by the Congress. The practical implication of the nondelegation doctrine is that statutory language spelling out the actions to be undertaken by the executive must be clear and detailed, lest broad and vague language in effect delegate too much discretionary authority to the executive Until the early twentieth century, statutes tended to allow the executive branch little discretion during the process of implementation, and the courts zealously protected the nondelegation doctrine.

During the New Deal era, however, as the complexity of economic and social legislation increased and the federal bureaucracy grew in size and complexity, Congress began to delegate more and more power to executive agencies by providing them with broad statutory mandates to develop rules and regulations. This practice was challenged in a number of court cases, and, initially, the Supreme Court employed the doctrine of nondelegation to strike down several major pieces of New Deal legislation. President Roosevelt's threat to "pack" the Court with pro–New Deal justices along with personnel changes on the Court led to a majority willing to support FDR and to accept broad delegations of power to administrative agencies. While the Court preserved the nondelegation doctrine as a "theoretical facade," it lost interest in interfering with the workings of the executive branch or attempting to force Congress to write precise rules into statutory language.[45]

A number of academic critics, most notably Theodore Lowi and David Schoenbrod, have argued for a return to enforcement of the nondelegation doctrine, asserting that this would enhance congressional power over rulemaking.[46]

In point of fact, Congress has written specific standards into many statutes in recent years precisely in order to delimit agency discretion.[47] The problem with this approach, though, is that agencies continue to write rules years and even decades after a statute's initial enactment. Agencies quite properly assert that changing times and circumstances necessitate new rules not anticipated by the Congress of some earlier era. The federal courts will, also quite reasonably, defer to agency judgments, and, for all intents and purposes, the statute will have been "captured" by the agency, however careful Congress was not to delegate too much power when the statute was enacted.

A third approach employed by Congress to maintain some semblance of control over agency rulemaking involves the use of statutory devices. One such device inserted into many statutes, until it was invalidated by the Supreme Court in 1983, was the legislative veto. A statute containing legislative veto provisions required agencies to submit rules proposed under the authority of that statute to Congress for review. Though there were many variations, most of these provisions gave one or both houses of Congress an opportunity to block implementation of proposed rules by majority vote. Congress incorporated legislative veto provisions into at least two hundred statutes. The veto was seldom employed but nonetheless had some effect. Typically, the threat of a veto led to negotiations between the agency and Congress and the elimination or modification of the rule in question.[48] In 1983, of course, the Supreme Court determined that the legislative veto violated the Constitution's two Presentment Clauses insofar as it was an attempt to exercise legislative power without the participation of the president as called for twice in Article I, which declares that bills passed by both Houses of Congress must be *presented* to the president for signature and which stipulates that a presidential veto can only be overridden by a two-thirds vote of both Houses.[49] As Justice White noted at the time, the *Chadha* decision invalidated provisions of some two hundred laws, more laws, White said, than the Court had cumulatively invalidated in its entire prior history.[50]

The Congressional Review Act, the REINS Act, and the SCRUB Act

The *Chadha* decision impelled Congress to consider other approaches to the question of supervision of agency rulemaking. One approach, discussed earlier, was embodied in the 1996 Congressional Review Act (CRA). This act requires agencies to submit proposed rules, accompanied by written reports, to the GAO. Congress then has sixty "session days" (days in which Congress is in session) to object to major rules. If passed by simple majorities of both houses—and the rules do not permit a Senate filibuster of such a resolution—a congressional resolution of disapproval is sent to the president, who may sign or veto the joint resolution. Once a rule is disallowed, it cannot be reissued. This procedure was designed to allow Congress to review proposed agency rules and unpublished guidance letters, while avoiding the issues raised by *Chadha*. However, the requirement that rules be disallowed by both houses of Congress and the president makes it extremely unlikely that the CRA will have any impact unless the president and both Houses of Congress are in agreement.[51] Indeed, in the twenty years after the enactment of the CRA, only one rule was actually disallowed. During the Obama presidency Congress used the CRA five times to disapprove proposed regulations. The president, however, vetoed all five resolutions. In the opening weeks of the Trump administration, with both Houses of Congress in GOP hands, Congress prepared joint resolutions disallowing a number of rules adopted during the closing sixty days of the Obama administration. President Trump signed the resolutions and thereby eliminated some 180 rules promulgated by the Interior Department, the Labor Department, and the Environmental Protection Agency since June 2016.

Some Republicans argued that a host of other Obama-era regulations and guidance letters were also vulnerable to the CRA procedure. The law requires an agency promulgating a new rule to submit a report to Congress and starts the sixty-day clock for congressional consideration when the report is received. Apparently, during the Obama years, many agencies never submitted the required reports, potentially making thousands of rules, going back at least to 2009 and possibly to 1996, vulnerable to review and possible disallowance.[52] Such an aggressive interpretation of the CRA would undoubtedly set off major partisan struggles as well as a good deal of litigation.

Still another approach considered by Congress was embodied in the proposed 2011 Regulations from the Executive in Need of Scrutiny (REINS) Act, which was passed by House Republicans on a party-line vote but was not taken up by the Democrat-controlled Senate. Under the terms of this proposed act, agencies would have been required to report proposed major rules to each House of Congress. Standing the CRA procedure on its head, under REINS, a rule would only take effect upon the enactment of a joint congressional resolution of approval and the signature of the president.[53] Republicans strongly favored the REINS concept, but Democrats viewed the bill as an effort to curb social policy, and

President Obama declared that he would veto the bill if it reached his desk. With Trump's election in 2016, congressional Republicans promised to seek enactment of legislation incorporating the REINS concept. President Trump has expressed his support for the idea.

A third legislative approach aimed at enhancing congressional control over agency rulemaking is exemplified by the 2016 Searching for and Cutting Regulations that are Unnecessarily Burdensome (SCRUB) Act. The SCRUB Act calls for the creation of a bipartisan commission to review all existing federal regulations and to identify those deemed to be unnecessary or unduly burdensome on the nation's economy. The commission's goal would be a 15 percent cut in the overall cost of federal regulation. The commission is empowered to make a recommendation to Congress, which would be enacted in total or in part by a joint resolution signed by the president. The SCRUB Act died in the 114th Congress and was reintroduced in the 115th without success.

Congressional Oversight of the Bureaucracy

Even putting aside the CRA, REINS, and SCRUB concepts, Congress possesses substantial oversight power vis-à-vis the bureaucracy. Congress can hold hearings, enact new legislation, and, if it so desires, slash agency budgets. In recent years, oversight hearings into such topics as the long waits that veterans were forced to endure before receiving care in VA hospitals, failures on the part of the Federal Emergency Management Agency (FEMA) in the wake of Hurricane Katrina, and the Defense Department's handling of the Abu Ghraib prison scandal in Iraq ended the careers of agency officials and forced all three agencies to adopt new procedures.

Congress, though, is better able to respond to heavily publicized abuses and crises than to engage in day-to-day supervision of the bureaucracy. Routine oversight is often conducted by a committee that is inclined to be friendly to the agency in question or to the interest groups that support that agency.[54] Members of Congress, moreover, seldom see much political advantage to be gained from devoting time, energy, and effort to oversight, particularly if their own party is in power. As one Republican member said during the Bush administration, "Our party controls the levers of government. We're not about to go out and look beneath a bunch of rocks to cause heartburn."[55] Even during the 1990s, a period of divided party government, the number of oversight hearings in both the House and Senate declined sharply as members decided that there was little political payoff to be derived from routine supervision of executive agencies.[56] Congress's chief instruments of bureaucratic control—statutory and budgetary sanctions—require the approval of majorities in both houses and the signature of the president, difficult to achieve in today's fragmented Congress.

Of course, Congress exercises power informally too, by the threat of budgetary sanction. For example, a GAO report criticizing an agency's contracting practices is only advisory and does not have the force of law. Agencies, however, will usually follow the GAO's recommendations, especially if these are supported by powerful committee chairs who might be in a position to threaten the agency's budget.

Bureaucratic Power

In principle, as Lowi, Schoenbrod, and others have suggested, Congress could write narrowly drawn statutes that limited bureaucratic discretion. In principle, the courts could reinstitute the nondelegation doctrine and stop deferring to administrative interpretations of statutory mandates. In principle, Congress might invest more time and energy in oversight of the administrative agencies. But the reality is that the more ambitious the programs and policies Congress develops, the more power it must delegate to the bureaucracy. And the more power it delegates to the bureaucracy, the less able legislators will be to oversee their creations.

Once power is delegated to them, executive agencies inevitably have substantial control over its use and, in most instances, neither Congress nor the judiciary is able or willing to second-guess their actions. The result is that federal agencies typically write laws according to their own lights rather than those of the Congress. Indeed, whatever policy goals Congress may have had, after many years and many Congresses have passed, often all that remains of a statute is its delegation of power to the executive branch.

Take, for example, the Family and Medical Leave Act of 1993 (FMLA).[57] The act requires employers to allow employees to take up to twelve weeks of unpaid leave each year to deal with childbirth, health problems, family emergencies, and other serious matters that might render employees temporarily unable to perform their duties.[58] In its report on the proposed legislation, the Senate Committee on Health, Education, Labor and Pensions indicated that problems justifying leave under the law would include such matters as heart attacks, strokes, spinal injuries, recovery from childbirth, and other serious conditions that clearly justified an extended period of absence from work. Congress delegated authority to the Department of Labor to develop appropriate rules and regulations to implement the act. The record of legislative hearings attendant to the act, though, makes it clear that Congress intended the legislation to cover only serious problems, not short-term conditions or minor illnesses. The Labor Department, however, had other ideas.

Each year that the department developed new rules, it expanded the scope of the act's coverage and even the number of weeks of leave to which employees were entitled. For example, under rules adopted by the department, a case of flu was considered a medical condition covered by the act. This expansion of the FMLA was upheld by a federal court, which, citing the *Chevron* doctrine, deferred to the agency's interpretation of the statute.[59] Subsequently the Labor Department ruled medical leave granted by employers under their own plans would be in addition to rather than concurrent with the leave required under the FMLA.[60] This rule meant that some employees might be entitled to considerably more than the twelve weeks mandated by Congress. Perhaps the Labor Department should not be faulted for its generosity. No doubt, ill employees are more deserving of sympathy than giant corporations are. Nevertheless, in this, as in so many other instances, a bureaucratic agency ignored congressional intent and wrote its own laws. When Congress delegated power it gave up control. It seems unlikely that the CRA, the REINS Act, or the SCRUB Act individually or in combination can fully reassert congressional control over America's bureaucratic behemoth.

9

Congress and the Courts

IN *FEDERALIST* 78, ALEXANDER HAMILTON's long essay defending the judicial branch of the proposed new government under the Constitution, Hamilton sought to refute critics who feared that the judiciary would pose a threat to popular rights and liberties. Hamilton was forced to admit, however, that although "liberty can have nothing to fear from the judiciary alone, but [it] would have every thing to fear from its union with either of the other departments."[1] As we shall see, in contemporary America the judiciary has formed a de facto "union" with the executive and has in some respects helped to diminish the role of Congress in the American governmental system.

Congress's Constitutional Power over the Courts

As we saw in chapter 1, the constitutional system of checks and balances assigns Congress a good deal of power over the judiciary. The Supreme Court was established by Article III of the Constitution, but the "inferior" federal courts were, as authorized by the Constitution, created by statute and can be modified or even abolished in the same way. Congress has made major changes to the court system several times in U.S. history, most recently by creating a system of specialized courts, known as the Article I courts, which include the U.S. Court of Federal Claims, the U.S. Court of International Trade, and the Court of Appeals for Veterans Claims, with a designated appellate court, the U.S. Court of Appeals for the Federal Circuit.

Judges and justices, moreover, must be approved by the Senate before they can don their robes or can be impeached by the Congress and so compelled to doff those same robes. In recent decades Supreme Court appointments, in particular, have sparked intense partisan struggles within Congress and between Congress and the White House. Justice Clarence Thomas was appointed after an epic battle while several other presidential nominees, including Zoë Baird, Robert Bork, Douglas Ginsburg, Harriet Miers, and Kimba Wood, who went down to defeat in the Senate or had their names withdrawn in the face of Senate opposition. Congress has delayed action on judicial nominations and, in several cases, compelled presidents to withdraw these nominations. In 2016, after the death of Justice Antonin Scalia, the Senate's Republican leadership refused to act on President Obama's nominee, Judge Merrick Garland, to replace Scalia. Republican senators hoped that a Republican president might be elected later in the year. While Republican leaders were widely criticized for this tactic, it proved successful, and newly elected President Trump nominated a conservative justice, Neil Gorsuch, who would bolster the Court's conservative majority. With the subsequent appointment of Justice Brett Kavanaugh, despite a vehement Democratic effort to block the appointment, the Court's swing to the right seemed assured.

A third congressional power is Congress's ability to alter the jurisdictions of federal tribunals and the rules of the judicial process. In chapter 1 we considered the example of the Sentencing Act of 1987, through which Congress endeavored to impose mandatory sentencing "guidelines" upon federal judges, eliminating all judicial discretion in the realm of sentencing. Though the Supreme Court eventually declared that mandatory guidelines were constitutionally impermissible, the guidelines remain in place as strong recommendations that most federal judges follow when imposing criminal penalties.

Finally, Congress can attempt to overturn even Supreme Court decisions by writing new legislation that contravenes the Court's edict. One well-known congressional effort came in response to the Supreme Court's decision in the 1990 case of *Employment Division v. Smith*.[2] This case involved a claim by defendants fired from their jobs for drug abuse that the drugs had been intended for religious purposes. The Court said that the state's duty to prevent the abuse of dangerous drugs should be given more weight than the claimed religious exercise. This opinion angered some members of Congress, who saw it as an attack on the First Amendment's guarantee of free religious exercise.

Congress responded with legislation, the Religious Freedom Restoration Act (RFRA), requiring a "compelling government interest" to be demonstrated before any limitations could be placed upon free exercise of religion. The Supreme Court, though, had the last word. It used its power of judicial review to overturn the RFRA, asserting that Congress had usurped the powers of the judiciary.[3] This decision brings us to a very important topic—judicial review of acts of Congress.

Why Can the Courts Overturn Acts of Congress?

Americans have come to accept the idea that the federal courts can declare acts of Congress to be inconsistent with the Constitution and, therefore, null and void. This idea, however, was not generally held at the time of the nation's founding and is not standard practice in other democracies. For example, if the Canadian Supreme Court strikes down an act of their parliament on constitutional grounds, the legislature has the power to reenact the invalidated legislation and bar further court challenges.[4]

When they created the Constitution's system of separated powers and checks and balances, the framers, as we saw, regarded the Congress as the branch most likely to seek to expand its power and the judiciary as the "least dangerous branch." "The judiciary," Alexander Hamilton wrote, "has no influence over either the sword or the purse; no direction either of the strength or of the wealth of the society; and can take no active resolution, whatever." He goes on to write, "[It] is beyond comparison the weakest of the three departments . . . [and] can never attack with success either of the other two."[5]

Today, of course, the federal courts claim the power to rule upon the constitutionality of acts of Congress. Using the power of *judicial review,* federal courts can decide whether congressional statutes pass constitutional muster. In an overwhelming majority of cases, the courts affirm the constitutionality of a contested statute. In some 170 instances over the course of American history, however—some very important—the Supreme Court has struck down statutes, in whole or in part, after determining that they were inconsistent with the federal Constitution.

It might be argued that judicial review and the invalidation of an act of Congress constituted just the sort of attack on another branch of government Hamilton deemed unlikely. When it makes use of judicial review, the Court is valorizing its own will and judgment and nullifying the actions of another branch. Indeed, to the Anti-Federalist critics of the proposed constitution, this aspect of the document was among its least democratic and most "aristocratic" elements. During the debates at the state ratifying conventions called to consider the proposed constitution, a number of Anti-Federalists asserted that the document gave far too much power to the unelected judiciary relative to the elected Congress. A well-known pamphleteer writing under the name Brutus declared, "If . . . the legislature pass any laws, inconsistent with the sense the judges put upon the constitution, they will declare it void; and therefore in this respect their power is superior to that of the legislature."[6]

Hamilton, however, replied that no legislative act contrary to the Constitution could be valid. Hence, as an element of the constitutional system of checks and balances, it was appropriate for judges to keep the legislature within the limits of its proper constitutional authority and protect the Constitution from "legislative encroachments." Hamilton's view was not universally accepted. Judicial review was nowhere mentioned in the Constitution, and James Madison, chief author of the Constitution, averred that each of the branches of the federal government "must in the exercise of its functions be guided by the text of the Constitution according to its own interpretation."[7] Thomas Jefferson objected even more vehemently to the idea that the judiciary, alone, had the power to interpret the Constitution. "But the opinion," declared Jefferson, "which gives to the Judges the right to decide what Laws are constitutional, and what not, not only for themselves in their own sphere of action, but for the Legislative and the Executive also in their spheres, would make the Judiciary a despotic branch."[8]

This view is sometimes called a *departmentalist* perspective. Departmentalists did not deny that the courts could rule on the applicability of a given law to a particular case but declared that the courts could not determine the validity of the law itself. This idea surfaces from time to time today. For example, before the Court again upheld the constitutionality of Obamacare in 2015 (*King v. Burwell*), one prominent law professor, William Baude of the University of Chicago, suggested that if the administration lost it should accept the result with regard to the four plaintiffs named in the case but not recognize the decision's general applicability.[9]

Despite early differences of opinion, the idea of judicial review came to be gradually accepted in the wake of the Supreme Court's 1803 *Marbury v. Madison* decision.[10] The proximate issue in the case concerned William Marbury's petition to the Court for a writ of mandamus ordering Secretary of State James Madison to deliver Marbury's commission as a justice of the peace in the District of Columbia. Marbury had been appointed by outgoing Federalist President John Adams—one of Adams's so-called midnight appointments—but his commission had not yet been delivered when President Jefferson assumed office. The Jeffersonians seemed to have no inclination to formalize Marbury's appointment. Marbury brought his claim to the Supreme Court under a provision of the Judiciary Act of 1789, which added to the High Court's original jurisdiction as defined by Article III of the Constitution by giving it the power to issue such writs.

Chief Justice Marshall declared that Madison's unwillingness to deliver Marbury's appointment documents was illegal. However, said Marshall, the portion of the Judiciary Act expanding the Supreme Court's original jurisdiction was unconstitutional. Congress, said the chief justice, had the power to define the Supreme Court's appellate jurisdiction but lacked the power to change the Court's constitutionally defined original jurisdiction. In this decision, Marshall restricted the power of Congress and claimed the power of judicial review but avoided issuing an order that President Jefferson might have refused to carry out and, by so doing, possibly undermining the Court's credibility. Marshall's decision is usually seen as one of the great judicial masterstrokes of American history.

The Supreme Court refrained from invalidating any other acts of Congress until 1857, when its decision in the *Dred Scott* case, holding that slaves were not citizens and striking down the Fugitive Slave Law, played a role in precipitating the Civil War.[11] The *Marbury* and *Dred Scott* decisions, though, did not completely settle the issue of judicial review. In his 1832 message explaining his veto of the rechartering of the Bank of the United States, some three decades after *Marbury,* President Andrew Jackson reaffirmed departmentalism, declaring that each branch of government had the authority to decide on the constitutionality of laws in its own domain. "The opinion of the judges," said Jackson, "has no more authority over Congress than the opinion of Congress has over the judges, and on that point the President is independent of both."[12] Similarly, Abraham Lincoln declared that the Court's decision in *Dred Scott* had been binding upon the litigants but not upon the legislative branch. Congress later overturned *Dred Scott* when it enacted the 1866 Civil Rights Act declaring all persons born in the United States to be citizens.[13]

Over the course of two centuries, nevertheless, the departmentalist conception of constitutional interpretation, though never completely disappearing, receded into the background, and the preeminence of judicial review came to be
an accepted fact. Political scientist Mark Graber has argued that judicial review
became established in the United States because sharp conflicts within Congressional coalitions sometimes impelled Congress to invite the judiciary to resolve
disputes that were too divisive for the legislative branch to handle.[14] *Dred
Scott* is such an example. The issue of slavery in the territories divided both
parties in Congress and led both Democratic and Whig leaders to hope the
courts could settle the matter. Invited several times, the Court, by establishing
precedents, came to stay, and the idea that the courts had the final say in interpreting the Constitution became firmly entrenched in American legal and political culture. Graber's explanation has much merit, but as we will see, the Court
is not simply what Graber characterizes as "a guest who would not leave." Instead, the primacy of judicial, as opposed to departmental, review became secure because it has generally served the interests of another institutional actor,
namely the president. Let us return to that point later in the chapter.

How Judicial Review Affects the Congress

Whatever its historic roots, judicial review of acts of Congress affects the
legislature in several ways. First, when the courts affirm the constitutionality of
a statute, they are, in effect, validating and legitimating the lawmaking process.
In ancient times, and even today, religious leaders were asked to bless the work
of lawmakers in order to assure citizens that the laws they were asked to obey
had divine sanction. In the United States, the Constitution is a revered text, and
when the courts affirm that legislative enactments are consistent with the Constitution, they are conferring a secular blessing upon the legislature and its works.

In the course of reviewing acts of Congress, however, the courts occasionally
find these in whole or in part inconsistent with the Constitution. In these instances, as Jefferson, Madison, Jackson, and Lincoln pointed out, the courts are
substituting their own judgment regarding constitutionality for those of the legislature. In many instances, this amounts to little more than a substitution of judicial policy preferences for those of the Congress in the guise of constitutional
interpretation. Between the 1890s and 1937, for example, the Court struck down
a number of laws on the grounds that Congress had exceeded its power under

the Commerce Clause. For the most part, these laws involved efforts by Congress to regulate business practices. Such regulation was supported by so-called progressive forces in the nation, and opposed by proponents of a laissez-faire philosophy.

Regardless of a reader's position on the substance of the economic questions before the Court, the point is that in a series of cases the justices generally seemed to elucidate constitutional principles crafted in order to support laissez-faire principles. Take the famous case of *Lochner v. New York.*[15] In this case, the Court struck down a New York law limiting the number of hours a baker could work to ten each day and sixty each week. The sponsors of the statute had a variety of motives, including the health of bakers, but the Court determined that the law intruded upon freedom of contract. This ruling drew a famous dissent from Justice Oliver Wendell Holmes, who wrote, "[t]he Fourteenth Amendment does not enact Mr. Herbert Spencer's *Social Statistics,*"[16] referring to a book in which Spencer advocated a laissez-faire perspective. Holmes went on to assert that the majority opinion represented little more than an effort to wrap a particular economic perspective in the mantle of the Constitution.

Lochner involved a state law. The Supreme Court, however, was no more friendly toward congressional enactments that seemed to intrude upon private economic activity. Thus, for example, in the 1895 case of *Pollock v. Farmers' Loan and Trust Co.,* the Court invalidated a newly enacted federal income tax.[17] The majority found a variety of constitutional reasons for the decision, ignoring the fact that a previous income tax levied during the Civil War had remained in effect until 1872 and had been found constitutional in a unanimous 1881 decision.[18] In the 1918 case of *Hammer v. Dagenhart,* the Court struck down a congressionally enacted child labor law prohibiting the interstate shipment of goods manufactured using child labor. The Court declared that manufacturing was not interstate commerce, the later shipment of the goods being merely incidental.[19] Generally, the Court opposed government intervention into private markets and the activities of industrial corporations, but where that intervention seemed to serve the interests of such corporations, the Court found reason to approve government action, as in the case of the government's action to end the 1895 Pullman Strike.[20]

Again, the point here is not whether the Court's economic judgment was better or worse than that of Congress. Instead, what is important is the Court's ability to use judicial review to substitute its own judgment for that of the Congress. As one group of constitutional authorities put it, "Instead of confining itself to the question of whether a legislative power was constitutional, the Supreme Court increasingly concerned itself with the wisdom of the legislation."[21]

Similar points could be made about the actions of the contemporary Supreme Court in a number of realms. For example, the Court's campaign finance decisions, striking down sections of the Bipartisan Campaign Reform Act (BCRA) on free-speech grounds, might be said to be judgments about the political process disguised in constitutional language. Congress had enacted campaign finance regulations designed to diminish the power of money in the political process. As noted in chapter 3, the authors are not fully convinced of the wisdom of such regulations. Campaign finance reform tends to reduce electoral competition and serves the interests of those currently in power. The Court's majority declared restrictions on campaign spending by wealthy individuals, corporations, and labor unions to be impermissible limits on free speech. The Court's majority, along with the authors, may view high levels of spending to be conducive to a vigorous and open political process. Many Americans, on the other hand, regard high levels of campaign spending to amount to little more than efforts by wealthy interests to buy elections. Reasonable people may disagree on this issue. However, in developing a free-speech rationale for its decisions, the Court simply found a constitutional rubric to justify substituting its own judgment for that of Congress. A different Supreme Court could just as easily argue that imbalances of spending inhibit free speech, and thereby wrap its preferences in a constitutional mantle. The late Justice Antonin Scalia made just this point in his dissent in the Court's 2015 decision in the case of *Obergefell v. Hodges,* striking down gay-marriage bans. Scalia declared that the Court's majority had simply substituted is own social views for those of most Americans.

Demise of the Political-Questions Doctrine

One example of the judiciary's increasing willingness to substitute its own views for those of Congress is the demise of the political-questions doctrine. In recent decades, the federal courts have regularly intruded into a number of areas that once would clearly have been considered political—more specifically, congressional—domains. For example, in the 1962 case of *Baker v. Carr,* the U.S. Supreme Court held that legislative apportionment, a matter the Court had previously said was left by the Constitution to Congress and the state legislatures, could, in fact, be determined by the federal courts.[22] Similarly, in the 1969 case of *Powell v. McCormack,* the Court heard, on the merits, former representative Adam Clayton Powell's claim that he had been improperly denied his seat in the Congress.[23] The House had voted to exclude Powell after it found that he had misappropriated congressional funds for personal use. Article I, Section 5, of the U.S. Constitution, of course, states explicitly that each house of Congress is empowered to judge the qualifications of its own members. The Supreme Court, nevertheless, held that it, rather than the Congress, should determine whether Powell was entitled to his seat.

Perhaps the most striking example of judicial intervention into the political arena in recent years was the Supreme Court's decision in the case of *Bush v. Gore,* one of several state and federal cases arising from the 2000 presidential election in the state of Florida. Here the Court, de facto if not de jure, awarded Florida's electoral votes to George W. Bush in the disputed 2000 Florida presidential vote count.[24] On its face, the issue of whether Florida's electoral votes belonged to Bush or Gore seems to be precisely the sort of political question that the Court had generally assigned to Congress and the state legislatures for the past century and a half. Though dismissed by the mainstream media—one national columnist referred to the state's legislative proceedings as "off-the-wall"— and the political establishment, the Florida legislature claimed to be prepared to resolve the issue, as might have appeared to be its constitutional and legal right.[25] Alternatively, Congress might have settled the outcome. In a similar situation following the disputed 1876 presidential election, the U.S. Congress devised a procedure that ultimately awarded disputed electoral votes to Republican candidate Rutherford B. Hayes. In 2000, however, neither the Florida Supreme Court nor the U.S. Supreme Court saw any reason to even consider deferring to meddlesome "off-the-wall" legislative bodies. Both courts entered the Florida recount fray, and eventually the U.S. Supreme Court let stand George W. Bush's narrow and much-disputed win in the state, giving Bush Florida's electoral votes and the presidency.

In 2016, state and federal courts in Michigan and Pennsylvania turned back demands by Green Party presidential candidate Jill Stein for recounts of both states' popular votes. Trump had carried the two states, along with Wisconsin, by narrow margins after polls had suggested that Clinton was ahead in all three. Stein was able to secure a recount in Wisconsin, which resulted in Trump actually picking up a few votes. In Michigan and Pennsylvania, state law seemed to offer Stein no grounds for a challenge, and the courts declined to intervene.

Civil Rights and Civil Liberties

Of course, there have been periods in American history, most notably in the 1960s, when the Court stood at the forefront of civil rights and civil liberties against attempts by some in Congress to curb both. On the other hand, there have periods in American history, such as the decades following Reconstruction, when the Supreme Court stood in the way of rights and liberties that had been initiated by the Congress, such as the Fourteenth Amendment, which was eviscerated by the Supreme Court. Thus, a number of commentators question the commonly held idea that the Supreme Court is a better defender of Americans' constitutional rights than the Congress. Mark V. Tushnet asserts that the Court at its best is better than Congress at its worst, but Congress at its best is better than the Court at its worst.[26] Surveying the cases, legal scholar William Glidden concludes that the United States functions well enough through ordinary legislative processes to decide contested rights issues. On balance, he declares, "representative democracy has lost much more than it has gained from the Court's invalidations of federal statutes regulating or protecting rights."[27] In his most recent book, constitutional scholar Louis Fisher comments that Congress has a "long and distinguished history" of protecting individual liberties and civil rights. While the courts have played a role, writes Fisher, "little in the record over the past two centuries offers convincing evidence that courts are particularly gifted or reliable" in this realm.[28] If Tushnet, Glidden, Fisher, and other scholars, including the distinguished legal philosopher Jeremy Waldron, are correct, the substitution of judicial review for congressional authority in the realm of rights and liberties has perhaps not been the unqualified success story Americans are accustomed to learning.[29]

Limiting the Power of Congress while Empowering the Executive

Not only have the courts generally been willing to substitute their own judgments for those of Congress, they have also amended the constitutional distribution of institutional power by constraining legislative power and enhancing the power of the executive. Some critics of the Supreme Court have often accused the High Court of judicial imperialism for expanding its own power relative to the other branches of government.[30] If this imperialism exists, it seems limited in scope, indeed, mainly confined to wearing away the prerogatives of the Congress. When it comes to the actions of the executive branch, however, the federal courts have in recent decades been far more tolerant. Indeed, as judicial deference to Congress has waned, so has its solicitude for the presidency grown. Let us examine four areas—foreign policy, war and national emergency powers, the president's legislative powers, and administrative power—in which the federal courts have acceded to and encouraged the expansion of executive power while reducing the power of Congress.

Foreign Policy

Foreign policy has come to be seen as a presidential preserve, but, of course, the Constitution assigns important foreign policy powers to the Congress. And from the birth of the Republic through the early years of the twentieth century, the federal courts recognized Congress's role in shaping American policy toward other nations. For example, in the 1795 case of *Penhallow v. Doane,* the Supreme Court specifically held that the Constitution required the president and the Congress to share foreign policy-making authority.[31] Over the ensuing decades, the courts continued to emphasize congressional power. In the 1829 case of *Foster v. Neilson,* the Court indicated that Congress had the ultimate power to interpret the meaning of language in treaties between the United States and other nations.[32] In the 1850 case of *Fleming v. Page,* the Court held that only Congress, not the president, had the power to annex territory to the United States.[33] In the 1893 Chinese Exclusion Case, the Court reaffirmed the dominance of Congress in the realm of international relations. Justice Gray, for the Court, said, "The power [in this instance, to exclude aliens] is vested in the political departments of the government, and is to be regulated by treaty or by Act of Congress."[34] In a similar vein, the 1901 Insular Cases conceded to Congress the power to determine the constitutional rights of the inhabitants of America's territories.[35]

This nineteenth-century deference to Congress in the realm of foreign relations gave way in the twentieth century to a distinct judicial presumption in favor of executive power in foreign affairs. The turning point was the 1936 case of *U.S. v. Curtiss-Wright Export Corp.*[36] The company had been charged with conspiring to sell fifteen machine guns to Bolivia. This sale violated a May 1934 presidential proclamation issued pursuant to a congressional resolution authorizing the president to prohibit arms sales to Paraguay and Bolivia, which were then engaged in a cross-border conflict. Attorneys for the company argued that the congressional resolution allowing the president discretion in the matter of arms sales was an unlawful delegation of legislative power to the executive branch. As we shall see, in two earlier cases, *A. L. A. Schechter Poultry Corp. v. U.S.* and *Panama Refining Co. v. Ryan,* the Court had struck down acts of Congress on the grounds that they represented unconstitutionally broad delegations of legislative power to the executive branch.[37] Both decisions had prompted severe criticism from the White House and from congressional Democrats. Perhaps for that reason, the Court seemed anxious to distinguish the present case from the earlier decisions without seeming to retreat from its former position.

The Court might have accomplished this objective merely by asserting that the discretion allowed the executive branch under the 1936 act was more narrowly defined than the president's authority under the earlier acts. However, the author of the Court's opinion, Justice George Sutherland, had long believed that America should pursue an active foreign policy guided by the president and the judiciary and free from the parochial concerns that, in his view, often dominated congressional policy making. In essence, Sutherland thought politics should stop at the water's edge.[38] Thus, writing for the Court, Justice Sutherland made a sharp distinction between internal and external affairs. The congressional resolution delegating power to the executive, said Sutherland, might have been unlawful if it had "related solely to internal affairs." In the realm of foreign affairs, however, different standards and rules applied, permitting Congress to delegate powers to the president with only very general standards or even leaving "the exercise of power to his unrestricted judgment." The difference between foreign and domestic affairs, moreover, did not end here. In the realm of foreign policy, the powers Congress could appropriately exercise, and presumably delegate to the president, were not limited to the express and implied powers granted in the Constitution. This limitation was said to apply "only in respect to our internal affairs." Finally, in the realm of foreign affairs, said the Court, the president exercised "plenary and exclusive power," independent of any legislative authority as "the sole organ of the federal government in the field of international relations."

Taken together, these three principles laid the legal groundwork for many of the claims of executive power made by presidents and sustained by the federal courts in subsequent years. The *Curtiss-Wright* decision implied that Congress, through action or inaction, could grant nearly any legislative authority to the president.[39] The president, moreover, possessing "plenary" powers, might in some instances act on his own authority without legislative authorization or even contrary to the express will of Congress. In particular, *Curtiss-Wright* helped to set the stage for presidential arrogation of one of Congress's most important foreign policy instruments—the treaty power—as well as the notion that presidential foreign policy actions not specifically prohibited by Congress had been tacitly approved through congressional acquiescence to the president's decisions.

With regard to the treaty power, Article II of the U.S. Constitution provides that proposed treaties between the United States and foreign states must be ratified by a two-thirds vote in the Senate before having the effect of law. On numerous occasions the Senate has exercised its Article II powers by refusing to ratify treaties negotiated and signed by the president. In recent years, the Senate has been especially unwilling to ratify human rights treaties and conventions that Senate Republicans have regarded as impositions on American sovereignty. These include the 1979 Convention on the Elimination of All Forms of Discrimination Against Women, the 1989 Convention on the Rights of the Child, the 1978 American Convention on Human Rights, and the 2000 treaty creating a permanent International Criminal Court. After President Clinton signed the last agreement, Senator Jesse Helms, who then chaired the Senate Foreign Relations Committee, announced it would be "dead on arrival" in the U.S. Senate.

In order to circumvent the Senate's Article II treaty powers, presidents have turned to the device of executive agreements with other nations. Largely at the president's discretion and based mainly on political considerations, these may be executive-congressional agreements, requiring a simple majority vote in each house of Congress, or sole executive agreements, which are never submitted for congressional approval.[40] In the nineteenth and early twentieth centuries, executive agreements were most often trade pacts linked to prior congressional legislation.[41] For example, the Tariff Act of 1897 authorized the president to negotiate certain types of commercial agreements with other nations.[42] Though the resulting agreements were not submitted for ratification, their underlying purpose had been affirmed by the Congress and the president's discretionary authority limited.[43] There are, to be sure, nineteenth- or early-twentieth-century examples of executive agreements undertaken by presidents on their own authority, sometimes at least nominally linked to the president's duties as commander in chief. For example, in 1900, without asking for authorization, President McKinley signed an agreement to cooperate with other nations to send troops to China to protect European legations during the Boxer Rebellion. Subsequently, in 1901, McKinley signed the Boxer Indemnity Protocol between China and other powers, again without seeking Senate approval. Despite these and other exceptions, though, the norm was that compacts between the United States and foreign nations were submitted to the Senate as required by the Constitution.

After taking office in 1933, President Franklin D. Roosevelt had no intention of allowing a small number of senators to block his foreign policy decisions and initiated what is now the standard practice of conducting foreign policy via executive agreement rather than by an Article II treaty. During his first year in office, Roosevelt signed what came to be known as the Litvinov Assignment, which, among other things, provided for American recognition of the Soviet Union and assigned to the government of the United States all Soviet claims against American nationals. When the U.S. government ordered New York's Belmont Bank to turn over certain Russian assets, the bank refused to comply, asserting that the executive agreement upon which the government's claim was based was not the equivalent of an Article II treaty and did not have the force of law. The case reached the Supreme Court in 1937 as *U.S. v. Belmont*.[44] In its decision, the Court not only upheld the government's claim, but it affirmed the president's power to negotiate agreements without Senate approval, which for all intents and purposes would have the legal effect of Article II treaties. Justice Sutherland, writing for the Court, reaffirmed his position in *Curtiss-Wright,* asserting that the president possessed the plenary authority to speak as the "sole organ" of the U.S. government in its foreign relations.[45] As such, the president had the power to make binding international agreements that did not require Senate ratification. This decision was reaffirmed four years later in *U.S. v. Pink,* which also dealt with the disposition of Russian assets in the United States.[46]

Beginning with these decisions, the federal courts have nearly always accepted sole executive agreements and executive-congressional agreements as the equivalents of Article II treaties. A handful of cases, to be sure, have qualified executive agreements or limited their scope. In *Swearingen v. U.S.,* for example, an appeals court held that a sole executive agreement could not supersede the tax code.[47] Such cases, however, are the occasional exceptions. For the most part, the courts have held that, like treaties, executive agreements supersede previously enacted federal and state laws unless they are subsequently disallowed by the Congress. Thus, for example, in *Bercut-Vandervoort & Co. v. U.S.,* the Court of Customs and Patent Appeals ruled that a provision of the Internal Revenue Code must be interpreted in a manner consistent with GATT, though the latter was a sole executive agreement.[48] And in *Coplin v. U.S.,* the Court of Federal Claims ruled that an executive agreement exempting some Americans working in the Panama Canal Zone from U.S. income taxes effectively repealed prior portions of the Internal Revenue Code with which it was inconsistent. Interestingly, the court reached this conclusion even though attorneys for the government actually argued that the president had exceeded his authority.[49] Congress can, through the ordinary legislative process, seek to repeal or qualify an executive agreement. Where Congress fails to take action and specifically prohibit a presidential initiative, the Supreme Court has held that inaction constitutes a form of congressional acceptance or acquiescence.[50] In recent years, President Obama signed a number of executive agreements, including the Enduring Strategic Partnership Agreement with Afghanistan and several trade agreements. Members of Congress grumbled, but grumbling has never been seen by the courts as a form of nonacquiescence. Most recently, the 2015 nuclear accord between the United States and Iran took the form of an agreement. Congress hypothetically had the power to reject the agreement, but such a rejection was subject to a presidential veto that could only have been overridden by a near impossible two-thirds vote of both houses. Had the Iran accord been brought to Congress as a proposed treaty, it could never have mustered the two-thirds vote of the Senate necessary for its ratification under the constitutional formula.

At the same time that they have allowed presidents to substitute executive agreements for treaties when doing so suited the chief executive's purposes, the federal courts have also given the president broad latitude in interpreting existing treaties.[51] In one important case, the Supreme Court actually declined to intervene to block the president from unilaterally terminating an existing treaty.[52] When President Jimmy Carter decided to recognize the People's Republic of China, he also recognized China's claim to sovereignty over Taiwan and accordingly withdrew American recognition from the Taiwan government and terminated America's mutual defense treaty with the island's regime.[53] This precedent was then cited by the Bush administration in support of the president's decision in 2001 to unilaterally terminate the 1972 Anti-Ballistic Missile Treaty.[54]

If one common theme unites the numerous cases affirming the president's dominance in the realm of foreign policy, it is the theme of expertise. In case

after case, the federal courts are moved to declare that the president and, by implication, only the president, possesses adequate knowledge, information, and
judgment to make foreign policy decisions. Legal historian Joel R. Paul calls
this often-expressed judicial presumption "the discourse of executive expediency."[55] Thus, in *Curtiss-Wright,* Justice Sutherland refers to the special information the president may have and to the "unwisdom" of requiring too much
congressional involvement in decision-making. In *Pink,* Justice Douglas writes
that presidential primacy in the realm of external relations is necessary to promote "effectiveness in handling the delicate problems of foreign affairs."[56] In
Dames & Moore, Chief Justice Rehnquist is concerned that Congress continue
to allow the president the discretion he needs to conduct the nation's foreign
policies and to meet the "challenges" with which he must deal.[57] The courts
plainly see that they cannot conduct the nation's foreign policy, and so they
turn—as they see it—of necessity to the president. "The conduct of foreign relations is not open to judicial inquiry" and must be left to the president, Justice
Sutherland said in *Belmont,*[58] and Justice Douglas reiterated in *Pink.*

But what of the Congress? Contemporary courts do not seem to take seriously
the notion that Congress should play a major role in conducting the nation's
foreign affairs. This was seen most recently in the 2015 "Jerusalem passport
case." Congress had enacted a statute declaring that the United States recognized Jerusalem as the capital of Israel. The president considered Tel Aviv to be
the Israeli capital and Jerusalem to be an international city, not formally part
of Israel. Accordingly, the State Department would not issue a Jerusalem-born
American citizen a passport indicating that Israel was his place of birth. The
Supreme Court overturned the congressional act and reaffirmed presidential primacy in matters of foreign policy.[59] As we shall see, this judicial notion of presidential primacy is even more pronounced when contemporary federal courts
consider issues of war and emergency power.

War and National Emergency

Contemporary presidents often behave as though they alone possess the authority to deploy military forces and lead the nation into war. Article I of the
Constitution, however, seems to assign Congress the central role in this area.
The framers gave Congress the power to declare war, to raise and support armies,
to maintain a navy, to make rules for the conduct of the army and navy, to call
out the militia, and to grant letters of marque and reprisal. Only Congress,

moreover, can appropriate funds for the support of military forces. Article II, by contrast, appears to assign the president a lesser role. The president is to serve as commander in chief of the nation's military forces and to see to it that the nation's laws are faithfully executed. On the basis of the Constitution's text and from the debates at the Constitutional Convention, it appears that most of the framers intended Congress to decide whether, how, and when to go to war. The president's role as commander in chief would consist mainly of implementing congressional decisions by organizing actual military campaigns.[60] In addition, the president's duty to see to the faithful execution of the laws might include the task of responding to civil disorder or to foreign attack when Congress could not be convened in a timely manner.[61]

This was certainly the view expressed by James Madison at the Constitutional Convention's committee on drafting when he moved to give Congress the power to declare war while leaving to the executive only the power to "repel sudden attacks."[62] Thomas Jefferson saw Madison's handiwork as an important means of preventing the nation from becoming embroiled in conflicts. "We have already given in example," Jefferson wrote to James Madison, "one effectual check to the Dog of war by transferring the power of letting him loose from those who are to spend to those who are to pay."[63] In modern times, however, the federal courts have been reluctant to rule against the president or in favor of Congress, perhaps unmuzzling the dogs of war more than Jefferson or Madison might have expected.

The early decisions of the federal courts supported this original conception of the distribution of war powers under the Constitution. In recent decades, however, as Gordon Silverstein has observed, the Supreme Court has given wide latitude to the president while reducing the sphere of congressional power in the realm of foreign policy.[64] Indeed, presidential action is generally only prohibited when the courts determine that Congress has formally and explicitly forbidden the action in question. The Supreme Court has interpreted anything short of unambiguous formal prohibition as tacit approval. Thus, the Court held that the absence of congressional disapproval of the president's actions could be constituted as approval. The Court came to a similar conclusion in the 1981 case of *Haig v. Agee,* where it held that the failure of Congress to give the president authority for his actions, "especially in the areas of foreign policy and national security," does not imply congressional disapproval of the president's actions.[65] Subsequently, in *Crockett v. Reagan,* a case in which several members of Congress claimed that the president was violating the War Powers Resolution (WPR) by supplying military assistance to El Salvador, the district court found that before a court could intervene, Congress must take explicit action to apply the WPR to the matter at hand.[66] Similar conclusions were reached by the court in 1987 in *Lowry v. Reagan* and in 1990 in *Dellums v. Bush.*[67] In 1999, several members of Congress brought suit against President Clinton, seeking to compel an end to the air war in Yugoslavia on the grounds that it had not been authorized by Congress and that the president's actions violated the WPR. Here again, both the district and appellate courts held that in the absence of clear-cut evidence of congressional disallowance of the president's actions, no action could be taken by the judiciary.[68]

The President's Legislative Powers

A third area in which the federal courts have helped to expand presidential influence is the realm of the president's legislative powers. The Constitution assigns the president significant legislative power in the form of the right to veto bills of which he disapproves. Over time, and with the help of the courts, presidents have acquired additional legislative power. To begin with, presidents often recommend bundles of programs and policies, such as Roosevelt's New Deal or Johnson's War on Poverty, that shape Congress's legislative agenda. Second, under the terms of the 1921 Budget and Accounting Act, moreover, the president develops and submits to the Congress a unified executive budget.[69] Though Congress may revise the president's estimates, the executive budget usually becomes the template from which Congress works. Third, Congress is usually compelled to delegate considerable legislative power to the president to allow the executive branch to implement congressional programs. For example, if Congress wishes to improve air quality it cannot possibly anticipate all the conditions and circumstances that may arise over the years with respect to its general goal. Inevitably, Congress must delegate to the executive substantial discretionary power to make judgments about the best ways to bring about congressional aims in the face of unforeseen and changing circumstances. Thus, over the years, almost any congressional program will result in thousands and thousands of pages of administrative regulations developed by executive agencies nominally seeking to implement the will of the Congress.

Such delegation is inescapable in the modern era. Congress can hardly administer the thousands of programs it has enacted, and it must delegate power to the president and to a huge bureaucracy to achieve its purposes. Delegation of power to the executive, however, also poses a number of problems for the Congress. If Congress delegates broad and discretionary authority to the executive, it risks seeing its goals subordinated to and subverted by those of the executive branch.[70] If, on the other hand, Congress attempts to limit executive discretion by enacting very precise rules and standards to govern the conduct of the president and the executive branch, it risks writing laws that do not conform to real-world conditions and that are too rigid to be adapted to changing circumstances.[71]

The issue of delegation of power has led to a number of court decisions over the past two centuries generally revolving around the question of the scope of the delegation. As a legal principle, the power delegated to Congress by the people through the Constitution cannot be redelegated by the Congress. This principle implies that directives from Congress to the executive should be narrowly defined and give the latter little or no discretionary power. A broad delegation of congressional authority to the executive branch could be construed as an impermissible redelegation of constitutional power. A second and related question sometimes brought before the courts is whether the rules and regulations adopted by administrators are consistent with Congress's express or implied intent. This question is closely related to the first because the broader the delegation to the executive, the more difficult it is to determine whether the actions of the executive comport with the intent of Congress. The nondelegation doctrine, however, seems to be a relic of the past.[72]

Nevertheless, on matters of agency interpretation, the Supreme Court has weighed in to remind presidents that the executive branch does not have the authority "to decide not to decide" if the statute is clear about a delegated task. In 2007, the Court ruled in *Massachusetts v. EPA* (549 U.S. 497) that the Environmental Protection Agency (EPA) had to regulate carbon dioxide and other greenhouse gases as pollutants according to the authority delegated to it under the Clean Air Act. Twelve states, three cities, and a number of citizen groups sued the EPA, which had been directed by President George W. Bush (R) not to regulate carbon dioxide and other greenhouse gases. The Court ruled, however, that this violated the terms of the Clean Air Act, which requires emission standards to be set for any "air pollution which may reasonably be anticipated to endanger public health or welfare." The question of how much deference is given to executive agencies continues to be worked out in the courts. It is always within the power of Congress, though, through clear statutory language to better control administrative outcomes. There is always some gap between what Congress intends a law to achieve and what an agency actually does to implement it, but the clearer the statutory language is, the smaller that implementation gap will be.

Administrative Power

A fourth realm in which the courts have helped to enhance the authority of the president is the area of administrative power. Three issues, in particular, have been important. These are executive privilege, the appointment and removal power, and executive orders. As to executive privilege, this concept had no firm standing in law until the Supreme Court's decision in *U.S. v. Nixon.* The actual term "executive privilege" was coined by President Eisenhower, who frequently refused to provide information to Congress when to do so, in his view, would violate the confidentiality of deliberations in the executive branch.[73] But long before Eisenhower introduced the phrase, presidents claimed the power to withhold materials from Congress and from the courts.[74] George Washington, for example, refused congressional requests for information about a disastrous campaign against the Indians and about the circumstances surrounding the negotiation of the Jay Treaty between the United States and Britain.

In the course of presiding over the criminal case against Aaron Burr, Chief Justice John Marshall gave some standing to such claims. Marshall indicated that in criminal cases the president could not be treated like an ordinary individual and might only be compelled to produce evidence if it was clearly shown by affidavit to be essential to the conduct of the case.[75] Because of the Watergate affair, the term "executive privilege" has developed a bad odor, and subsequent presidents have sometimes used other phrases to deny congressional or judicial requests for information. For example, in refusing to allow the director of Homeland Security to testify before Congress in March 2002, President Bush asserted a claim of "executive prerogative."[76] In 2014, however, President Obama did use the term "executive privilege" in refusing to provide Congress with documents pertaining to an abortive "sting operation" by the Bureau of Alcohol, Tobacco, Firearms and Explosives (ATF), which may have resulted in a Mexican drug gang acquiring firearms used, among other criminal matters, in the murder of a U.S. Border Patrol agent.

In *U.S. v. Nixon,* the Court for the first time explicitly recognized executive privilege as a valid presidential claim to be balanced against competing claims. The Court indicated that where important issues were at stake, especially foreign policy questions as well as military and state secrets, presidential claims of privilege should be given great deference by the courts. Finding no such issues in the present case, though, the Court ruled against Nixon. In a subsequent case, *Nixon v. Administrator of General Services,* the Court held that the former president's records were not privileged communications and could be transferred to the General Services Administration.[77] Once again, though, the Court recognized the existence of executive privilege and said it could be used to protect the president's communications "in performance of [his] responsibilities . . . and made in the process of shaping policy and making decisions." Thus, in both *Nixon* cases, precedents were established for claims of privilege, and in subsequent years the federal courts have upheld several such claims made by the president and other executive branch officials acting at the president's behest. For example, in *U.S. v. American Telephone & Telegraph,* in response to a presidential claim of privilege, the district court enjoined AT&T from providing a congressional subcommittee with the contents of a number of wiretaps conducted by the FBI.[78] Similarly, in *U.S. v. House of Representatives,* the district court refused to compel EPA administrator Anne Gorsuch to hand over what she claimed were privileged documents to a House subcommittee.[79]

In their more recent decisions, federal courts have continued to rule in favor of executive privilege in national security cases and others as well.[80] Both presidential deliberations and those of presidential advisers and their staffs have been held to be privileged.[81] In a recent case, the Vice President claimed privilege. This is the case of *U.S. v. District Court of the District of Columbia.*[82] In this case, a coalition of public interest groups, including Judicial Watch and the Sierra Club, sought to obtain the records of an energy task force led by Vice President Dick Cheney in 2001. The public interest groups brought the suit after a similar suit brought by the director of the Government Accountability Office was dismissed for want of standing. The Cheney energy task force had been formed to make recommendations to the administration regarding federal energy policy. The public interest coalition charged that the task force gave inordinate influence to energy producers at the expense of consumer and environmental interests. A federal district court ordered Cheney to turn over his records.

In a 7–2 opinion, however, the Supreme Court ruled that the vice president was entitled to the protection of executive privilege in order "to protect the executive branch from vexatious litigation that might distract it from the energetic performance of its constitutional duties."[83]

Another administrative realm in which the Supreme Court has generally shown deference to the president in recent decades is the area of appointment and removal. The president's appointment powers are defined in the Constitution and have produced little litigation. One important recent case, however, is *Buckley v. Valeo,* in which the Court ruled that Congress was not entitled to give itself the power to appoint members of the Federal Election Commission, an agency of the executive branch.[84] The removal power, by contrast, is not defined in the Constitution and has been a topic of some conflict between the president and Congress. In 1833, Congress censured President Jackson for removing the secretary of the Treasury. In 1867, Congress enacted the Tenure of Office Act, which required Senate consent for the removal of cabinet officers over Andrew Johnson's veto. Johnson's subsequent attempt to remove Secretary of War Stanton played a major role in the president's impeachment. Congress enacted legislation in 1872 and 1876 requiring Senate consent for the removal of postmasters but did, however, repeal the Tenure of Office Act in 1887.[85]

The Supreme Court has made a number of decisions regarding the removal power, which for the most part have supported the president. In the 1926 case of *Myers v. U.S.,* the Court struck down the 1876 law, ruling that the power to remove executive officials "is vested in the president alone."[86] In the 1935 case of *Humphrey's Executor v. U.S.,* however, the Court ruled against Franklin D. Roosevelt's efforts to remove a Federal Trade Commission (FTC) member before his term had expired. The Court noted that the FTC Act required the president to show cause for such actions and upheld Congress's right to impose such a requirement.[87] More recently, however, in the case of *Bowsher v. Synar,* the Court struck down a portion of the Gramm-Rudman-Hollings Balanced Budget Act, which authorized the comptroller general, an official removable only by Congress, to review executive decisions.[88] And in *Mistretta v. U.S.,* the Court upheld the president's power under the Sentencing Reform Act to remove members of the U.S. Sentencing Commission, including federal judges.[89] In recent years, only in the politically charged cases involving special prosecutors have the courts significantly restricted presidential removal powers. In *Nader v. Bork,* the district court held that President Nixon's firing of the Watergate special prosecutor, Archibald Cox, was illegal.[90] And in *Morrison v. Olson,* the Supreme Court held that restrictions on the president's power to remove a special prosecutor did not invalidate the appointment.[91]

Finally, as to executive orders, it is sufficient to note that of the thousands of such orders and presidential memoranda issued from the birth of the Republic through 1999, the overwhelming majority of which have been since 1933, one systematic study found that only fourteen were actually overturned by the courts. Of these fourteen, the federal judiciary struck down portions of twelve orders and overturned two others in their entirety.[92] One additional executive order was invalidated by a lower court in 2001.[93] In 2015, a federal circuit court struck down President Obama's order on immigration, and, on the basis of a 4–4 tie vote, the Supreme Court left the decision in place. Also in 2015, as we saw in chapter 6, the Supreme Court blocked enforcement of Obama's 2013 orders mandating new carbon-emissions rules until they received further judicial scrutiny, a matter that became moot after Obama left office and President Trump rescinded the orders. During his first two years in office, President Trump made extensive use of executive orders. Lower federal courts blocked portions of his orders on immigration and the rights of federal employees, but as of October 2018, in the one case heard by the Supreme Court, the president's actions were upheld. In 2017, several lower federal courts had blocked implementation of President Trump's executive orders imposing restrictions on visitors from several mainly Muslim countries. The president said that his travel ban was needed to prevent terrorism, but several judges found that the ban was discriminatory and in violation of federal law. In June 2018, however, the Supreme Court ruled that the president's actions were consistent with the executive's broad power over immigration matters.[94]

One important executive order overturned in its entirety was Truman's directive seizing the nation's steel mills, which was struck down in the 1952 case of *Youngstown Sheet & Tube v. Sawyer.*[95] A second was President Clinton's order prohibiting the federal government from hiring permanent replacements for striking workers. This order, which contradicted both a Supreme Court ruling and specific federal legislation, was invalidated in the 1996 case of *Chamber of Commerce v. Reich.*[96] For the most part, the courts have been reluctant to examine executive orders, often ruling that the plaintiff lacked standing or that the dispute involved a political question. And where they have heard the case, they have almost always upheld the president's directive.[97]

Why the Courts Support the President and Not the Congress

For the past century or so, the federal courts have generally used their power of judicial review to strengthen the presidency and reduce the role of Congress. Occasionally, the judiciary does show a willingness to confront the president. Perhaps the most dramatic instance since the New Deal when the Court directly confronted a sitting president was the Watergate tapes case, in which the Supreme Court ordered President Nixon to give congressional investigators the secret Oval Office tapes that had been subpoenaed by the Congress.[98] In this instance the Court could count on the support of the Congress as well as backing from leaders of both political parties and most of the national news media. Nixon, moreover, would have been certain of impeachment if he had refused the order. Even so, there was no guarantee that the president would obey, and, as we shall see, in its opinion the Court was deferential to the idea of presidential power. In 1975, the Court ruled against Nixon's practice of impounding funds that Congress had appropriated when he did not approve of their use.[99] By this time, however, Nixon had already resigned and Congress had already placed restrictions on impoundment in the 1974 Budget Act. The Court's decision was anticlimactic, to say the least.

Against this backdrop of conflict avoidance, Chief Justice Roberts's 2012 decision to uphold the constitutionality of the 2010 Affordable Care Act, the central focus of President Obama's legislative agenda, seems consistent with the historic pattern. Many commentators expected the Court, with its conservative majority, to strike down major portions of the act on the grounds that the individual mandate (requirement that individuals purchase health insurance) imposed by the legislation was inconsistent with congressional power under the Commerce Clause. In his opinion for the Court, though, Chief Justice Roberts asserted that the mandate was actually a tax, not an unwarranted expansion of congressional regulatory powers.[100] As a tax, the mandate was well within the scope of congressional authority. Some critics pointed out that if the mandate was a tax, it violated the constitutional requirement that tax bills originate in the House. The Affordable Care Act originated in the Senate. But whatever the constitutional niceties, the Chief Justice seemed determined to avoid a direct clash with the president and so found reason to uphold the act. This position was affirmed in 2015 when the Court again upheld the Affordable Care Act in the case of *King v. Burwell*.[101]

In a much less important case, Justice Roberts *was* willing to rebuke the president. As we saw in chapter 2, the Court ruled unanimously in 2014 that a ten-day recess had been "presumptively too short" to permit the president to make three recess appointments to the National Labor Relations Board. The president was annoyed, but the White House had merely been testing the limits of its power with no real expectation that its ploy would succeed.

The federal courts generally support the president and the executive branch not simply because they are afraid not to do so, but because they think they should. The support given the executive branch by the federal courts has often been noted by legal scholars with a number of explanations offered for the phenomenon. For example, the late constitutional historian Edward Corwin thought that the courts tended to defer to the president because presidential exercises of power often produced some change in the world that the judiciary felt powerless to negate.[102] Political scientists Terry Moe and William Howell, on the other hand, point to the dependence of the courts upon the goodwill of the executive branch for enforcement of their decisions.[103] Other scholars emphasize the reluctance of the courts to risk their prestige in disputes with popular presidents.[104]

All these explanations have some merit, but there is another factor that has played an even more important role in linking the courts to the White House. This element is the process of judicial appointment. While much has been written about the appointment process, its political significance has often been misunderstood. Presidents obviously seek to appoint judges who will support them in the years to come but, as has often been noted, this expectation is the equivalent of an unenforceable contract.[105] There is no guarantee that once ensconced in office jurists will support their patrons, much less their patrons' successors. And, often enough, judges have surprised and disappointed the presidents who nominated them. We need look no further than the late Supreme Court chief justice Earl Warren or former justice David Souter for two recent examples.

The actual significance of the appointment process, especially as it pertains to presidential power, is, however, somewhat more subtle. In their overall pattern, judicial appointments reflect the political milieu from which judges are drawn and to which they are tied. During the nineteenth century, federal judges were typically drawn from—and often had continuing ties to—the nation's electoral and representative systems. Not only were most judicial nominees active in party politics, but before their appointment to the bench, many district and circuit court judges, and even a number of Supreme Court justices, had run for elective office and had served in the state legislators. Some had served in the U.S. Congress. Chief Justice John Marshall, for example, served in both the Virginia House of Delegates and the U.S. House of Representatives. His successor, Roger Brooke Taney, had served in the Maryland General Assembly and the Maryland State Senate. Indeed, one comprehensive study has shown that among the two hundred district court judges appointed between 1829 and 1861, not only were the jurists themselves veterans of the electoral and legislative arenas, but more than 60 percent even had fathers who had been active in electoral and legislative politics.[106]

The legislative experience once possessed by judges is now largely a thing of the past. Before the Civil War, more than 50 percent of all federal judges had previously served in a representative assembly, while today barely 4 percent have ever held elective office.[107] Contemporary federal judges are drawn mainly from the executive and judicial branches and have little experience in the realm of legislative politics. This shift in the political backgrounds of federal judges, of course, reflects changes in the character of the American party system as well as the place of legislatures in the American institutional framework. In the nineteenth century, presidents looked to legislatures as a source of party notables whose appointment to the bench would strengthen their own political position. In the twentieth and twenty-first centuries, political parties and legislatures have declined in importance and presidents are more likely to seek the favor of important interest and constituency groups, like environmentalists and consumer activists (if they are Democrats), or antiabortionists and pro-business forces (if they are Republicans). Unlike the old-time party leaders, these new political notables are often likely to be found in the executive and judicial branches, where such movements have sought and won privileged access. Many important political forces in recent years have been eschewing legislative combat in favor of bureaucratic politics and litigation, where they have been able to achieve satisfactory results without risking their fate to the vicissitudes of democratic politics.[108]

Does the institutional wellhead from which judges are drawn make a difference in their behavior on the bench? Conclusive proof would be difficult to offer, but everyone who has lived and worked in Washington, D.C., sooner or later learns that most employees of the executive and judicial branches of the government are rather disdainful of the Congress and, if they notice them at all, dismissive of the state legislatures. Indeed, from the perspective of many offi-cials of the other two branches of government, the nation's elected representa-tives are mainly a collection of meddlers and bunglers who almost invariably place political considerations ahead of important national goals and priorities. It is revealing to read the unflattering assessment of Congress offered by the late Harold Seidman, one of the nation's greatest scholars of governmental or-ganization and, for twenty-five years, a senior executive-branch official in the Bureau of the Budget (now called the White House Office of Management and Budget). "Within the Congress," Seidman asserts, "words are sometimes equated with deeds . . . [and] . . . concern . . . is focused principally on those elements [of public policy] that directly affect constituency interests or committee juris-dictions." He continues: "Legislative proposals are seldom debated from the viewpoint of their administrative feasibility. . . . If things go wrong, failure can always be attributed to [others]."[109]

Seidman's views probably reflect the Washington consensus. It would be dif-ficult to find any official with an executive or judicial background who has much respect for Congress, its processes, and—with a few exceptions—its members. Disparaging comments about legislative "interference" in the orderly processes of government are commonly heard in both formal and informal Washington settings. As the late senator Robert Byrd (D-WV) complained after White House officials referred to congressional rules and procedures as a set of, "Lilliputian do's and don'ts": "Some of these people [executive branch officials] have com-plete disdain for Congress. They are contemptuous of Congress."[110]

Nineteenth-century judges often had legislative backgrounds and were re-cruited from a political milieu in which legislatures were respected and power-ful institutions. Accordingly, they had little difficulty deferring to legislative judgments. Contemporary judges, by contrast, seldom have served as members of representative bodies. They are not even accustomed to viewing legislatures as institutions capable of taking sound and decisive actions. Perhaps the most significant exception to this rule was former Supreme Court Justice Sandra Day O'Connor who was the principal author of a number of decisions seeking to return power to the state legislatures. Perhaps it is no coincidence that Justice O'Connor was among the rare federal judges with state legislative experience, having served as a member and majority leader of the Arizona State Legislature in the 1970s.

To a substantial extent, indeed, many federal judges have come to embrace a set of beliefs that were first fully articulated in the United States during the Progressive Era. In the Progressive vision, only the judiciary and the executive branch are capable of dealing effectively with important national problems. Legislatures, by contrast, are inefficient, fit only to represent parochial, as opposed to broad, public interests, and are often corrupt. As one prominent federal appeals court judge observed, many contemporary federal judges, influenced by Progressive modes of thought, seek "rationality" in public policy and have an attitude of "hostility to a pluralist, party dominated, political process."[111] Such views are, of course, likely to find expression in distaste for legislatures and a preference for decision-making by courts and the executive—the nation's "rational" institutions. Recently, for example, a number of judges have objected vigorously to congressional efforts to control the policies of the United States Sentencing Commission, created by Congress in 1984 to ensure some measure of nationwide uniformity in sentencing for federal crimes. Though setting the appropriate penalties for violations of statutes would seem to lie within the purview of the nation's legislature, some federal judges seem to regard congressional efforts to establish sentencing rules as wholly misguided and illegitimate, and the rules were eventually modified and power restored to the bench by a series of Supreme Court decisions.[112]

What Can Congress Do?

The Constitution gave Congress a number of powers that it might use vis-à-vis the courts. Congress can alter the jurisdiction of the federal courts, including the appellate jurisdiction of the Supreme Court; Congress can impeach federal judges; and Congress can launch an effort to amend the Constitution, as it did after the Supreme Court struck down the income tax in 1885. Through legislation, moreover, Congress may endeavor to overturn a judicial holding or modify judicial procedure, as in the case of the sentencing guidelines. All these weapons are cumbersome to use and rather weak in the face of the giant cannon wielded by the court—the power of judicial review.

Presidents and their congressional supporters, moreover, generally oppose efforts in Congress to attack the judiciary. Every student learns the story of President Andrew Jackson's defiance of the Supreme Court, but Jackson was the rare—and perhaps lone—exception. Generally speaking, presidents have seen it as consistent with their broader interests to support the Court. As observed by

Lyle Denniston of the National Constitution Center, presidents in general have tended to see it as their duty to obey Supreme Court rulings and to enforce them. For example, despite his own doubts about the wisdom of school desegregation, President Dwight Eisenhower called out the military in 1957 to enforce the Supreme Court's order to racially integrate the Little Rock, Arkansas, public schools. Eisenhower told the nation, "Whenever normal agencies prove inadequate to the task and it becomes necessary for the Executive Branch of the Federal Government to use its powers and authority to uphold Federal Courts, the President's responsibility is inescapable."[113] Indeed, between 1957 and 1960, when important forces in Congress fulminated against the High Court and looked for legislative mechanisms to curb judicial power, the Court was rather steadfastly defended by the executive branch.[114] In October 2018, a bitter partisan struggle over the appointment of Brett Kavanaugh to the Supreme Court ended with Kavanaugh's confirmation and a solid conservative majority on the Court. Some Democratic pundits recommended that the next Democratic president seek to increase the number of justices in order to tip the Court's ideological balance or otherwise reduce the Supreme Court's power in American affairs. Against the historical backdrop, this would seem to be an unlikely development.

On a year-in, year-out basis, the executive defends the Court in another way. Recall the suggestion made by University of Chicago law professor William Baude cited at the beginning of this chapter. Baude proposed a return to the departmentalist view in which presidents, while obeying the specifics, might refuse to accept as binding precedent Court decisions they did not like. Generally speaking, presidents do not take this position, though it is a position with historic and constitutional justification that would weaken the courts and that the judiciary would have enormous difficulty circumventing. The fact that presidents are not departmentalists speaks volumes about their view that judicial power generally serves their interests. Perhaps we have reached the situation Hamilton feared—the judiciary firmly allied with one institution against the other.

Reflections on Congress

IN RECENT YEARS, AMERICANS HAVE been sharply divided on many political questions. They have disagreed about social policy, foreign policy, health policy, crime, guns, immigration, and issues of race and gender. If there is, however, one political matter that seems to unite Americans, it is contempt for Congress. Less than 17 percent of the public thinks Congress is doing a good job, and nearly 75 percent say they have an unfavorable view of Congress. Some academics seem to share this perspective, calling Congress a "broken branch."[1]

When Americans are asked why they have a negative image of the Congress, three factors appear to stand out. First, Congress is seen as having slow and cumbersome procedures that interfere with "getting the job done." Former talk show host Jay Leno once claimed, "according to a *Washington Post* poll, 84 percent of Americans did not approve of the way Congress was doing its job. Sixteen percent weren't even aware Congress was doing a job." Second, Congress is seen as polarized, with members unwilling to develop the compromises needed to serve the public interest. High levels of polarization are exemplified by frequent name calling on the Hill, such as the recent exchange between then Senate minority leader Harry Reid and several GOP colleagues. Reid declared that Republicans wanted to make the economy worse to embarrass the president. Republicans replied to Reid's comment by asserting that Reid frequently espoused "bullshit." Third, Congress is seen as corrupt, serving lobbyists, special interests, and campaign contributors rather than the American people. The late senator Ted Kennedy captured this sentiment when he described America's representative assembly as "the best Congress money can buy."

There is obviously some truth to each of these charges. Congressional procedures can be slow and cumbersome, Congress is ideologically polarized, and various forms of corruption can be found on Capitol Hill. Let us consider, however, whether these charges amount to a serious indictment of Congress, its members, and its procedures.

Not Getting the Job Done

During each recent session of Congress, more than 10,000 bills and resolutions have been introduced by senators and representatives. Of these thousands of potential pieces of legislation, typically only 3 or 4 percent have been actually voted upon, and only 2 or 3 percent eventually enacted into law. The two most recent Congresses were especially unproductive. The 112th Congress (2011–2013) voted on 390 of 12,299 bills introduced, enacting 284, or 2 percent, while the 113th Congress (2013–2014) voted on 474 bills of the 10,637 introduced during its two-year life. Only 296 of these bills, or 3 percent, passed both houses and were signed into law by the president. The current Congress is likely to be no different and, in fact, may reach the newest low in terms of productivity in at least forty years.

Why are so few bills enacted into law? As noted earlier, in many cases, members introduce legislation mainly for symbolic purposes, say to demonstrate to a constituency group that the member is cognizant of their views, without having any particular expectation that the bill will be enacted or signed into law.[2] But even when a bill's sponsors are actually hopeful of writing a new law, they face many hurdles. Legislation proposed by members of the minority party is unlikely ever to be reported out of committee. Legislation proposed by members of the majority party may be out of step with the leadership's agenda and, as a result, blocked by a committee chairman or the Speaker or majority leader, all of whom, as we saw in chapters 4 and 5, have considerable power to prevent a bill from coming up for a vote, much less becoming a law. In the 1990s, as we saw, Congress adopted a number of reforms ostensibly designed to streamline the legislative process and to give rank-and-file members a greater opportunity to see their proposals enacted. And, today, some members of Congress and academic experts have proposed quite a few more well-intentioned reforms that, if adopted, might speed the flow of business through Congress and result in more legislation.[3]

The question, though, begged by demands that Congress be reformed, is whether the congressional process is actually "snarled and broken," as some say. On the face of it, perhaps: only 296 bills enacted after more than 10,000 were introduced in the 113th Congress might suggest an overly cumbersome legislative process, but how many laws should Congress have enacted? During roughly the same period, the Supreme Court granted certiorari (agreement to hear and decide) to only about 1 percent of the more than nine thousand cases filed by petitioners. No one suggests that the High Court is broken, even though its level of productivity might be said to be only one-third that of the Congress.

The charge that Congress does not do enough, to some extent, reflects what might be called a "legislationist" bias that evaluates Congress on the basis of the quantity of legislation it produces. But shouldn't Congress be credited for blocking proposals as well as enacting them? Recall that during the four years of the 112th and 113th Congresses, Republicans controlled the House of Representatives and worked diligently to block policy initiatives emanating from the Democratic White House. The fact that relatively few laws were enacted should be no surprise. From a Republican perspective, Congress was hardly a broken branch—it was vigorously doing its job as Dr. No!

The framers of the Constitution, it might be recalled, were hardly legislationists. They thought one advantage of America's complicated system of checks and balances was precisely the fact that it would make it difficult to enact new legislation. We might all benefit from rereading James Madison's views, expressed in *Federalist* 62. Madison wrote, "It will be of little avail to the people that the laws are made by men of their own choice, if the laws be so voluminous that they cannot be read, or so incoherent that they cannot be understood; if they be repealed or revised before they are promulgated, or undergo such incessant changes that no man, who knows what the law is to-day, can guess what it will be to-morrow." Such a state of affairs, according to Madison, can reduce popular respect for government. Thus, by Madisonian standards, Congress is not exactly a broken branch.

Polarization

A second charge frequently leveled against the Congress is that its members are so polarized that they cannot work together to achieve the level of consensus and compromise needed to legislate. There is certainly a good deal of truth to

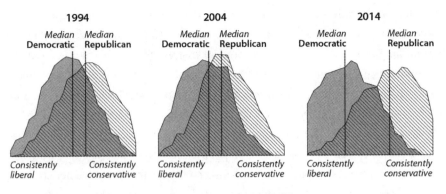

Figure 10.1. "Political Polarization in the American Public," 1994, 2004, and 2014, Pew Research Center, June 12, 2014. http://www.people-press.org/2014 /06/12/political-polarization-in-the-american-public/.

this assertion. As many studies have indicated, Congress is more ideologically polarized today than at any time since the end of Reconstruction.

This high level of polarization, however, does not indicate some aberration unique to Capitol Hill. The fact is that Americans are deeply polarized and Congress reflects that fact. According to a recent Pew study, Democrats and Republicans in the general population are more deeply divided than in the past, with 27 percent of Democrats surveyed saying that the Republican Party is a threat to the nation's well-being, and 36 percent of Republicans holding a similar view about the Democrats (see fig. 10.1). President Trump's actions to sharply reduce immigration were viewed as matters of common sense or perceived security needs by most Republicans and as antidemocratic, if not outright racist, by most Democrats. Cross-party conversations on the matter, whether across the aisle or over the fence, often devolve into shouting matches.

This high level of ideological polarization within the general public is, in no small part, a result of changes in the mass media over the past several decades. As recently as the end of the twentieth century, most Americans obtained their news from a small number of television networks—NBC, CBS, and ABC. These networks competed directly with one another for a national audience and tailored their news and public affairs coverage for what they saw as the median viewer. The result was that all three offered similar content and moderate opinions. Today, Americans can choose from among a number of media outlets, and most receive their news and information from the Internet and from cable news networks.

This proliferation of media outlets has meant that rather than compete for a national audience, each has chosen an ideological niche and developed programming to satisfy the predispositions of that group. The best known outlets employing this strategy are FOX, which aims its programming at conservatives, and MSNBC, which serves a politically liberal audience. Many Americans obtain their information from even more stridently liberal or conservative radio hosts and bloggers. The result is that the media has a radicalizing rather than moderating effect. And as levels of polarization have increased, Americans have chosen to cluster together in like-minded groups in choosing where to worship, where to shop, and even where to live.[4]

Of course, as we saw in chapter 3, polarization on Capitol Hill is exacerbated by gerrymandering (controlled by the state legislatures), which has tended to produce ideologically homogeneous districts that demand ideological purity from their representatives. The point is, nevertheless, that ideological polarization on Capitol Hill reflects the state of affairs in the nation. In America today, congressional moderates and partisans who reach across the aisle to vote with the members of the other party are likely to be castigated as spineless, as turncoats or flip-floppers, and worse. We should not complain about ideological polarization and demand ideological purity.

Corruption

A third charge frequently leveled against Congress concerns corruption. In a recent survey, more than half of all Americans said that most members of Congress were corrupt, and a third thought that even their own representative was corrupt. Two-thirds thought that Congress was focused on the needs of special interests rather than the needs of its ordinary constituents (see table 10.1).

It is certainly easy to understand why Americans view Congress as a corrupt institution. As we saw in chapter 3, special interests contribute hundreds of millions of dollars to congressional campaigns. And, as we saw in chapter 5, lobbyists representing those selfsame interests actively seek to influence the legislative process. Even the least engaged citizen can connect these two very large dots. Concrete evidence of wrongdoing on Capitol Hill, such as scandals involving bribes, payoffs, kickbacks, and so forth seems to erupt every eight or ten years. In the 1980 "Abscam" scandal, six House members and one senator

Table 10.1. Is Congress Corrupt?

	Your Member %	Most Members %
Corrupt or Not Corrupt?		
Corrupt	32	52
Not Corrupt	59	42
Focused on the Needs of Special Interests, or Focused On Needs of Constituents in Your/Their District?		
Special interests	47	69
Constituents	43	25
Generally Out of Touch with Average Americans or Generally in Touch?		
Out of touch	48	79
In touch	47	20

Source: Adapted from: Andrew Dugan, "Majority of Americans See Congress as Out of Touch, Corrupt," September 28, 2015, Gallup poll at https://news.gallup.com/poll/185918/majority-americans-congress-touch-corrupt.aspx.

were videotaped accepting bribes. The 1991 House Post Office scandal and the 1992 House banking scandal revealed that some members misused their privileges at the two institutions. The most recent of these scandals involved the activities of Washington super lobbyist Jack Abramoff, who, along with several associates, including Michael Scanlon, a former staffer for House majority leader Tom DeLay (R-TX), took more than $80 million in payments from several Native American tribes to win approval to establish gambling casinos on their reservations or, in some cases, to block other tribes from so doing. In some instances, Abramoff and Scanlon apparently accepted money from competing tribes, promising to both further and block the same casino project.

In 2006, Abramoff and Scanlon were convicted of various criminal offenses, and DeLay was charged and convicted in 2010 of money laundering and conspiracy. After a series of appeals, however, DeLay's conviction was reversed in 2014. During the course of the investigation, Abramoff apparently implicated a number of other members of Congress, including former Democratic Senate majority leader Harry Reid, in illegal activities. The only member found guilty of illicit activities was Representative Bob Ney (R-OH), convicted of conspiracy and making false statements to a federal investigator.

Of course, Congress has developed a variety of rules designed to reassure the public that their senators and representatives are honest and ethical. The 1995 Lobbying Disclosure Act is designed to produce transparency regarding the activities of Capitol Hill lobbyists. (Campaign finance rules were discussed in chapter 3.) Each House of Congress, moreover, has adopted voluminous ethics rules governing the activities of its members. House ethics rules, for example, prohibit members from accepting gifts and gratuities, regulate attendance at private events and travel, prohibit the acceptance of honoraria for speeches, monitor potential conflicts of interest, and so forth.[5]

Do these rules guarantee completely honest and ethical conduct on the part of members of Congress? Absolutely not. All human beings, whether legislators, bureaucrats, members of the clergy, or even college professors are capable of behaving in a corrupt and venal manner. Most will be discouraged from engaging in illicit conduct by fear of disclosure and punishment. Some believe themselves sufficiently clever to evade detection or are so venal that they will accept considerable risk in exchange for the possibility of making a quick dollar. The idea of halting all corruption is a mirage, and a dangerous one. To secure absolute integrity we would be forced to accept a level of surveillance and oversight that would stifle the activities of a representative body.[6]

The question we should ask ourselves is not whether Congress is an absolutely ethical body, but rather whether Congress is less ethical than other institutions or so unethical as to be unworthy of its place in the governance of the United States. If we consider the matter from this perspective, the answer, though somewhat ambiguous, does not represent a searing indictment of the U.S. Congress. Between 1993 and 2014, 18 members of the Congress were convicted of various forms of official misconduct—most on charges stemming from the scandals mentioned earlier. During the same period, 9,088 officials of the executive branch, 1,990 state officials, and 5,146 local officials were convicted on various federal corruption charges.[7] Of course, the number of federal, state, and local officials is far greater than the number of members of Congress, but one might also argue that members of Congress are subjected to far more official and media scrutiny than the others. The point here is not to absolve members of Congress of all their sins. It is rather to suggest that the Congress is not the den of iniquity imagined by the media.

Congressional Gridlock and the Rise of Presidentialism

The various charges frequently leveled against Congress by the media and by academic critics, as just discussed, contribute to the public's sense that Congress is a broken institution, incapable of playing a meaningful role in the governance of the United States. We believe that these charges are not only overstated but destructive to democratic government in America. If Congress is incompetent, polarized, and corrupt, it seems to follow that Americans should give up on democratic government and look to the president and the bureaucracy and the courts for leadership. Some might welcome this change. We submit, however, that neither the president nor the bureaucracy nor the courts are democratic institutions, nor are they free of their own forms of incompetence and corruption. Congress, warts and all, *is* a democratic institution. Its faults are the faults of democracy. Democracy is messy; it can become polarized and gridlocked; its politicians can be venal. It is, as Winston Churchill quipped, the worst of all possible forms of government except all the others. We might do well to remember that Congress is not only the first branch but also the democratic branch of American government. If Congress is broken, then democracy in America is broken.

The widespread perception, fostered by journalists and pundits, that Congress is broken has emboldened presidents to ignore the Congress and seek to govern unilaterally. Each year, presidents issue dozens if not hundreds of executive orders and memoranda, claiming that their action was necessary because Congress had been unable to act. In 2015, for example, President Obama issued an executive order blocking the deportation of large numbers of undocumented immigrants. The president said he had no choice but to act on his own because Congress had proven unable to take action. The president's claim was a bit disingenuous. A bill proposing congressional action had failed to pass. It would be more correct to say that Congress had declined to take the action favored by the president rather than declare that Congress had shown an inability to act. Nevertheless, consistent with the broken-Congress thesis, most pundits accepted the president's assertion.

Presidents attempt to make domestic policy by executive order. President Trump issued fifteen executive orders in just his first nine days in office—some reversing orders issued by former president Obama. They attempt to make foreign policy, as we have seen, by executive agreement, thus circumventing the constitutional treaty power. Presidents use signing statements to rewrite statutes enacted by Congress and, in a process called regulatory review, attempt to write their own laws by taking control of the bureaucratic rulemaking process we examined in chapter 7. Executive power seems to be on the march, and the challenge to Congress is to preserve democratic government in the face of presidentialism.

There is no shortage of proposals for reforms that could potentially strengthen Congress and enhance its power over the executive branch. In June 2016, then House Speaker Ryan frequently lamented the decline of congressional power under the pressure of presidents of both political parties and unveiled a set of such proposals.[8] The Ryan proposals consisted of four major elements. First, the Speaker proposed greater restrictions on the authority of federal agencies through statutory language that spelled out in greater detail an agency's duties and powers under any piece of legislation. Second, Ryan called for greater congressional and judicial oversight over agency rulemaking, including more aggressive use of the Congressional Review Act and enactment of the REINS Act (see chapter 8). REINS would require agencies to obtain congressional approval before adopting major new rules, while the CRA gives Congress an opportunity to disallow major and minor rules that have been adopted. The Speaker also sketched out ways in which spending bills might better specify what the executive is and is not allowed to do with authorized funds and called for more systematic congressional oversight of executive agencies. This would include expedited use of the subpoena power and more authority for agencies' own inspectors general to investigate fraud and abuse and to report it to Congress.

During the first weeks of the 115th Congress, the CRA was used to negate a number of regulations adopted in the closing months of the Obama administration. These included rules on the environment, education, gun ownership, financial protections, and Internet privacy. President Trump then signed bills erasing these rules and fulfilling his campaign promise to curb government regulation. Perhaps Speaker Ryan's aggressive use of the CRA suggests that Congress can reassert its authority over the executive branch, but we should be mindful of the fact that the success of the CRA depends upon presidential cooperation. Had President Trump chosen to veto the bills instead of sign them, the rules would have remained in effect. This, in fact, could happen if the two branches are held by different parties. Thus, the CRA illustrates the limits as well as the possibilities of congressional power.

Some congressional analysts, though, such as Kevin Kosar, president of the think tank R Street Institute, argue that Congress can "curb a runaway president." Kosar outlines six ways in which the institution can achieve this, and several are consistent with Ryan's proposals: leveraging the nomination process by the majority party to better influence presidential picks for key administrative positions; restricting executive branch regulatory power by passing the REINS Act and related measures; increasing the staff and thereby the capacity of the legislative branch; insisting that agencies' public communications and actions are "objective and balanced in tone and are not intended to the 'sell' the policies" of a particular president; taking back "some power over the purse" by insisting that agencies return to the Treasury Department funds that a president decides not to spend so the Congress can reappropriate them; and clarifying what an impeachable offense is so that Congress is "publicly on the hook to consider impeachment when a president crosses the line."[9] Congress is the most dynamic of our political institutions and will need to continue to adapt to changes within our country and beyond our borders. It remains the first branch, and it behooves all of us to help ensure its vitality within our political system of checks and balances.

As students of Congress, we should put partisanship aside and perhaps consider Ryan's comments as he introduced his various proposals. In presenting his proposals, Ryan declared, "The people granted Congress the power to write laws, raise revenues, and spend and borrow money on behalf of the United States. There is no power more consequential. . . . Yet for decades Congress has let this power atrophy—thereby depriving the people of their voice."[10] From what we have seen in this book, is Speaker Ryan wrong? We will see what the new Congress elected in 2018 does, but whatever the partisan composition of a particular Congress, we might go a step further and say that the friends of democracy should wish Congress well and perhaps congratulate Congress for its virtues rather than simply rehearse its faults.

NOTES

Chapter 1. Congress

1. Thomas E. Mann and Norman J. Ornstein, *The Broken Branch: How Congress Is Failing America and How to Get It on Track* (New York: Oxford University Press, 2006).
2. Eric A. Posner and Adrian Vermeule, *The Executive Unbound: After the Madisonian Republic* (New York: Oxford University Press, 2010), 16.
3. William J. Keefe and Morris S. Ogul, *The American Legislative Process* (Upper Saddle River, NJ: Prentice-Hall, 2001), 236.
4. Christopher Simpson, *National Security Directives of the Reagan and Bush Administrations* (Boulder, CO: Westview Press, 1995).
5. Edward Mead Earle, ed., *The Federalist,* No. 70 (New York: Modern Library, 1937), 458.
6. Ibid.
7. Vote Smart Facts Matter, 2007–2008, https://votesmart.org/interest-group/1475/rating/4275?p=2&of=#.VU0oaflVhBc.
8. Earle, ed., *The Federalist,* No. 57, 372.
9. Angus Campbell, Philip E. Converse, Warren E. Miller, and Donald E. Stokes, *Elections and the Political Order* (New York: Wiley, 1966), 194–211.
10. Nick Freiling, "Just 37% of Americans Can Name Their Representative," Haven Insights, May 31, 2017, https://www.haveninsights.com/just-37-percent-name-representative/.
11. Max Farrand, ed., *The Records of the Federal Convention of 1787,* vol. 1 (New Haven, CT: Yale University Press, 1966), 49.
12. Ibid., 48
13. Ralph Rossum, *Federalism, the Supreme Court, and the Seventeenth Amendment: The Irony of Constitutional Democracy* (New York: Lexington Books, 2001).
14. Farrand, *Records of the Federal Convention,* 48.
15. Ibid., 49.
16. 17 U.S. 316 (1819).
17. *McCulloch v. Maryland* 17 U.S. (4 Wheat.) 316 (1819).

18. Alexander Hamilton and James Madison, *Letters of Pacificus and Helvidius* (New York: Scholars Facsimiles & Reprint, 1999).

19. Ibid., 13.

20. Edward S. Corwin, *The President: Office and Powers* (New York: NYU Press, 1957), 181.

21. Hamilton and Madison, *Letters of Pacificus and Helvidius,* 57.

22. Corwin, *The President,* 189.

23. Leonard White, *The Federalists: A Study in Administrative History, 1789–1901* (New York: Free Press, 1948), 64.

24. Louis Fisher, *The Politics of Shared Power,* 4th ed. (College Station: Texas A&M University Press, 1998), 186.

25. Earle, ed., *The Federalist,* No. 69, 445.

26. Max Boot, *The Savage Wars of Peace: Small Wars and the Rise of American Power* (New York: Basic Books, 2002).

27. From Tenth Amendment Center, with additions made by the author, http://tenthamendment center.com/historical-documents/united-states-constitution/thirty-enumerated-powers/.

28. Jonathan Simon, *Governing Through Crime* (New York: Oxford, 2007), chap. 4.

29. 543 U.S. 220 (2005).

30. Farrand, *Records of the Federal Convention,* vol. 2, 65.

31. Ibid., 66.

32. William G. Howell and David E. Lewis, "Agencies by Presidential Design," *Journal of Politics* 64, no. 4 (Nov. 2002), 1095–1114.

33. John Yoo, *The Powers of War and Peace* (Chicago: University of Chicago Press, 2003).

34. Eric Posner and Adrian Vermeule, *The Executive Unbound: After the Madisonian Republic* (Chicago: University of Chicago Press, 2011).

35. "Unchecked Abuse," *Washington Post,* Jan. 11, 2006, http://www.washingtonpost.com /wp-dyn/content/article/2006/01/10/AR2006011001536.html.

36. Alexander Hamilton, "Pacificus Letter I," in *Letters of Pacificus and Helvidius,* 11.

37. John Stuart Mill, *Considerations on Representative Government* (London: Parker, Son and Bourne, 1861), 104.

38. 273 U.S. 135 (1927).

39. 10 Annals of Cong. 613 (1800).

40. Louis Fisher, "Presidential Inherent Power: The 'Sole Organ' Doctrine," *Presidential Studies Quarterly* 37, no. 1 (Mar. 2007), 139.

41. *United States v. Curtiss-Wright Corp.,* 299 U.S. 304 (1936).

42. Earle, ed., *The Federalist,* No. 51, 337.

43. U.S. Senate, http://www.senate.gov/artandhistory/history/common/briefing/Nominations .htm.

44. U.S. Senate, http://www.senate.gov/pagelayout/reference/nominations/Nominations.htm #official.

45. James Wallner, "Unring the Bell," Legislative Procedure, Sept. 6, 2018, LegBranch.org, https://www.legbranch.org/theblog/2018/9/6/unring-the-bell/.

46. Robert Pear, "President Protests Limits on His Power to Fill Posts," *New York Times,* Feb. 29, 2016, A10.

47. Jonathan P. Kastellec, Jeffrey Lax, and Justin Phillips, "Public Opinion and Senate Confirmation of Supreme Court Nominees," *Journal of Politics,* 72, no. 3 (July 2010), 767–84.

48. Jan C. Greenburg, *Supreme Conflict* (New York: Penguin, 2007), 281.

49. Earle, ed., *The Federalist,* No. 48.

50. Ibid.

51. Farrand, *Records of the Federal Convention,* vol. 2, 66.

Chapter 2. A Brief History of Congress

1. Leonard D. White, *The Republican Era: A Study in Administrative History, 1869–1901* (New York: Free Press, 1958), 101.

2. Edward Corwin, *The President: Office and Powers* (New York: New York University Press, 1957), 171.

3. "No More Gerrymanders: Congressional Representation in the Seven At-Large States," FairVote, Dec. 30, 2011, http://www.fairvote.org/research-and-analysis/blog/no-more -gerrymanders-at-large-states/.

4. Randall B. Ripley, *Congress: Process and Policy* (New York: Norton, 1988), 50.

5. Ibid., 61.

6. Jeffrey Tulis, *The Rhetorical Presidency* (Princeton, NJ: Princeton University Press, 1987), 69.

7. Fred Greenstein, *Inventing the Job of President: Leadership Style from George Washington to Andrew Jackson* (Princeton, NJ: Princeton University Press, 2009).

8. 418 U.S. 663 (1974).

9. Worthington Chauncy Ford, ed., *The Writings of George Washington* (New York: G. P. Putnam's, 1889), vol. 33, 96.

10. Quoted in White, *The Federalists,* 68.

11. Ibid., 70.

12. Ibid., 71.

13. Ralph Ketcham, *James Madison: A Biography* (Charlottesville: University Press of Virginia, 1990), 329.

14. Noble Cunningham Jr., "The Election of 1800," in *History of American Presidential Elections,* vol. 1, ed. Arthur Schlesinger Jr. (New York: Chelsea House, 1972), 101–34.

15. James Roger Sharp, *The Deadlocked Election of 1800: Jefferson, Burr, and the Union in Balance* (Lawrence: University Press of Kansas, 2010).

16. Jeremy Bailey, *Thomas Jefferson and Executive Power* (New York: Cambridge University Press, 2007).

17. Leonard White, *The Jeffersonians: A Study in Administrative History, 1801–1829* (New York: Free Press, 1951), 99.

18. James F. Hopkins, "Election of 1824," in *History of American Presidential Elections,* vol. 1, ed. Schlesinger, 361–64.

19. Samuel P. Huntington, "Congressional Responses to the Twentieth Century," in *The Congress and America's Future,* ed. David Truman (New York: Columbia University Press, 1965), 5–31.

20. Matthew Crenson and Benjamin Ginsberg, *Presidential Power: Unchecked and Unbalanced* (New York: W. W. Norton, 2007), 76–77.

21. Hal Morris, "The Hayne-Webster Debate," 1996, http://jmisc.net/hwdebate.htm.

22. Quoted in Leonard D. White, *The Jacksonians: A Study in Administrative History, 1829–1861* (New York: Free Press, 1954), 122.

23. Christopher Deering and Stephen Smith, *Committees in Congress* (Washington, DC: CQ Press, 1997), 28.

24. White, *The Jacksonians,* 127.

25. Ibid., 129.

26. Michael P. Riccards, *The Ferocious Engine of Democracy: A History of the American Presidency,* vol. 1 (Lanham, MD: Madison Books, 1995), 162–63.

27. Walter R. Borneman, *Polk: The Man Who Transformed the Presidency and America* (New York: Random House, 2009).

28. 60 U.S. 393 (1857).

29. Eric Foner, *Free Soil, Free Labor, Free Men: Ideology of the Republican Party Before the Civil War* (New York: Oxford University Press, 1995).

30. James G. Randall, *Constitutional Problems under Lincoln* (New York: Appleton, 1926), chap. 1.

31. David Donald, *Lincoln Reconsidered: Essays on the Civil War Era* (New York: Vintage, 2001), 191–92.

32. 2 Bl. 635 (1863).

33. 4 Wall. 2 (1866).

34. Michael Welsh, "An Overview of the Development of U.S. Congressional Committees" (Washington, DC: Law Librarians Society, 2008), http://www.llsdc.org/assets/sourcebook/cong-cmte-overview.pdf.

35. "The Wade-Davis Manifesto, Aug. 5, 1864," American History, http://www.let.rug.nl/usa/documents/1851-1875/the-wade-davis-manifesto-august-5-1864.php.

36. George F. Hoar, *Autobiography of Seventy Years,* vol. 2 (New York: Scribners, 1903), 46.

37. White, *Republican Era,* 23.

38. Wilfred E. Binkley, *President and Congress* (New York: Knopf, 1947), 155.

39. White, *Republican Era,* 33–34.

40. Lewis L. Gould, *The Spanish-American War and President McKinley* (Lawrence: University Press of Kansas, 1982).

41. Quoted in White, *Republican Era,* 41.

42. Woodrow Wilson, *Congressional Government* (Los Angeles: University of California Libraries, 1885), 10–11.

43. White, *Republican Era,* 68.

44. Ibid.

45. "How a Building Changed the House," History, Art & Archives, United States House of Representatives, Oct. 12, 2018, http://history.house.gov/Exhibitions-and-Publications/Cannon-Building/Cannon-Building/.

46. Arthur W. Dunn, *From Harrison to Harding* (New York: G. P. Putnam's, 1922), 334–35.

47. Jeffrey K. Tulis, *The Rhetorical Presidency* (Princeton, NJ: Princeton University Press, 1987), chap. 4.

48. Ibid., 118.

49. Peri Arnold, *Making the Managerial Presidency* (Lawrence: University Press of Kansas, 1998), 54.

50. U.S. Census, "Statistical Abstract," table 176, 1945, http://www2.census.gov/prod2/stat comp/documents/1944–04.pdf.

51. Paul C. Light, *The True Size of Government* (Washington, DC: Brookings, 1999).

52. Mathew McCubbins and Thomas Schwartz, "Congressional Oversight Overlooked: Police Patrols v. Fire Alarms," *American Journal of Political Science* 28, no. 1 (Feb. 1984), 165–79.

53. Richard P. Nathan, *The Plot That Failed: Nixon and the Administrative Presidency* (New York: Wiley, 1975).

54. Gordon Crovitz and Jeremy Rabkin, *The Fettered Presidency: Legal Constraints on the Executive Branch* (Washington, DC: American Enterprise Institute, 1989).

55. Lydia DePillis, "End Run on Overtime Pay Has Lobbyists Rushing," *Washington Post,* Sept. 5, 2015, A2.

Chapter 3. Congressional Elections

1. Edward Mead Earle, ed., *The Federalist,* No. 62 (New York: Modern Library, 1937) 62, 400.

2. Tamara El Waylly, "SIPA Student Runs for Congress," *Morningside Post,* Mar. 7, 2014.

3. Emma Harris, "Med Student Sets Sights on Congress," *Brown Daily Herald,* Feb. 10, 2014, http://www.browndailyherald.com/2014/02/10/med-school-student-sets-sights -congress/.

4. Lauren Oliver, "Miami Professor Runs for Congress," *Miami Student,* June 1, 2015, http://miamistudent.net/?p=17002589.

5. For incumbents running unopposed, see Ballotpedia, https://ballotpedia.org/U.S._House _elections_without_a_Democratic_or_Republican_candidate,_2018.

6. Antoinette Pole, "Antoinette Pole: Congressional Blogging: Advertising, Credit Claiming and Position Taking," 2010, http://www.researchgate.net/profile/Antoinette_Pole /publication/266464189_Congressional_Blogging_Advertising_Credit_Claiming__Po sition_Taking/links/54e74a8e0cf2cd2e0292ac8c.pdf.

7. Adam Johnson, "Union Sanitary District Dedicates New Green Energy Facility, *Union City Patch,* Apr. 6, 2015, http://patch.com/california/unioncity/union-sanitary-district -dedicates-new-green-energy-facility.

8. David Mayhew, *Congress: The Electoral Connection* (New Haven, CT: Yale University Press, 1974).

9. Diana Evans, *Greasing the Wheels: Using Pork Barrel Projects to Build Majority Coalitions in Congress* (New York: Cambridge University Press, 2004).

10. Andrea Kelly, "Tucson Streetcar Stop Dedicated to Congressman Grijalva," Arizona Public Media, July 21, 2014, https://news.azpm.org/p/news-spots/2014/7/21/39994 -tucson-streetcar-stop-dedicated-to-conrgessman-grijalva/.

11. Al Kamen and Colby Itkowitz, "In the Loop," *Washington Post,* June 2, 2015, A11.

12. Paul S. Herrnson, *Congressional Elections: Campaigning at Home and in Washington* (Washington, DC: Sage, 2012), chap. 9.

13. Shane Goldmacher, "Why Would Anyone Ever Want to Run for Congress?," *The Atlantic,* Apr. 19, 2013, http://www.theatlantic.com/politics/archive/2013/04/why-would-any one-ever-want-to-run-for-congress/275135/.

14. Ibid.

15. Sandy Maisel, *From Obscurity to Oblivion: Running in the Congressional Primary* (Knoxville: University of Tennessee Press, 1982), 23.

16. Greg Giroux, "Republicans Win Congress as Democrats Get Most Votes," *Bloomberg News,* Mar. 18, 2013, http://www.bloomberg.com/news/articles/2013–03–19/republicans -win-congress-as-democrats-get-most-votes.

17. 515 U.S. 900 (1995).

18. Maggie Haberman, "A Deep Pocket for Democrats to Open Polls," *New York Times,* June 6, 2015, A1.

19. Sean Sullivan, "Republican Ernst Draws on Experience 'Castrating Hogs' in Iowa Senate Cable Ad," *Washington Post,* Mar. 25, 2014, https://www.washingtonpost.com/news /post-politics/wp/2014/03/25/republican-ernst-draws-on-experience-castrating-hogs-in -iowa-senate-cable-ad/?utm_term=.7edfe06f6e4a.

20. Hannah Wise, "These Texans' Campaign Ads Run Gamut from Funny to Downright Bizarre," *Dallas News,* Oct. 2016, https://www.dallasnews.com/news/politics/2016/10/26 /texans-campaign-ads-run-gamut-funny-downright-bizarre.

21. Aliyah Frumin, "The 9 Most Memorable Campaign Ads of 2014," MSNBC, Oct. 20, 2014, http://www.msnbc.com/msnbc/the-9-most-memorable-campaign-ads-2014.

22. Julia Caplan, "Social Media and Politics," *Elon Journal of Undergraduate Research in Communication* 4, no. 1 (Spring 2013), http://www.elon.edu/docs/e-web/academics/com munications/research/vol4no1/01CaplanEJSpring13.pdf.

23. V. O. Key Jr., *The Responsible Electorate* (Cambridge, MA: Harvard University Press, 1966).

24. Tim Murphy, "Can This Oppo Research Guru Survive the Mudslinging in Her GOP Primary?," *Mother Jones,* Apr. 25, 2014, http://www.motherjones.com/politics/2014/04 /barbara-comstock-bob-marshall-congressional-race.

25. Ibid.

26. Gary Jacobson, *The Politics of Congressional Elections,* 8th ed. (Saddle River, NJ: Pearson, 2013), 57.

27. 572 U.S. 185 (2014).

28. 558 U.S. 310 (2010).

29. Jacobson, *Politics of Congressional Elections,* 78.

30. Ibid., 86.

31. Mayhew, *Congress,* 40.

32. Ibid., 116–19.

33. Jeffrey H. Birnbaum, *The Money Men* (New York: Crown, 2000), 75.

34. Jeffrey Birnbaum, "'Client' Rewards Keep K Street Lobbyists Thriving," *Washington Post,* Feb. 14, 2006, A1.

35. 424 U.S. 1 (1976).

36. Jennifer Bachner and Benjamin Ginsberg, *What the Government Thinks of the People* (New Haven. CT: Yale University Press, 2016).

37. Matthew Glassman and Amber Wilhelm, *Congressional Careers: Service Tenure and Patterns of Member Service, 1789–2015* (Washington, DC: Congressional Research Service, 2015).

Chapter 4. Political Parties and the Organization of Congress

1. Quoted in Robert V. Remini, *The History of the House of Representatives* (New York: HarperCollins, 2006), 76.
2. Joseph Cooper and David Brady, "Institutional Context and Leadership Style: The House from Cannon to Rayburn," *American Political Science Review* 75, no. 2 (1981), 411–25 (413).
3. Peter Sullivan, "Rift Opens in GOP Over Zika Funding," *The Hill,* Apr. 26, 2016, http://thehill.com/policy/healthcare/277732-rift-opens-in-gop-over-zika-funding.
4. Judy Schneider and Michel L. Koempel, *Congressional Deskbook: The Practical and Comprehensive Guide to Congress,* 6th ed. (Alexandria, VA: TheCapitol.Net, 2012,) 200.
5. Walter J. Oleszek, *Congressional Procedures and the Policy Process,* 9th ed. (Washington, DC: CQ Press, 2014), 433ff; see also Thomas E. Mann and Norman J. Ornstein, *The Broken Branch: How Congress Is Failing America and How to Get It Back on Track* (New York: Oxford University Press, 2008), 7ff.
6. Quoted in Greg Jaffe, "What a Divided America Hears When Obama Speaks," *Washington Post,* Feb. 14, 2016, A1.
7. Emily Goodin, "Weekly Lunches Give Senators a Chance to Air Their Differences," *The Hill,* May 7, 2013.
8. Ibid.
9. Kristina Peterson, "Parliamentarian at Center of Overhaul," *Wall Street Journal,* Jan. 18, 2017, A6.
10. Quoted in Oleszek, *Congressional Procedures,* 429.
11. Peter Wehner, "The Party of Reagan Is No More," *Time,* Mar. 21, 2016.
12. Ibid.
13. Burgess Everett, "Senate Woes Abound for Dems in 2016," *Politico* 10, no. 9 (Feb. 9, 2016), 1, 14.
14. In the House, the political parties categorize the committees as "exclusive," "nonexclusive," and "exempt." Members can serve on one exclusive committee but can also serve on the Budget Committee and House Administration panel while doing so, and on two nonexclusive committees. There are a few other technical limitations that apply as well. See Schneider and Koempel, *Congressional Deskbook,* 208–12.
15. In the Senate, rules distinguish "A," "B," and "C" categories of committees and each party designates "Super A" committees. Senators can usually only serve on two "A" committees, one "B" committee, and one "Super A" committee, with no restrictions on "C" committees. See Ibid., 213–14.
16. Ibid., 202.
17. Ibid., 202–5.
18. Mann and Ornstein, *Broken Branch,* 27ff.

19. Woodrow Wilson, *Congressional Government* (Boston: Houghton, Mifflin, 1885; repr. Baltimore: Johns Hopkins University Press, 1981), 69.

20. Anne-Laure Beaussier, "The Patient Protection and Affordable Care Act: The Victory of Unorthodox Lawmaking," *Journal of Health Politics, Policy and Law* 37, no. 5 (Oct. 2012), 741–78 (760ff).

21. Ibid., 761.

22. Schneider and Koempel, *Congressional Deskbook,* 202.

23. *Constitution, Jefferson's Manual, and Rules of the House of Representatives* (Washington, DC: Government Printing Office, 2011).

24. *House Practice: A Guide to the Rules, Precedents, and Procedures of the House* (Washington, DC: Government Printing Office, 2011); *Procedure in the U.S. House of Representatives, 97th Congress: A Summary of the Modern Precedents and Practices of the House, 86th Congress–97th Congress* (Washington, DC: Government Printing Office, 2017); see also the House's "The Legislative Process" website at clerk.house.gov/legislative/legprocess.aspx.

25. *Senate Manual* (Washington, DC: Government Printing Office, 2011).

26. Floyd M. Riddick and Alan S. Frumin, *Riddick's Senate Procedure: Precedents and Practices* (Washington, DC: Government Printing Office, 1992); *Senate Cloture Rule* (Washington, DC: Government Printing Office, 2011); see also the Senate's "Legislative Process" website at https://www.senate.gov/legislative/process.htm.

27. Donald R. Wolfensberger, *A Brief History of Congressional Reform Efforts,* paper prepared for the Bipartisan Policy Center and the Woodrow Wilson Center, Washington, DC, Feb. 22, 2013, iv.

28. Ibid., 1–2; Judy Schneider, Christopher David, and Betsy Palmer, "Reorganization of the House of Representatives: Modern Reform Efforts" (Washington, DC: Congressional Research Service, Oct. 2003), http://archives.democrats.rules.house.gov/archives/rl31835.pdf; and Judy Schneider, Colton Campbell, Christopher Davis, and Betsy Palmer, Reorganization of the Senate: Modern Reform Efforts (Washington, DC: Congressional Research Service, Oct. 2003).

29. James Wallner, "Reforming the Senate's Hotline System," LegislativeProcedure, Oct. 31, 2018, LegBranch.org, https://www.legbranch.org/2018-10-31-reforming-the-senates-hotline-system/.

30. Zach Graves and Daniel Schuman, "The Decline of Congressional Expertise Explained in 10 Charts," Oct. 18, 2018, TechDirt, https://www.techdirt.com/articles/20181018/10204640869/decline-congressional-expertise-explained-10-charts.shtml.

31. Philip Joyce, "The Congressional Budget Office at Middle Age" (Working Paper #9, Hutchins Center on Fiscal and Monetary Policy at the Brookings Institution, Washington, DC, Feb. 2015), 1.

32. Ibid.

33. Ibid., 11; quoted in Philip Joyce, *The Congressional Budget Office: Honest Numbers, Power, and Policymaking* (Washington, DC: Georgetown University Press, 2011).

34. Thomas Jefferson, Jefferson's Library, Library of Congress, http://www.loc.gov/exhibits/jefferson/jefflib.html#219.

35. Kevin Kosar, "Why I Quit the Congressional Research Service: How Congress's Dys-

function Has Degraded Its Own In-House Think Tank," *Washington Monthly,* Jan.–Feb. 2015.

36. "Congressional Staff: 1979–2011," *Vital Statistics on Congress,* 2018, www.brookings .edu/vitalstats.

37. Representatives and Senators make $174,000 per year, and this has not changed since 2009.

38. Jon Wonderlich, "Keeping Congress Competent: Staff Pay, Turnover, and What It Means for Democracy," Sunlight Foundation, Dec. 2010, https://sunlightfoundation.com/policy /documents/keeping_congress_competent/.

39. Ibid.

40. Abner J. Mikva and Patti B. Saris, *The American Congress: The First Branch* (New York: Franklin Watts, 1983), 162ff.

41. Susan Webb Hammond, *Congressional Caucuses in National Policy Making* (Baltimore: Johns Hopkins University Press), 1998, 11, xi; see also DeWayne Lucas and Iva Ellen Deutchman, "Five Factions, Two Parties: Caucus Membership in the House of Representatives, 1994–2002," *Congress & the Presidency* 36 (2009), 58–79.

42. Lucas and Deutchman, "Five Factions," 76.

43. Chris Den Hartog and Timothy Nokken, "More Heat Than Light: New Conservative Amending Activity in the U.S. House," Committees & Caucuses, Oct. 24, 2018, LegBranch.org, https://www.legbranch.org/2018-10-22-more-heat-than-light-new-conservative-amending -activity-in-the-us-house/.

44. Schneider and Koempel, *Congressional Deskbook,* 214–17.

45. Ibid., 216–17.

46. Diane M. Francis, "How to Fix America's Gridlock," *HuffPost,* Sept. 18, 2014, http:// www.huffingtonpost.com/diane-m-francis/how-to-fix-americas-gridl_b_5842756.html.

Chapter 5. The Legislative Process

1. Note that the overall number of bills introduced and passed has steadily declined in recent years. Forty years ago, in the 1970s, about 24,000 bills and resolutions were introduced and about 768 bills were enacted per two-year Congress. Since 2010, only about half that number, 12,000 bills and resolutions, have been introduced and approximately 322 become law per Congress. (See "Historical Statistics about Legislation in the U.S. Congress," https://www.govtrack.us/congress/bills/statistics, accessed Oct. 12, 2018.) This decline in legislative productivity reflects both the partisan "gridlock" of recent years and changes in congressional procedure.

2. See Thomas E. Mann and Norman J. Ornstein, *The Broken Branch: How Congress Is Failing American and How to Get It Back on Track* (New York: Oxford University Press, 2008); and Barbara Sinclair, *Unorthodox Lawmaking: New Legislative Procedures in the U.S. Congress* (Washington, DC: CQ Press, 2012).

3. Walter J. Oleszek, *Congressional Procedures and the Policy Process,* 9th ed. (Washington, DC: CQ Press, 2014), 14; see also Doug Andres, "Congress and Why Process Matters" (master's in government thesis, Johns Hopkins University, 2016).

4. See generally Judy Schneider and Michael Koempel, *The Congressional Deskbook: The*

Practical and Comprehensive Guide to Congress, 6th ed. (Alexandria, VA: TheCapitol .Net, 2012).

5. "Open plus" rules refer to those rules that allow for the offering of amendments that are in compliance, as in any open rule *plus* any amendments for which a special rule granted waivers of points of order.

6. A legislative day is from the time the Senate convenes until it adjourns. It may last more than a calendar day, and it is not unusual for the Senate to be in session past midnight when considering a major bill or motion.

7. Filibusters are not allowed during the consideration of budget bills, because they are governed under a special rule process called "reconciliation," which limits debate to twenty hours.

8. If the issue at hand involves a change in Senate rules, then a two-thirds majority is needed to end the filibuster.

9. In the Senate, if there is a tie, then the vice president casts the deciding vote. If, however, the vice president is not present, then the vote is resolved in the negative.

10. Lindsey McPherson, "Paul Ryan Talks Up Return to Regular Order," *Roll Call,* Dec. 16, 2015, https://www.rollcall.com/news/paul-ryan-talks-return-regular-order; see also *A Better Way: Our Vision for A Confident America* (Washington, DC: Better.gop, 2016), issued June 16 by Speaker Ryan's Office and the Republican leadership of the House of Representatives.

11. See Sinclair, *Unorthodox Lawmaking.*

12. Donald Wolfensberger, *Changing Cultures in Congress: From Fair Play to Power Plays* (New York: Columbia University Press, 2018).

13. Oleszek, *Congressional Procedures,* 15ff; Mann and Ornstein, *Broken Branch,* 7ff; and Sinclair, *Unorthodox Lawmaking,* 160ff.

14. Oleszek, *Congressional Procedures,* 170.

15. Ibid., 180.

16. Glenn Thrush, "55 Dems (plus Hoyer?) Want 'Regular Order,'" *Politico,* Nov. 29, 2013.

17. Ibid.

18. Jake Sherman and Heather Caygle, "Paul Ryan Proposes Blocking Amendments That Could Kill Spending Bills," *Politico,* June 8, 2016, http://www.politico.com/story/2016 /06/paul-ryan-block-amendments-spending-bills-224061.

19. Eric Schickler, *Disjointed Pluralism* (Princeton, NJ: Princeton University Press, 2011), 203.

20. Sinclair, *Unorthodox Lawmaking,* 186–234; see also Anne-Laure Beaussier, "The Patient Protection and Affordable Care Act: The Victory of Unorthodox Lawmaking," *Journal of Health Politics, Policy and Law* 37, no. 5 (2012), 741–78.

21. Walter Oleszek, "Whither the Role of Conference Committees: An Analysis," CRS Report RL34611, Aug. 12, 2008, U.S. Library of Congress, Congressional Research Service (Washington, DC: Office of Congressional Information and Publishing, 2008); and Andres, "Congress and Why Process Matters," chap. 1.

22. Ruth Bloch Rubin, *Building the Bloc: Intraparty Organization in the U.S. Congress* (Cambridge: Cambridge University Press, 2017).

23. There is also "delegate representation," in which a member votes based on constituent preferences that are counter to his or her own, and "trustee representation," in which a member votes based on his or her own views that are contrary to those of the constituents. See Kim Quaile Hill, "'Models of Representation' Reflected in the Roll Call Votes of House Members," Sept. 26, 2018, https://www.legbranch.org/2018-9-20-models-of -representation-reflected-in-the-roll-call-votes-of-house-members/.

24. Sinclair, *Unorthodox Lawmaking,* 136.

25. Ibid.

26. Richard Fenno, "The Senate Through the Looking Glass: The Debate over Television," *Legislative Studies Quarterly* 14, no. 3 (Aug. 1989), 316. See also Molly E. Reynolds, *Exceptions to the Rule: The Politics of Filibuster Limitations in the U.S. Senate* (Washington, DC: Brookings Institution Press, 2017).

27. Ezra Klein, "The History of the Filibuster, in One Graph," *Washington Post,* May 15, 2012, www.washingtonpost.com/blogs/wonkblog/post/the-history-of-the-filibuster-in-one -graph/2012/05/15/gIQAVHfoRU_blog.html, accessed June 6, 2016.

28. Sarah A. Binder and Steve S. Smith, *Politics or Principle? Filibustering in the United States Senate* (Washington, DC: Brookings Institution, 1996); see also Sinclair, *Unorthodox Lawmaking,* 136ff.

29. Philip Wegmann, "12 Bills That the Filibuster Stopped from Becoming Law," *Daily Signal,* Nov. 11, 2015,

30. Burgess Everett, "Democrats Learn to Love the Filibuster: Party Leaders Change Tune Now That They Are in Minority," *Politico,* Feb. 3, 2015, www.politico.com/story/2015/02 /senate-democrats-filibuster-114888.

31. Rachael Bade and Heather Caygle, "How Democrats Mounted Their Dramatic Guns Sit-In," *Politico* 10, no. 74 (June 23, 2016), 1, 13.

32. See Richard B. Doyle, "The Rise and (Relative) Fall of Earmarks: Congress and Reform, 2006–2010," *Public Budgeting & Finance* 31, no. 1 (Mar. 2011), 1–22; and Rob Porter and Sam Walsh, "Earmarks in the Federal Budget Process" (Briefing Paper No. 16, Federal Budget Policy Seminar, Harvard Law School, Cambridge, MA, 2008), last updated by Robert Allen and Robert Brown.

33. Steven S. Smith, Jason M. Roberts, and Ryan J. Vander Wielen, *The American Congress,* 8th ed. (New York: Cambridge University Press, 2013), 396; see also Lee Drutman, *The Business of America Is Lobbying: How Corporations Became Politicized and Politics Became More Corporate* (New York: Oxford University Press, 2015), 227.

34. Steven Gordon, "What Did the Earmark Ban Do? Evidence from Intergovernmental Grants," *Journal of Regional Analysis & Policy* 18, no. 3 (2016), 20–40.

35. "Earmark Spending: 1991 to 2018" and "Number of Earmarks, 1991 to 2016," Citizens Against Government Waste, Washington, DC, 2018, https://www.cagw.org/reporting /2016-pig-book.

36. Austin Clemens, Michael Crespin, and Charles J. Finocchiaro, "Earmarks and Subcommittee Government in the U.S. Congress," *American Politics Research* 43, no. 6 (2015), 1074–1106.

37. Ibid.

38. Steven Gordon, "The Great Earmark Debate: Who Should Determine Federal Spending Priorities?" Oct. 16, 2018, https://www.legbranch.org/2018-10-16-the-great-earmark-debate-or-who-should-determine-federal-spending-priorities/.

39. Office of the President, Office of Management and Budget, Budget of the United States Government, Fiscal Year 2019 (Feb. 2018).

40. "Budget Basics," National Priorities Project, 2016, https://www.nationalpriorities.org/budget-basics; see also Schneider and Koempel, *Congressional Deskbook,* 322–23, and Oleszek, *Congressional Procedures,* 73–76.

41. David M. Herszenhorn, "Failed Spending Bills Pile Up in Senate as Budget Agreement Breaks Down," *New York Times,* July 12, 2016, A11.

42. Natalie Andrews and Kristina Peterson, "Lawmakers Make Deal to Avoid Shutdown," *Wall Street Journal,* Sept. 14, 2018, A4; Erica Werner, "A Tug of War with Massive Implications," *Washington Post,* Sept. 6, 2018, A1 and 7.

43. Smith, Roberts, and Vander Wielen, *American Congress,* 353.

44. Pamela Ban, Daniel J. Moskowitz, and James M. Snyder Jr., "The Changing Relative Power of Party Leaders in Congress" (draft working paper, Feb. 2, 2016, scholar.harvard.edu/files/jsnyder/files/pac_leadership_draft.pdf?m=1460063073).

45. Oleszek, *Congressional Procedures,* 40.

46. Paul Burstein, *American Public Opinion, Advocacy, and Policy in Congress: What the Public Wants and What It Gets* (New York: Cambridge University Press, 2014).

47. Mann and Ornstein, *Broken Branch;* David E. Price, "Congressional-Executive Balance in an Era of Congressional Dysfunction," *PS: Political Science & Politics* 49, no. 3 (July 2016), 485–89; Dina Titus, "Is Congress the 'Broken Branch' of Government?," *PS: Political Science & Politics* 49, no. 3 (July 2016), 490–94; and Mike Lee, "Curing the Cancer of Congressional Dysfunction," *PS: Political Science & Politics* 49, no. 3 (July 2016), 481–84.

48. Peri Arnold, *Making the Managerial Presidency* (Lawrence: University Press of Kansas, 1998), 319.

49. Drew DeSilver, "Congressional Productivity Is Up—But Many New Laws Overturn Obama-Era Rules," Pew Research Center, Aug. 29, 2017, http://www.pewresearch.org/fact-tank/2017/08/29/115th-congress-productivity/.

50. Sinclair, *Unorthodox Lawmaking,* 149–51.

Chapter 6. Congress, the President, and Domestic Policy

1. Ralph Carter and James Scott, "Taking the Lead: Congressional Foreign Policy Entrepreneurs in U.S. Foreign Policy," *Politics and Policy* 32, no. 1 (Mar. 2004), 34–71.

2. Matthew N. Beckmann, *Pushing the Agenda: Presidential Leadership in U.S. Lawmaking, 1953–2004* (New York: Cambridge University Press, 2010); see also Jeffrey E. Cohen, *The President's Legislative Policy Agenda, 1789–2002* (New York, Cambridge University Press, 2012); George C. Edwards III, *The Strategic President: Persuasion and Opportunity in Presidential Leadership* (Princeton, NJ: Princeton University Press, 2009); Paul Light, *The President's Agenda,* 3rd. ed. (Baltimore: Johns Hopkins University Press, 1999).

3. Gary C. Jacobson, "Partisan Polarization in Presidential Support: The Electoral Connection," *Congress and the Presidency* 30, no. 1 (2003), 1–36; see also Gary C. Jacobson, "The President's Effect on Partisan Attitudes," *Presidential Studies Quarterly* 42, no. 4 (Dec. 2012), 683–718; Matthew Lebo and Andrew J. O'Geen, "The President's Role in the Partisan Congressional Arena," *Journal of Politics* 73, no. 3 (July 2011), 718–34; Frances E. Lee, "Dividers, Not Uniters: Presidential Leadership and Senate Partisanship," *Journal of Politics* 70, no. 4 (Oct. 2008), 914–28.

4. Stephen Skowronek, *The Politics Presidents Make* (Cambridge: Belknap Press, 1997).

5. David Mayhew, *Congress: The Electoral Connection* (New Haven, CT: Yale University Press, 1974).

6. Justin Grimmer, Solomon Messing, and Sean J. Westwood, "How Words and Money Cultivate a Personal Vote: The Effect of Legislator Credit Claiming on Constituent Credit Allocation," *American Political Science Review* 106, no. 4 (Nov. 2012), 703–19.

7. Stephen Frantzich, "Congress, the Houses of Ill Repute: Editorial Cartoonists Take On the House and Senate," *Congress and the Presidency* 40, no. 2 (2012), 152–64.

8. W. G. Howell and J. C. Rogowski, "War, the Presidency, and Legislative Voting Behavior," *American Journal of Political Science* 57 (2013), 150–66.

9. Bruce Jepson, "Obamacare Will Bring Drug Industry $35 Billion in Profits," *Forbes,* May 25, 2013, http://www.forbes.com/sites/brucejapsen/2013/05/25/obamacare-will-bring-drug-industry-35-billion-in-profits/.

10. Edward Mead Earle, ed., *The Federalist,* No. 71 (New York: Modern Library, 1937), 464.11; G. C. Jacobson, "Partisan Polarization in American Politics: A Background Paper." *Presidential Studies Quarterly* 43 (2013), 688–708.

11. Gary Cox and Jonathan Katz, *Elbridge Gerry's Salamander: The Electoral Consequences of the Reapportionment Revolution* (New York: Cambridge, 2002).

12. N. McCarty, K. T. Poole, and H. Rosenthal, "Does Gerrymandering Cause Polarization?," *American Journal of Political Science* 53 (2009), 666–80; see also Jamie Carson, Michael H. Crespin, Charles J. Finocchiaro, and David W. Rohde, "Redistricting and Party Polarization in the U.S. House of Representatives, *American Politics Research* 35, no. 6 (2007), 878–904; Morris Fiorina, with Samuel J. Abrams and Jeremy C. Pope, *Culture War? The Myth of a Polarized America* (New York: Longman, 2004).

13. T. Skocpol and L. R. Jacobs, "Accomplished and Embattled: Understanding Obama's Presidency," *Political Science Quarterly* 127 (2012), 1–24.

14. Andrew Rudalevige, "The Executive Branch and the Legislative Process," in *The Executive Branch,* ed. Joel Aberbach and Mark Peterson (New York: Oxford, 2005), 421.

15. Ibid.

16. Ibid., 423.

17. Russell L. Riley, *Bridging the Constitutional Divide: Inside the White House Office of Legislative Affairs* (College Station: Texas A&M University Press, 2010); see also Matthew N. Beckmann, "The President's Playbook: White House Strategies For Lobbying Congress," *Journal of Politics* 70, no. 2 (Apr. 2008), 407–19.

18. Ben Terris, "A Congress Too Pathetic to Picket: Political Gridlock Has Turned a Onetime Magnet for Protest into a Virtual Ghost Town," *Washington Post,* July 23, 2014, C1.

19. *Clinton v. City of New York,* 524 U.S. 417 (1998).

20. 576 U.S. [unassigned] (2015).

21. Phillip J. Cooper, *By Order of the President* (Lawrence: University Press of Kansas, 2002), 206.

22. Elisabeth Bumiller, "For President, Final Say on a Bill Sometimes Comes after the Signing," *New York Times,* Jan. 16, 2006, A11.

23. Steve Friess, "Obama's Policy Strategy: Ignore Laws," *Politico,* June 16, 2012.

24. Elena Kagan, "Presidential Administration," *Harvard Law Review* 114 (June 2001), 2245.

25. 420 U.S. 35 (1975).

26. David Bridge, "Presidential Power Denied: A New Model of Veto Overrides Using Political Time," *Congress and the Presidency* 41, no. 2 (2014), 149–66.

27. Kenneth Mayer and Thomas Weko, "The Institutionalization of Power," in *Presidential Power,* ed. Robert Y. Shapiro et al. (New York: Columbia University Press, 2000), 195.

28. Leonard D. White, *The Republican Era: A Study in Administrative History, 1869–1901* (New York: Free Press, 1958), 55.

29. Louis Fisher, "Presidential Budgetary Duties," *Presidential Studies Quarterly* 42, no. 4 (Dec. 2012), 754–90.

30. Jason A. MacDonald, "Limitation Riders and Congressional Influence over Bureaucratic Policy Decisions," *American Political Science Review* 104 (2010), 766–82.

31. Charles Dawes, *The First Year of the Budget of the United States* (New York: Harper, 1923).

32. Philip G. Joyce, *The Congressional Budget Office: Honest Numbers, Power and Policymaking* (Washington, DC: Georgetown University Press, 2011).

33. Leonard D. White, *The Federalists: A Study in Administrative History, 1789–1801* (New York: Free Press, 1948), 80.

34. Ibid., 81.

35. *U.S. v. Nixon,* 418 U.S. 683 (1974).

36. Leonard D. White, *The Jeffersonians: A Study in Administrative History, 1801–1829* (New York: Free Press, 1951), 94.

37. Ibid., 96.

38. Ibid., 102.

39. Joel D. Aberbach, "What's Happened to the Watchful Eye? *Congress and the Presidency* 29, no. 1 (2002), 3–23.

40. Maggie Fox, "GAO Sting Finds It Easy to Fake It, Get Obamacare Premiums," *NBC News,* July 22, 2014, https://www.nbcnews.com/health/health-news/gao-sting-finds-it-easy-fake-it-get-obamacare-premiums-n162456.

41. Morton Rosenberg, "The Congressional Review Act after 15 Years: Background and Considerations for Reform," Administrative Conference of the United States, Sept. 16, 2011, http://www.acus.gov/sites/default/files/documents/COJR-Draft-CRA-Report-9-16-11.pdf.

42. Cornelius M. Kerwin and Scott R. Furlong, *Rulemaking: How Government Agencies Write Law and Make Policy* (Washington, DC: CQ Press, 2011), 231.

43. Juliet Eilperin, "Technically, Hundreds of Administration Rules Are Invalid," *Washington Post,* July 31, 2014, A19.

44. Morris S. Ogul, *Congress Oversees the Bureaucracy: Studies in Legislative Supervision* (Pittsburgh, PA: University of Pittsburgh Press, 1976).

45. Mathew McCubbins and Thomas Schwartz, "Congressional Oversight Overlooked: Police Patrols versus Fire Alarms," *American Journal of Political Science* 28, no. 1 (Feb. 1984), 165–79.

46. Steven Balla and Christopher Deering, "Police Patrols and Fire Alarms: An Empirical Examination of the Legislative Preference for Oversight," *Congress and the Presidency* 40, no. 1 (2013), 27–40.

47. Connor Radnovich, "Cruise Passengers Recount Horror Stories to Senate," *Seattle Times,* July 24, 2014, https://www.seattletimes.com/business/cruise-passengers-recount-horror -stories-to-senate/.

48. Douglas Kriner and Eric Schickler, "Investigating the President: Committee Probes and Presidential Approval, 1953–2006," *Journal of Politics* 76, no. 2 (Apr. 2014), 521–34.

49. White, *Jeffersonians,* 99.

50. Josh Hicks, "Rep. Issa Ends Hearing after White House Defies Subpoena," *Washington Post,* July 17, 2014, A15.

51. David A. Yaloff, *Prosecution among Friends: Presidents, Attorneys General, and Executive Branch Wrongdoing* (College Station: Texas A&M University Press, 2012).

52. Michael Gerhardt, *The Federal Impeachment Process,* 2nd ed. (Chicago: University of Chicago Press, 2000).

53. Remarks in the U.S. House of Representatives in an effort to impeach Supreme Court Justice William O. Douglas (Apr. 15, 1970), Cong. Rec. 116, 11913.

54. Nia-Malika Henderson and Wesley Lowery, "Talk of Impeaching Obama Could Help, Not Hurt Democrats," *Washington Post,* July 24, 2014, A4.

55. Peter Baker and Susan Schmidt, "Starr Searches for Sources of Staff Criticism: Private Investigator Says Clinton Team Hired Him," *Washington Post,* Feb. 24, 1998, 1.

56. John F. Harris, "Office of Damage Control," *Washington Post,* Jan. 31, 1998, 1.

57. Earle, ed., *The Federalist,* No. 51.

58. Ibid.

Chapter 7. Congress and Foreign Policy

1. Edward S. Corwin, *The President: Office and Powers,* 4th rev. ed. (New York: New York University Press, 1957), 171.

2. James W. Davis, *The American Presidency* (Westport, CT: Praeger, 1995), 246.

3. Corwin, *The President,* 178–79.

4. Ibid., 182.

5. Leonard White, *The Federalists: A Study in Administrative History, 1789–1801* (New York: Free Press, 1948), 55.

6. Alexander Hamilton and James Madison, *Letters of Pacificus and Helvidius* (New York: Scholars Facsimiles & Reprints, 1999).

7. Corwin, *The President,* 181.

8. Sidney M. Milkis and Michael Nelson, *The American Presidency: Origins and Development* (Washington, DC: Congressional Quarterly Press, 1999), 91.

9. Leonard White, *The Jeffersonians: A Study in Administrative History, 1801–1829* (New York: Free Press, 1951), 32.

10. Davis, *American Presidency,* 242.

11. *United States v. Curtiss-Wright Export Corp.,* 209 U.S. 304 (1936).

12. Jessica T. Matthews, "The Death of Our Treaties," *New York Review of Books,* Mar. 24, 2016, 28–30.

13. Hamilton and Madison, *Letters of Pacificus and Helvidius,* 66.

14. Corwin, *The President,* 189.

15. White, *The Federalists,* 64.

16. Louis Fisher, *The Politics of Shared Power,* 4th ed. (College Station: Texas A&M University Press, 1998), 186.

17. United States Senate, Committee on Foreign Relations, Washington, DC, Document No. 105-28, 1999, http://www.foreign.senate.gov/imo/media/doc/CDOC-105sdoc28.pdf.

18. Walter A. McDougall, *Promised Land, Crusader State: The American Encounter with the World since 1776* (New York: Houghton Mifflin, 1997), 144.

19. United States Senate, "Convention on the Rights of Persons With Disabilities," Washington, DC, 2012, http://www.foreign.senate.gov/imo/media/doc/CDOC-105sdoc28.pdf, 7.

20. Steven Lee Myers, "U.S. Move to Give Egypt $450 Million in Aid Meets Resistance," *Washington Post,* Sept. 28, 2012, http://www.nytimes.com/2012/09/29/world/middleeast/white-house-move-to-give-egypt-450-million-in-aid-meets-resistance.html?_r=0.

21. Austin Wright, "House GOPers Dig in on Defense Cuts," *Politico,* Nov. 15, 2012, http://www.politico.com/news/stories/1112/83863.html.

22. Bill Gertz, "Congress: U.S. Military Highly Vulnerable to Cyber Attacks," *Washington Free Beacon,* June 1, 2015, http://freebeacon.com/national-security/congress-u-s-military-highly-vulnerable-to-cyber-attacks/.

23. Quoted in Daniel J. Solove, *Nothing to Hide* (New Haven: Yale University Press, 2011), 10.

24. James Bamford, "The Agency That Could Be Big Brother," *New York Times,* Dec. 25, 2005.

25. James Bamford, "They Know Much More Than You Think," *New York Review of Books,* Aug. 15, 2013, 4, http://www.nybooks.com/articles/archives/2013/aug/15/nsa-they-know-much-more-you-think/.

26. Mollie Reilly, "James Clapper: I Gave 'Least Untruthful' Answer Possible on NSA Surveillance," *HuffPost,* June 12, 2013, https://www.huffingtonpost.com/2013/06/11/james-clapper-nsa-surveillance_n_3424620.html.

27. Dan Nosowitz, "Congress Was Not Really Briefed on PRISM," *Popular Science,* June 12, 2013, http://www.popsci.com/technology/article/2013-06/obama-said-all-congress-was-briefed-prism-nonsense.

28. See Max Boot, *The Savage Wars of Peace: Small Wars and the Rise of American Power* (New York: Basic Books, 2002).

29. Arthur M. Schlesinger Jr., *The Imperial Presidency* (Boston: Houghton Mifflin, 1973), 166.

30. Joel R. Paul, "The Geopolitical Constitution: Executive Expediency and Executive Agreements," *University of California Law Review* 86 (July 1998), 713–14.

31. Ibid., 720–21.

32. Ibid., sect. 3; see also Fisher, *Politics of Shared Power,* 190–91.

33. Harold W. Stanley and Richard Niemi, *Vital Statistics on American Politics, 2001–2002* (Washington, DC: Congressional Quarterly Press, 2001), 334.

34. John C. Yoo, "Laws as Treaties?: The Constitutionality of Congressional-Executive Agreements," *University of Michigan Law Review* 73 (Feb. 2001), 757.

35. Phillip J. Cooper, *By Order of the President* (Lawrence: University Press of Kansas, 2002), 144.

36. Ibid., 158.

37. Charles E. Bohlen, *Witness to History* (New York: Norton, 1973), 210.

38. George Q. Flynn, *The Draft* (Lawrence: University Press of Kansas, 1973), 265.

39. Douglas Bandow, "Fixing What Ain't Broke: The Renewed Call for Conscription," *Policy Analysis,* no. 351 (Aug. 31, 1999), 2.

40. Charles B. Rangel, "Bring Back the Draft," *New York Times,* Dec. 31, 2002, A21.

41. Thomas E. Ricks, *Making the Corps* (New York: Simon & Schuster, 1997), chap. 5.

42. Ole R. Holsti, "Of Chasms and Convergences: Attitudes and Beliefs of Civilians and Military Elites at the Start of a New Millennium," in *Soldiers and Civilians,* ed. Peter D. Feaver and Richard H. Kohn (Cambridge, MA: MIT Press, 2001), 15–100.

43. James R. Locher III, *Victory on the Potomac: The Goldwater-Nichols Act Unifies the Pentagon* (College Station: Texas A&M University Press, 2002).

44. Franklin C. Spinney, "Notes on Close Air Support," in *Spirit, Blood and Treasure: The American Cost of Battle in the 21st Century,* ed. Donald Vandergriff (Novato, CA: Presidio Press, 2001), 199–213.

45. Gordon Silverstein, *Imbalance of Powers: Constitutional Interpretation and the Making of American Foreign Policy* (New York: Oxford University Press, 1997), 145.

46. Lori F. Damrosch, "Covert Operations," in *Foreign Affairs and the U.S. Constitution,* ed. Louis Henkin, Michael J. Glennon, and William D. Rogers (Ardsley-on-Hudson, NY: Transnational Publishers, 1990), 87–97.

47. 453 U.S. 654 (1981).

48. 462 U.S. 919 (1983).

49. Christopher N. May, *In the Name of War: Judicial Review and the War Powers since 1918* (Cambridge, MA: Harvard University Press, 1989), 256.

50. Thomas M. Franck, "Rethinking War Powers: By Law or by 'Thaumaturgic Invocation,'?" in Henkin, Glennon, and Rogers, *Foreign Affairs,* 59.

51. Caspar W. Weinberger, "Dangerous Constraints on the President's War Powers," in *The Fettered Presidency: Legal Constraints on the Executive Branch,* ed. L. Gordon Crovitz and Jeremy Rabkin (Washington, DC: American Enterprise Institute, 1989), 95–116.

52. Louis Fisher, *Congressional Abdication On War and Spending* (College Station: Texas A&M University Press, 2000), 68.

53. Ibid., 75–76.

54. Ibid., 77.

55. George Bush and Brent Scowcroft, *A World Transformed* (New York: Knopf, 1998), 441.

56. Robert J. Delahunty and John C. Yoo, "The President's Constitutional Authority to Conduct Military Operations Against Terrorist Organizations and the Nations That Harbor Them," *Harvard Journal of Law and Public Policy* 25 (Spring 2002), 487.

57. For an analysis of the act, see Michael T. McCarthy, "USA Patriot Act," *Harvard Journal on Legislation* 39 (Summer 2002), 435.
58. See, for example, Ronald Dworkin, "Terror and the Attack on Civil Liberties," *New York Review of Books,* Nov. 6, 2003, 37–41.
59. Eric Lichtblau, "U.S. Uses Terror Law to Pursue Crimes from Drugs to Swindling," *New York Times,* Sept. 28, 2003, 1.

Chapter 8. Congress and the Bureaucracy

1. Robert Higgs, *Crisis and Leviathan: Critical Episodes in the Growth of American Government* (New York: Oxford University Press, 1987).
2. Daniel P. Carpenter, *The Forging of Bureaucratic Autonomy* (Princeton, NJ: Princeton University Press, 2001).
3. C. R. Berry, B. C. Burden, and W. G. Howell, "After Enactment: The Lives and Deaths of Federal Programs," *American Journal of Political Science* 54 (2010), 1–17.
4. Congress.gov Resources, Calendars and Schedules, https://www.congress.gov/resources /display/content/Calendars+and+Schedules.
5. David Oshinsky, *A Conspiracy So Immense* (New York: Free Press, 1985).
6. Wilfred Binkley, "The Decline of the Executive," *New Republic,* May 18, 1953.
7. Robert Pear, "Ambiguity in Health Law Could Make Family Coverage Too Costly for Many," *New York Times,* Aug. 12, 2012, 10.
8. Jerry L. Mashaw, *Greed, Chaos, & Governance: Using Public Choice to Improve Public Law* (New Haven, CT: Yale University Press, 1997), 106.
9. Kimberly Johnson, *Governing the American State* (Princeton, NJ: Princeton University Press, 2006); see also Elizabeth Sanders, *Roots of Reform: Farmers, Workers, and the American State* (Chicago: University of Chicago Press, 1999); and Theda Skocpol, *Protecting Soldiers and Mothers: The Political Origins of Social Policy in the United States* (Cambridge, MA: Harvard University Press, 1995).
10. Daniel Carpenter, *The Forging of Bureaucratic Autonomy* (Princeton, NJ: Princeton University Press, 2001).
11. See Theodore J. Lowi, *The End of Liberalism,* 2nd. ed. (New York: Norton, 1979); see also David Schoenbrod, *Power Without Responsibility: How Congress Abuses the People Through Delegation* (New Haven, CT: Yale University Press, 1993).
12. Kenneth Culp Davis, *Discretionary Justice* (Baton Rouge: Louisiana State University Press, 1969), 15–21.
13. *Mistretta v. U.S.,* 488 U.S. 361, 372 (1989).
14. Schoenbrod, *Power Without Responsibility,* chap. 2.
15. Ibid., 61.
16. William F. Fox, *Understanding Administrative Law,* 4th ed. (New York: Lexis Publishing, 2000), 36–37.
17. Kara Scannell and Deborah Soloman, "Business Wins Its Battle to Ease a Costly Sarbanes-Oxley Rule," *Wall Street Journal,* Nov. 10, 2006, 1.
18. Harold W. Stanley and Richard G. Niemi, *Vital Statistics on American Politics* (Washington, DC: Congressional Quarterly Press, 2001), 262.

19. James L. Gattuso and Diane Katz, "Red Tape Rising: Regulation in Obama's First Term," *Heritage Foundation Backgrounder,* no. 2793 (May 1, 2013), http://www.heritage.org /research/reports/2013/05/red-tape-rising-regulation-in-obamas-first-term.

20. "2013 Draft Report to Congress on the Benefits and Costs of Federal Regulations and Agency Compliance with the Uniform Mandates Reform Act," White House Office of Management and Budget, http://www.whitehouse.gov/sites/default/files/omb/inforeg /2013_cb/draft_2013_cost_benefit_report.pdf.

21. Ibid., 4.

22. Cornelius M. Kerwin and Scott R. Furlong, *Rulemaking: How Government Agencies Write Law and Make Policy* (Washington, DC: CQ Press, 2011), 226.

23. William F. West and Connor Raso, "Who Shapes the Rulemaking Agenda?: Implications for Bureaucratic Responsiveness and Bureaucratic Control," *Journal of Public Administration Research and Theory* 23 (Oct. 2012), 495–519.

24. Christopher Foreman, for example, was able to identify efforts by the committees overseeing the Food and Drug Administration to induce the agency to develop new rules. Christopher Foreman, *Signals from the Hill: Congressional Oversight and the Challenge of Social* Regulation (New Haven, CT: Yale University Press, 1988).

25. West and Raso, "Who Shapes the Rulemaking Agenda?," 504.

26. Joel Aberbach, *Keeping a Watchful Eye: The Politics of Congressional Oversight* (Washington, DC: Brookings Institution, 1990).

27. David M. O'Brien, *Constitutional Law and Politics,* vol. 1, 4th ed. (New York: Norton, 2000), 368.

28. Lowi, *End of Liberalism,* 94–97.

29. Jeffrey A. Wertkin, "Reintroducing Compromise to the Nondelegation Doctrine," 98 *Georgetown Law Journal* 98 (Apr. 2002), 1012–13.

30. 143 U.S. 649 (1892).

31. 23 U.S. 1 (1825).

32. 276 U.S. 394 (1928).

33. 56 Stat. 23 (Jan. 30, 1942).

34. *Panama Refining Co. v. Ryan,* 293 U.S 388 (1933).

35. *Schechter Poultry v. U.S.,* 295 U.S. 496 (1935).

36. 298 U.S. 238 (1936).

37. *Yakus v. U.S.,* 321 U.S. 414, 425 (1944).

38. 488 U.S. 361 (1989).

39. *U.S. v. Booker,* 125 S. Ct. 738 (2005).

40. 467 U.S. 837 (1984).

41. See *Whitman v. American Trucking Associations,* 531 U.S. 457 (2001); see also *AT&T Corp. v. Iowa Utilities Board,* 525 U.S.366 (1999).

42. 533 U.S. 218 (2001).

43. 133 S. Ct. 1863 (2013).

44. *Michigan v. EPA,* 576 U.S. [unassigned] (2015).

45. Fox, *Understanding Administrative Law,* 27.

46. Lowi, *End of Liberalism;* Schoenbrod, *Power Without Responsibility.*

47. Kerwin and Furlong, *Rulemaking,* 223.

48. Harold Bruff and Ernest Gellhorn, "Congressional Control of Administrative Regulation: A Study of Legislative Vetoes," *Harvard Law Review* 90 (May 1977), 1369.
49. *Immigration and Naturalization Service v. Chadha,* 462 U.S. 919 (1983).
50. 462 U.S. 919, 2002.
51. Morton Rosenberg, "The Congressional Review Act after 15 Years: Background and Considerations for Reform," Administrative Conference of the United States, Sept. 16, 2011," http://www.acus.gov/sites/default/files/documents/COJR-Draft-CRA-Report-9-16 -11.pdf, 13.
52. Kimberley Strassel, "A GOP Regulatory Game Changer," *Wall Street Journal,* Jan. 27, 2017, A13.
53. Curtis W. Copeland and Maeve P. Carey, "REINS Act," Congressional Research Service, Feb. 24, 2011, http://www.speaker.gov/sites/speaker.house.gov/files/UploadedFiles /110830_crs_majorrules.pdf.
54. Elena Kagan, "Presidential Administration," *Harvard Law Review* 114 (2001), 2347.
55. Henry A. Waxman, "Free Pass from Congress," *Washington Post,* July 6, 2004, A19.
56. Shailagh Murray, "Storms Show a System Out of Balance," *Washington Post,* Oct. 5, 2005, A21.
57. 29 U.S.C. 2601.
58. Caitlyn M. Campbell, "Overstepping One's Bounds: The Department of Labor and the Family and Medical Leave Act," *Boston University Law Review* 84 (Oct. 2004), 1077.
59. *Miller v. AT&T Corp.,* 250 F.3d 820 (2001).
60. Campbell, "Overstepping One's Bounds," 1088.

Chapter 9. Congress and the Courts

1. Edward Mead Earle, ed., *The Federalist,* No. 78 (New York: Modern Library, 1937).
2. 494 U.S. 872 (1990).
3. *City of Boerne v. Flores,* 521 U.S. 507 (1997).
4. Mark V. Tushnet, "New Forms of Judicial Review and the Persistence of Rights and Democracy-Based Worries," *Wake Forest Law Review* 38 (2003), 813.
5. Earle, ed., *The Federalist,* No. 78.
6. Herbert J. Storing, *What the Anti-Federalists Were For* (Chicago: University of Chicago Press, 1981), 50.
7. Quoted in William B. Glidden, *The Supreme Court versus Congress: Disrupting the Balance of Power, 1789–2014* (Santa Barbara, CA: Praeger, 2015), chap. 1.
8. Ibid., 5.
9. William Baude, "Could Obama Bypass the Supreme Court?," *New York Times,* Mar. 17, 2015, http://www.nytimes.com/2015/03/17/opinion/could-obama-bypass-the-supreme -court.html?_r=0.
10. 5 U.S. 137 (1803)
11. 60 U.S. 393 (1857).
12. Quoted in Glidden, *Supreme Court,* chap. 2.
13. Ibid.

14. Mark A. Graber, "The Nonmajoritarian Difficulty: Legislative Deference to the Judiciary," *Studies in American Political Development* 7 (1993), 35.

15. *Lochner v. New York,* 198 U.S. 45 (1905).

16. Ibid.

17. 158 U.S. 601 (1895).

18. *Springer v. United States,* 102 U.S. 586 (1881).

19. 247 U.S. 251 (1918).

20. *In re Debs,* 158 U.S. 564 (1895).

21. Alfred H. Kelly, Winfred A. Harbison, and Herman Belz, *The American Constitution: Its Origins and Development* (New York: W. W. Norton, 1983).

22. 369 U.S. 186 (1962).

23. 395 U.S. 486 (1969).

24. 531 U.S. 98 (2000). For the background and details of the case, see E. J. Dionne and William Kristol, eds., *Bush v. Gore: The Court Cases and the Commentary* (Washington, DC: Brookings Institution, 2001). For a defense of the Court's actions, see Richard Posner, *Breaking the Deadlock: The 2000 Election, the Constitution, and the Courts* (Princeton, NJ: Princeton University Press, 2001).

25. Benjamin Ginsberg and Martin Shefter, *Politics by Other Means* (New York: W. W. Norton, 2002), chap. 6. The quoted comment regarding the Florida legislature is from Thomas Oliphant, "Gov. Bush's Cynical End-Around in the Florida Legislature," *Boston Globe,* Dec. 3, 2000, D8.

26. Mark V. Tushnet, *Taking the Constitution Away from the Courts* (Princeton, NJ: Princeton University Press, 2000).

27. Glidden, *Supreme Court,* chap. 11.

28. Louis Fisher, *Congress: Protecting Individual Rights* (Lawrence: University Press of Kansas, 2016), xii.

29. Jeremy Waldron, *Law and Disagreement* (New York: Oxford University Press, 1999).

30. For a critique of the notion of judicial imperialism, see Mark Kozloski and Anthony Lewis, *The Myth of the Imperial Judiciary* (New York: New York University Press, 2003).

31. 3 Dall. 54 (1795).

32. 2 Pet. 253 (1829).

33. 50 U.S. 602 (1850).

34. *Fong Yue Ting v. U.S.,* 149 U.S. 698 (1893).

35. 182 U.S. 1 (1901)

36. 299 U.S. 304 (1936).

37. *A. L. A. Schechter Poultry Corp. v. U.S.,* 295 U.S. 495 (1935); *Panama Refining Co. v. Ryan,* 293 U.S. 388 (1935).

38. Gordon Silverstein, "Judicial Enhancement of Executive Power," in *The President, the Congress, and the Making of Foreign Policy,* ed. Paul Peterson (Norman: University of Oklahoma Press, 1994), 28–29.

39. Randall W. Bland, *The Black Robe and the Bald Eagle: The Supreme Court and the Foreign Policy of the United States, 1789–1953* (San Francisco: Austin & Winfield, 1996), 172.

40. John C. Yoo, "Laws as Treaties?: The Constitutionality of Congressional-Executive Agreements," *Michigan Law Review* 99 (Feb. 2001), 757.

41. Edward Corwin, *The President: Office and Powers,* 4th rev. ed. (New York: New York University Press, 1957), 212–13.

42. Bland, *Black Robe,* 177.

43. See *Field v. Clark,* 143 U.S. 649 (1892).

44. 301 U.S. 324 (1937).

45. *United States v. Curtiss-Wright Export Corp.,* 299 U.S. 304 (1936).

46. 315 U.S. 203 (1942).

47. 565 F. Supp. 1019 (D. Colo. 1983).

48. 151 F. Supp. 942 (1957).

49. 6 Cl. Ct. 115 (1984). The decision was later reversed on appeal by the U.S. Court of Appeals for the Federal Circuit primarily because both the U.S. and Panamanian governments asserted that the executive agreement had not been intended to relieve Canal Zone workers of their federal tax obligations. See 761 F. 2nd. 688 (1985).

50. *Dames & Moore v. Regan,* 453 U.S. 654 (1981).

51. Relevant cases include *Rust v. Sullivan,* 500 U.S. 173 (1991), and *U.S. v. Alvarez-Machain,* 504 U.S. 655 (1992).

52. *Goldwater v. Carter,* 444 U.S. 996 (1979).

53. Victoria M. Kraft, *The U.S. Constitution and Foreign Policy: Terminating the Taiwan Treaty* (New York: Greenwood, 1991), chap. 3.

54. Joshua P. O'Donnell, "The Anti-Ballistic Missile Treaty Debate: Time for Some Clarification of the President's Authority to Terminate a Treaty," *Vanderbilt Journal of Transnational Law* 35 (Nov. 2002), 1601.

55. Joel R. Paul, "The Geopolitical Constitution," *California Law Review* 86 (July 1998), 672.

56. *United States v. Pink,* 315 U.S. 203 (1942).

57. *Dames & Moore v. Regan,* 453 U.S. 654 (1981).

58. *United States v. Belmont,* 301 U.S. 324 (1937).

59. Robert Barnes, "Supreme Court Says President's Powers Prevail on Foreign Borders," *Washington Post,* June 8, 2015, http://www.washingtonpost.com/politics/courts_law/supreme-court-strikes-down-born-in-jerusalem-passport-law/2015/06/08/19562bb2-d71d-11e4-ba28-f2a685dc7f89_story.html.

60. Ronald J. Sievert, "*Campbell v. Clinton* and the Continuing Effort to Reassert Congress' Predominant Constitutional Authority to Commence, or Prevent, War," *Dickinson Law Review* 105 (Winter 2001), 157.

61. D. A. Jeremy Telman, "A Truism That Isn't True? The Tenth Amendment and Executive War Power," *Catholic University Law Review* 51 (Fall 2001), 135.

62. Max Farrand, ed., *The Records of the Federal Convention of 1787,* vol. 2 (New Haven, CT: Yale University Press, 1937), 318.

63. Julian C. Boyd, ed., *The Papers of Thomas Jefferson,* vol. 15 (Princeton, NJ: Princeton University Press, 1950), 397.

64. Gordon Silverstein, *Imbalance of Powers: Constitutional Interpretation and the Making of American Foreign Policy* (New York: Oxford University Press, 1996).

65. 453 U.S. 280 (1981).

66. 558 F. Supp. 893 (1982).

67. *Lowry v. Reagan,* 676 F. Supp. 333 (1987); *Dellums v. Bush,* 752 F. Supp. 1141 (1990).

68. 340 U.S. App. D.C. 149 (2000).

69. Several agencies, however, are not subject to presidential budgetary review. See Louis Fisher, *Constitutional Conflicts Between Congress and the President,* 4th ed. (Lawrence: University Press of Kansas, 1997), 201.

70. See Theodore J. Lowi, *The End of Liberalism,* 2nd. ed. (New York: Norton, 1979); see also David Schoenbrod, *Power Without Responsibility: How Congress Abuses the People Through Delegation* (New Haven, CT: Yale University Press, 1993).

71. Kenneth Culp Davis, *Discretionary Justice* (Baton Rouge: Louisiana State University Press, 1969), 15–21.

72. David M. O'Brien, *Constitutional Law and Politics,* vol. 1, 4th ed. (New York: Norton, 2000), 368.

73. Archibald Cox, "Executive Privilege," *University of Pennsylvania Law Review* 122 (1974), 1383.

74. Raoul Berger, *Executive Privilege* (Cambridge, MA: Harvard University Press, 1974).

75. *U.S. v. Burr,* 25 F. Cas. 187 (1807).

76. Jeffrey P. Carlin, "Walker v. Cheney: Politics, Posturing and Executive Privilege," *Southern California Law Review* 76 (Nov. 2002), 245.

77. 433 U.S. 425 (1977).

78. The appeals court, however, developed a procedure that gave the subcommittee limited access to documents under court supervision. 551 F.2nd 384 (D.C. Cir. 1976).

79. 556 F. Supp. 150 (D.D.C. 1983). As in the *AT&T* case, the court developed a procedure providing limited access to the contested documents.

80. See, for example, *Bareford v. General Dynamics Corp.,* 973 F.2nd 1138 (5th Cir. 1992).

81. See *In re Sealed Case,* 121 F.3rd 729 (D.C. Cir. 1997).

82. 124 S. Ct. 1391 (2004).

83. *Cheney v. United States District Court,* 542 U.S. 367 (2004).

84. 424 U.S. 1 (1976).

85. Robert V. Percival, "Presidential Management of the Administrative State: The Not-So-Unitary Executive," *Duke Law Journal* 51 (Dec. 2001), 972.

86. 272 U.S. 52 (1926).

87. 295 U.S. 602 (1935).

88. 478 U.S. 714 (1986).

89. 48 U.S. 361 (1989).

90. 366 F. Supp. 104 (D.D.C., 1973).

91. 487 U.S. 654 (1988).

92. William J. Olson and Alan Woll, *How Presidents Have Come to Run the Country by Usurping Legislative Power* (Washington, DC: Cato Institute, 1999).

93. *Building and Construction Trades Department v. Allbaugh,* 172 F. Supp. 2nd 138 (D.D.C., 2001).

94. *Trump v. Hawaii,* 585 U.S. [unassigned] (2018).

95. 343 U.S. 579 (1952).

96. 74 F. 3rd 1322 (D.C. Cir. 1996).
97. Tara L. Branum, "President or King? The Use and Abuse of Executive Orders in Modern-Day America," *Journal of Legislation* 28 (2002), 18.
98. *U.S. v. Nixon,* 418 U.S. 683 (1974).
99. *Train v. City of New York,* 420 U.S. 35 (1975).
100. *National Federation of Independent Business v. Sebelius,* 567 U.S. 519 (2012).
101. 576 U.S. [unassigned] (2015).
102. Corwin, *The President,* 16.
103. Terry M. Moe and William G. Howell, "The Presidential Power of Unilateral Action," *Journal of Law, Economics and Organization* 15, no. 1 (1999), 151–52.
104. Thomas E. Cronin and Michael A. Genovese, *The Paradoxes of the American Presidency* (New York: Oxford University Press, 1998), 271.
105. Moe and Howell, *Presidential Power,* 150.
106. Kermit L. Hall, *The Politics of Justice: Lower Federal Judicial Selection and the Second Party System, 1829–1861* (Lincoln: University of Nebraska Press, 1979), 152–56.
107. Matthew Crenson and Benjamin Ginsberg, *Presidential Power: Unchecked and Unbalanced* (New York: W. W. Norton, 2007), 313.
108. Matthew A. Crenson and Benjamin Ginsberg, *Downsizing Democracy: How America Sidelined Its Citizens and Privatized Its Public* (Baltimore: Johns Hopkins University Press, 2002), 14–19.
109. Harold Seidman, *Politics, Position, and Power: The Dynamics of Federal Organization,* 5th ed. (New York: Oxford University Press, 1998), 52.
110. David Baumann, "Budget Debates Leave White House with Foes in Both Parties," Government Executive, Feb. 15, 2002, https://www.govexec.com/federal-news/2002/02/budget-debates-leave-white-house-with-foes-in-both-parties/11072/.
111. Ralph K. Winter, "The Activist Judicial Mind," in *Views From the Bench,* ed. Mark W. Cannon and David M. O'Brien (Chatham, NJ: Chatham House, 1985), 291.
112. John S. Martin Jr., "Let Judges Do Their Jobs," *New York Times,* June 24, 2003, A31.
113. Lyle Denniston, "Can the President Ignore Supreme Court Rulings?," *HuffPost,* Oct. 18, 2011, http://www.huffingtonpost.com/lyle-denniston/gingrich-supreme-court_b_1017418.html.
114. C. Herman Pritchett, *Congress versus the Supreme Court* (Minneapolis: University of Minnesota Press, 1961).

Chapter 10. Reflections on Congress

1. Thomas E. Mann and Norman J. Ornstein, *The Broken Branch* (New York: Oxford University Press, 2008).
2. David Mayhew, *Congress: The Electoral Connection* (New Haven, CT: Yale University Press, 1974).
3. Richard Dorment, "22 Simple Reforms That Could #FixCongress Now, *Esquire,* Oct. 15, 2014, http://www.esquire.com/news-politics/news/a32838/congress-the-report-reforms-fixcongress-1114/.

4. Bill Bishop, *The Big Sort: Why the Clustering of Like-Minded America Is Tearing Us Apart* (New York: Mariner Books, 2009).

5. U.S. House of Representatives, Committee on Ethics, "Highlights of the House Ethics Rules," May 2015, https://ethics.house.gov/sites/ethics.house.gov/files/Final%20Version%20of%20the%20Highlights%20Overview%20Booklet%202015.pdf.

6. Frank Anechiarico and James B. Jacobs, *The Pursuit of Absolute Integrity: How Corruption Control Makes Government Ineffective* (Chicago: University of Chicago Press, 1998).

7. U.S. Department of Justice, Office of Public Integrity, "Report to Congress on the Activities and Operations of the Public Integrity Section for 2013," https://www.justice.gov/sites/default/files/criminal/legacy/2014/09/09/2013-Annual-Report.pdf.

8. Speaker Paul Ryan, "A Better Way: Our Vision for a Confident America," 2016, https://abetterway.speaker.gov.

9. Kevin Kosar, "Six Ways Congress Can Curb a Runaway President," *Politico,* Jan. 21. 2017.

10. Mike DeBonis, "House Republicans Lay Out Proposals to Rein in Presidential Power," *Washington Post,* June 16, 2016, https://www.washingtonpost.com/news/powerpost/wp/2016/06/16/house-republicans-lay-out-proposals-to-rein-in-presidential-power/?utm_term=.d560195ce38f.

INDEX

9/11 terror attacks, 76, 187, 215, 235–36. *See also* terrorism
106th Congress (1999–2000), 248
110th Congress (2007–2009), 165. *See also specific individuals*
111th Congress (2009–2011), 168, 169, 181(tbl.), 182
112th Congress (2011–2013), 291
113th Congress (2013–2014), 291, 292
115th Congress (2017–2019), 125(tbl.), 163, 173, 176, 177, 181, 188. *See also specific individuals*

AARP, 117
abolitionists, 58, 59, 60. *See also* slavery: debate over
Abramoff, Jack, 295
Abscam scandal, 294–95
ACA. *See* Affordable Care Act
accountability, of politicians, 115–18
Acheson, Dean, 191
Adams, Henry, 65
Adams, John, 40, 46, 52, 199(tbl.), 214, 265
Adams, John Quincy, 50, 51, 52, 199(tbl.)
ad hoc groups, 149–50. *See also specific groups and caucuses*

Administrative Procedure Act (APA; 1946), 71, 76–77, 254
advertisements, 106–7, 118
Affordable Care Act (Obamacare; ACA; 2010): committees involved in crafting, 167; constitutionality, 264, 284; efforts to repeal/revise, 129, 185, 188; executive branch's power increased by, 35; fraud reported, 205; insider lobbying and the battle over, 178–79; IRS eligibility rules, 245; poorly understood by Congress members, 245; and Republican holds on Obama nominees, 29–30; tactics used to pass, 132, 187; tax credit implementation, 193–94
Afghanistan, 185, 215, 235, 275
African Americans: anti-discrimination laws, 73; civil rights activism, 109; and the Clarence Thomas nomination, 32; Congressional Black Caucus, 129; Democratic Party and, 95, 110; segregation and desegregation, 109, 289; suffrage, 11; three-fifths compromise and, 10, 58; and voting rights, 99. *See also* slavery; *and specific individuals*